Antifeminism in America

A Collection of Readings from the Literature
of the Opponents to U.S. Feminism, 1848 to the Present

Series Editors

Angela Howard and Sasha Ranaé Adams Tarrant
University of Houston Clear Lake

A GARLAND SERIES

Contents of the Series

Reaction to the Modern Women's Movement, 1963 to the Present

Edited with introductions by

Angela Howard and **Sasha Ranaé Adams Tarrant**
University of Houston Clear Lake

GARLAND PUBLISHING, INC.
A MEMBER OF THE TAYLOR & FRANCIS GROUP
New York & London
1997

Library of Congress Cataloging-in-Publication Data

Reaction to the modern women's movement, 1963 to the present /
edited with introductions by Angela Howard and Sasha Ranaé
Adams Tarrant.
    p. cm. — (Antifeminism in America ; 3)
    Includes bibliographical references.
    ISBN 0-8153-2715-3 (alk. paper)
    1. Anti-feminism—United States. 2. Feminism—United States.
3. Women—United States—Social conditions. I. Howard, Angela.
II. Tarrant, Sasha Ranaé Adams. III. Series.
HQ1426.R416 1997
305.42—dc21   97-38205
                            CIP

Printed on acid-free, 250-year-life paper
Manufactured in the United States of America

Contents

Series Introduction

Understanding the Opposition to U.S. Feminism

The purpose of this three-volume collection of primary sources is to generate a more complete understanding and appreciation of the social and political context in which the advocates of women's rights have labored and labor from 1848 to the present. The editors have selected original documents from mainstream literature to allow the reader immediate access to this continuing public discourse that accompanies the prospective and the real changes in women's role and status in the United States. Those opposed to the feminist goal of women's equality have addressed to the public, directly through contemporary popular books and magazines, their concerns regarding the particular nineteenth-century issues of the woman's rights movement. These include woman suffrage and dress reform, as well as topics relating to the discerning and enforcing the proper role and status of women. Public discourse over such topics has extended into the twentieth century, as opponents raised arguments against increased opportunities in women's employment and education, denied the propriety and practice of family planning, and admonished against women's involvement in political issues and activities. In these three volumes, the opponents of feminism speak directly to the reader who is free to evaluate the merits of each author's arguments.

Diversity of opinion and perspective has persisted among those who oppose the assertion of women's rights as reform movement, which challenges the concepts and institutions of patriarchy as well as the gender system that supports and perpetuates a gender-defined, limited, and segregated existence for women. The constellation of conservative definitions of proper womanhood has varied widely in approach, intent, and intensity. Over the past two-hundred years the critics of feminism, of advances in women's rights, and of the increased opportunity in education and employment for women have had to absorb changes in the status of middle-class women. These critics therefore have co-opted and redefined some of the fait accompli changes to maintain that contemporary practices uphold the primary limitation for women in any century, that for women "biology is destiny." All these opponents to sexual equality ultimately assert that an inescapable maternal duty grounds every woman's identity in her relationships to others and especially to men: each woman's usefulness to society through filial, uxorial, maternal, professional, and civic responsibilities define and limit her identity as an individual.

Some opponents merely dismissed or ridiculed advocates for changes in women's status, and eschewed the need to specify particular flaws in the feminist position on any particular issue. Others relied on interpretations of divine ordination, appeals to natural law, and manipulations of public fears of familial and social disintegration. Often opponents sought to discredit the propriety or to challenge the necessity of any change in the gender system proposed by advocates of women's rights. They utilized divisive tactics to separate women by race or ethnic group, religion, or economic class. Frequently, these critics resorted to ad hominum charges of lesbianism, communism, and socialism, or disgruntled spinsterhood against the advocates of women's rights and against the movement itself. Opponents defined the effort to promote the women's movement out of the domestic sphere and into the public arena of political, economic, and social reform as inherently destructive of social order. By focusing on maintaining a limited role for women, adversaries of the women's movement, both women and men, expressed their common fear that has been created by ongoing social, economic, and political changes beyond their control.

Therefore, much of the value in reading these sources is to experience the variety of perspectives that provide the historical and intellectual context for these documents from the distant and near past. The editors offer this varied selection of sources to allow the reader to assess the merit and validity of the arguments presented by these representative opponents of women's rights and equality. Not all opponents of specific feminist reforms would define themselves as antifeminist; most would deny that they are anti-woman, although opposed to expanding women's rights. For the student of women's history, the temptation to look for patterns of opposition will become irresistible. To facilitate an evaluation of the texts in their own historical context, the editors have grouped the documents within three major historical periods. Because the sources of mainstream opponents were more readily available, we elected to focus on the debate among writers who represented the middle class and who exerted a presence in the popular press. Especially for students of American women's history, this collection provides the opportunity to encounter directly the opinions of those who resisted and criticized the goals as well as the tactics of feminism in all its forms.

The documents in volume one, *Opposition to the Women's Movement in the United States, 1848–1929*, cover the initial era of the woman's movement, which began in the antebellum period and produced the *Declaration of Sentiments* of the Seneca Falls Woman's Rights Convention in 1848 as well as the Cult of True Womanhood (1820–1860). The sources in volume one extend through the culmination of the ratification of the Nineteenth Amendment to the U.S. Constitution that enfranchised women. The nineteenth-century critics of the emerging women's movement launched the conservative defense of a delineated woman's sphere and redefined the cult of domesticity with appeals to scripture and history, as well as to contemporary scientific theories that emphasized the physical-gender differences. By the twentieth century, the opponents of women's rights and equality faced formidable challenges to the validity of these translations of scripture, interpretations of historical development, and questionable "scientific" evidence and conclusions.

The sources provided in volume two, *Redefining the New Woman, 1920–1963*, offer reflections of the twentieth-century era from the "Roaring Twenties" through the

World War II period to the rise of the Civil Rights Movement. Both the 1920s and the 1950s were decades characterized by post-war antifeminism and a trend toward intellectually stifling social conformity for women and men; the maintenance of patriarchal values justified this repression. Those opposed to feminism added applications of Freudian psychology to the arguments based on biological and physiological "facts," firmly established before World War I. This psycho-biological approach reaffirmed that "biology is destiny" for women of the twentieth century as well as for the nineteenth. But developments in the postindustrial economy of the mid-twentieth century U.S. fostered changes in the middle class that redounded to increased women's opportunity in employment and education; the consequences of these changes seemed to threaten to lessen women's economic dependence upon men.

In volume three, *Reaction to the Modern Women's Movement, 1963 to the Present*, the readings span an era contemporary to the publication of Betty Friedan's *The Feminine Mystique* (1963), the so-called sexual revolution (in which women were more prisoners of war than combatants), and the rise of the modern women's movement. The impact of the Civil Rights Act of 1964, Title VII especially, no less than the rise of the women's liberation movement (1968–1972) and the development of women's studies within the standard curriculum of higher education created a climate for change that continues to occur throughout the last decade in the twentieth century. The 1980s ushered in the Reagan era with a backlash against the women's movement that capitalized on the insecurities of middle-class women, especially homemakers, that they would be discarded, abandoned, and stranded as single heads of households and the sole support of their children; middle-class men were told to fear the added economic competition of women and men of color. Conservatives reacted to the legacy of the 1970s—the questioning of authority—and bristled at the challenge of the women's liberation movement to patriarchal institutions and values. This generation of defenders of the gender system articulated the threat feminism posed to organized religion, "traditional" family values, the nation's future, and the free-enterprise economy.

This collection of readings developed from a shared experience and exasperation of a professor and her graduate student in a course on U.S. feminism. Dissatisfied with the limited sources available for studying contemporary criticism of the women's movement and feminism in U.S. history, the editors collaborated to find, edit, and present to the reader the kinds of sources that often appear in women's history courses as handouts—assorted items gathered over time and informally assembled. Our division of labor reflected our individual strengths: the professor brought the expertise gained from decades of teaching women's history as well as editorial experience; the graduate student (now well on her way to completing her Ph.D.) contributed impressive state-of-the-art researching skills and determination to locate, screen, and recommend documents most likely to represent the trends and standard arguments of the critics of the women's movement and feminism. From experience, the former knew that good intentions notwithstanding, "no good deed goes unpunished" and therefore anticipated that the best efforts would still garner candid criticism of purpose and selections; the latter maintained a conviction that this "good deed" needed doing regardless of the time and effort demanded. The idealism of youth won out. We drew into our quixotic vision other graduate students who provided crucial research as assistants to the editors:

Pamela F. Wille, Rae Fuller Wilson, and Susanne Grooms. All of us relied on the kindness and expertise of the professional librarians at U.H.C.L., including Susan Steele, and the professional staff of other libraries. The editors therefore accept any compliments on the results of the collaboration as only proportionally ours while we assert our sole claim of accountability for the inevitable errors (which we trust our readers will bring to our attention and that will be corrected in future editions).

Volume Introduction

From 1963 to the mid-1990s, opponents of the contemporary women's movement, such as Phyllis Schlafly, Jerry Falwell, Midge Decter, and Rush Limbaugh, pondered the wisdom of changes wrought by changes in the postwar economy as well as proposed reforms of women's status and role after 1963. These authors exploited public concern over implications of the Equal Rights Amendment and significant alterations to the nuclear family structure by rephrasing the enduring approaches of those who opposed feminism in theory and in practice: Had feminists gone too far? What had reform done to families and society? Would the feminists' desire for reform ever be satisfied? These critics brought full circle the initial opposition to the feminist challenge to patriarchy and the gender system that limited women to a domestic role.

The two parts of volume three contain sources that expressed the criticism of the modern women's movement before the failed attempt to ratify the Equal Rights Amendment (from 1963 to 1982) and readings that were published during the subsequent "backlash" era that extends from the 1980s into the 1990s. The general availability of "the pill" merged women's increased control over reproduction with a mainstream reaction to the sexual repression of the 1950s: thus, the sexual revolution of the 1960s challenged social taboos of all kinds. However, access to contraception did not obviate the influence of sexist socialization during the 1950s and 1960s of girls and women who were not necessarily empowered to decide for themselves whether or when to become sexually active. The civil rights and student movements prepared a generation of women leaders of the modern women's movement. The short-lived women's liberation movement, which applied the tactics and methodology of "anti-establishment" dissent to challenge patriarchal values, especially provoked the ire of the resurgent right. Political fundamentalists and conservative opponents of women's rights and feminism recruited middle-class and working-class women, previously unpoliticized, by adroit manipulation of the issue of women's reproductive rights, as defined in *Roe* v. *Wade* (1973). These critics mobilized middle-class and working-class men against women's rights, as in the case of affirmative action, by arguing that such policies promoted unnatural roles for women and thus would weaken the traditional patriarchal "family values" which affirmed religious and political fundamentalism.

Reaction to the
Modern Women's Movement,
1963 to the Present

THE WOMAN'S VOTE

Has It Made Any Difference?

LENA JEGER MP

So what about some women having had a vote for 50 years? The golden jubilee has been a gift for the glossies, the colour supplements, for radio and TV. The subject has been dealt with flippantly, stupidly, respectfully, nostalgically, regretfully, hopefully, reproachfully, boringly, superficially. But the central question usually has a common core. What difference has the woman's vote made? From some of the assessments of the disappointed, one would have thought we were considering the anniversary of women growing an Adam's rib or a unicorn's horn instead of a delayed extension of ordinary citizenship. Historically it is much more interesting to consider what difference the man's vote has made to human progress, for he has had it longer. But the fact that this question is so seldom asked and the anniversaries of male franchise so meanly celebrated indicates a persistent dichotomy.

Whatever some early suffragettes may have claimed in the stress of campaigning, the only valid claim for women being included on the electoral register was not that they were different from men, but that they were the same in the context of the franchise and in their common humanity. This is older doctrine than the suffragettes, older than Mary Wollstonecraft. But to many people who had not followed the arguments closely there was a novelty of presentation in Ibsen's *The Doll's House* in 1879. Torvald tells his restless wife: 'Before all else, you are a wife and mother.' And thousands of playgoers heard Nora's cry of revolution: 'I believe that before all else I am a reasonable human being . . .'

It is as human beings, reasonable or unreasonable, that women have a claim to equal responsibilities, to equal status. This is not feminism. It is part of a total battle against prejudice in human affairs, of the need to assert that discrimination between one being and another is vulgar and irrelevant, if it is based on sex or class or colour or race or creed. This approach was part of the charm of Pethick-Lawrence, the Daniel of suffrage. He wrote in his autobiography: 'I venture to assert that, unless an individual can transcend the limits of sex, class, race, age and creed, his personality remains of necessity to that extent incomplete.'

So what are all these brittle young commentators trying to assess in their anniversary computations? Rich women probably vote differently from poor men and poor women from rich men. Unless we start a system of pink and blue ballot papers we shall never be certain about the sexual basis of voting behaviour. A sample survey in an LCC election in Battersea some years ago indicated that fewer women voted than men; and that among the women older women had a better record. There are generalisations about women who copy their husbands – I have often been asked when canvassing to 'come back when my husband is home'. But that might well be because the kettle is boiling or the baby crying. I have heard women telling me that they usually vote Conservative but they are supporting me because they think there should be more women in the House. And I recall the railwayman's wife who said she was usually Labour, but she 'would rather have a man'.

What effect did anybody expect from female enfranchisement? There were some who thought that not only would it differentiate women from the voting status which they shared with infants, felons and idiots, but that it would raise women to high public status, humanise society and bring peace on earth. Not everybody agreed. In 1889 Beatrice Webb was among the signatories of a manifesto drafted by Mrs Humphry Ward against the political enfranchisement of women. It was 20 years before she publicly recanted. She wrote in *Our Partnership*:

> Conservative by temperament and anti-democratic through social environment, I reacted against the narrow outlook and exasperated tone of some of the pioneers of women's suffrage . . . But the root of my anti-feminism lay in the fact that I had never myself suffered the disabilities assumed to arise from my sex.

Women's rights, it was said, 'is a subject which makes the Queen so furious that she cannot contain herself'. But there she was, safely underground, before women of 30 and over were granted the vote in 1919. Now there's a fascinating question. What was magic about 30? Was a woman over 30 invariably less flighty, more responsible than a man of 21? Whatever the reason, the 'flappers' had to wait until 1928. And at a time when Parliament will have to consider giving votes at 18 it is of course unthinkable that a different age should be fixed for young men and women. This, at least, is progress.

G. D. H. Cole used to say, as a strong supporter of votes for women, that women ought to have the vote as a matter of socialist principle; but that the result of giving it to them would be disastrous because the bulk of women were (a) unintelligent and (b) reactionary, and that they would hold back progress. Certainly there is no more reactionary human being than a reactionary woman. The hardest women are more granite than hard men. Sex is no criterion of progress in politics. All we have done is to enlarge the stage to make room for Lady Macbeth and Portia, for Martha and for Mary, for Jezebel and Naomi, for Eleanor Rathbone and for Florence Horsbrugh. And there is old Shaw laughing in the wings because he wrote in *The Intelligent Woman's Guide*:

> Historians, and journalists and political orators may assure you that the defeat of the armada, the cutting off of King Charles's head, the substitution of Dutch William for Scottish James on the throne, the passing of the Married Women's Property Acts and the conquest by the suffragettes of votes for women, have set you free . . . but all these events have added nothing to your leisure and therefore nothing to your liberty.

Nothing to your leisure. That is really

the heart of the problem. We have worked our way out of the coal mines and into a widening diversity of occupations without always solving the problem of the double job which then results. This is nothing new – the poorest women have always worked outside their homes as well as inside (sometimes doing outwork at home), and so have some of the most talented. But the main difference between today and 50 years ago is that now millions of women are involved. Half of our working woman-power now consists of married women. An unknown number of single women workers come home to care for elderly dependants at the end of a long day. For all these women the most intractable problem remains the maintenance of leisure and of liberty. This is where we need to make progress. I do not believe that the arithmetic of women's advance can be counted in terms of women MPs (which is just as well, as the number is declining) or of women poets or women bank managers or women airline pilots. There is no automatic osmosis of success which conveys the benefit of achievement to the poorest women. Here is where the assessors of progress must look – to the million women who earn less than five shillings an hour, for example.

Politics is only one aspect of power, but in this anniversary flotsam it is bound to demand the most attention. In the articles and at the meetings the number of women MPs is counted up as if it were an index of progress. But they might, after all, be entirely Conservative and not all as pleasant as Irene Ward or as fair-minded as Joan Vickers. I think it is a measure of unsureness that people do this. Of course, there should be more women in government and in local government simply because there are a lot of good human beings, who happen to be women, not yet participating.

The main reason why there are not more women in the House of Commons is that many women are not able to play a very active part in the chores of party politics – travelling, speaking, organising – while they are busy with their families and often with a job as well. If, when the children are off their hands, they decide they would like to go into Parliament they will find themselves right at the bottom of the ladder and regarded by patronising young men on selection committees as too old to begin. There is no more difficult job to combine with motherhood – not impossible, as women like Judith Hart and Shirley Williams and Margaret Thatcher can demonstrate. But not easy. This is partly because Parliament is run on a bachelor masculine timetable – its programme is not geared to mothers (or fathers) who might want to tuck up their babies or help with the homework. More normal working hours might well transform the personnel.

There is one achievement of the suffrage movement in this country too often overlooked. Because women here had won the vote, universal adult suffrage was automatically written into the constitutions of most Commonwealth countries as they became independent. And let us lay another flower on the graves of the brave. The glib may say that it was women's work in the war of 1914-18 which won them the vote and that the suffragettes were a waste of time. But how do we know that without their campaign public opinion would have connected war work with the franchise? After all, women had worked in earlier wars. Florence Nightingale never had a vote.

The Employment of Wives, Dominance, and Fertility[*]

ROBERT H. WELLER[**]

Using survey data collected in predominantly lower- and middle-income neighborhoods of San Juan, Puerto Rico, the author tests three propositions. (1) Participation in the labor force is associated with increased influence by the wife in family decision-making, particularly with respect to having additional children. (2) This increased influence in decision-making is associated with lower fertility among working women. (3) The negative relationship between labor-force status and fertility is stronger among wife-dominant and egalitarian families than among husband-dominant couples. Empirical support is present for each proposition.

CENSUS as well as survey data collected in Puerto Rico indicate that there is a negative relationship between female labor-force participation and fertility.[1] A similar relationship has been observed in numerous other countries.[2] Although the Puerto Rican experience suggests that this relationship is produced by voluntary factors rather than by involuntary, biological factors,[3] the explanatory intermediate variables have not been defined completely. Thus, reflecting on the experience of the United States, Jaffe writes that our knowledge is deficient concerning "the exact interrelationship between fertility rates and patterns and the participation of women in the working force."[4]

One variable that may help to explain the relationship between female labor-force participation and fertility is the pattern of family decision-making, particularly with respect to having children. Although some studies have offered little support for this proposition,[5] Kligler,[6] Heer,[7] and others[8] have reported that labor-

[*] This is a slightly revised version of a paper presented at the annual meetings of the American Sociological Association in August, 1968. Substantial portions of this paper are contained in the author's unpublished doctoral dissertation, *Female Work Experience and Fertility in San Juan, Puerto Rico: A Study of Selected Lower and Middle Income Neighborhoods*, Cornell University, 1967. The data reported in this paper were collected in the summer of 1966 under support by the Agency for International Development under Contract #AID/csd-817 with the Center for Housing and Environmental Studies at Cornell University. The author is grateful for permission to use these data. The author also wishes to express his appreciation to Professor George C. Myers of Cornell University for commenting critically upon this paper. Of course the author retains sole responsibility for any shortcomings that may exist.

[**] *Robert H. Weller, Ph.D., is Assistant Professor, Department of Sociology and Anthropology, Brown University.*

[1] A. J. Jaffe, *People, Jobs and Economic Development*, New York: Free Press, 1959; Jose Vasquez, *The Demographic Evolution of Puerto Rico*, unpublished Ph.D. dissertation, The University of Chicago, 1964, pp. 218-220; Ishmael Okraku, *Regional Variations in Puerto Rican Fertility Levels*, unpublished M.A. thesis, Cornell University, 1965; and Robert Hubert Weller, *Female Work Experience and Fertility in San Juan, Puerto Rico: A Study of Selected Lower and Middle Income Neighborhoods*, unpublished Ph.D., dissertation, Cornell University, 1967, pp. 83, 131-134.

[2] Ronald Freedman, "American Studies of Family Planning and Fertility: A Review of Major Trends and Issues," in *Research in Family Planning*, ed. by Clyde V. Kiser, Princeton, New Jersey: Princeton University Press, 1962, p. 223; Ronald Freedman, G. Baumert, and M. Bolte, "Expected Family Size and Family Size Values in West Germany," *Population Studies*, 13:2 (November, 1959), pp. 136-150; Murray Gendell, *Swedish Working Wives: A Study of Determinants and Consequences*, Totowa, New Jersey: Bedminster Press, 1963, pp. 145-148; Andras Klinger, "Trends of Differential Fertility by Social Strata in Hungary," *International Population Conference: New York, 1961*, London: UNESCO, 1963, pp. 93-94; David Heer, "Fertility Differences Between Indian and Spanish Speaking Parts of Andean Countries," *Population Studies*, 18:1 (July, 1964), pp. 71-84; and Carmen A. Miro, "Some Misconceptions Disproved: A Program of Comparative Fertility Surveys in Latin America," in *Family Planning and Population Problems: A*

Review of World Developments, ed. by Bernard Berelson *et al.*, Chicago: University of Chicago Press, 1966, pp. 615-634.

[3] Jaffe, *op. cit.*, p. 188; and Weller, *op. cit.*, chaps. 4 and 5. Data from the United States also indicate the importance of voluntary factors. Ronald Freedman, Pascal K. Whelpton, and Arthur A. Campbell, *Family Planning, Sterility and Population Growth*, New York: McGraw-Hill, 1959; Pascal K. Whelpton, Arthur A. Campbell, and John E. Patterson, *Fertility and Family Planning in the United States*, Princeton: Princeton University Press, 1966; and Judith Blake, "Demographic Science and the Redirection of Population Policy," *Journal of Chronic Diseases*, 18 (1965), pp. 1181-1200.

[4] A. J. Jaffe, "Working Force," in *The Study of Population: An Inventory and Appraisal*, ed. by Philip M. Hauser and Otis Dudley Duncan, Chicago: University of Chicago Press, 1959, p. 615.

[5] Gendell, *op. cit.*, pp. 130-133; Lois W. Hoffman, "Effects of the Employment of Mothers on Parental Power Relations and the Division of Household Tasks," *Marriage and Family Living*, 22:1 (February, 1960), pp. 27-35; and Constantina Safilios-Rothschild, "Some Aspects of Fertility in Urban Greece," *Proceedings of the World Population Conference*, New York: United Nations, 1967, Vol. 2, pp. 128-131.

[6] Deborah H. Kligler, *The Effects of the Employment of Married Women on Husband and Wife Roles*, unpublished Ph.D. dissertation, Yale University, 1954.

[7] David M. Heer, "Dominance and the Working Wife," *Social Forces*, 35 (May, 1958), pp. 341-347.

[8] Pierre Fougeyrollas, "Predominance du mari ou de la femme dans le menage," *Population*, 6 (1951), pp. 83-102; and Constantina Safilios-Rothschild, "A Comparison of

force participation by the wife lowers the degree of authority exercised by the husband and that the working wife exercises more influence in making decisions than the nonworking wife. Although it could be argued that authority is a characteristic possessed from childhood and that a husband with authority will resist his wife's desire to work, earlier research by Heer indicates that the greater influence of working wives is a consequence of their employment and is not an association due to the fact that a woman who goes out of the home to work is by nature more dominant in her dealings with other people than is her husband.[9]

Given this assumption, one link between the employment of wives and lower fertility becomes clear. Employment leads to greater influence in decision-making in general. If having additional children conflicts with the wife's desire to continue employment, the wife is better able to resist any pressures for additional children that her husband may exert.

Research in this substantive area has been limited. After finding no relationship between female labor-force status and completed fertility, Goldberg notes that the proportion of home- and family-centered activities was related to decisions about family size *only* among wife-dominant couples and among couples at early stages of their marriage. For husband-dominant couples, the expected number of children was found to be a direct function of the socioeconomic status characteristics of the family.[10]

This suggests the following propositions:

Participation in the labor force is associated with increased influence by the wife in family decision-making, particularly with respect to decisions regarding having additional children.

This increased influence in decision-making is associated with lower fertility among working women.

The last proposition assumes that additional fertility and continued employment are relatively incompatible. If these propositions are valid, then it follows that:

The negative relationship between labor-force status and fertility is stronger among wife-dominant and egalitarian families than among husband-dominant couples.

Power Structure and Marital Satisfaction in Urban Greek and French Families," paper presented at the Sixth World Congress of Sociology, Evian, France, 1966.

[9] Heer, "Dominance and the Working Wife," *op. cit.*

[10] David Goldberg, *Family Role Structure and Fertility,* unpublished Ph.D. dissertation, The University of Michigan, 1958.

SOURCE OF DATA

During the summer of 1966, a sample survey of 1,022 female mates of the head of household (or the female head of household if there was no male head) was conducted in San Juan, Puerto Rico, under the sponsorship of the Agency for International Development by a team of investigators from Cornell University. The principal goal of the research team was to assess the demographic, social, and political effects of various types of housing.

Seven areas representing four types of neighborhoods—middle class, lower class, lower-class slum, and public housing—were selected by the principal investigators, and systematic sampling was performed within each area.

As part of the survey, fertility and employment histories were obtained from the 650 ever-married women under 50 years of age. In the present report, analysis is limited to currently mated women (consensual as well as legal) between the ages of 15 and 49. Of the 577 respondents satisfying these criteria, the fertility histories obtained from 18 women were not complete (numerical expressions of children ever born, ideal and expected family size, and number of months married); therefore these have been excluded from analysis. Additional restrictions are made later for conceptual purposes.

It is believed that the portion of the sample used in this report can be regarded as representative of the currently mated women between the ages of 15 and 49 who are resident in these lower- and middle-class neighborhoods, but extreme care should be taken in generalizing beyond that universe.[11] As upper-class and suburban families are excluded from the universe of the sample, it is not representative of the total San Juan metropolitan population.

In addition to questions on fertility and employment, the questionnaire contained several items that were designed to reveal the pattern of family decision-making. These concerned the following: weekly food expenditures; having another child; buying something new, such as a radio or mirror; raising the children; time expenditure on holidays; and neighborhood of residence. The following question was used:

In each family someone has to decide matters such as where the family lives and in what manner. Many couples discuss the matter first, but the final decision

---

[11] For a more detailed description of the organizational features of the project as well as an analysis of the sample's representativeness, see Weller, *op. cit.,* pp. 56-63.

6

has to be made by the husband or wife. For example, who in your family finally decides matters like the following?

The response categories were: husband always, husband more than wife, husband and wife about equally, wife more than husband, wife always, and other. The last category was included to accommodate responses such as "don't know" or "God decides such things."

A Likert-type index has been formed by assigning values from one to five to each response, with one designating "husband always" and five designating "wife always." Respondents classified as "other" on one or more items have been excluded from the computation of this index; this was particularly likely with respect to the item on whether or not to have another child. The possible values of the index range from six to 30. The higher the score, the more a wife reports that she influences family decisions with respect to these particular items.

RESULTS

In Table 1 it can be seen that participation in the labor force is associated with greater influence by the wife in family decision-making at all levels of educational attainment. Unexpectedly, there is no systematic increase in the wife's influence with education.

A large proportion of the respondents report that the decision on having another child is made jointly by the husband and wife. Given that this decision is not made jointly, the wife is more likely to make the final decision. The same pattern is present in the item on raising children and is in sharp contrast with the pattern of responses in the other four items.

The pattern of decision-making by education and labor-force status with respect to having another child is shown in Table 3. For conceptual clarity, 100 respondents who have been classi-

TABLE 1. MEDIAN INDEX OF DECISION-MAKING BY LABOR-FORCE STATUS AND EDUCATION FOR ALL CURRENTLY MATED WOMEN

Years of Schooling	Labor Force	Non-Labor Force
0–5	17.6 (27)	15.3 (168)
6–8	18.2 (21)	15.1 (111)
9+	18.1 (71)	17.6 (123)
Total	18.0	15.7

Number of cases shown in parentheses.

fied as involuntarily sterile or subfecund have been excluded from this and subsequent analyses.[12] The author feels that for these families decisions on additional children are either unlikely because of the apparent impossibility of realization of the decision or unrealistic in that they would not reflect the family and socioeconomic situation of the persons involved. An additional 40 respondents have been excluded from analysis because their answer was such that the pattern of family decison-making could not be ascertained. In Table 3 these are reported as "Other." The 418 remaining respondents are currently mated women with complete fertility histories who are either fecund or voluntarily sterile and who indicated that the de-

[12] A system of classification has been used that is similar conceptually to the Growth of American Family (1960) study. Parameters of involuntary sterility and subfecundability have been obtained that are very close to the GAF estimates for the United States. For an elaboration of the scheme as well as a comparison with the GAF results, see *ibid.*, pp. 87-93.

TABLE 2. FAMILY DECISION-MAKING ON SELECTED ITEMS

	Having Children		Raising Children		Food Expenditure		Buying Things		Holiday Time		Residence	
	LF*	NLF†	LF	NLF	LF	NLF	LF	NLF	LF	NLF	LF	NLF
Husband always	7%	14%	5%	11%	28%	37%	17%	43%	17%	34%	18%	43%
Husband more than wife	4	6	4	6	9	11	11	12	9	13	13	12
Husband and wife about equally	59	57	66	68	32	30	42	33	53	44	47	37
Wife more than husband	14	14	16	11	16	11	18	7	12	5	11	5
Wife always	15	9	9	4	15	12	13	5	8	4	10	4
Total	100%	100%	100%	100%	100%	100%	100%	100%	100%	100%	100%	100%
Other	13	42	4	14	1	2	1	4	2	13	1	3
Number of cases	132	445										

* Labor force.
† Non-labor force.

TABLE 3. PATTERN OF DECISION-MAKING ON WHETHER TO HAVE ANOTHER CHILD, BY LABOR-FORCE STATUS AND YEARS OF SCHOOLING—NORMALLY FECUND WOMEN ONLY

Decision-Making	Labor Force				Non-Labor Force			
	0–5	6–8	9+	All	0–5	6–8	9+	All
Husband always	13%	5%	7%	7%	12%	20%	12%	14%
Husband more than wife	0	5	5	4	9	8	4	7
Husband and wife about equally	69	58	58	60	53	46	61	53
Wife more than husband	0	16	17	14	15	15	15	15
Wife always	18	16	13	15	11	11	8	11
	100%	100%	100%	100%	100%	100%	100%	100%
Number of cases	16	19	59	94	133	91	100	324
Other	3	3	5	11	12	8	9	29

cion on whether or not to have another child customarily is made by either the husband or wife (or both).

At all levels of educational attainment, workers are less likely than nonworkers to report that the husband makes the final decision concerning having another child. Moreover, workers are more likely than nonworkers to report that they make this decision more often than their husbands. This applies to all categories of educational attainment except the lowest.

Therefore, empirical support is present for the proposition that working is associated with greater influence by the wife in family decision-making.

In subsequent analyses, the respondents are divided into three groups. The husband is considered the dominant partner with respect to having another child if the respondent replied "husband always" or "husband more than wife." Those answering "husband and wife about equally" are classified as egalitarian. The wife is considered the dominant partner if she replied "wife always" or "wife more than husband" to the item on having another child.

The meaningfulness of this distinction is ex-amined in Table 4. If this trichotomy measures the relative influence of the wife in family decisions, then it is reasonable to assert that wives who influence decisions about having additional children also exercise increased influence over other family decisions. The Likert index scores offer support for this proposition, even when the item on having additional children is omitted from computation. The crucial distinction is between husband-dominant couples and other families, with the former having markedly lower scores. This generalization holds *within* labor-force categories, even though labor-force participants in general exhibit much higher scores.

It is also a plausible proposition that husbands who dominate family decisions should be less likely than other husbands to assist in performing domestic chores, as such husbands are likely to be authoritarian and traditionally oriented. Support for this proposition is present, although the frequency with which the husband helps with the domestic chores apparently is unrelated to labor-force status. As in decision-making, the important distinction seems to be that between husband-dominant and other cou-

TABLE 4. SELECTED VARIABLES BY PATTERN OF FAMILY DECISION-MAKING AND LABOR-FORCE STATUS

	All Women			Labor Force			Non-Labor Force		
	Husband	Equal	Wife	Husband	Equal	Wife	Husband	Equal	Wife
Likert index score*	11.9	17.5	17.0	13.5	18.0	19.7	11.7	16.8	16.0
Transformed score	10.1	14.5	12.6	12.5	15.1	15.5	9.9	13.8	11.7
Percent reporting husband helps with chores "sometime" or "frequently"	36	44	45	36	48	48	36	42	44
Number of cases	80	229	109	11	56	27	69	173	82

* Both of these scores are medians derived from the six items on family decision-making described earlier. The transformed score is the total score less the score for the item on having another child.

8

TABLE 5. SELECTED ASPECTS OF FERTILITY AND DURATION OF MARRIAGE BY LABOR-FORCE STATUS AND HUSBAND-WIFE DOMINANCE

Selected Variables	All Women			Husband			Equal			Wife		
	Hus-band	Equal	Wife	NLF†	LF*	Ratio of LF:NLF	NLF	LF	Ratio of LF:NLF	NLF	LF	Ratio of LF:NLF
Children ever born	3.7	3.6	3.4	3.7	3.5	.95	3.8	3.0	.79	3.6	2.7	.75
Expected family size	4.3	4.3	4.5	4.4	3.6	.82	4.5	3.7	.82	4.9	3.3	.67
Ideal family size	4.0	4.1	4.2	3.9	4.2	1.08	4.1	3.9	.95	4.3	3.9	.91
CEB/1,000 months married	24	23	26	25	19	.76	24	18	.75	28	19	.68
Percent desiring more children	20	19	26	20	22	1.10	21	14	.67	28	22	.79
Number times married	1.3	1.2	1.2	1.3	1.4	—	1.2	1.2	—	1.2	1.2	—
Age at marriage	19.2	19.2	19.0	19.1	20.6	—	18.9	20.1	—	18.5	20.7	—
Current age	32.9	32.7	31.0	32.4	38.4	—	32.2	34.6	—	30.3	32.8	—
Number months married	155	158	134	150	182	—	156	169	—	131	142	—
Years of schooling	6.4	7.3	7.1	6.0	8.7	—	6.7	9.2	—	6.2	9.9	—

* Labor force.
† Non-labor force.

ples. This suggests that the decisive distinction with respect to differential fertility by labor-force status may be the same one. Specifically, the relationship between working and fertility should be weakest among husband-dominant couples and about equally strong among other couples.

Table 5 shows that the pattern of dominance per se apparently bears little relation to fertility behavior.[13] Among workers, however, the husband-dominant couples exhibit much higher fertility than the other couples. This is interpreted as support for the second proposition, that increased influence in decision-making is associated with lower fertility among working women.

Current age and age at marriage do not differ greatly by dominance category. Although differences in educational attainment by labor-force status are present, differences by dominance category are small. Therefore, education cannot be a confounding variable. It would be interesting to examine these relationships by level of education, for the relationship itself may vary with the educational attainment of the marital partners. However, the small number of cases in some cells precludes such analysis.

In previous research, Goldberg has indicated that, among wife-dominant couples, participation in the labor force is associated with lower fertility but that this relationship is absent among husband-dominant couples.[14] In the present study, a somewhat different pattern is observed. Differential fertility by labor-force status is present among all three types of families; but this relation is weakest among husband-dominant couples and is totally absent with respect to desired fertility. This lends support to the third proposition, that the negative relationship between labor-force status and fertility is stronger among the wife-dominant and egalitarian families than among those classified as husband-dominant.

In conclusion, participation in the labor force apparently leads to increased influence by the wife in family decision-making. This is true particularly with respect to having additional children—a decision that is reported predominantly as being made upon an egalitarian basis. Although the pattern of dominance per se appears to be unrelated to fertility behavior, among workers the husband-dominant couples exhibit fertility markedly higher than that of other families. Differential fertility by labor-force status also is weakest among husband-dominant couples.

In general, respondents in husband-dominant families possess less knowledge of birth-control technology than do other respondents. Nevertheless, the relationship between working and increased knowledge of birth control is not weaker among the husband-dominant couples than among the others. In some instances it is stronger. However, when use of birth control is considered, the relationship between employment and use is considerably weaker among husband-dominant couples. This is true regarding regularity of current use as well as the parity at which contraception was first used. This suggests the importance of motivation to utilize existing knowledge rather than differential knowledge per se as accounting for differential fertility by labor-force status and is similar to

[13] Analysis of data from the Detroit Area Study also indicates this lack of association. Although the questions used in this paper are very similar to those used by Blood and Wolfe, a completely different method of classifying couples by dominance characteristics has been employed. Robert O. Blood, Jr. and Donald M. Wolfe, *Husbands and Wives: The Dynamics of Married Living*, New York: Free Press, 1960, p. 133.

[14] Goldberg, *op. cit.*

9

TABLE 6. KNOWLEDGE AND USE OF BIRTH CONTROL BY HUSBAND-
WIFE DOMINANCE AND LABOR-FORCE STATUS

	All Women			Husband			Equal			Wife		
	Hus-band	Equal	Wife	NLF†	LF*	Ratio of LF:NLF	NLF	LF	Ratio of LF:NLF	NLF	LF	Ratio of LF:NLF
% Ever read about birth control	46	53	54	42	73	1.74	49	66	1.35	49	70	1.43
% Heard about oral pills	81	87	84	83	73	.88	87	84	.97	84	85	1.01
% Knows how pills work	26	28	30	25	36	1.44	25	38	1.52	30	30	1.00
% Heard of diaphragm	60	72	83	55	91	1.65	68	86	1.26	52	85	1.63
% Ever talked with husband about number of children she would like to have	70	71	72	70	73	1.04	72	70	.97	72	70	.97
% Ever talked with doctor, nurse, or social worker about birth control	46	56	59	41	82	2.00	54	63	1.17	59	59	1.00
% Ever talked with spouse about birth control	59	64	69	57	73	1.28	63	70	1.11	67	74	1.10
% Ever talked with anyone about birth control	77	87	90	76	82	1.08	86	89	1.03	87	96	1.10
% Ever using birth control	80	79	83	81	73	.90	75	93	1.24	81	89	1.10
Mean parity before which ever-users first used birth control	4.1	3.6	3.5	4.0	4.6	—	3.6	3.6	—	3.9	2.6	—
% Currently "always" using a method	68	62	69	67	73	1.09	57	79	1.39	67	75	1.12
% Non-sterilized women currently "always" using a method	42	37	48	42	40	.95	32	56	1.75	46	56	1.22

* Labor force.
† Non-labor force.

the relationship between dominance and fertility discussed above.

SUMMARY

Participation in the labor force is associated with increased influence by the wife in family decision-making, particularly with respect to having additional children. This increased influence in decision-making is associated with lower fertility among working women. The negative relation between labor-force status and fertility is stronger among the wife-dominant and egalitarian families than among the husband-dominant couples. Although the pattern of family decision-making apparently is not related to knowledge of contraceptive techniques, the differential use of birth control is weakest among the husband-dominant couples.

Therefore, the pattern of family decision-making appears to be a crucial intermediate variable in the relationship between employment of the wife and fertility. This is related to alterations in the customary cultural alignment of marital roles and may result in role strain within the marital relationship itself. More research is needed on this point before a definite statement can be made. Due to the emphasis placed upon interviewing the female mate of the head of household, the present data are not appropriate for examining this question. The author would have preferred to include items measuring marital satisfaction, but this was not possible because of the length of the questionnaire as well as the multiplicity of topics it covered. In addition, it is necessary to make the methodological distinction between marital satisfaction as reported by the wife and that reported by the husband; for quite different measures might be obtained if the wife is content with her influential position vis-à-vis the husband, who may be quite dissatisfied. The same criticism may be made about indicators of dominance that rely solely upon the responses of one partner. These are issues that must be resolved before the causal links between working dominance, role strain or conflict, and fertility are known completely. Moreover, the need for temporal research is clear. Does labor-force participation lead to increased influence by the wife, or is the relationship between dominance and employment produced by the selection of dominant women into the labor force? On the basis of limited research in the United States, the proposition of selectivity seems unlikely. However, the situation in societies characterized as male authoritarian may be quite different. Only temporal studies utilizing proper experimental design can answer these questions properly.

10

Sex Unwanted

The Economist (December 7, 1968)

It is now against government rules to specify that males or females are preferred when job vacancies are advertised in America. An exception is to be made for those jobs necessarily limited to one sex or the other—models for women's clothes, perhaps, or coaches for boys' football teams. But in general, starting last Sunday, employers, employment agencies and newspapers which carry "help wanted" advertising must either avoid mentioning sex or be ready to prove that it is the actual demands of the job, rather than prejudice, that gives a job a sexual classification.

The ruling is an outgrowth of the Civil Rights Act of 1964. That prohibited employers from discriminating in hiring because of an applicant's race, religion or sex (the latter being tucked into the Act as an afterthought). Until this year, the federal Equal Employment Opportunity Commission had been lenient, allowing the segregation of male and female advertisements on the grounds that they helped applicants locate the jobs that were most likely to be attractive to them. But after thinking it over, the commission decided last summer that the practice was discriminatory and set December 1st as the deadline for it to be abolished.

For women, the tougher policy of the commission should mean a lot of teasing and greater equality as well. One woman has succeeded in getting a jockey's license from the Maryland racing commission, while another has made headlines by failing in Kentucky (male jockeys refused to ride with her in the races that she needed to qualify). Airline stewardesses will no longer have to suffer under the regulations which took their jobs away when they married or turned 35. The question now is whether the state laws concerning the employment of women can survive; some insist on early retirement, others on rest periods, some even that there be day beds in women's rest rooms. In California three women have challenged the law which says that in general women may not work more than eight hours a day; they claim that this restricts their ability to do overtime and to earn as much as men.

A similar kind of federal protection has been given to older workers. The 1967 Age Discrimination Act went into effect in June and employers now risk penalties if they refuse to hire a worker because of his advanced age or if they use his age as an excuse for paying him less. (The older worker, incidentally, is somebody over 40.) Like the laws against discrimination because of race or sex, this one will prove hard to administer. There can be fines against employers found guilty in court and on occasion the offenders have been required to pay the applicant the wages that he would have earned.

THE ABORTION DEBATE

by Ralph B. Potter, Jr.

The right wing of the spectrum is defended most relentlessly in public debate by Roman Catholic spokesmen. It should not be overlooked, however, that some members of the Protestant and

95

13

Jewish communities join in defense of the present laws regulating abortion. Nevertheless, most of the right-wing arguments stated here are to be attributed to Roman Catholic commentators who, by and large, have set the terms of debate over and against left-wing advocates.

As one moves toward the right end of the spectrum, certainty increases that it is the proper function of the state to intervene in the matter of abortion in order to prevent harm. The harm envisioned may be inflicted upon the mother, the medical profession, the family, society at large, the fetus, or what might best be described as "the cultural ethos."

The nub of the right-wing argument, as presented to contemporary Americans, is simple and stark: the condoning of widespread resort to abortion would undermine civilization. The argument is couched in theological terms; it leads, however, to conclusions in the realm of cultural anthropology. The path of reasoning sometimes twists through philosophical thickets. But the destination is a flat prediction concerning consequences for all human relationships if a significant number of people come to accept abortion in good conscience. There are many distractive bypaths along the route to be traversed in argument. But the constant goal is to convince hearers, by whatever arguments carry force in their generation, that the practice of abortion is incompatible with the attainment of man's true humanity. At stake in controversies over abortion law reform is the definition of the vision of what man should be. Urgency arises from the conviction that the content of that vision will shape the actual quality of human relationships in decades to come.

The profundity of the right-wing argument is its greatest weakness. Many of the injuries described by controversialists on the right take place in a dimension of existence unknown or unexplored by their fellow citizens. Indeed, when the particular "harms" are analyzed closely, they are seen to consist ultimately of a deprivation of a greater good, a good which may transcend the concern of a secular, pluralistic state. Can the prevention of such a harm, or the realization of such a good, be considered a valid legislative purpose sufficient to overrule the strong desires

96

of innumerable pregnant women? Analysis of the difficulties experienced by right-wing critics in dramatizing the injuries they presume to be wrought upon mothers by abortion will suggest the perils of profundity and illustrate the dynamics of the abortion debate.

The harm that is most vivid and imaginable to typical onlookers is injury to the health and welfare of the mother. Spokesmen for the left wing generate great dramatic impact by portraying very palpable injuries to mothers. They depict vivid harm to victims with whom readers can readily identify. The power of immediacy is exploited also in their outline of causes and cures. The harm is attributed directly to the lack of legal access to medically competent abortions performed in hospital settings. A prompt remedy is offered through "legalization of abortion now." In the effort to recoup the title of "defenders of the public welfare," right-wing advocates are obliged, by contrast, to depict either very subtle injuries to real persons or somewhat less subtle harm to less vividly imaginable entities such as "society," "civilization," or "the fetus." Indeed, the attempt to overcome the seeming inability of many people to visualize the fetus as an object of real injury accounts for many of the intellectual and rhetorical maneuvers in the battle over abortion law reform.

Both the left and the right wings of the abortion spectrum would like to enjoy a reputation as guardians of the life and health of mothers. But how are life and health truly protected? Members of the left wing join with many moderates of the middle segment in urging that permission for abortion should be granted when the measure is deemed necessary by physicians to spare a woman from a nonlethal threat to her health. Going beyond that, the left wing emphasizes the need to protect women from the risk to life and health incurred through criminal abortion. The right wing asserts that true life and health are best served by guarding women from abortion in any circumstance.

To reinforce its claim to be the true guardian of the mother, each side provides empirical data concerning the incidence of abortion, both legal and illegal, and the medical and psychiatric

97

effects of abortion performed under various circumstances. The left wing must overcome public inertia. Its spokesmen are compelled to show that a massive problem exists that ought not to be ignored. Hence, their estimates of the incidence of criminal abortion tend to be high. Moreover, their statistics must indicate that criminal abortions are very dangerous while hospital abortions are medically safe and seldom give rise to untoward psychological effects.

Conversely, statistics presented by the right wing diminish the danger gap between hospital and extrahospital abortions. Emphasis is placed by right-wing spokesmen upon the residual risk of the operation under even the best medical conditions. It is asserted that "sound medical practice" would require abortion only in exceedingly rare circumstances. With the advance of medical skill, strictly medical indications have been reduced. It is rare that life or health is seriously jeopardized in well attended pregnancy. Moreover, it is claimed, there is no strong evidence of significant therapeutic gain through abortion. There is a lack of due proportion between the undoubted risk and the uncertain gain.

The right wing's first line of defense — that abortion, as a medical procedure, is both dangerous and superfluous — seems to be crumbling under an avalanche of statistics from Eastern Europe and other regions where abortion is widely practiced and new techniques are being developed through research. The level of medical danger there is not high. Also, it can be argued that abortion is not totally superfluous. If it is seldom necessary, abortion may nevertheless be occasionally necessary, and the law should not bar physicians from attempting to preserve the life and health of their patients.

There is a second line of defense. The dangers of abortion may be more subtle. The unhappy effects may be delayed in time and buried in the recesses of the personality, accessible only to those armed with psychiatric skill. Many on the right wing insist that, no matter where, or by whom, or for what reason abortion is performed, it inflicts a scar upon the conscience of the woman and places her mental health in jeopardy by exposing her to the harsh retribution of guilt.

A considerable body of literature deals with the psychiatric effects of abortion. From this literature adherents of the left wing extract evidence that the incidence of serious psychological after-effects is relatively low. They go on to argue that the incidence would be much lower still if right-wing propaganda did not perpetuate the self-fulfilling prophecy that induces symptoms of guilt by contending that such symptoms are virtually inevitable. They hold that guilt over abortion is a cultural legacy that will become increasingly rare as societies adopt a more "enlightened" and therefore more tolerant attitude toward abortion.

The reply of those on the right wing is to make the injury from abortion appear more subtle still. They hold that some psychiatrists cannot detect the full extent of the harm to mothers because they maintain a superficial view of the full components of true health. True health involves more than "a state of complete physical and mental wellbeing." It has a spiritual dimension. The injury to the spirit of one who violates the law of nature and commandment of God by indulging in abortion may escape the notice of observers who employ less sensitive indices of affliction.

The depth of the disagreement which leads to strikingly different estimates of how harm to mothers is to be avoided comes clearly into view in debate over the meaning and function of guilt. All agree that women should be spared the experience of guilt. The left would remove the cultural inducement to exhibit this learned response. Adherents of the right wing insist that the only way to be rid of guilt is to avoid the occasion of guilt. In their view, guilt is not simply a legacy from an unenlightened past. It is a sign of latent health, a danger signal that the law of nature cannot be violated with impunity. Given the reality of abortion as the extermination of innocent life for self-centered purposes, women *ought* to feel guilty. Indeed, the *absence* of guilt is a grievous symptom which reveals that callousness and spiritual sclerosis are far advanced. Women should be spared the

99

occasion of guilt by the refusal of abortion. But, if abortions are to be performed, the entire community must be saved from experiencing a *lack* of guilt.

The third line of defense of the right-wing claim to be the true guardian of women is the claim that the practice of abortion frustrates the realization of man's true humanity. Evidence for this is not easily given. It is difficult to muster "hard empirical data" to convince those who, on other bases, do not already share a particular view of men. The difficulty exposes the true nature of the dispute and demonstrates the burden of profundity.

With regard to the protection of mothers, as on other issues, participants in the abortion controversy talk past one another. Reformers on the left gather statistics which purport to prove that, at least in certain nations, few women experience deep remorse after an abortion. But the statistics, even if acknowledged as accurate, have little effect upon right-wing commentators. Their arguments are not grounded in such observations. Their line can be defended with the aid of statistics that show abortion *does* have ill effects. But it cannot be overthrown by empirical evidence that abortion does *not* have bad medical or psychiatric consequences. Only the outer defenses can be endangered by the attack of epidemiologists and sociologists. The inner defense is founded firmly upon theological ground. The battle is being fought over questions of theological anthropology and ethics. The issue is: What ought man to be? What style of life represents the realization of true humanity?

HIGH STAKES

The central claim of the right wing is that abortion is evil because it deprives an individual of the greater good of becoming a more selfless creature. Abortion, in killing the actual self of the fetus, kills the potential higher self of the mother. Abortion is inimical to the attainment of "a generous spirit" which wel-

100

comes new life and accepts the occasion of redemptive suffering and sacrifice.

At stake in the abortion debate is not simply the fate of individual women or even the destiny of individual nations and cultures. It is difficult to demonstrate that acceptance of the most extreme proposal for abortion on demand would establish a clear and present danger to the civil harmony necessary for the maintenance of a tranquil state. Nations that have lenient abortion laws do function. But if abortion is not an actual threat to minimal public order, it may nevertheless be a symbolic threat to the ideal moral order espoused by Christians for two millennia. Abortion does not merely contradict specific mores and moral teachings pertaining to sexuality, marriage, and procreation or endanger a system of law built upon "respect for life." It implies the rejection of a world view which has sustained a way of life, a mode of being in the world, a pattern of response to the human condition.

Abortion is a symbolic threat to an entire system of thought and meaning. The willingness to practice abortion, or even to condone resort to abortion by others, signals that the high Christian vision of selfless charity has become despised and rejected of men. The Christian portrayal of the true man as one characterized by selflessness, sacrifice, concern for the weak and the unlovely, and a willingness to accept and transcend allotted afflictions through the power of redemptive suffering has faded in public consciousness to the point that it can seldom induce willing imitation. For many people there is simply no meaning in putting up with an unwanted circumstance when recourse is available without a high probability of temporal retribution.

For Christians, an entire system of meaning may be at stake in the abortion debate; but is anything at stake for a secular, pluralistic state?

SOURCES OF THE ABHORRENCE OF ABORTION

Christians frequently are delighted to take credit for instilling into the Western tradition a deep abhorrence of abortion. This

I O I

affirmation of the historical relevance of Christianity may do wonders for Christian pride and morale, but it makes it more, rather than less, difficult to maintain antiabortion laws in a secular, pluralistic setting. Norman St. John-Stevas, a British Roman Catholic barrister and member of Parliament, has celebrated the role attributed to Christian faith in the emergence of respect for the fundamental value of "the right to life."

> The respect for human life and personality that distinguishes Western society from the totalitarian societies of the East did not spring up out of nothing. It is deeply rooted in experience and history. Above all it is rooted in religion. Ultimately the idea of the right to life, as is the case with other human rights, is traceable to the Christian doctrine of man. . . . The value of human life for the Christian in the first century A.D., as today, rested not on its development of a superior sentience but on its unique character of the union of body and soul, both destined for eternal life. The right to life thus has a theological foundation. . . . Respect for the lives of *others* because of their eternal destiny is the essence of the Christian teaching. Its other aspect is the emphasis on the creatureliness of man. Man is not absolutely master of his own life and body, he has no *dominion* over it but holds it in trust for God's purposes.
>   This respect for human life has become part of the moral consensus of Western society [34:16, 17].

By this account, a ban on abortion might seem to be a particular application of the fundamental principle ascribed to Christian influence. But St. John-Stevas suggests that the sentiments which lead to sanctions against abortion have a more general source.

> This attitude to young life undoubtedly has in part a Christian foundation but it goes back beyond the Christian era to earlier civilizations. Rejection of abortion seems to result from the nature of man himself. . . . With the coming of Christianity condemnation of abortion was reinforced and became absolute [34:36].

Is the rejection of abortion really rooted in the nature of man himself? Or does it derive from a response to the image of man

102

portrayed in the Gospels? The issue cannot be settled by available anthropological data which seem to indicate a general ambivalence towards the practice of abortion within societies which differ greatly in the rate of occurrence and the severity of the sanctions imposed [8:97–152; 9].

The more emphasis is placed upon the distinctively Christian roots of the ban on abortion, the more difficult it becomes to argue that the restrictions can or should be maintained if the theological roots from which they sprang have now been eroded. St. John-Stevas observes that the concept of the right to life "is accepted by many who would reject the Christian doctrine on which it is based." But he implies, nevertheless, that the pillars of Christian faith are necessary props for the ban upon abortion: ". . . the right to life is ceaselessly challenged. . . . Against these attacks the Christian doctrine of man, as a being destined for eternal life, and therefore of unique value, provides the most effective bulwark" [34:127]. An increasingly shaky popular belief in man's eternal destiny is, in these days, an unsteady foundation for domestic legislation.

It seems credible that Christian apologists are correct in the historical judgment that the harsh condemnation of abortion expressed in our laws is the precipitate of Western exposure to Christian moral teaching. An evangelical vision of how men ought to behave has been imposed as the legal norm of how they must behave. The requirements of love have been confused with the demands of natural justice.

In an extensive law journal article, Eugene Quay provides an example of the extent to which Christian expectations of self-sacrificing charity have crept into Roman Catholic definitions of conduct to be required by legal enactment.

> A mother who would sacrifice the life of her unborn child for her own health is lacking in something. If there could be any authority to destroy an innocent life for social considerations, it would still be in the interests of society to sacrifice such a mother rather than the child who might otherwise prove to be normal and decent and an asset [30:234].

103

Willingness to sacrifice one's health for the sake of an unborn child would seem to many people to represent an heroic achievement rather than a minimal gesture necessary to qualify one as "an asset" to society. Quay's rendition of the natural law and the nature of man has been skewed by Christian norms; the model of charity has been taken as the mandate of the law.

Through the teaching of the church, the faithful may come to look upon self-sacrifice as "normal and decent." It is difficult to convince the unfaithful, who may not share the prior conviction that man should be something more than he is, that abortion makes man something less than he ought to be. The mother who refuses to sacrifice her health may be "lacking in something," but that something is superadded to the level of morality that the state must require in order to preserve its stable existence.

The teaching of the church generated the sentiments expressed through the ban upon abortion. Abortion is a practice which seems incongruous with the profession of faith of those who live under the sign of the cross. But the nation does not live under the sign of the cross. Why, then, should there be laws restricting abortion? Do such statutes serve any secular purpose which may invest them with binding force in a society no longer willing to submit to the tutelage of the church?

WHAT VALUES DO ABORTION LAWS PROTECT?

The harm attributed to abortion by right-wing critics of legal reform is subtle and profound; it is the deprivation of man's greatest good — a character formed by charity and humble obedience to the commandments of God. But the very nobility of the vision places it beyond the protective concern of the law.

The state cannot command charity, but it can enforce justice. If it could be demonstrated that abortion did injury to some proper subject of the law's protection, a more solid foundation for antiabortion statutes could be constructed. This is the challenge to the right wing and to the middle: they must indicate

104

a harm the law cannot ignore to a victim the law is bound to protect. The Christian commentator is goaded by a moral abhorrence of abortion derived from the charitable lesson of the Gospel. But to defend public laws against abortion he needs legal arguments derived from the universal norms of natural justice.

105

THE PRESERVATION OF INDIVIDUAL CHARACTER

In order to provide a secular purpose for the legislative restriction of abortion, those sharing the inclinations of the right wing can argue that the ban on abortion functions not simply to uphold a particular code of behavior, let alone a peculiar code of sexual behavior. It upholds character, the type of character that is indispensable to good citizenship. The virtues necessary to sustain the true family are the virtues necessary to sustain the state. The virtues and vices exposed in dealing with matters of sex, family life, and procreation pervade the entire character and find expression in civic relations. The state has a stake in the promotion of self-restraint rather than self-indulgence, responsibility rather than irresponsibility, and selfless adaptability rather than selfish rigidity.

There is more to this phase of the argument than the cry that acceptance of abortion will lead to sexual promiscuity. The fear is rather that it will lead to a general decline of individual character through lax enforcement of responsibility. The issue is not whether sex is to be separated from procreation, but whether procreation can be divorced from the responsibility to nurture new life.

Most commentators at every point across the spectrum might be willing to concede that in American society, by and large, sex has already been separated from procreation. This can be accomplished, with fair reliability, by practice of the rhythm method, which is cheap, simple, available without reliance upon a supplier, and is well advertised in literature widely distributed by the Roman Catholic Church. The new sexual mores that may evolve will doubtless be labeled "promiscuous" by some moralists and welcomed by others. In either case, it is too late to suppress the knowledge that, except for occasional "accidents," sexual inter-

109

course need not result in procreation. The small but enduring margin of error gives rise to the question, "Who will bear the risk of contraceptive failure?"

Right-wing commentators insist that the woman must bear the residual risk of pregnancy because her dismissal from that responsibility would bring on a widespread eagerness to evade every troublesome inconvenience which members of society must bear. To this, critics reply that the desire to escape the "natural consequences" of our actions is not only common and in most circumstances approved; it is, in fact, the stimulus to research and progress. The progress attained by permitting abortion as an emergency backstop to contraception would be the upgrading of parenthood and the realization of a happy family in a home in which every child would be wanted and welcomed. Men applaud the extension of human control into all other areas. Advocates of reform ask, "Why should this one act be set off as inaccessible to control?" The answer from the right wing is that life is present. No matter how tenuous the existence of a newly formed embryo, its creation is an event of moral import that cannot be totally ignored or despised.

The battle line is drawn at the point at which the relentless extension of self-determination and control over nature collides with the fundamental principle of "respect for life." Should there be no limit to willful manipulation, no inclination to concede that there are boundaries to the power that may safely be entrusted to men? The fear expressed by the right wing is that if the law does not contest a woman's claim that she has a right to dispose as she wishes of that "piece of tissue" which contains the seed of a full grown person, we shall plummet ever faster towards a brave new world in which the only barrier to the manipulation of fellow human beings will be lack of power and technique.

Opponents of abortion fear that the inhabitants of the brave new world will be possessed and driven by a type of character that will brook no interference with their ambitions from nature, man, or God. If the dystopia they envision were a certain consequence of present toleration of abortion, many moderates might reconsider their mild reformist views. But the consequences are

110

not inevitable nor would they be horrifying to all. In light of the broad and intense demand for abortion, can the state withhold permission solely on the basis of speculation about the possible effects of abortion upon individual character?

The argument that "easy abortion" will undermine a quality of individual character necessary to uphold civic virtue suffices only to gain a place for abortion within the category of "crimes without victims." In that category, antiabortion legislation maintains a perennially perilous existence in company with laws against drug addiction, homosexuality, prostitution, and gambling. The paternalistic style of such laws is deemed old fashioned by many citizens who are only slightly to the left of the center of the spectrum. In their minds, what a man chooses to do to his individual character ought to be considered a private affair. If there is to be a justification of antiabortion legislation grounded firmly in the defense of the public interest, the search must go on.

REFERENCES

8. Devereux, George: A Typological Study of Abortion in 350 Primitive, Ancient, and Pre-Industrial Societies, in Harold Rosen, ed: *Therapeutic Abortion: Medical, Psychiatric, Legal, Anthropological and Religious Considerations* (The Julian Press, New York, New York) 1954, pp 97–152.

9. Devereux, George: *A Study of Abortion in Primitive Societies* (The Julian Press, New York, New York) 1955.

30. Quay, Eugene: Justifiable Abortion: Medical and Legal Foundations, *The Georgetown Law Journal*, vol 49, no 2, Winter 1960, pp 173–256, see also reference 31.

31. Quay, Eugene: Justifiable Abortion: Medical and Legal Foundations, *The Georgetown Law Journal*, vol 49, no 3, Spring 1961, pp 395–538. An extensive bibliography accompanies the article, the first portion of which is in reference 30. A 73-page summary of laws governing abortion in the United States and its territories is contained in an appendix.

34. St John-Stevas, Norman: *The Right to Life* (Hodder & Stoughton, Ltd, London, England) 1963, pp 16, 17, 36, 127.

Introduction

It is time to declare that sex is too important a subject to leave to the myopic crowd of happy hookers, Dr. Feelgoods, black panthers, white rats, answer men, evangelical lesbians, sensuous psychiatrists, retired baseball players, pornographers, dolphins, swinging priests, displaced revolutionaries, polymorphous perverts, and *Playboy* philosophers—all bouncing around on waterbeds and typewriters and television talk shows, making "freedom" ring the cash registers of the revolution.

Nothing is free, least of all sex, which is bound to our deepest sources of energy, identity, and emotion. Sex can be cheapened, of course, but then, inevitably, it becomes extremely costly to the society as a whole. For sex is the life force—and cohesive impulse—of a people, and their very character will be deeply affected by how sexuality is managed, sublimated, expressed, denied, and propagated. When sex is devalued, propagandized, and deformed, as at present, the quality of our lives declines and our social fabric deteriorates.

Even the attitude toward sex and sexuality as concepts illustrates the problem. The words no longer evoke an image of a broad pageant of relations and differences between the sexes, embracing every aspect of our lives. Instead "sex" and "sexuality" are assumed to refer chiefly to copulation, as if our sexual lives were restricted to the male limits—as if the experiences of maternity were not paramount sexual events. In fact, however, our whole lives are sexual. Sexual energy animates most of our activities and connects every individual to a family and a community. Sexuality is best examined not in terms of sexology, physiology, or psychology, but as a study encompassing all the ulterior life of our society.

Our current deformities make a familiar catalogue. This has been the decade when priests and homosexuals marry and politicians divorce; when *Playboy* philosophers in pulpits preach situational ethics ("if you itch, scratch") to dwindling audiences, who are already sore from scratching. It has been a period when all the technology of advertising and publicity has been applied to arousing sexual excitement, while nothing new at all has been offered for the relief of the man with his hand on the bottleneck; a period when every group of complainants and protesters, however well situated—from Ivy League students to suburban women—are decked out in the heroic vestments of the civil rights movement: "the [student] [woman] [junior professor] [professional baseball player] is the nigger of the world"; when the whole crowd is fitted with the Marxist trappings of a "new proletariat": Women, students, children of the world, unite; you have nothing to lose.

It has been a time when fashionable psychologists proclaim that all orifices were created equal ("I'm okay, you're okay"), and the "missionary position" (which we are all presumed to know means the man upstairs) is casually dismissed as the way squares peg round holes. It is a time of wife swapping, group swinging, and gay liberation; a time of dildoes in drugstore windows and perfume sprays in men's rooms; a time of oral sex and vaginal sundaes, with a Howard Johnson's array of flavors advertised in *McCall's*.

It is a time when few things are as they seem—and when appearances are propagated everywhere. In no realm are things less as they seem to the media—to the observer-kings of the American consciousness—than in sex. What is described as the sexual revolution is a terminal spinning, without traction: the sexual suicide society.

Among the popular books of the day is Dr. Phyllis Chesler's *Women and Madness*.[1] A professor of psychology and a poet, she believes that American society is driving women crazy by sexist discrimination and oppression. The only solution she offers is sexual suicide: the abolition of biological differences between men and women. "Science must be used," she says, "to either release women from biological reproduction—or to allow men to experience the process also" [*sic*].[2] At the end of her book is one of those analogies to Nazism. "How does the Nazi use of the human body for industrial purposes . . ." she asks, "differ from [the American system's] female—or male—prostitution?" Ms. Chesler's incredible book, a best seller, was celebrated on the front page of *The New York Times Book Review*.

Also well received was a tract for lesbianism called *Sappho Was a Right-on Woman*.[3] Again *The Times* led the way. In the past, it observed in its *Book Review,* lesbianism had been a burden for the women's movement. But this book would change all that. In particular it would help overcome, in the words of *The Times* review, "the nuclear family, that cradle of evil." [4] *The Times* did not explain why the nuclear family is a "cradle of evil." Perhaps it has something to do with Nazi Germany (though the Nazis also opposed the nuclear family and encouraged illegitimate births to counteract it.)

A typical scene—a cocktail party in a fashionable Massachusetts suburb. The young woman's voice shook with emotion: "I couldn't bring a child into the world. I just couldn't do it. It wouldn't be fair." No one in the room seemed surprised. A few nodded assent. It is a common refrain of educated young women—from age 15 on—in current-day America. *I have no interest in having children.*

A less fashionable revolutionary mecca—the singles bar. Depicted as a great sexual marketplace in newspaper and magazine accounts, and groovy indeed to the tourist's eye, it is deadly to those who seriously partake. Most of them are essentially unavailable on any profound level. The men are self-pitying, impotent with girls they like; or they are married and searching for an image of sexual bliss advertised in all the magazines as a province of shapely youth performing sexual exotica. The stable and serious girls rarely come back. And the serious men drink and banter. The Stones' "I Can't Get No Satisfaction," is the national anthem of the "love generation." Most of the single men fill their throbbing vanities with alcohol and go home to their swinging bachelor digs, perhaps to beat off to the Playmate of the Month, who by 1972—as an index of thrilling liberation—was beginning to display pubic hair.

Life as a swingle means, for all too many of its devotees, a succession of neurotic women and men of dubious emotional and physical health alternating with muckish evenings of pornography and television. The promiscuous revels of urban and college youth conveyed by the media are actually enjoyed by only a few erotic aristocrats and voyeurs. For the rest of us it is a sick joke, which makes us sickest if we are foolish enough to believe it and invest it with our money and aspirations.

The swinging existence—the *Playboy* ideal and image of youthful urbanity—is pursued chiefly by those who have no choice: various classes of neurotics and losers. But it is, nevertheless, maintained as the standard. Though it is hard to find people who are truly enjoying the culturally ordained images of carefree sex, few can assert a plausible alternative.

Try another famous center of liberation, the great Eastern University. Here differences between the sexes are systematically suppressed. In general, men and women go to classes together, few form families, birth control is ubiquitous. It is a perfect scene for sexual emancipation. And yet—birth control is repeatedly botched; pornography and masturbation are pervasive forms of sex; and impotence is the chief male complaint at the psychological clinic.[5] One discovers a widespread sense of pessimism and demoralization, a fascination with violence, revolution, drugs, and the occult—and a strangely desperate loneliness.

Promiscuity is tried and usually rejected. Monogamous relationships are intensely sought, but increasingly difficult to sustain. The revels of co-ed dormitories, on closer inspection, consist of marijuana reveries and traffic tie-ups at the door of the common bathroom. Otherwise what is really happening is a feverish, if often unsuccessful, pursuit of stable sexuality in a world of polygamous fantasies. The mass culture is increasingy promiscuous; thus marriage and procreative love are becoming a countercultural assertion. The remarkable fact is the tenacity of the quest for it.

Nonetheless, a kind of Gresham's law applies. Bad sex drives out the good, and the worst of all—philandering and homosexuality—are exalted. Gay liberation, pornographic glut, and one-night trysts are all indices of sexual frustration; all usually disclose a failure to achieve profound and loving sexuality. When a society deliberately affirms these failures—contemplates legislation of homosexual marriage, celebrates the women who denounce the family, and indulges pornography as a manifestation of sexual health and a release from repression—the culture is promoting a form of erotic suicide. For it is destroying the cultural preconditions of profound love and sexuality: the durable heterosexual relationships necessary to a community of emotional investments and continuities in which children can find a secure place.

The inflation and devaluation of sexual currency leads to a failure of marriage that subverts the entire society. The increasing incidence of divorce, desertion, illegitimacy, and venereal disease produces a chaotic biological arena. Anyone may be cut and slashed by the shards of broken families in the streets of our cities. When sex becomes a temporary release, to be prompted as well by one woman as by another, or by sex magazines; when sex becomes a kind of massage, which can be administered as well by a member of the same sex or by a machine for that matter—one's whole emotional existence is depleted. We can no longer fathom the depths of our biological beings, which are open only to loving sexual experience. Drugs and alcohol can substitute for erotic activity; and with a cheapened sexual currency, couples can no longer afford children emotionally. Babies come as mistakes, misconceived and misbegotten. They come back to get theirs later.

All these social problems are ultimately erotic. The frustration of the affluent young and their resort to drugs, the breakdown of the family among both the rich and poor, the rising rate of crime and violence—all the clichés of our social crisis spring from, or reflect and reinforce, a fundamental deformation of sexuality.

The chief perpetrators of these problems are men: [6] Men commit over 90 percent of major crimes of violence, 100 percent of the rapes, 95 percent of the burglaries. They comprise 94 percent of our drunken drivers, 70 percent of suicides, 91 percent of offenders against family and children.[7] More specifically, the chief perpetrators are *single* men. Single men comprise between 80 and 90 percent of most of the categories of social pathology, and on the average they make less money than any other group in the society—yes, less than single women or married women.[8] As any insurance actuary will tell you, single men are also less responsible about their bills, their driving, and other personal conduct. Together with the disintegration of the family, they constitute our leading social problem. For there has emerged no institution that can replace the family in turning children into civilized human beings or in retrieving the wreckage of our current disorder.

Yet what is our new leading social movement? It's Women's Liberation, with a whole array of nostrums designed to emancipate us. From what? From the very institution that is most indispensable to overcoming our present social crisis: the family. They want to make marriage more open, flexible, revokable, at a time when it is already opening up all over the country and spewing forth swarms of delinquents and neurotics, or swarms of middle-aged men and women looking for a sexual utopia that is advertised everywhere, delivered nowhere, but paid for through the nose (and other improbable erogenous zones). At a time when modernity is placing ever greater strains on the institutions of male socialization—our families, sports, men's organizations—the women's movement wants to weaken them further, make them optional, bisexual, androgynous. Most of the books of the feminists speak of the need to "humanize" (emasculate?) men.

Surely women's liberation is a most unpromising panacea. But the movement is working politically, because our sexuality is so confused, our masculinity so uncertain, and our families so beleaguered that no one knows what they are for or how they are sustained. Against a fetish of individualism and a spurious equality, against an economic emphasis on sexless efficiency, against an erotic hedonism that sees sex as a mere sensuality, against such ideological abstractions and glandular pulsations, our social fabric seems invisible. Like the Pentagon, our social science often reduces all phenomena to dollars and body counts. Sexuality, family unity, kinship, masculine solidarity, maternity, motivation, nurturing, all the rituals of personal identity and development, all the bonds of community, seem "sexist," "superstitious," "mystical," "inefficient," "discriminatory." And, of course, they are—and they are also indispensable to a civilized society.

So the way is opened for the feminists. The movement barges into all the private ceremonies, sexual mystiques, and religious devotions of the society as if they were optional indulgences rather than the definitive processes of our lives. In a world in which most men and women everywhere, throughout history, have spent most of their time and energy in elaborate rituals of differentiation, the feminists advance the preposterous idea that we are all just individual "human beings," only secondarily identified by sex or family. This assumption is statistically convenient. But it is a myth. And this myth makes the women unable to understand almost everything that happens in the society or to comprehend what is important in motivating men and women.

Perhaps the epitome of this attitude was the statement by *Esquire*'s house feminist, Nora Ephron, in a column on sex after liberation. "What will happen to sex after liberation?" she asks. "Frankly, I don't know. It is a great mystery to all of us." [9]

Since sex in all its dimensions is the single most important motivating force in human life, what happens to sex after liberation will largely determine what happens to everything else. But Ms. Ephron is honest and right. The liberationists have no idea where their program would take us. The movement is counseling us to walk off a cliff, in the evident wish that our society can be kept afloat on feminist hot air.

Demographers, historians, anthropologists, and zoologists have often observed that both human and animal societies sometimes reach a condition of demoralization in which they have difficulty reproducing themselves. The cause is a collapse of the future: a group no longer believes in a better world to come. The French aristocrats before the revolution, American Indians after the closing of the frontier, European towns faced with starvation and plague, tribes in the Pacific shaken by a Western intrusion on their religious rites—even animals moved to zoos or other alien conditions—all experienced a crisis of procreation.

We may soon be able to add to that somber list the American intelligentsia. Contrary to popular belief, many influential groups in this society are already failing to reproduce themselves, and the country as a whole is now at a level approaching zero population growth. Any increase of this trend would signify a serious national demoralization.[10]

In the most elemental sense, the sex drive is the survival instinct: the primal tie to the future. When people lose faith in themselves and their prospects, they also lose their procreative energy. They commit sexual suicide. They just cannot bear the idea of "bringing children into the world." Such people may indulge a lot in what they call sex. But it is a kind of aimless copulation having little to do with the deeper currents of sexuality and love that carry a community into the future.

The Woman's Role

We're very biological animals. We always tend to
think that if one is in a violent state of emotional need,
it is our unique emotional need or state, when in
fact it is probably just the emotions of a young woman
whose body is demanding that she have children . . . Anna and
Molly [Communist heroines of *The Golden Notebook*]
are women who are conditioned to be one way and are trying to
be another. I know lots of girls who don't want to
get married or have children. And very vocal they are about
it. Well, they're trying to cheat on their biology . . .

Doris Lessing
Harper's, *June 1973*

The average American woman who looks into the media —that vivid trick mirror of her society—finds a cluster of negative images. Gloria Steinem has memorably declared her, in essence, a "prostitute." [1] Germaine Greer thinks she is "a female eunuch," not even being paid.[2] After depicting her as a hapless victim of history, Kate Millett defined the problem as Norman Mailer, Henry Miller, and D. H. Lawrence, and the solution as Genet;[3] she then came helpfully out of the closet herself.[4] Betty Friedan envisages woman as a vain gull of male exploitation, frittering away her talents in boredom and drudgery.[5] Ellen Peck sees her remorselessly trapped by babies.[6] Susan Brownmiller sees her relentlessly tweaked by goosers (no kidding, almost everywhere, all the time).[7]

The beat goes on. John and Yoko scream, "Woman is the Nigger of the World." Others more delicately describe her as the permanent proletariat. Esther Vilar, supposedly antifeminist, finds the average woman a "parasite." [8] Greer, in debate with her, shrewdly agrees.[9] Popular singers find woman in a state of alternating and converging sexual pain and desire. Natalie Gittelson finds her in a state of continuous sexual frustration and incipient or active promiscuity.[10] Philip Roth in *Portnoy's Complaint* vividly depicts that style of maternal "oppression" which has produced by far the most successful single group of Americans. [11]

Meanwhile, having grandly urged, in *Ms.*, that women dispense with underwear, Germaine Greer returns to the fray in *Harper's* to depict Gloria Steinem and all the other women at the Democratic convention as being "screwed" by Frank Mankiewicz and the Democratic establishment.[12] (Greer, however, narrowly escaped a similar fate at the hands of a panty-raiding movie star.) [13] In case anything was unclear in the *Harper's* piece, she continued to undress her *weltanschauung* afterwards in *Playboy*—$3,000 being $3,000—maintaining that almost all heterosexual screwing is rape.[14] Thus she added to her pejorative edge on Gloria Steinem's unhappy hookings and Susan Brownmiller's prickly heat, but still lagged behind, in polemical pith, Abby Rockefeller's view of sex as a "debilitating and counterrevolutionary" distraction.

Ingrid Bengis, who can write, finds woman hateful and angry; [15] Phyllis Chesler finds her psychopathic but curable by the creation of artificial wombs.[16] Greer puts it more intricately: Women are sick, but only when the society deems them healthy, or when they are dull and happy and impotent, if you get it.[17] A thousand writers find them hopeless puppets of Madison Avenue, hapless victims of sexism, reluctant prisoners of suburbia. And many of these negatives, widely propagated by the media, influence the self-image of millions of women, pursuing good and constructive lives under difficult conditions. They are distracted and confused, moreover, by the corollary illusions of "liberation." [18]

Most of the proponents are graduate students, assistant professors, journalists, and various lumpen litterateurs; products of distended education and stinted experience, permissive sex and cynical love; or else they are wives and mothers manqué, having their revenge on the world of men. An indefatigable few are lesbians or dildotage activists.

But mostly they are young and intellectual, suffering from the simultaneous contraction of opportunity and inflation of prestige affecting most of their age and profession. Spoiled by doting parents during the postwar binge of pretentious motherhood, beneficiaries of a steadily ascending familial affluence, taught to expect too much of life, educated to believe that qualifications decide, and qualified as no previous female generation—these women simply have no idea how most people live, or why. Their catalogue of pejoratives neatly replaces their elders' social snobbism (which they regard as utterly despicable) with a new idiom of intellectual snobbism, conveniently directed toward many of the very same people: those same poor, status-seeking, materialistic, insensitive, dull inhabitants of America's suburbs. But it is no use asking these poor suburbanites about their lives. Why, they *must* be unhappy—they're not like *us*. And if they aren't unhappy, they must be sick (i.e., suffering from false or "lowered consciousness").

Okay. Enough for the *ad feminam* approach. Midge Decter has done it much better. The essential point is that for the liberationists, their two subjects, America and sex, are great *terra incognita*. They think sex is some kind of pleasurable massage and sexual differences an invention of "sexists"; and they think the United States is some kind of protofascist society, for which problems of scarcity and growth should no longer be of concern. They also think motherhood is a secondary role because of the population explosion (which has inflicted as much brain damage as ecological strain). Thus they cannot understand the American woman, who like the American man, is in the largest sense a sexual rather than an ideological being, who devotes a large proportion of her energies to maternal roles, who senses that sex is a product of crucial differences, and who still relentlessly lives in a world of scarcity.

Take that American suburban housewife, for example. She has been closely studied, in the general context of her suburban environment, by Herbert J. Gans,[19] and in 573 close and specific personal interviews by Helen Znaniecki Lopata.[20] They conclude, like many other observers, that people deeply enjoy suburban living, most particularly women, and that suburbanites tend to be among the happiest Americans. In addition, the sociologists show, the suburbs are particularly notable for the lack of isolation of women there. The city dweller and the farmer tend to be far more devoid of social aid and involvement. A few newcomers and misfits, often intellectual, are lonely and dissident, and they are all too often allowed to speak for the rest. Some women give the impression they would not venture forth under any conditions.

But in general, Lopata and Gans both depict a panorama of social engagement, community concern, cooperative activity and even, in many cases, cultural and intellectual animation: a realm of options that substantially exceeds those of either men or working women. Mrs. Lopata, for instance, found that suburban housewives, by a significant margin, were more likely than working women to be using their education in their lives, to be reading widely and curiously, to be maintaining close and varied friendships, and to be involved in community affairs. "The role of housewife provides her a base for building a many faceted life, an opportunity few other vocational roles allow, because they are tied down to single organizational structures and goals." [21] Working women normally looked forward to leaving their jobs. Gans found that only 10 percent of suburban women reported frequent loneliness or boredom.[22]

That such observations may be viewed as surprising suggests the unreality of the notions of so many of the fashionably intellectual. It is really absurd to suppose that American women, educated extensively and in many cases more successfully than men, would move massively to the suburbs and then sit there and do nothing. It takes a really peculiarly mercenary or elite perspective to suppose that the workaday world of business and bureaucracy, where individuals tend to be fungible units, is more challenging and important than the realm of the home. The disparagement of the role of wife, mother, and homemaker—and the celebration of careers—is in fact the single most reprehensible aspect of the so-called women's movement. It is chiefly a way by which the new generation of the privileged—often in perfect innocence, like the upper-class woman who asks a poorer acquaintance where she went to college—displays the often spurious advantages of wealth and education. The insult is not changed in essence by attaching it to an ideology of liberation that can be fulfilled, and then often unhappily, only by an elite. The fact is that the role of the housewife is more important than any other broad category of work in the society, certainly more important than the combination of academic maneuvering and morbid radical politics much favored by the movement.

Of course, one should not replace the eunuch image with one of suburban eudaemonia. Life is tough all over. Jessie Bernard has found a pattern of nervous strain more serious among American housewives with children than among married men or single women. Only single men, by every measure the most afflicted Americans, show mental stresses substantially more acute.[23] One should differentiate between those two distressed groups, however, in social terms. The single men are in trouble because their lives violate the sexual constitution; they are failures in the most important realm of manhood in civilized society, the maintenance of a family. By contrast, the substantially lesser but still serious problem of the mothers reflects the inherent difficulty of a role that is fully positive but that modern conditions, including liberationist propaganda, have made more demanding.

The changes have often been remarked. In the past a mother role may have evolved naturally from one's experience in an extended family. One's entire education and range of expectations prepared one for it. As Midge Decter has observed, motherhood was regarded as inevitable; one didn't choose it; one accepted it.[24] Thus the strain was less. Modernity, moreover, has expanded the dimensions of maternal work. In the past, sickness, mortality, slow-learning, and other childhood afflictions were taken for granted as part of life. Today the mother is expected to control them. To the difficult tasks of physical support are now added burdens of medical diagnosis, psychological analysis, and early education.

Although new technology aids to some degree in performing the perfunctory work of the household, the woman's overall responsibilities are not suspended during the early stages of child-rearing. The mother is still expected to maintain an aesthetically pleasing home for child and husband, to prepare most meals, to maintain social connections, and to continue her own private education and development. Women's lib might call it "shitwork," and it certainly is hard work. But in a sense it is the best and most important work of the society.

There is no question at all that too many husbands have neglected their own role in this process. But feminists do not help matters by claiming complete procreative control of their bodies and praising women who raise children without fathers (all the while incongruously demanding that husbands assume new child care responsibilities like changing diapers). Nevertheless fathers are taking their parental role more seriously and will continue to do so as the workweek shortens for many jobholders in coming years. Airline pilots, for example, one of our most leisured working groups, with supremely masculine jobs (the number-one choice of teen-agers), are notably attentive fathers.[25] More support from husbands and from the society, perhaps in the form of child and maternity allowances, would be of significant help in relieving the burdens of motherhood.

But it is foolish to imagine that the complex roles and relationships sustained by the housewife can be abolished or assumed by outside agencies. Her role is nothing less than the central activity of the human community. All the other work— the business and politics and entertainment and service performed in the society—finds its ultimate test in the quality of the home. The home is where we finally and privately live, where we express our individuality, where we display our aesthetic choices, where we make and enjoy love, and where we cultivate our children as individuals. All very pedestrian, perhaps, but there is not very much more in civilized life.

The central position of the woman in the home parallels her central position in all civilized society. Both derive from her necessary role in procreation and from the most primary and inviolable of human ties, the one between mother and child. In those extraordinary circumstances when this tie is broken—as with some disintegrating tribes—broken as well is the human identity of the group. Most of the characteristics we define as humane and individual originate in the mother's love for her children.

Deriving from this love are the other civilizing concerns of maternity: the desire for male protection and support, the hope for a stable community life, and the aspiration for a better future. The success or failure of civilized society depends on how well the women can transmit these values to the men, to whom they come less naturally. The woman's sexual life and how she manages it is crucial to this process of male socialization. The males have no ties to women and children—or to long-term human community—so deep or tenacious as the mother's to her child. That is primary in society; all else is contingent and derivative.

This essential female role has become much more sophisticated and refined in the modern world. But its essence is the same. The woman assumes charge of what may be described as the domestic values of the community; its moral, aesthetic, religious, nurturant, social, and sexual concerns. In these values consist the ultimate goals of human life: all those matters that we consider of such supreme importance that we do not ascribe a financial worth to them. Paramount is the worth of the human individual, enshrined in the home, and in the connection between a woman and child. These values transcend the marketplace. In fact, to enter them in commercial traffic is considered a major evil in civilized society. Whether one proposes to sell a baby or a body or a religious blessing, one is conscious of a deep moral perversion.

The woman's place in this scheme is deeply individual.

She is valued for her uniqueness. Only a specific woman can bear a specific child, and her tie to it is personal and infrangible. When she raises the child she imparts in privacy her own individual values. She can create children who transcend consensus and prefigure the future: children of private singularity rather than "child development policy."

Even the husband ultimately validates his individual worth through the woman. He chooses her for her special qualities and she chooses him to submit his marketplace reward to her—and to her individual values. A man in courtship offers not chiefly his work but his individuality to the woman. In his entire adult life, it may be only his wife who receives him as a whole human being.

One of the roles of the woman as arbiter, therefore, is to cultivate herself: to fulfill her moral, aesthetic, and expressive being as an individual. There is no standard beyond her. She is the vessel of the ultimate values of the society. The society is what she is and what she demands in men. She does her work because it is of primary rather than instrumental value. The woman in the home with her child is the last bastion against the technocratic marketplace.

The man's role is indispensable as well. But it is relatively fungible and derivative. He is in charge of the instrumental realm: the world of work and the marketplace. Here, individuality is much less in demand. Just as any particular hunter might kill an animal, so within obvious bounds any workman can be trained to do most jobs. The marketplace is the realm of utility, adaptability, and convertibility—of money. It is also the realm of objective power, where the organization of individuals by others with special knowledge or vision can lead to increased production of utility to the entire society. But ultimately not the man himself but the marketplace defines the value of the work.

Jobs rarely afford room for the whole man. Even highly paid work often creates what Ortega y Gasset called "barbarians of specialization." One may become a scientist, doctor, or lawyer, for example, chiefly by narrowing the mind, by excluding personal idiosyncrasies and visions in order to master the disciplines and technicalities of one's trade. This process does not fulfill the individual in any profound way. Nor does it usually make him interesting or whole. In fact, he is likely to succeed precisely to the extent he is willing to subordinate himself to the narrow impersonal categories of his specialty, precisely to the extent he foregoes the distractions and impulses of the integral personality.

Among men, the term dilettante may be a pejorative. Yet, because the range of human knowledge and experience is so broad, the best that most people can ever achieve if they respond as whole persons to their lives, is the curiosity, openness, and eclectic knowledge of the dilettante at her best. Most men have to forego this form of individual fulfillment. They have to limit themselves, at great psychological cost, in order to fit the functions of the economic division of labor. Most of them endure their submission to the marketplace chiefly in order to make enough money to sustain a home, to earn a place in the household, to be needed by women.

"Women's liberation" entails a profound dislocation. Women, uniquely in charge of the central activities of human life, are exalting instead the peripheral values—values that have meaning only in relation to the role they would disparage or abandon. Through the women's movement, moreover, the society is being asked to dispense with most of the devices and conventions by which it was ensured that women perform their indispensable work and by which men have been induced to support it. Among those devices and conventions is the system the feminists call sexism, which in fact, is based on the exaltation of women, acknowledgment of the supremacy of domestic values, and the necessity of inducing men to support them in civilized society.

In effect, the system of discrimination, which the movement is perfectly right in finding nearly ubiquitous, tells women that if they enter the marketplace they will often receive less pay than a man, not because they could do the job less well but because they have an alternative role of incomparable value to the society as a whole. The man, on the other hand, is paid more not because of special virtue but because of the key importance of socializing his naturally disruptive energies. In addition, his possession of a margin of financial superiority endows his role as provider or social and sexual initiator.

In practice, this system has not imposed any very grievous hardship on many women who desire to work. It has merely given them a mild burden of proof: to show their work is financially indispensable to themselves and their families; or to show that it is essentially devoted to domestic rather than marketplace values; or to show that it is of such unique quality or productivity that it justifies compromise of other responsibilities. These criteria mean that women are mildly discouraged from taking fungible jobs of an ascribed masculine character, with primary incentives of pay and status. These values are more important to the provider and initiator males. But women are encouraged to make unique contributions in the realm of aesthetics, literature, art, and entertainment, and are paid just as much as men when they do. They can conduct enterpreneurial activity when they have a marketplace idea that will enrich the community. They are also assigned a variety of nurturant and service jobs for which they are judged to have special competence.

Needless to say, moreover, women are not excluded from the work that might be described as essentially masculine. If their motivation and skill are sufficient, they can overcome almost any of the barriers the society has rather fecklessly erected against them. Females in virtually every arena of economic and social activity confute the stupid feminist charges of carefully cultivated impotence and ineptitude. Again the key test is an especially intense motivation, an exceptionally strong talent, an extraordinary resolve. These qualities are amply found in American women.

Nonetheless, the woman's place *is* in the home, and she does her best when she can get the man there too. That, she cannot easily do alone. The society has to provide a role for him, usually as provider, that connects him to the family in a masculine way. But if social conditions are right, the woman can induce the man to submit most human activity to the domestic values of civilization.

Thus in a sense she also brings the home into the society. The radiance of the values the home embodies can give meaning and illumination not only to male sexuality but also to all other masculine enterprises. Male work is most valuable when it is imbued with long-term love and communal concern of femininity, when it is brought back to the home. Otherwise masculine activity is apt to degenerate quickly to the level of a game, and unless closely regulated, games have a way of deteriorating into the vain pursuit of power. Male games are kept in socially affirmative modes by the judgment of women. Men come to learn that their activity will be best received if it partakes of the value of the home. If they think the work itself is unworthy, they try to conceal it and bring home the money alone. Like the legendary Mafiosi, they try to please their women by elaborate submission to domestic values in the home, while scrupulously keeping the women out of the male realm of work. But in almost every instance, they pay tribute to the moral superiority of women.

The feminist answer to such arguments is usually a flip question: If the woman's role is so great, why don't men want it? One answer is that in a sense men unconsciously do want it. Their desire is shown in the character of primitive male initiation rites, in which all the processes of childbirth are simulated; it is shown in the ritual of couvade, in which men actually undergo labor; [26] it is shown perhaps in the tendency of men, more than women, to turn transvestite; it is shown in love, focused on the procreative and nurturant formations of the woman's body and mind. But nevertheless it is, unimpeachably, the woman's role, and males have to be taught by women even its derivative values. In addition, when men too intimately emulate the woman's role, they endanger their masculinity. The aggressiveness and extroversion of males is most useful to the society when it is submitted to, but not absorbed by, female sexual values. The transvestite is at best a barren parody.

The fact is that there is no way that women can escape their supreme responsibilities in civilized society without endangering civilization itself. The most chilling portent of our current crises, therefore, is the conjuncture of a movement of female abdication with a new biochemistry, which shines direct and deadly beams of technocratic light on the very crux of human identity, the tie between the mother and her child.

With the possible creation of clones and artificial wombs, human reproduction is on the not-so-distant verge of becoming a branch of laboratory husbandry. It is the ultimate scandal of the women's movement that it doesn't seem to care. In fact,

Shulamith Firestone of the New York Liberationists joins the Central Committee of the Chinese Communist Party in hailing the impending technology as "a happy day for women." [27] Ms. Firestone and the Chinese have long been concerned by the number of working days lost through pregnancy and childbirth.

But forgetting the Chinese, perhaps the women's movement might be more concerned if they understood that what is happening can be accurately described as the effort of a small group of male scientists to achieve the sexual nullification of women. The statement might seem extreme. Yet to "separate, for once and for all," as Edward Grossman puts it, "intercourse and reproduction" [28]—to perfect *in vitro* fertilization, artificial wombs, cloning, and other biomedical techniques of human manufacture—is to destroy the meaning and utility of much of the female body. (If you don't know what the biomedical terms mean—or if you think they merely comprise a panoply of inviting new options—you illustrate the extent of the threat). It is a concerted attack on the physical constitution of women. Female psychology could not help but suffer grave strains as a result.

Except in the case of cloning, the limited sexual circuits of males are less affected. Masturbation will still be a convenient way to collect semen. But, of course, the destruction of female sexuality would mean also the destruction of its male counterpart in all its significant dimensions. The sexual suicide of the human race would be a *fait accompli*. If we underestimate the danger and fail to act, merely because it is only future generations that will be directly affected, we may by omission commit an act of genocide that dwarfs any in human history. Perhaps that should be considered an evil—in the view of political woman—comparable even to sexism.

Notes

Introduction

1. Phyllis Chesler, *Women and Madness*. Garden City, N.Y.: Doubleday, 1972.

2. Ibid., pp. 299, 304.

3. Sidney Abbott and Barbara Love, *Sappho Was a Right-On Woman: A Liberated View of Lesbianism.* New York: Stein & Day, 1972.

4. *New York Times Book Review*, February 25, 1973: 39, 40.

5. Philip Nobile, "What's the New Impotence and Who's Got It?" *Esquire*, October 1972: 95 ff.; see also, Joseph Adelson, "Is Women's Lib a Passing Phase?" *The New York Times Magazine*, March 19, 1972: 26 ff.

6. The overwhelming preponderance of males among criminals is summarized by Edwin H. Sutherland and Donald R. Cressy, *Principles of Criminology*, Philadelphia: Lippincott, 1966, p. 138: "The crime rate for men is greatly in excess of the crime rate for women—in all nations, all communities within a nation, all age groups, all periods of history for which statistics are available, and for all types of crime except those peculiar to women, such as infanticide and abortion." Edwin M. Schur points out that there are 20 times as many men as women in major prisons and reformatories and 15 times as many men in local jails (*Our Criminal Society, The Social and Legal Sources of Crime in America*, Englewood Cliffs, N.J.: Prentice-Hall, 1969, p. 41). Later statistics indicate a ratio of 25 to 1 for federal and state prisons in 1970 (*The American Almanac, The U.S. Book of Statistics and Information*, New York: Grosset and Dunlap, 1973, from The Statistical Abstract of the U.S. prepared by the Department of the Census, U.S. Department of Commerce, issued September 1972, current to September 1973, p. 160).

7. Arrest statistics by sex and category may be found in *American Almanac*, op. cit., p. 151.

8. Jessie Bernard, *The Future of Marriage*, New York: World, 1972, Table 20 (page 341 in Bantam Books edition). About twice as many single women as single men held professional jobs (ibid.), and single men are almost eight times as likely as single women to show severe neurotic symptoms and about 60 percent more likely to suffer from depression and various psychopathic conditions (ibid., Tables 18, 19).

Bachelors are 21 times as likely as married men to be incarcerated in correctional or mental institutions. Hugh Carter and Paul C. Glick, *Marriage and Divorce: A Social and Economic Study*, Cambridge, Mass.: Harvard University Press, 1970, p. 410.

9. Nora Ephron, "Women," *Esquire*, July 1972: 42.

10. Ellen Goodman, "Occupation Housewife," *Boston Globe*, June 5, 1973. This account of the Radcliffe class of 1963 discloses the impact

of the women's movement on elite women. The 400 parents involved had produced only 224 children; the housewives felt defensive; and the achievers felt frustrated. "The anxieties of achieving women . . . hang out all over the pages."

Chapter 18—The Woman's Role

1. Leonard Levitt, "She," *Esquire,* October 1971: 210.

2. Germaine Greer, *The Female Eunuch.* New York: McGraw-Hill, 1971.

3. Kate Millett, *Sexual Politics.* Garden City, N.Y.: Doubleday, 1969.

4. *Time,* cover story, August 31, 1970.

5. Betty Friedan, *The Feminine Mystique.* New York: Norton, 1963.

6. Ellen Peck, *The Baby Trap.* New York: Bernard Geis, 1971.

7. Susan Brownmiller, "On Goosing," *The Village Voice,* April 15, 1971: 5.

8. Esther Vilar, *The Manipulated Male.* New York: Farrar, Straus and Giroux, 1972.

9. Greer, *Female Eunuch,* op. cit.

10. Natalie Gittelson, *The Erotic Life of the American Wife.* New York: Delacorte, 1972.

11. Philip Roth, *Portnoy's Complaint.* New York: Random House, 1969.

12. Greer, "Down with Panties," *Ms.,* July 1972: 8; "At the Democratic National Convention," *Harper's,* October 1972.

13. Greer, "Democratic Convention," op. cit.

14. Greer, "On Rape," *Playboy,* January 1973.

15. Ingrid Bengis, *Combat in the Erogenous Zone.* New York: Knopf, 1973.

16. Phyllis Chesler, *Women and Madness.* Garden City, N.Y.: Doubleday, 1972.

17. Greer, *Female Eunuch,* op. cit.

18. Helen Lopata, *Occupation Housewife.* New York: Oxford University Press, 1971, p. 376.

19. Herbert J. Gans, *The Levittowners*. New York: Pantheon, 1967.

20. Lopata, *Housewife*, op. cit.

21. Lopata, *Housewife*, op. cit., p. 373.

22. Gans, *Levittowners*, op. cit., pp. 230, 231.

23. Jessie Bernard, *The Future of Marriage*. New York: World, 1972, pp. 336, 338, 339.

24. Midge Decter, *The New Chastity and Other Arguments Against Women's Liberation*. New York: Coward, McCann and Geoghegan, 1972.

25. Harvey Swados, *A Radical's America*. Boston: Little, Brown, 1962, pp. 302–316.

26. Theodore Reik, *Ritual*. New York: International Universities Press, 1946, pp. 27–90.

27. Edward Grossman, "The Obsolescent Mother," *Atlantic*, May 1971: 39–50.

28. Ibid.

Accept Him

Salad, Sex, and Sports

Your husband is what he is. Accept him as that. This principle is as old as life itself. God accepts us as we are. Even though we don't deserve it, He still loves us. He has no angle. His love is unconditional. Because He accepts us, through His power we can love and accept others, including our husbands.

One woman balked at this idea. "I don't even love my husband anymore, let alone accept him," she said. "He doesn't deserve to be accepted." This seems to be the case in so many homes. What's the cure for this marital malady?

First of all, the Bible says that wives should love their husbands. If you've lost the love for your husband, why not ask God to restore it? Secondly, if you want your marriage to succeed, you must choose to accept him, knowing that your relationship will probably not improve if you don't. The choice is yours—you can choose to either go on living with resentment or accept your husband.

If you choose the latter course, how do you start? Simply make up your mind to accept him just as he is. By an act of your will, determine that you won't try to change him no matter what. That's supreme love.

The change I saw in one couple was remarkable. The wife had thought long and hard before making this decision. But once she did, her husband spotted the difference immediately. "*He* has changed so much," she told me. "He's so much more loving and generous. He wants to give me money all the time! I'm going to start taking it just to make him happy!"

Some women don't nag verbally, but their nonaccepting vibrations communicate loud and clear. With heaving sighs over the kitchen sink, the martyr silently nurses her woes. "I do accept my husband," she thinks. "I've been putting up with his faults for years without saying a word, but he'll never change. I won't say anything. I'll just carry on for the sake of the children."

Tolerance is not acceptance. Your tolerance only makes your husband feel incomplete and unworthy. He can sense when he's not being accepted, and is not able to love you fully.

Your husband needs your acceptance most of all during his times of apparent failure. If he's already low, don't put him down further. Never compare him with another man. And remember, he'll never confide in you if he feels that you are being critical or are trying to change him.

Life is too short to dwell on another's weaknesses. Concentrate on his strengths.

Your man needs to feel important, loved, and accepted. If you won't accept his idiosyncrasies, who will? A Total Woman caters to her man's special quirks, whether it be in salads, sex, or sports. She makes his home his haven, a place to which he can run. She allows him that priceless luxury of unqualified acceptance.

The Man, not the Plan

Having lived on both sides of the fence, I can tell you where the greener pastures are. During my early years of married life, I led a one-woman crusade to make my man into my mold. One particular irritation was that Charlie was constantly on the phone with his stockbroker. A dozen times a day they conspired, and each time I became more and more upset. First of all, I was jealous of the time Charlie spent on the phone. Secondly, I was worried sick that he'd gamble away all our savings.

One day the broker, who also happened to be a family friend, called me on the phone. He knew that Charlie was at work and he gave me some advice: "Let your husband do what he wants in the market. Don't ever tell him what to do with his money. You stay out of it and take care of the kitchen."

Oh, boy, did that burn me up! I was furious at both of them! But the wise, old gentleman had sensed my animosity. He had seen that I wasn't accepting Charlie's role as provider, nor was I submitting to his family leadership.

Today my attitudes have changed, and we're both much happier because of it. I have determined to support my husband's plan, and if that seems impossible, at least I'll support the *man!*

If you too make this decision, be sincere. Your husband may be surprised by your change of attitude, and react with suspicion. His love cannot be aroused by something contrived by a manipulative wife.

One wife said accusingly to her husband, "I've made radical changes around here for two whole weeks, and you haven't changed at all." He replied, "You've made two-week changes before; I'm waiting to see if it's permanent." His coals of love had been dormant for so many years that it took more than a spark to relight his fire. Her attempted manipulation fizzled; he had been burned before.

Once you begin accepting your husband, you can stop worrying about your role as his chief advisor. He doesn't need your advice; he needs your acceptance. Tremendous pressure will be lifted from you, not to mention the pressure lifted from him! He will probably begin to reveal his thoughts to you, and he may even choose to do exactly what you've been wanting!

Accepting your husband is the first step in making your man come alive, and it works. It frees him to become a Total Man. He has that potential, but is unable to attain it until you allow him to be himself. Accept him, just as he is today. Accept his strengths and weaknesses, ". . . for better for worse, for richer for poorer, in sickness and in health . . . from this day forward."

Admire Him

Psychiatrists tell us that a man's most basic needs, outside of warm sexual love, are approval and admiration. Women need to be loved; men need to be admired. We women would do well to remember this one important difference between us and the other half.

Just the other day a woman told me, "My husband doesn't fulfill me. He never tells me his real feelings; he never expresses his love. He's about as warm as a cold fish!"

Your man, like so many American males, may be like an empty cup emotionally. He may seem void of emotions, unable to properly express his real feelings to you. Why is this? Remember that he grew up in a culture that taught him not to cry when he scratched his leg. Instead of hugging Uncle Jack, he shook hands. Grown-ups were generally unavailable to listen, so he learned to keep his feelings to himself.

We girls, on the other hand, were allowed to cry and

throw temper tantrums. We were encouraged to kiss baby
dolls, Aunt Susie, and the baby-sitter. We grew up full of
emotions and knew basically how to express love. Then
one day the fun began. Mr. Cool married Miss Passion.
Is it any wonder that she felt unfulfilled because he never
showed her any emotion?

Have you ever wondered why your husband doesn't
just melt when you tell him how much you love him?
But try saying, "I admire you," and see what happens.
If you want to free him to express his thoughts and emotions, begin by filling up his empty cup with admiration.
He must be filled first, for he has nothing to give until
this need is met. And when his cup runs over, guess who
lives in the overflow? Why, the very one who has been
filling up the cup—you!

Love your husband and hold him in reverence, it says
in the Bible. That means admire him. *Reverence,* according to the dictionary, means "To respect, honor, esteem,
adore, praise, enjoy, and admire."

As a woman, you yearn to be loved by that man, right?
He, being a man, yearns to be admired by you. And he
needs it first. This irritates some women until they see
that they have certain strengths that a man doesn't have.
It's a great strength, not a weakness, to give for the sheer
sake of giving. It is your nature to give. Calvin Coolidge
once said, "No person was ever honored for what he received. Honor has been the reward for what he gave."

You are the one person your husband needs to make
him feel special. He married you because he thought you

were the most enchanting girl of all. The world may bestow awards on him, but above all others, he needs your admiration. He needs it to live. Without it his motivation is gone.

A young executive was literally starved for admiration from his wife. She wanted him to fulfill her before she met his needs. She explained, "Why should I give in first? Marriage is a fifty-fifty deal. I'm not about to give everything." Her husband threw himself into his business, working extra-long hours. He hoped his work would fill up that inner emptiness.

During a Total Woman class, this wife realized that she had the power to pour into him the admiration he needed. She began to admire him. Their relationship began to change. One evening he told her, "Something beautiful is happening. I don't know what it is, but it's great. You seem more alive for some reason."

Hero Worship

Try this test for a week. Starting tonight determine that you will admire your husband. By an act of your will, determine to fill up his cup, which may be bone dry. Be positive. Remember that compliments will encourage him to talk.

Admire him as he talks to you. Concentrate on what he's saying. Let him know you care. Put your magazine down and look at him. Even if you don't care who won

yesterday's football game, your attention is important to
him and he needs you. Let him know he's your hero.

Don't interrupt or be preoccupied. A pilot told me,
"When my wife is indifferent and doesn't respond to what
I'm saying, it shatters me for two or three days. Indiffer-
ence is the worst pain of all."

Another woman called me the night she was sued for
divorce. When she asked her husband why, she was
shocked at his reply: "You've always been completely indifferent to my life. You never cared what I did or
thought."

Every marriage needs tact—that special ability to describe another person as he sees himself. Your husband
needs you to see him as he sees himself. For example, take
a good look at him. He happens to love his body. It's the
only one he has and he lives in there. He wants you to
love it too. The only way he'll ever know that you do is
for you to tell him.

Perhaps this sounds very foreign to you. You may even
think it vulgar. If so, your husband is probably long over-
due for some badly needed praise. It is your highest privilege to assure him that he is as special as he hoped he
was.

Tonight when he comes home, concentrate on his body.
Look at him, really observe him. It may have been years
since you actually looked at him with eyes that see. Try
looking at him through another woman's eyes—his secretary's or your neighbor's. That might help bring him into
focus.

Tell him you love his body. If you choke on that phrase, practice until it comes out naturally. If you haven't admired him lately, he's probably starving emotionally. He can't take too much at once, so start slowly. Give him one good compliment a day and watch him blossom right before your eyes.

Look for his admirable qualities. Even the ugliest man has certain qualities worth admiring, but we're talking about the dream man you married. Compliment that one who used to make your heart pound and make your lips stammer. Admire that one who stood far above the crowd of common men.

Pick out his most masculine characteristics and let him know they please you. His whiskers, for instance. The day he shaved for the first time was a milestone in his life. But have you ever complained with irritation, "Ouch, why don't you shave once in awhile? You're rubbing my face raw"? Instead, try telling him nicely, "Honey, your scratchy beard is too strong for my tender skin." You can compliment your husband into shaving off his weekend whiskers by reinforcing his masculine image.

Thin Arms, Full Heart

Admire him *personally*. This is what he is yearning for. When he comes home tonight would you rather have him admire your newly waxed floor, or tell you how great you look? In the same way, he'd rather hear how handsome he is, than how great his corporation is.

Tomorrow morning watch your husband when he looks in the mirror. He sees an eighteen-year-old youth, with firm stomach muscles and a full head of hair. No matter what his age, he doesn't see his pouch or receding hairline. He sees what he wants to see, and wants you to see that eighteen-year-old, too. Of course, this isn't really so strange. What age girl do you see in the mirror? My own grandmother admitted to feeling that she was not much past twenty-one.

A dentist's wife told me she had blurted out one night, "Look, you're getting fat and bald. It's disgusting. Why don't you just face the truth? You're not a kid anymore." The first shot had been fired. Her husband felt devastated and to protect himself, he lashed out at her weaknesses in a brutal way that only he could do. He could not rationally answer her comment but instead struck out at her personally.

In class one day, I gave the assignment for the girls to admire their husband's body that night. One girl went right to work on her homework. Her husband was shorter than she, but quite handsome. In all their years together she had never put her admiration into words. It was a big step for her. She didn't quite know how to start, even though it was her own husband. That evening while he was reading the paper, she sat down next to him on the sofa and began stroking his arm. After a bit, she stopped at the bicep and squeezed. He unconsciously flexed his muscle and she said, "Oh, I never knew you were so muscular!" He put down the paper, looked at her, and inquired, "What else?" He was so starved for admiration, he wanted to hear more!

The next day, she told this to her girl friend, who also decided to try it. Her husband had thin arms, but she admired his muscles anyway. Two nights later she couldn't find him at dinner time. He was out lifting his new set of weights in the garage! He wanted to build more muscles for her to admire.

By the way, admiration can also work wonders for your children. For example, one mother always nagged her son to hop out of the car to open the garage door. One afternoon she said, "Tommy, I'll bet a boy with muscles like yours could flip that garage door up in nothing flat." That's all she said, and that's all he needed. She never again had to ask him to open the door.

Your husband won't mind helping you either, if he's approached in the proper way. Instead of struggling with a jar and breaking a fingernail, ask him to loan you his strong hands for a minute. He derives pleasure from showing off his strength, even on a little old jar.

I know of only one case where this principle backfired. One wife asked her husband, one of the Miami Dolphin football players, to give her a muscular hand with the jars. Finally he asked, "Say, what's with you? You've been opening these baby food jars for five months and now all of a sudden you can't seem to manage them." So don't overdo it. Give him only the jars you really can't handle.

Rebuilding a Partial Man

I heard one wife say, "I feel guilty using feminine wiles on my husband. It seems dishonest. Anyway, his ego is so big, it doesn't need expanding. His body is not all that great. Why should I lie to build him up? I want to be honest, but still meet his needs."

If you're secure within yourself, you won't be afraid to give your husband credit. Instead of feeling threatened, you will feel joy in meeting his needs. As you know, you cannot express love to your husband until you really love yourself. But once you do, you can give with abandon. In fact, you can give with no thought of what you'll receive in return.

I am not advocating that you lie to give your husband a superficial ego boost; even a fool will see through flattery. But I am saying he has a deep need for sincere admiration. Look for new parts to compliment as you see him with new eyes.

Consider his weaknesses and things about which he may be self-conscious. Larry had a nasty scar on his neck as the result of an accident. His wife knew that it upset him and saw that he kept rubbing it. She said, "I really love your scar, honey. It makes you look so rugged." Her admiration made him feel relieved inside and less self-conscious.

If you haven't been communicating much lately with your husband, you may have trouble finding something to compliment. If that's your case, think back to those days when you were first convinced that he was the one. What did you love about him then?

An older couple was so estranged that the wife could not see anything to admire about her husband. She forced herself to think back, all the way to the Depression days, when he frugally kept the family together with shrewd business management. Now, nearly forty years later, she shyly mentioned how she had admired his financial leadership during that time. Those were the first appreciative words he had heard in years, and his reaction was pitiful. He looked at her with disbelieving eyes, tears welled up, and though he found no way of verbally expressing his appreciation, he was very tender that evening. The wife was amazed that such a little remark from the distant past could cause this behavior. It was a turning point in their marriage.

A marriage must not remain stagnant. You can keep yours exciting and growing, and in order to succeed, you must. At the end of a long day, your husband especially needs your compliments. One husband called his wife just before quitting time to say, "This is a partial man looking for a Total Woman; be prepared!"

Put your husband's tattered ego back together again at the end of each day. That's not using feminine wiles; that is the very nature of love. If you fulfill his needs, he won't have to escape some other way.

On the other hand, you may have a husband who does not do anything but stay home drinking beer in his underwear. The responsibility of the family may rest on your back because somewhere along the line you usurped his role. Your nagging may have taken the wind out of his sails and now he has no desire to keep working for you. If so, he needs your compliments to restart his engine, regardless of the distance or bitterness between you.

Life is made up of seemingly inconsequential things, but often it's a little thing that can turn the tide. Behind every great man is a great woman, loving him and meeting his needs. There are some exceptions to this, but very few.

Self cries, "Love me, meet my needs." Love says, "Allow me to meet your needs." Dish out some sincere compliments to your man tonight, and watch his cup fill up and overflow. What nagging cannot do, admiration will!

Adapt to Him

One Monday morning Bobbie Evans, the wife of Miami Dolphins tackle Norm Evans, arrived at my doorstep fed up and resentful. The football team was flying in at noon and she was picking up Norm at the airport. Bobbie needed to talk out her anger to a buddy before she unloaded it on her husband. She was tired of Norm's never-ending football schedule, his endless appearances and speaking engagements, and her having to bear sole responsibility for disciplining the children. In fact, the heartbreaking question of her little boy, "Isn't Daddy ever coming home for dinner again?" prompted her to seek a solution.

She felt lonely, neglected, and unloved. The situation didn't look good. I wondered what to tell her—put her foot down? insist that he quit football? demand that he spend more time at home? threaten him? She had already tried that for two years, but of course nothing had changed. Should I tell her to withhold her love? make him come begging to her? play the martyr? She had tried that too. Result? No change.

What I told her, she didn't like. Later she admitted, "I was so mad, I almost got up and walked out. I certainly hadn't come over to hear that *I* should adapt to *Norm's* life."

Adapting was the only thing I knew that would work. "Bobbie," I told her, "adapt to his way of life wholeheartedly, even if he doesn't come home for weeks. When he is home, make life so attractive he won't want to leave. Don't make him feel guilty and don't complain. Instead, treat him like a king and cater to his needs."

Bobbie cried a little, but finally dried her eyes and smiled. "I'm going to do it," she said. The first thing Norm said when he got off the plane and saw her radiant face was, "Hey, what's happened to you?" Nothing had changed except Bobbie's attitude. The unreal schedule was still the same, but Bobbie had determined to adapt.

Two years later, Norm told her one night during sweet communion, "I love you so much right now that if you asked me to quit playing football, I'd do it." She wouldn't ask him to; she has adapted to his way of life. By the way, he has become an All-Pro NFL player, a Total Tackle, and she, a Total Woman teacher. They've never been happier together.

My Way

What causes most of the problems in your marriage? I find that the conflict between two separate egos is usually the culprit—your viewpoint versus his viewpoint. If they happen to be the same, fine. If not, as so often is the case, conflict results.

For instance, your weary man comes home from the office longing for a quiet evening. You've been cooped up in the house all day and want to get out. There's instant conflict with two egos, each shouting, "Me, me, me."

Or you have a little extra money. He wants that new car and you have your heart set on new carpeting. Conflict. He wants to go to the game Saturday and you want to go shopping. And so it goes.

Every couple has this problem. How can two different egos fuse their two different opinions into one? Some don't. Often these conflicts are "resolved" when the parties go their separate ways, instead of growing together.

The biblical remedy for marital conflict is stated, "You wives must submit to your husbands' leadership in the same way you submit to the Lord" (6). God planned for woman to be under her husband's rule.

Now before you scream and throw this book away, hear me out. First of all, no one says you have to get married. If you do not wish to adapt to a man, the negative implication is to stay single. If you are married but not adapting, you probably already know that marriage isn't the glorious experience you anticipated.

Secondly, you may think, "That's not fair. I have my rights. Why shouldn't he adapt to my way first, and then maybe I'll consider doing something to please him?" I have seen many couples try this new arrangement, unsuccessfully. Unless the wife adapts to his way of life, there's no way to avoid the conflict that is certain to occur.

Thirdly, please note that I did not say a woman is inferior to man, or even that a woman should be subservient to all men, but that a wife should be under her own husband's leadership.

Fourthly, another little phrase may cause some consternation: ". . . in the same way you submit to the Lord." Perhaps you are thinking, "I don't submit to the Lord. I don't even know Him. How archaic can you get? Even if you believe in Him, who submits to Him?"

The fact is that God originally ordained marriage. He gave certain ground rules and if they are applied, a marriage will work. Otherwise, the marriage cannot be closely knit because of the inherent conflict between your husband's will and yours. The evidence is all too clearly visible. In some cities there are now more people getting divorced each day than getting married.

Man and woman, although equal in status, are different in function. God ordained man to be the head of the family, its president, and his wife to be the executive vice-president. Every organization has a leader and the family unit is no exception. There is no way you can alter or improve this arrangement. On occasion, families have tried to reverse this and have elected a woman as president. When this order is turned around, the family is upside down. The system usually breaks down within a short period of time. Allowing your husband to be your family president is just good business.

Oh, King, Live Forever

I have been asked if this process of adapting places a woman on a slave-master basis with her husband. A Total Woman is not a slave. She graciously chooses to adapt to her husband's way, even though at times she desperately may not want to. He in turn will gratefully respond by trying to make it up to her and grant her desires. He may even want to spoil her with goodies.

Marriage has also been likened to a monarchy, where the husband is king, and his wife is queen. In a royal marriage, the king's decision is the final word, for his country and his queen alike. The queen is certainly not his slave, for she knows where her powers lie. She is queen. She, too, sits on a throne. She has the right, and in fact, the responsibility to express her feelings, but of course, she does so in a regal way. Though the king relies heavily on her judgment, if there is a difference of opinion, it is the king who makes the final decision.

Now hold on, I know just what you're thinking; remember, I've been through all of this, too. What if the king makes the wrong decision? Oh, that's a hard one, especially when you *know* you're right, and there are times when that is the case. The queen is still to follow him, forthwith. A queen shall not nag or buck her king's decision after it is decreed. Remember those speedy trials, gals!

In so many marriages today, the woman rules the roost.

In others, there are two coequal rulers, whose decisions often clash. In still others, only the fittest survive. None of these cases enhance romance. Emotions are sent plummeting to zero, and the husband is left wondering, "How did I get into this mess?"

A lawyer's wife told me after a class, "I wasn't brought up to adapt to any man; in fact, just the opposite. I was taught as a small girl that no man is to be trusted. Men are only out for what they can get, and if you shack up with one for life, do him before he can do you." Having this propaganda piped into her little computer as a child has certainly caused her great obstacles today.

I would like to say right here, that in the beginning I was as dubious as anyone about adapting. But wow, has my thinking changed! I see now that a man does not want a nagging wife, nor does he want a doormat. He wants one with dignity and opinions and spunk, but one who will leave the final decision to him.

On January 15, 1972, Margrethe Alexandrine Thórhildur Ingrid became Queen Margrethe II of Denmark. Since childhood she had been groomed for the task of being queen someday. She had the finest education, received military training, and was prepared in every way to be a queen.

Her husband, Prince Hendrik, has no function constitutionally, other than as husband of the queen. But it is no secret that Hendrik wears the trousers at home. "Ever since I was a little girl," Margrethe said on the day of her engagement, "I have believed that even though I must officially take first place, it would be possible for me to take second place in marriage."

If a real live queen who could *demand* subservience from her husband feels that way, can we queens do less?

Lord, Teach Me to Submit

"Know how you can tell if somebody's really a Christian? Go home with him!"

Brother Bill's humor really hits home. As self-conscious laughter rippled around the room, I silently agreed. *Yes. Talk to the husband and children.*

So much I read, heard, and studied those days led straight to a road marked WITNESS AT HOME. It amounted to a continuous challenge. Our home appeared to be a normal, happy, Christian place. Bob and I had no exceptional amounts of friction—only occasional blowups, which by day's end always seemed to smooth out okay.

". . . let not the sun go down upon your wrath" (Ephesians 5:26) is something Bob and I heed. We don't often harbor a grudge; both forgive easily. We had no serious problems, I supposed. It was more a desire to perfect our day-to-day walk with Christ.

Marabel Morgan increased that desire in me as she talked about her course entitled "The Total Woman." Marabel not only is my darling friend and Christian sister, but also my prayer buddy. She based her course on the Bible, and I like the subtitle: "How to Make Your Husband Adore You." ·

Marabel researches continually, and shares her discoveries with me. Her enthusiasm is so contagious, so upbeat and optimistic, I just knew all that womanliness was bound to rub off on me. Much as I kidded her, however—and I kid Marabel unmercifully—at the same time, I knew God was dealing with me in those very same areas of my life. And Marabel, naturally, is one of His instruments.

So I prayed and studied the Bible a great deal, and God gave me one amazing insight after another—a series of personal revelations about my needs and failings as a woman, a wife, and a mother.

To add even further impetus to my desire to grow, Brother Bill began teaching the New Members Class lessons—Bible-based, of course—expounding what Christ expects of wives, husbands, parents, and children. Sometimes God just seems to bombard you from all sides!

All this began to change my heart. I became convinced women must study the Bible in order to learn how God wants us to live. That's the only way we'll ever find real fulfillment as females.

An enormous problem in America today—and it's man's fault as well as woman's—is our sinfulness against God as each of us individually persists in carving out his own personal set of rules, his own so-called rights. This is no small matter. I've come to believe America ultimately will be endangered unless each of us endeavors to become a really strong, godly man or woman.

Many who profess and call themselves Christians absolutely flinch at God's requirements for full manhood and womanhood. For example, consider Ephesians 5:22–24:

> Wives, submit yourselves unto your own husbands, as unto the Lord.
> For the husband is the head of the wife, even as Christ is the head of the church: and he is the saviour of the body.
> Therefore as the church is subject unto Christ, so let the wives be to their own husbands in every thing.

How much plainer could it be stated? I thought I'd never describe myself as submissive. But *submissive,* I was to learn, doesn't mean *timid.* It doesn't mean a woman is meant to be overrun, downtrodden, and all that. To submit is a voluntary act of love and trust. It's a deliberate yielding and deferring to your husband, in obedience to God's plan for your life. Until we do that, we can't please God.

Think of today's unhappy women who struggle to usurp men's authority. Their efforts can only be fruitless and result in self-defeat and misery because I can't see where they're supported by God's Word.

Though most of us women don't consider ourselves activists in that sort of struggle, we may actually end up in the same camp—if we nag, bicker, criticize, and undercut the man God gave us to love, rather than submitting our lives and hearts in perfect trust and support.

Marabel's life dramatically illustrates what I mean. In fact, her resolution to stop nagging Charlie Morgan led to her researching and developing her own wife-to-husband approach. These eventually evolved into her Total Woman classes which became tremendously successful here in Miami Beach.

See if her story parallels yours in any way. It really hit home with me!

Charlie and I loved one another, but he never talked to me. We were "happily married." Anybody would say so. But why was I so uptight? I'd always pictured myself as a serene, loving woman who never got cross with her husband or children. Meanwhile, Charlie often said, "Gee, you sure come unglued easily, don't you?"

One day I realized I *nagged* Charlie. I constantly tried to remake him. I was always telling him small things I disliked about him—things he ought to improve. I saw he had begun to crawl into a shell. He had begun to think of me as a second mother. I could see *I* was the one cutting down the flame of our romance.

That day Marabel made a drastic decision:

I promised myself I'd never nag Charlie Morgan again.

That night I told my husband I'd never nag him again but was going to accept him *exactly as he was*. I'm certain he didn't believe me. I stuck to it, however. From that day to this, our lives, our marriage, and everything else has become fantastically better.

There's much, much more to Marabel's amazing story. In her very first lesson she makes an extremely significant point, and reiterates it often: "You must accept your husband as he is. The reason you can is that God loves you and accepts you just as you are!"

That's exactly the principle God showed me. I realized I must stop criticizing Bob's lack of spiritual development and work only on my own. I could see my carping literally undercut my husband's confidence, desire, and ability to grow in Christ. Of course I mentally defended that nagging as something I had to do for Bob's good, but that's because I didn't know the Bible very well.

I'd never try to get away with that now. The Bible doesn't uphold a nagging wife *anywhere*—and Bob knows it. The devil can disrupt many a would-be Christian household via the woman's tongue. Unfortunately, he's done some damage this way at Villa Verde. Nagging, anger, criticism, sharp remarks, negative ideas—oh, that tongue is as a sharp-edged sword!

In Ephesians (such a rich book!) Paul speaks directly to that. In chapter 4, verses 31 and 32, he says:

> Let all bitterness, and wrath, and anger, and clamour, and evil speaking, be put away from you, with all malice:
> And be ye kind one to another, tenderhearted, forgiving one another, even as God for Christ's sake hath forgiven you.

What if a wife truly lacks confidence in her husband? Perhaps he's critical of her, hard to please, unfair. Should she submit to that kind of man? The Bible says she should. The inference is plain: Live out your Christian life before Him so that you influence your partner for the good. God says that's a woman's responsibility.

Husbands can disappoint wives for many reasons and in many ways. Some women, especially those who lost their fathers in childhood due to death or divorce, really want a daddy more than a husband. Their search for lost childhood robs the husband. (After all, how can he meet the needs a father should have supplied—needs and dissatisfactions a woman probably isn't conscious of having and can't even express in words?)

Perhaps I've expected Bob to be Daddy. I don't know. My parents divorced when I was thirteen, and as so many girls do, I did miss my father.

Submission, in the Biblical meaning of the word, becomes the only answer to that sort of problem. "Looking up to" the man as head of the house constantly asserts and reaffirms him. As I can support him with faith and trust, he can protect and complete me.

Husbands don't come readymade, all packaged and prepared. Neither do wives. But as soon as one of them—either one—begins to follow the marital precepts outlined in the Bible, the other will desire to comply. That is, compliance follows where the first partner acts in love, as God would wish, rather than strict, joyless legalism.

Duty is stern; love is winsome. The loving wife always has more fun in marriage because God planned it that way. He really does provide us with joy and abundant life if we'll just follow His blueprints.

When we as wives decide to submit to the man we love, that means we're truly willing to change our natures. First, we need insight as to the places in life and marriage where we don't meet God's criteria. By reading the Bible we discover where these places are. Then we must learn, through reading the Word, how to overcome—which only can be done by the grace of God, diligent prayer, and faithfulness.

You'll find your prototype in the Bible, I discovered; not only the kind of person you are, but a description of your feelings, your condition, and how to deal with it. It's all there. If you're faithful about reading and praying about it, the Word will reveal what you need in your life.

In Sunday school we studied the four natures Christians display. I think mine is sanguine, like Peter's. In Matthew 26:33, he shows a quick display of emotion and is so outspoken and impetuous. I really identify with Peter!

Then there's the phlegmatic nature, the ho-hum sort of person who often follows the line of least resistance. This is described in 1 Timothy 4:14–16.

The Apostle Paul, as depicted in 2 Timothy 4:7 exemplifies the choleric nature; a strong, determined, bulldog sort of person.

The melancholy nature, as in 1 John 3:16–18, represents loyalty and love. This is a fragile spirit which easily can be offended. I identify with that, too. I can see something of myself in all these natures—especially Peter's.

Study the Bible enough, and I'm convinced you can become your own analyst. Jesus Christ is the perfect psychiatrist. By applying the Word of God to my life, knowing I'm born again, being lifted from sins through the blood of Christ, I see I can be delivered from the power of Satan, through Jesus. Miracles are possible. And sometimes, in any marriage, it takes a miracle.

People in the world can see this change. They comment that you're different, that your personality is emerging. They recognize your changed life, but don't know it's the Christ in you.

God has had to show me that after my finding the joy of Christian life, and after He started me digging in the Word, He would continue to point out areas which need changing. Challenge follows challenge. There's a Scripture text, Philippians 1:6, which speaks to that.

The woman who seriously intends to follow Jesus really desires to submit to her Lord. She knows that's the only way. She desires this because she loves Him.

Only as I practice yielding to Jesus can I learn to submit, as the Bible instructs me, to the loving leadership of my husband. Only the power of Christ can enable a woman like me to become submissive in the Lord.

Christ becomes the means, then, toward perfecting and sanctifying a woman's cherished relationship to her man. In this way He fuses the two of them and creates a Christian marriage.

CLASS AND RACIAL DIVISIONS IN THE FEMALE POPULATION: SOME PRACTICAL AND POLITICAL DILEMMAS FOR THE WOMEN'S MOVEMENT[1]

SCOTT CUMMINGS
University of Texas at Arlington

One of the professed goals of the women's movement is to liberate both men and women from the bonds of traditional attitudes which prevent females from actualizing their human potentialities. Consequently, an area of considerable interest among feminists is the extent to which the movement has changed traditional attitudes toward the place of women in society. An associated area of central importance is the attempt to identify those sectors of the population which rigidly cling to these traditional ideas. Although they do not typically allow one to reach conclusions about change over time, analysis of public opinion data is a useful way to estimate the impact of the women's movement on traditional attitudes toward females. Opinion surveys can also be used to identify those sectors in the population which exhibit the greatest resistance to the idea of more egalitarian relationships between the sexes.

This study reports the results of an analysis of recent opinion data dealing with traditional attitudes toward the place of women in society. No specific hypothesis are tested; no attempt is made to construct or evaluate a specific theory which purports to explain the causes of the women's movement. Instead, the data are discussed in terms of class and racial divisions in the female population, and the relevance of these divisions for the women's movement. The data are described, presented, and discussed briefly. Lastly, some speculation is offered concerning the implications the data suggest for the goals of the women's movement.

THE DATA

The data used to assess the impact of the feminist movement on traditional attitudes toward the place of women in society are drawn from the 1972 election study conducted by the Survey Research Center at the University of Michigan. The sample itself was drawn from a representative cross-section of households in the continental United States; persons 18 years or older were interviewed. The sample size was 2705, 1537 of whom were females and 1168 were males.

Among the various survey items included on the
original interview schedule, four were especially relevent
to the issues championed by feminists. They are presented
below and discussed briefly. The following item measured
variations in attitudes toward traditional sex roles:

> Recently there has been a lot of talk about
> women's rights. Some people feel that women
> should have an equal role with men in running
> business, industry, and government. Others
> feel that women's place is in the home. Where
> would you place yourself on this scale or
> haven't you thought much about it?

The actual scale ranged from 1 to 7. At one extreme (1),
appeared the position that women and men should have an
equal role; at the other extreme (7), was the position that
women's place is in the home (for reviews of recent sex role
research, see Boverman, et al., 1972; Freeman, 1970; Frieden,
1963; Hacker, 1957; Hochschild, 1973; Komarovsky, 1946;
Kenniston and Kenniston, 1964; Kirschner, 1973; Rossi, 1964).
Because natural cutting points appeared in the analysis of
the data, responses were collapsed in three categories: 1-2,
egalitarian; 3-5, transitional and; 6-7, traditional attitudes.
One-hundred sixty-one respondents had no opinion or did not
answer the question.

An item dealing with abortion also appeared in the
larger survey.

> There has been some discussion about abortion
> during the recent years. Which one of the
> following opinions best agrees with your view?
>
> 1. abortion should never be permitted
>
> 2. abortion should be permitted only if
>   the life and health of the women is in
>   danger
>
> 3. abortions should be permitted if, due to
>   personal reasons, the woman would have
>   difficulty in caring for the child
>
> 4. abortions should never be forbidden, since
>   one should not require a woman to have
>   a child she doesn't want

Eighty-six respondents did not answer the question or had no
opinion. While the item does not tap variations in attitudes
about heterosexual and homosexual behavior in general, it
does, nonetheless, get at one important issue championed by
the women's movement: the right to exercise control over

one's own body (Boston Women's Health Collective, 1972; Frankfort, 1972).

An important and precisely worded statement was included in the original survey which relates to the general issue of the economic exploitation of women and income inequality between sexes:

> Sometimes a company has to lay-off part of its labor force. Some people think that the first workers to be laid-off should be women whose husbands have jobs. Others think that male and female employees should be treated the same. Which of these opinions do you agree with?
>
> 1. lay off women first
> 2. treat male and female employees the same

This question in a rather direct manner indexes the issue of the economics of sexism, that is, it indicates the differential treatment of people in the work force purely on the basis of sex (Hacker, 1973; Epstein, 1970; Fuchs, 1971; Goldberg, 1969; Jordan, 1970; Levitin, et al., 1971; Loeb and Ferber, 1971; Oppenheimer, 1968; Peterson, 1964; Stevenson, 1974; Sutter and Miller, 1973; Weisskoff, 1972; Wilensky, 1968; Zellner, 1972). Ninety-two respondents did not answer the question or had no opinion on the issue.

Lastly, an item dealing with the participation of women in politics was included in the original survey. Like the previous question, this item was also simple, straightforward, and dealt directly with the traditional maxim that politics is men's business (Bourque and Grossholtz, 1974; Boyd, 1968; Bullock and Hayes, 1972; Constantini and Craik, 1972; Erskine, 1971; Werner, 1968, 1966).

> Do you agree or disagree with this statement?
> Women should stay out of politics.
>
> 1. agree
> 2. disagree

The data analysis was straightforward and direct. A comparison of the distribution of attitudes by sex was made. In addition, class and racial comparisons were made. Class position was determined on the basis of annual family income. This index was selected over measures of occupational status or educational attainment level because it is more sensitive to variations in economic insecurity. Discussions of variations in attitudes toward the issues championed by the women's movement have tended to focus upon affluence versus insecurity as casual factors. Thus, in cases where both the husband and the wife are employed, even though the status of the occupations may be low, the combined family income may be fairly substantial. Although many other factors are associated with the economic security, it was assumed that annual family income was the most precise measure among those available. Nineteen different levels of annual family income were included in the original survey; on the basis of natural cutting points, five levels of class position were ultimately created: low, less than $3,999; medium-low, $4,000 to $5,999; medium, $6,000 to $11,999; medium-high, $12,000 to $24,999 and; high, over $25,000 per year.

Sex, race, and class are obviously important variables to include in the analysis. Since male chauvinism is often identified as the chief barrier preventing the full emancipation of women, the attitudes of males should be singled out for special attention. In addition, class and racial cleavages and conflicts in the population have often been identified as being responsible for preventing widespread unity among women, thus reducing the idea of sisterhood to a myth. Consequently, the attitudes of working and lower-class men and women, as well as those of black and white men and women should be examined separately also.

RESULTS

Table 1 shows the distribution of attitudes on the four questions by sex. In terms of traditional sex roles, the two populations showed no significant differences. The same can be said in regard to attitudes about abortion. On the question dealing with the economics of sexism, however, men were slightly more egalitarian than women. The comparison of political attitudes showed no differences between the two groups. Overall, then, the data suggest, with the exception of the item dealing with the economics of sexism, the attitudes of men and women are very similar. Consequently, the idea that the female population in general is characterized by a commonly held set of attitudes and common interests created by exposure to sex discrimination is simply not supported by the data. Perhaps a more relevant interpretation, however, is not the fact that no large differences in attitudes were found between the two groups but that overall the general population itself appears very divided over the desirability of establishing more egalitarian relationships between the sexes. That is, if we assume that the four questions are components of a larger attitudinal complex which feminists call sexism, then one might conclude from the data that sexism itself appears firmly entrenched in both the male and female populations. The only exception to this observation was found in attitudes toward the participation of women in politics.

TABLE 1

SUPPORT FOR MORE EGALITARIAN RELATIONSHIPS BETWEEN
THE SEXES BY SEX

	Female	Male
traditional sex roles:		
traditional	25.3	22.8
transitional	34.2	32.9
egalitarian	40.5	44.3
	1434	1073

$$x^2 = 3.9$$
$$p < .20$$

abortion:		
never	11.8	10.7
health reasons	48.3	45.1
child care reasons	16.7	18.2
anytime	23.1	26.1
	1469	1110

$$x^2 = 5.34$$
$$p < .20$$

economics of sexism:		
fire women first	49.9	41.7
equal treatment	50.1	58.3
	1450	1127

$$x^2 = 17.4$$
$$p < .001$$

participation in politics:		
should not	20.5	18.4
should	79.5	81.6
	1490	1133

$$x^2 = 1.94$$
$$p < .20$$

Table 2 shows the comparison between males and
females, controlling for race. Generally, no strong differences were found in the attitudes of males and females in
either the black or white population. Some significant
differences did emerge, however, in the analysis of responses
by race. Whites were significantly more inclined than blacks
to express positive attitudes toward abortion (chi-square
significant beyond .001). This attitudinal difference is
probably accounted for by the genocide interpretation of birth
control in the black community. The work force participation
questions showed an important racial difference as well (chi-
square significant beyond .001). In fact, in comparison to
the three other groups, white females were less inclined to
endorse the idea that men and women should be treated equally
in the work force. These data suggest that bread and butter
issues are more important to blacks than whites, regardless
of sex. Referring solely to black females, however, it is
well documented that, in comparison to their white counterparts, they are called upon more frequently to provide income
to maintain the household (Aldous, 1969; Bock, 1969). In this
survey, for example, 46.5% of the black females reported being
employed full-time, whereas 37.8% of the white females reported being in the work force. Consequently, the economics
of sexism issues should be more salient to black as opposed
to white females.

Table 3 shows the comparison between males and
females, controlling for class position. Generally, no significant differences were found in the attitudes of males
and females regardless of class position. On the work force
participation question, however, higher status males tended
to be significantly more egalitarian than their female counterparts. Further analysis showed a slight relationship between
class position and the four dependent variables. Simply,
economically secure respondents appeared less committed to
traditional attitudes than their economically insecure counterparts.

Table 4 shows the degree of association between
class position and support for more egalitarian relationships,
separately by sex. In the male population, the relationship
between class position and the four dependent variables was
not strong and in some cases not systematic. In the female
population, however, the relationship between class and
attitudes was stronger. The major exception to this pattern
was found in the females' response to the question dealing
with the participation of women in the work force. For females,
the data showed no relationship between class and attitude
toward the equal treatment of the sexes in the work force.
That is, middle and upper status women were no different from
their working and lower-class counterparts on this particular
question. Apparently, the endorsement of more egalitarian
relationships between the sexes by higher status women does

TABLE 2

SUPPORT FOR MORE EGALITARIAN RELATIONSHIPS BETWEEN

THE SEXES BY SEX, CONTROLLING FOR RACE

	Blacks		Whites	
	females	males	females	males
traditional sex roles:				
traditional	29.6	22.0	24.8	22.9
transitional	26.3	28.6	35.1	33.3
egalitarian	44.1	49.5	40.1	43.8
	152	91	1282	982

$$x^2 = 1.7 \qquad\qquad x^2 = 3.18$$
$$p < .70 \qquad\qquad p < .30$$

abortion:				
never	21.4	18.2	10.7	9.8
health reasons	42.1	50.5	49.0	44.6
child care reasons	18.9	14.1	16.5	18.6
anytime	17.6	17.2	23.8	27.0
	159	99	1310	1011

$$x^2 = 2.06 \qquad\qquad x^2 = 6.54$$
$$p < .70 \qquad\qquad p < .10$$

economics of sexism:				
fire women first	29.0	32.7	52.4	42.5
equal treatment	71.0	67.3	47.6	57.5
	155	98	1295	1023

$$x^2 = .37 \qquad\qquad x^2 = 22.49$$
$$p < .70 \qquad\qquad p < .001$$

participation in politics:				
should not	23.0	15.0	20.2	18.7
should	77.0	85.0	79.8	81.3
	161	100	1329	1033

$$x^2 = 2.46 \qquad\qquad x^2 = .90$$
$$p < .20 \qquad\qquad p < .80$$

TABLE 3

SUPPORT FOR MORE EGALITARIAN RELATIONSHIPS
BETWEEN THE SEXES BY SEX, CONTROLLING FOR CLASS POSITION

Social Class Position

| | Low | | | | Middle | | High | | | |
| | 1 | | 2 | | 3 | | 4 | | 5 | |
	female	male	female	male	female	male	female	male	female	male
traditional sex roles:										
traditional	34.9	27.1	29.1	25.7	25.2	26.8	17.1	17.8	13.1	10.1
transitional	29.2	27.8	33.1	22.9	36.4	34.5	36.5	34.4	28.3	49.3
egalitarian	35.9	45.1	37.7	51.4	38.4	38.7	46.5	47.9	58.3	40.6
	298	144	175	109	500	406	340	326	60	69
abortion:										
never	21.9	19.0	12.6	15.1	9.4	9.5	5.8	7.9	8.5	4.6
health reasons	49.7	47.7	54.9	46.2	49.5	48.0	43.2	40.2	35.6	44.6
child care reasons	13.1	15.7	14.3	16.0	17.3	19.1	21.2	19.6	18.6	12.3
anytime	15.3	17.6	18.3	22.7	23.8	23.4	29.9	32.3	37.3	38.5
	320	153	175	119	509	423	345	331	59	65
economics of sexism:										
fire women first	50.0	46.4	48.8	42.7	48.9	43.7	50.6	39.1	49.1	31.3
equal treatment	50.0	53.6	51.2	57.3	51.1	56.3	49.9	60.9	50.9	68.7
	316	153	170	117	505	428	342	335	57	67
							p < .05		p < .05	
participation in politics:										
should not	38.2	26.8	25.7	21.7	16.5	20.9	9.2	12.5	6.6	10.1
should	61.8	73.2	74.3	78.3	83.5	79.1	90.8	87.5	93.4	89.9
	327	157	175	120	516	430	348	336	61	69

Note: Except where indicated, chi-square tests are not significant at the .05 level.

TABLE 4

THE RELATIONSHIP BETWEEN CLASS POSITION
AND SUPPORT FOR MORE EGALITARIAN RELATIONSHIPS
BETWEEN THE SEXES, SEPARATELY FOR FEMALES AND MALES
(gamma coefficients)

	Females	Males
traditional sex roles:	.17*	.07*
abortion:	.25*	.19*
economics of sexism:	.00	.10
participation in politics:	.48*	.26*

*Denotes statistical significance at the .05 level.

Note: Statistical significance determined by chi-square.

TABLE 5

SUPPORT FOR MORE EGALITARIAN RELATIONSHIPS BETWEEN
THE SEXES, CONTROLLING FOR CLASS POSITION AND RACIAL STATUS

BLACKS

Social Class Position

	Low 1		2		Middle 3		4		High 5*	
	female	male	female	male	female	male	female	male	female	male
traditional sex roles:										
traditional	35.4	26.1	19.2	29.4	30.6	19.4	21.2	12.5		
transitional	26.2	26.1	30.8	29.4	13.9	32.3	47.4	31.3		
egalitarian	38.5	47.8	50.0	41.2	55.6	48.4	31.6	56.3		
(N)	65	23	26	17	36	31	19	16	1	2
abortion:										
never	27.5	33.3	19.2	33.3	13.9	7.9	15.0	.0		
health reasons	42.0	45.8	42.3	44.4	50.0	57.9	30.0	50.0		
child care reasons	18.8	16.7	11.5	11.1	25.0	10.5	25.0	25.0		
anytime	11.6	4.2	26.9	11.1	11.1	23.7	30.0	25.0		
(N)	69	24	26	18	36	38	20	16	1	2
economics of sexism:										
fire women first	35.3	33.3	19.2	29.4	20.6	33.3	35.0	35.3		
equal treatment	64.7	66.7	80.8	70.6	79.4	66.7	65.0	64.7		
(N)	68	24	26	17	34	36	20	17	1	2
participation in politics:										
should not	30.0	29.2	19.2	22.2	18.9	10.8	10.0	.0		
should	70.0	70.8	80.8	77.8	81.1	89.2	90.0	100.0		
(N)	70	24	26	18	37	37	20	17	1	2

WHITES

traditional sex roles:										
traditional	34.8	27.3	30.9	25.0	24.8	27.5	16.8	18.1	11.9	9.0
transitional	30.0	28.1	33.6	21.7	38.1	34.7	35.8	34.5	28.8	51.7
egalitarian	35.2	44.6	35.6	53.3	37.1	37.9	47.4	47.4	59.3	40.5
	233	121	149	92	464	375	321	310	59	67
			p < .05						p	.05
abortion:										
never	20.3	16.3	11.4	11.9	9.1	9.6	5.2	8.3	8.6	4.8
health reasons	51.8	48.1	57.0	46.5	49.5	47.0	44.0	39.7	36.2	44.4
child care reasons	11.6	15.5	14.8	16.8	16.7	20.0	20.9	19.4	19.0	12.7
anytime	16.3	20.2	16.8	24.8	24.7	23.4	29.8	32.7	36.2	38.1
	251	129	149	101	473	385	325	315	58	63
economics of sexism:										
fire women first	54.0	48.8	54.2	44.0	51.0	44.6	51.6	39.3	48.2	30.8
equal treatment	46.0	51.2	45.8	55.0	49.0	55.4	48.4	60.7	51.8	69.2
	248	129	144	100	471	392	322	318	56	65
						p < .05			p <.05	
participation in politics:										
should not	40.5	26.3	26.8	21.6	16.3	21.9	9.1	13.2	5.0	7.5
should	59.5	73.7	73.2	78.4	83.7	78.1	90.9	86.8	95.0	92.5
	257	133	149	102	479	393	328	319	60	67
	p < .05									

Note: Except where indicated, chi-square tests are not significant at the .05 level.

*Too few cases to percentage.

91

TABLE 6

THE RELATIONSHIP BETWEEN CLASS POSITION
AND SUPPORT FOR MORE EGALITARIAN RELATIONSHIPS
BETWEEN THE SEXES, SEPARATELY FOR MALES AND FEMALES
WITHIN RACIAL GROUPS
(gamma coefficients)

	Blacks		Whites	
	females	males	females	males
traditional sex roles:	.20	.12	.19*	.07*
abortion:	.21	.41*	.25*	.16*
economics of sexism:	.14	.14	.04	.13
participation in politics:	.32	.32	.50*	.26*

*Denotes statistical significance at the .05 level.

Note: Statistical significance determined by chi-square.

not extend to issues relating to the hiring and firing of women. Perhaps economic self-interest explains this latter finding. Working and lower-class women, even though they may be economically insecure, may develop more conservative attitudes on this issue with the thought in mind that it may be their husband's job, hence their own economic security, which is at stake if women increase their participation in the work force. On the other hand, many middle and upper-class women, because they are economically secure, may perceive the economic issue as somewhat irrelevant to their own life circumstances, problems, and aspirations. In the male population, the findings also seem to support a self interest interpretation. That is, slightly lower levels of support shown for egalitarian relationships between the sexes among working and lower-class males may emerge as a response to limit the participation of another group, in this case women, in the competition over scarce resources (Bonacich, 1972). In summary, then, class differences do seem to divide the population, especially the female population, on many of the central issues championed by the women's movement.

Table 5 shows the analysis of responses by sex, controlling for class and race. Since class and racial status are related, this analysis was undertaken in order to determine if class or race was more influential in shaping attitudes. Like previous analysis, the data did not suggest that sex is an important factor dividing the population's attitudes toward the place of women in society. In the black sample, attitudes did not vary significantly according to the sex of the respondent. In the white sample, some significant differences did emerge in the analysis of responses by sex; however, the differences revealed no particular pattern and in most cases males expressed more egalitarian attitudes then females.

Table 6 shows the relationship between class position and the four dependent variables separately for males and females in each racial group. In the black population, for both males and females, there tended to be a systematic connection between class position and support of more egalitarian relationships between the sexes. Differences in attitudes between classes, however, approached but did not typically reach significance at the .05 level. Due to the small number of cases in the higher income levels of the black sample, more definite conclusions were difficult to reach. Nonetheless, economically secure blacks, regardless of sex, seemed to have more in common with their economically secure white counterparts than their economically insecure black counterparts. In the white population, the relationships between class position and the four dependent variables were strongest in the female sample.

These findings tend to support the idea that the most important cleavage in the white female population's orientation toward traditional sex roles is brought about by class position. On the abortion issue, a more general conclusion is suggested. In the black population, regardless of sex, the greater the degree of economic security, the more positive the attitude toward abortion. Thus, the analysis suggests, but not strongly, that abortion is more a class than a racial issue. Economically secure blacks, regardless of sex, tend to be more like their white counterparts when it comes to the abortion question.

The economic issue, however, seems to be characterized by a racial and not a class cleavage. In the white population, no significant class differences were found. In the black population, regardless of sex, no class differences were found. More importantly, though, the initial racial differences remained. In regard to bread and butter issues, the black respondents, regardless of sex or class status, were significantly more supportive of equal treatment of the sexes in the work force. The data showed as well that white females were more traditional on economic issues than both the black and the white male populations. On the political participation question, though, upper status women were significantly less traditional than their lower status counterparts, regardless of racial status.

In summary, then, the data suggest that class and racial status, and not sexual status, divide the population on many of the important issues championed by the women's movement.

PRACTICAL AND POLITICAL IMPLICATIONS OF THE FINDINGS FOR THE WOMEN'S MOVEMENT

The data show no support for the idea that sexual status is strongly associated with variations in attitudes toward the place of women in society. Many activists in the women's movement have asserted that all women suffer sex discrimination. If one assumes the validity of such an assertion, however, the data show quite clearly that exposure to sex discrimination does not produce in women a commonly held set of interest and orientations challenging the traditional maxims about the place of women in society. Rather, the data suggest that class position and racial status are far more important variables than is sex in explaining differences in attitudes toward women. More significant, however, is the fact that class position and racial status seem to produce differences, strains, and conflicting orientations among women rather than consensus and unity. If sisterhood is defined in terms of a commonly held set of values, a systematic set of maxims challenging the traditional place of women in society, then the data give little reason to conclude that such an ethic is very widespread in the female population.

In practical terms, such a conclusion suggests a dilemma for the women's movement. Specifically, in order to succeed and sustain itself, any social movement must recruit or attract converts; in order to recruit a following, it must appeal to the widest constituency possible. And most importantly, its cafeteria of appeals must validly reflect real issues and problems encountered by the audience it is attempting to reach. While it is certainly not necessary for a social movement to be homogeneous, it does have to orchestrate its members in such a way that they can act together in similar, supplementary, and complementary ways. Yet the data suggest that many of the issues championed by the women's movement have little or no appeal, or at least a differential appeal, to white, black, and working and lower-class women. Further, despite the fact that the most egalitarian sector of the female population was found at the upper levels of the class hierarchy, there still remained a sizable element in this group that appeared committed to traditional maxims and practices.

In a critical analysis of internal conflict within the movement, Dixon (1971-72:154) wrote:

> ...all women do not have the same interests, needs, and desires. Working class women and middle class women, student women and professional women, black women and white women have more conflicting interests than could ever be overcome by their common experience based upon sex discrimination.

Thus, she suggests, the conflicts within the movement may reflect important differences within the female population at large. The data reported in this study seem to support some of Dixon's critical observations.

FOOTNOTES

1. The data in this study were made available through the Inter-University Consortium for Political Research. I thank Jerold Heiss, Charlotte O'Kelly, Susan Spiggle, and an anonymous reviewer for *Sociological Symposium* for commenting helpfully on an earlier draft of this paper.

REFERENCES

Acker, Joan
    1973 "Women and social stratification: a case of
          intellectual sexism." American Journal of
          Sociology 78 (January):936-945

Aldous, Joan
    1969 "Wives' employment status and lower-class men as
          husband-fathers: support for the Moynihan thesis."
          Journal of Marriage and the Family 31 (August):
          469-476.

Bock, E. Wilbur
    1969 "Farmer's daughter effect: the case of the Negro
          female professional." Phylon 30 (Spring):17-26.

Bonacich, Edna
    1972 "A theory of ethnic antagonism: the split labor
          market." American Sociological Review 37 (October):
          547-559.

Boston Women's Health Collective
    1972 Our Bodies, Ourselves: A Book by and for Women.
          New York: Simon and Schuster.

Bourque, Susan and Jean Grossholtz
    1974 "Politics an unnatural practice: political science
          looks at female participation." Politics and Society
          4 (Winter):225-266.

Boyd, Rosamonde
    1968 "Women and politics in the U.S. and Canada."
          The Annals 375 (January):52-57.

Broverman, Inge,et al.
    1972 "Sex-role stereotypes: a current appraisal."
          Journal of Social Issues 28 (November):59-78.

Bullock, Charles and Patricia L.F. Hays
    1972 "Recruitment of women for congress: a research
          note." Western Political Quarterly 25 (September):
          416-423.

Costantini, Edmond and Kenneth H. Craik
    1972 "Women as politicians: the social background,
          personality, and political careers of female
          party leaders." Journal of Social Issues 28
          (November):217-236.

Dixon, Marlene
    1971 "Public ideology and the class composition of
          women's liberation." Berkeley Journal of Sociology:
          149-167.

97

Epstein, Cynthia
1970 "Encountering the male establishment: sex status limits on women's careers in the professions." American Journal of Sociology 75 (May):965-982.

Erskine, Helen
1971 "The polls: women's role." Public Opinion Quarterly 35 (Summer):275-290.

Frankfurt, Ellen
1972 Vaginal Politics. New York: Quadrangle Books.

Freeman, Jo
1970 "Growing up girlish." Transaction 8 36-43.

Friedan, Betty
1963 The Feminine Mystique. New York: Dell Publishing Company.

Fuchs, Victor
1971 "Differences in hourly earnings between men and women." Monthly Labor Review (May):9-15.

Goldberg, Marilyn
1969 "The economic exploitation of women." Pp. 113-117 in David Gordon (ed.), Problems in Political Economy. Lexington: D.C. Heath and Co.

Hacker, Helen
1957 "The new burdens of masculinity." Marriage and Family Living 19 227-233.

Hochschild, Arlie Russell
1973 "A review of sex role research." American Journal of Sociology 78 (January):1101-1129.

Jordan, Joan
1970 "Working women and the equal rights amendment." Transaction 8 16-22.

Kamarovsky, Mirra
1946 "Cultural contradictions and sex roles." American Journal of Sociology 52 184-190.

Kenniston, Ellen and Kenneth Kenniston
1964 "An American anachronism: the image of women and work." The American Scholar 33 (Summer):355-375.

Kirschner, Frankie
1973 "Introducing students to women's place in society." American Journal of Sociology 78 (January):1051-1054.

Levitin, Teresa, Robert Quinn and Graham L. Staines
    1971 "Sex discrimination against the American working
          women." American Behavioral Scientist 15 (November):
          237-254.

Loeb, Jane W. and Marianne Feber
    1971 "Sex as predictive of salary and status on a
          university faculty." Journal of Educational
          Measurement 8 (Winter):235-244.

Oppenheimer, Valerie Kincaid
    1968 "The sex-labeling of jobs." Industrial Relations
          7 (May):219-234.

Peterson, Esther
    1964 "Working women." Daedalus 93 (Spring):671-699.

Rossi, Alice
    1964 "Equality between the sexes: an immodest proposal."
          Daedalus 93 (Spring):607-652.

Stevenson, Mary
    1974 "Women's wages and job segregation." Politics
          and Society 4 (Fall):83-91.

Sutter, Larry E. and Herman P. Miller
    1973 "Income differences between men and career women."
          American Journal of Sociology 78 (January):962-981.

Weisskoff, Francine Blau
    1972 "Women's place in the labor market." The American
          Economic Review 62 (May):161-166.

Werner, Emmy E.
    1968 "Women in the state legislatures." Western Political
          Quarterly 21 (March):40-50.
          "Women in congress: 1917-1964." Western Political
          Quarterly 19 (March):16-30.

Wilensky, Harold
    1968 "Women's work: economic growth, ideology and
          structure." Industrial Relations 7 (May):235-248.

Zellner, Harriet
    1972 "Discrimination against women, occupational segre-
          gation and the relative wage." The American Economic
          Review 62 (May):157-160.

Preface

The cry of "women's liberation" leaps out from the "lifestyle" sections of newspapers and the pages of slick magazines, from radio speakers and television screens. Cut loose from past patterns of behavior and expectations, women of all ages are searching for their identity—the college woman who has new alternatives thrust upon her via "women's studies" courses, the young woman whose routine is shattered by a chance encounter with a "consciousness-raising session," the woman in her middle years who suddenly finds herself in the "empty-nest syndrome," the woman of any age whose lover or lifetime partner departs for greener pastures (and a younger crop).

All of these women, thanks to the women's liberation movement, no longer see their predicament in terms of personal problems to be confronted and solved. They see their own difficulties as a little cog in the big machine of establishment restraints and stereotypical injustice in which they have lost their own equilibrium. Who am I? Why am I here? Why am I just another faceless victim of society's oppression, a nameless prisoner behind walls too high for me to climb alone?

If I were stymied by a slice in my golf drive, I would seek lessons from a pro rather than join the postmortems in the bar at the "nineteenth hole." If I found a lump on my breast, I would run, not walk, to the best available physician, rather than join rap sessions with other women who had recently made similar discoveries. If my business were sliding into bankruptcy, I would ask advice from those whose companies operate in the black rather than in the red.

Likewise, it would seem that, for a woman to find her identity in the modern world, the path should be sought from the Positive Women who have found the road and possess the map, rather than from those who have not. In this spirit, I share with you the thoughts of one who loves life as a woman and lives love as a woman, whose credentials are from the school of practical experience, and who has learned that fulfillment as a woman is a journey, not a destination.

Like every human being born into this world, the Positive Woman has her share of sorrows and sufferings, of unfulfilled desires and bitter defeats. But she will never be crushed by life's disappointments, because her positive mental attitude has built her an inner security that the actions of other people can never fracture. To the Positive Woman, her particular set of problems is not a conspiracy against her, but a challenge to her character and her capabilities.

I

Understanding
the Difference

The first requirement for the acquisition of
power by the Positive Woman is to understand the differences
between men and women. Your outlook on life, your faith,
your behavior, your potential for fulfillment, all are determined by the parameters of your original premise. The Positive
Woman starts with the assumption that the world is her oyster.
She rejoices in the creative capability within her body and the
power potential of her mind and spirit. She understands that
men and women are different, and that those very differences
provide the key to her success as a person and fulfillment as a
woman.

The women's liberationist, on the other hand, is imprisoned
by her own negative view of herself and of her place in the
world around her. This view of women was most succinctly
expressed in an advertisement designed by the principal wom-
en's liberationist organization, the National Organization for
Women (NOW), and run in many magazines and newspapers
and as spot announcements on many television stations. The
advertisement showed a darling curlyheaded girl with the cap-
tion: "This healthy, normal baby has a handicap. She was born
female."

This is the self-articulated dog-in-the-manger, chip-on-the-
shoulder, fundamental dogma of the women's liberation movement. Someone—it is not clear who, perhaps God, perhaps the
"Establishment," perhaps a conspiracy of male chauvinist pigs
—dealt women a foul blow by making them female. It becomes
necessary, therefore, for women to agitate and demonstrate and
hurl demands on society in order to wrest from an oppressive

male-dominated social structure the status that has been wrongfully denied to women through the centuries.

By its very nature, therefore, the women's liberation movement precipitates a series of conflict situations—in the legislatures, in the courts, in the schools, in industry—with man targeted as the enemy. Confrontation replaces cooperation as the watchword of all relationships. Women and men become adversaries instead of partners.,

The second dogma of the women's liberationists is that, of all the injustices perpetrated upon women through the centuries, the most oppressive is the cruel fact that women have babies and men do not. Within the confines of the women's liberationist ideology, therefore, the abolition of this overriding inequality of women becomes the primary goal. This goal must be achieved at any and all costs—to the woman herself, to the baby, to the family, and to society. Women must be made equal to men in their ability *not* to become pregnant and *not* to be expected to care for babies they may bring into the world.

This is why women's liberationists are compulsively involved in the drive to make abortion and child-care centers for all women, regardless of religion or income, both socially acceptable and government-financed. Former Congresswoman Bella Abzug has defined the goal: "to enforce the constitutional right of females to terminate pregnancies that they do not wish to continue."

If man is targeted as the enemy, and the ultimate goal of women's liberation is independence from men and the avoidance of pregnancy and its consequences, then lesbianism is logically the highest form in the ritual of women's liberation. Many, such as Kate Millett, come to this conclusion, although many others do not.

The Positive Woman will never travel that dead-end road. It is self-evident to the Positive Woman that the female body with its baby-producing organs was not designed by a conspiracy of men but by the Divine Architect of the human race. Those who think it is unfair that women have babies, whereas men cannot, will have to take up their complaint with God because no other power is capable of changing that fundamental fact. On some college campuses, I have been assured that other methods of reproduction will be developed. But most of us must deal with the real world rather than with the imagination of dreamers.

Another feature of the woman's natural role is the obvious fact that women can breast-feed babies and men cannot. This functional role was not imposed by conspiratorial males seeking to burden women with confining chores, but must be recognized as part of the plan of the Divine Architect for the survival of the human race through the centuries and in the countries that know no pasteurization of milk or sterilization of bottles.

The Positive Woman looks upon her femaleness and her fertility as part of her purpose, her potential, and her power. She rejoices that she has a capability for creativity that men can never have.

The third basic dogma of the women's liberation movement is that there is no difference between male and female except the sex organs, and that all those physical, cognitive, and emotional differences you *think* are there, are merely the result of centuries of restraints imposed by a male-dominated society and sex-stereotyped schooling. The role imposed on women is, by definition, inferior, according to the women's liberationists.

The Positive Woman knows that, while there are some physical competitions in which women are better (and can command more money) than men, including those that put a premium on grace and beauty, such as figure skating, the superior physical strength of males over females in competitions of strength, speed, and short-term endurance is beyond rational dispute.

In the Olympic Games, women not only cannot win any medals in competition with men, the gulf between them is so great that they cannot even qualify for the contests with men. No amount of training from infancy can enable women to throw the discus as far as men, or to match men in push-ups or in lifting weights. In track and field events, individual male records surpass those of women by 10 to 20 percent.

Female swimmers today are beating Johnny Weissmuller's records, but today's male swimmers are better still. Chris Evert can never win a tennis match against Jimmy Connors. If we removed lady's tees from golf courses, women would be out of the game. Putting women in football or wrestling matches can only be an exercise in laughs.

The Olympic Games, whose rules require strict verification to ascertain that no male enters a female contest and, with his masculine advantage, unfairly captures a woman's medal, formerly insisted on a visual inspection of the contestants' bodies. Science, however, has discovered that men and women are so innately different physically that their maleness/femaleness can be conclusively established by means of a simple skin test of fully clothed persons.

If there is *anyone* who should oppose enforced sex-equality, it is the women athletes. Babe Didrickson, who played and defeated some of the great male athletes of her time, is unique in the history of sports.[1]

If sex equality were enforced in professional sports, it would mean that men could enter the women's tournaments and win most of the money. Bobby Riggs has already threatened: "I think that men 55 years and over should be allowed to play women's tournaments—like the Virginia Slims. Everybody ought to know there's no sex after 55 anyway."

The Positive Woman remembers the essential validity of the old prayer: "Lord, give me the strength to change what I can change, the serenity to accept what I cannot change, and the wisdom to discern the difference." The women's liberationists are expending their time and energies erecting a make-believe world in which they hypothesize that *if* schooling were gender-free, and *if* the same money were spent on male and female sports programs, and *if* women were permitted to compete on equal terms, *then* they would prove themselves to be physically equal. Meanwhile, the Positive Woman has put the ineradicable physical differences into her mental computer, programmed her plan of action, and is already on the way to personal achievement.

Thus, while some militant women spend their time demanding more money for professional sports, ice skater Janet Lynn, a truly Positive Woman, quietly signed the most profitable financial contract in the history of women's athletics. It was not the strident demands of the women's liberationists that brought high prizes to women's tennis, but the discovery by sports promoters that beautiful female legs gracefully moving around the court made women's tennis a highly marketable television production to delight male audiences.

Many people thought that the remarkable filly named Ruffian would prove that a female race horse could compete equally with a male. Even with the handicap of extra weights placed on the male horse, the race was a disaster for the female. The gallant Ruffian gave her all in a noble effort to compete, but broke a leg in the race and, despite the immediate attention of top veterinarians, had to be put away.

Despite the claims of the women's liberation movement, there are countless physical differences between men and women. The female body is 50 to 60 percent water, the male 60 to 70 percent water, which explains why males can dilute alcohol better than women and delay its effect. The average woman is about 25 percent fatty tissue, while the male is 15 percent, making women more buoyant in water and able to swim with less effort. Males have a tendency to color blindness. Only 5 percent of persons who get gout are female. Boys are born bigger. Women live longer in most countries of the world, not only in the United States where we have a hard-driving competitive pace. Women excel in manual dexterity, verbal skills, and memory recall.

Arianna Stassinopoulos in her book *The Female Woman* has done a good job of spelling out the many specific physical differences that are so innate and so all-pervasive that

> even if Women's Lib was given a hundred, a thousand, ten thousand years in which to eradicate *all* the differences between the sexes, it would still be an impossible undertaking. . . .
>
> It is inconceivable that millions of years of evolutionary selection during a period of marked sexual division of labor have not left pronounced traces on the innate character of men and women. Aggressiveness, and mechanical and spatial skills, a sense of direction, and physical strength—all masculine characteristics—are the qualities essential for a hunter; even food gatherers need these same qualities for defense and exploration. The prolonged period of dependence of human children, the difficulty of carrying the peculiarly heavy and inert human baby—a much heavier, clumsier burden than the monkey infant and much less able to cling on for safety—meant that women could not both look after their children and be hunters and explorers. Early humans learned to take advantage of this period of dependence to transmit rules, knowledge and skills to their offspring—women needed to develop verbal skills, a talent for personal relationships, and a predilection for nurturing going even beyond the maternal instinct.[2]

Does the physical advantage of men doom women to a life of servility and subservience? The Positive Woman knows that she has a complementary advantage which is at least as great—and, in the hands of a skillful woman, far greater. The Divine

Architect who gave men a superior strength to lift weights also gave women a different kind of superior strength.

The women's liberationists and their dupes who try to tell each other that the sexual drive of men and women is really the same, and that it is only societal restraints that inhibit women from an equal desire, an equal enjoyment, and an equal freedom from the consequences, are doomed to frustration forever. It just isn't so, and pretending cannot make it so. The differences are not a woman's weakness but her strength.

Dr. Robert Collins, who has had ten years' experience in listening to and advising young women at a large eastern university, put his finger on the reason why casual "sexual activity" is such a cheat on women:

> A basic flaw in this new morality is the assumption that males and females are the same sexually. The simplicity of the male anatomy and its operation suggest that to a man, sex can be an activity apart from his whole being, a drive related to the organs themselves.
>
> In a woman, the complex internal organization, correlated with her other hormonal systems, indicates her sexuality must involve her total self. On the other hand, the man is orgasm-oriented with a drive that ignores most other aspects of the relationship. The woman is almost totally different. She is engulfed in romanticism and tries to find and express her total feelings for her partner.
>
> A study at a midwestern school shows that 80 percent of the women who had intercourse hoped to marry their partner. Only 12 percent of the men expected the same.
>
> Women say that soft, warm promises and tender touches are delightful, but that the act itself usually leads to a "Is that all there is to it?" reaction. . . .
>
> [A typical reaction is]: "It sure wasn't worth it. It was no fun at the time. I've been worried ever since. . . ."
>
> The new morality is a fad. It ignores history, it denies the physical and mental composition of human beings, it is intolerant, exploitative, and is oriented toward intercourse, not love.[3]

The new generation can brag all it wants about the new liberation of the new morality, but it is still the woman who is hurt the most. The new morality isn't just a "fad"—it is a cheat and a thief. It robs the woman of her virtue, her youth, her beauty, and her love—for nothing, just nothing. It has produced a generation of young women searching for their identity, bored with sexual freedom, and despondent from the loneliness of living a life without commitment. They have abandoned the old commandments, but they can't find any new rules that work.

The Positive Woman recognizes the fact that, when it comes to sex, women are simply not the equal of men. The sexual drive of men is much stronger than that of women. That is how the human race was designed in order that it might perpetuate itself. The other side of the coin is that it is easier for women to control their sexual appetites. A Positive Woman cannot defeat a man in a wrestling or boxing match, but she can motivate him, inspire him, encourage him, teach him, restrain him, reward him, and have power over him that he can never achieve over her with all his muscle. How or whether a Positive Woman uses her power is determined solely by the way she alone defines her goals and develops her skills.

The differences between men and women are also emotional and psychological. Without woman's innate maternal instinct, the human race would have died out centuries ago. There is nothing so helpless in all earthly life as the newborn infant. It will die within hours if not cared for. Even in the most primitive, uneducated societies, women have always cared for their newborn babies. They didn't need any schooling to teach them how. They didn't need any welfare workers to tell them it is their social obligation. Even in societies to whom such concepts as "ought," "social responsibility," and "compassion for the helpless" were unknown, mothers cared for their new babies.

Why? Because caring for a baby serves the natural maternal need of a woman. Although not nearly so total as the baby's need, the woman's need is nonetheless real.

The overriding psychological need of a woman is to love something alive. A baby fulfills this need in the lives of most women. If a baby is not available to fill that need, women search for a baby-substitute. This is the reason why women have traditionally gone into teaching and nursing careers. They are doing what comes naturally to the female psyche. The schoolchild or the patient of any age provides an outlet for a woman to express her natural maternal need.

This maternal need in women is the reason why mothers whose children have grown up and flown from the nest are sometimes cut loose from their psychological moorings. The maternal need in women can show itself in love for grandchildren, nieces, nephews, or even neighbors' children. The maternal need in some women has even manifested itself in an extraordinary affection lavished on a dog, a cat, or a parakeet.

This is not to say that every woman must have a baby in order to be fulfilled. But it is to say that fulfillment for most women involves expressing their natural maternal urge by loving and caring for someone.

The women's liberation movement complains that traditional stereotyped roles assume that women are "passive" and that men are "aggressive." The anomaly is that a woman's most fundamental emotional need is not passive at all, but active. A woman naturally seeks to love affirmatively and to show that love in an active way by caring for the object of her affections.

The Positive Woman finds somebody on whom she can lavish her maternal love so that it doesn't well up inside her and cause psychological frustrations. Surely no woman is so isolated by geography or insulated by spirit that she cannot find someone worthy of her maternal love. All persons, men and women, gain by sharing something of themselves with their fellow humans, but women profit most of all because it is part of their very nature.

One of the strangest quirks of women's liberationists is their complaint that societal restraints prevent men from crying in public or showing their emotions, but permit women to do so, and that therefore we should "liberate" men to enable them, too, to cry in public. The public display of fear, sorrow, anger, and irritation reveals a lack of self-discipline that should be avoided by the Positive Woman just as much as by the Positive Man. Maternal love, however, is not a weakness but a manifestation of strength and service, and it should be nurtured by the Positive Woman.

Most women's organizations, recognizing the preference of most women to avoid hard-driving competition, handle the matter of succession of officers by the device of a nominating committee. This eliminates the unpleasantness and the tension of a competitive confrontation every year or two. Many women's organizations customarily use a prayer attributed to Mary, Queen of Scots, which is an excellent analysis by a woman of women's faults:

> Keep us, O God, from pettiness; let us be large in thought, in word, in deed. Let us be done with fault-finding and leave

off self-seeking. . . . Grant that we may realize it is the little things that create differences, that in the big things of life we are at one.

Another silliness of the women's liberationists is their frenetic desire to force all women to accept the title *Ms* in place of *Miss* or *Mrs.* If Gloria Steinem and Betty Friedan want to call themselves *Ms* in order to conceal their marital status, their wishes should be respected.

But that doesn't satisfy the women's liberationists. They want all women to be compelled to use *Ms* whether they like it or not. The women's liberation movement has been waging a persistent campaign to browbeat the media into using *Ms* as the standard title for all women. The women's liberationists have already succeeding in getting the Department of Health, Education and Welfare to forbid schools and colleges from identifying women students as *Miss* or *Mrs.*[4]

All polls show that the majority of women do not care to be called *Ms.* A Roper poll indicated that 81 percent of the women questioned said they prefer *Miss* or *Mrs.* to *Ms.* Most married women feel they worked hard for the *r* in their names, and they don't care to be gratuitously deprived of it. Most single women don't care to have their name changed to an unfamiliar title that at best conveys overtones of feminist ideology and is polemical in meaning, and at worst connotes misery instead of joy. Thus, Kate Smith, a very Positive Woman, proudly proclaimed on television that she is "Miss Kate Smith, not Ms." Like other Positive Women, she has been succeeding while negative women have been complaining.

Finally, women are different from men in dealing with the fundamentals of life itself. Men are philosophers, women are practical, and 'twas ever thus. Men may philosophize about how life began and where we are heading; women are concerned about feeding the kids today. No woman would ever, as Karl Marx did, spend years reading political philosophy in the British Museum while her child starved to death. Women don't take naturally to a search for the intangible and the abstract. The Positive Woman knows who she is and where she is going, and she will reach her goal because the longest journey starts with a very practical first step.

Amaury de Riencourt, in his book *Sex and Power in History,* shows that a successful society depends on a delicate balancing of different male and female factors, and that the women's liberation movement, which promotes unisexual values and androgyny, contains within it "a social and cultural death wish and the end of the civilization that endorses it."

One of the few scholarly works dealing with woman's role, *Sex and Power in History* synthesizes research from a variety of disciplines—sociology, biology, history, anthropology, religion, philosophy, and psychology. De Riencourt traces distinguishable types of women in different periods in history, from prehistoric to modern times. The "liberated" Roman matron, who is most similar to the present-day feminist, helped bring about the fall of Rome through her unnatural emulation of masculine qualities, which resulted in a large-scale breakdown of the family and ultimately of the empire.

De Riencourt examines the fundamental, inherent differences between men and women. He argues that man is the more aggressive, rational, mentally creative, analytical-minded sex because of his early biological role as hunter and provider. Woman, on the other hand, represents stability, flexibility, reliance on intuition, and harmony with nature, stemming from her procreative function.

Where man is discursive, logical, abstract, or philosophical, woman tends to be emotional, personal, practical, or mystical. Each set of qualities is vital and complements the other. Among the many differences explained in de Riencourt's book are the following:

> Women tend more toward conformity than men—which is why they often excel in such disciplines as spelling and punctuation where there is only one correct answer, determined by social authority. Higher intellectual activities, however, require a mental independence and power of abstraction that they usually lack, not to mention a certain form of aggressive boldness of the imagination which can only exist in a sex that is basically aggressive for biological reasons.
>
> To sum up: The masculine proclivity in problem solving is analytical and categorical; the feminine, synthetic and contextual. . . . Deep down, man tends to focus on the object, on external results and achievements; woman focuses on subjective motives and feelings. If life can be compared to a play, man focuses on the theme and structure of the play, woman on the innermost feelings displayed by the actors.[5]

De Riencourt provides impressive refutation of two of the

basic errors of the women's liberation movement: (1) that there are no emotional or cognitive differences between the sexes, and (2) that women should strive to be like men.

A more colloquial way of expressing the de Riencourt conclusion that men are more analytical and women more personal and practical is in the different answers that one is likely to get to the question, "Where did you get that steak?" A man will reply, "At the corner market," or wherever he bought it. A woman will usually answer, "Why? What's the matter with it?"

An effort to eliminate the differences by social engineering or legislative or constitutional tinkering cannot succeed, which is fortunate, but social relationships and spiritual values can be ruptured in the attempt. Thus the role reversals being forced upon high school students, under which guidance counselors urge reluctant girls to take "shop" and boys to take "home economics," further confuse a generation already unsure about its identity. They are as wrong as efforts to make a left-handed child right-handed.[6]

The Economics of Middle-Income Family Life: Working Women During the Great Depression

WINIFRED D. WANDERSEE BOLIN

THE history of women and work is becoming an increasingly fertile field of research for historians, and the interest in this topic has generated a great deal of valuable scholarship. If there is one theme that emerges, it is that women's work outside of the home has been an extension of their family role and a reflection of their economic need. From the historian's point of view, the "pin-money theory" is dead.[1] Long before the depression of the 1930s, married women left their homes to work in the factories and fields, in the homes of other women, and, increasingly during the twentieth century, in clerical and service occupations. In the decade between 1930 and 1940, the number of married women in the labor force increased by nearly 50 percent, while their numbers in the population increased by only 15 percent. By 1940 married women were 35 percent of the female labor force, in comparison to 29 percent in 1930 (see Table 1).

Thus, in spite of the oversupply of labor and the underemployment of the population as a whole, married women workers made substantial numerical gains during the depression decade. It would be a mistake to suggest that the 1930s represented a new direction; rather, the labor force behavior of these years was a continuation of long-term trends that had been developing since the turn of the century. In fact, the gains of

Winifred D. Wandersee Bolin, Minneapolis, Minnesota, received a Ph.D. in American history at the University of Minnesota.

[1] Several historians discuss the "pin-money theory" in the context of broader social issues. See Clarke A. Chambers, *Seedtime of Reform: American Social Service and Social Action, 1918–1933* (Minneaplis, 1963), 62–63; and William H. Chafe, *The American Woman: Her Changing Social, Economic, and Political Roles, 1920–1970* (New York, 1972), 62–65. The relationship between work and family is the basic theme of several recent studies in women's history: Virginia Yans McLaughlin, "Patterns of Work and Family Organization: Buffalo's Italians," *Journal of Interdisciplinary History*, II (Autumn 1971), 299–314; Daniel J. Walkowitz, "Working-Class Women in the Gilded Age: Factory, Community, and Family Life among Cohoes, New York, Cotton Workers," *Journal of Social History*, 5 (Summer 1972), 464–90; Joan W. Scott and Louise A. Tilly, "Women's Work and the Family in Nineteenth-Century Europe," *Comparative Studies in Society and History*, 17 (Jan. 1975), 36–64; and Thomas Dublin, "Women, Work, and the Family: Women Operatives in the Lowell Mills, 1830–1860," *Feminist Studies*, 3 (Fall 1975).

TABLE 1
Number and Proportion of Women 15 Years Old and Over, Gainfully Occupied, by Marital Condition, for the United States, 1890–1940

Census Year and Marital Status	Total Number*	Gainfully Occupied		% Distr. of Gainfully Occupied
		Number*	Percent	
1890				
Females 15 and over	19.6	3.7	18.9	100.0
Single and unknown	6.3	2.5	40.5	68.2
Married	11.1	0.5	4.6	13.9
Widowed and divorced	2.2	0.7	29.9	17.9
1900				
Females 15 and over	24.2	5.0	20.6	100.0
Single and unknown	7.6	3.3	43.5	66.2
Married	13.8	0.8	5.6	15.4
Widowed and divorced	2.8	0.9	32.5	18.4
1910				
Females 15 and over	30.0	7.6	25.4	100.0
Single and unknown	9.0	4.6	51.1	60.2
Married	17.7	1.9	10.7	24.7
Widowed and divorced	3.4	1.2	34.1	15.0
1920				
Females 15 and over	35.2	8.3	23.7	100.0
Single, widowed, divorced and unknown	13.9	6.4	46.4	77.0
Married	21.3	1.9	9.0	23.0
1930				
Females 15 and over	42.8	10.6	24.8	100.0
Single and unknown	11.4	5.7	50.5	53.9
Married	26.2	3.1	11.7	28.9
Widowed and divorced	5.3	1.8	24.4	17.2
1940				
Females 14 and over**	50.5	12.8	25.3	100.0
Single	13.9	6.3	45.0	49.4
Married	30.1	4.6	15.3	35.5
Husband present	28.5	3.8	13.3	29.6
Husband absent	1.6	0.8	46.9	5.9
Widowed and divorced	6.5	1.9	29.2	15.1

* Numbers in millions.

** 1940 age category differs from other census years.

Source: 16th Census of the United States, 1940, *Population*. Vol. III: *The Labor Force: Industry, Employment, and Income*. Part I: *United States Summary* (Washington, 1943), Table 9, p. 26; 15th Census of the United States, 1930, *Population*. Vol. V: *General Report on Occupations* (Washington, 1933), Table I, 272; and Gertrude Bancroft, *The American Labor Force: Its Growth and Changing Composition* (New York, 1958), Table 25, p. 45.

the 1930s were not nearly as dramatic as those of two earlier decades— 1900 to 1910 and 1920 to 1930. What is significant is that they were made at a time of economic stagnation—at a time when women were under a great deal of public pressure to leave the labor market in order to avoid competing with men for the short supply of jobs.

The majority of married women workers during these years were working because of economic necessity. The investigations conducted by the Women's Bureau were devoted to proving that point, and even a cursory glance at the census data on the female labor force would support the bureau's interpretation. For instance, in 1930, about 3.9 million women combined the roles of homemaker and wage earner;

TABLE 2

Family Income Distribution, 1929

Income Level (in dollars)	No. of Families (in thousands)	Percent at Each Level	Cumulative Percent
Under 0	120	0.4	0.4
0 to 500	1,982	7.2	7.6
500 to 1,000	3,797	13.8	21.5
1,000 to 1,500	5,754	21.0	42.4
1,500 to 2,000	4,701	17.1	59.5
2,000 to 2,500	3,204	11.6	71.2
2,500 to 3,000	1,988	7.2	78.4
3,000 to 3,500	1,447	5.3	83.7
3,500 to 4,000	993	3.6	87.3
4,000 to 4,500	718	2.6	89.9
4,500 to 5,000	514	1.9	91.8
Over 5,000	2,256	8.2	100.0
Total	27,474	100.0	

Source: Maurice Leven, Harold G. Moulton, and Clark Warburton, *America's Capacity to Consume* (Washington, 1934), 54.

TABLE 3

Family Income Distribution, 1935–1936

Income Level (in dollars)	No. of Families (in thousands)	Percent at Each Level	Cumulative Percent
Under 250	1,163	4.0	4.0
250 to 500	3,015	10.3	14.2
500 to 750	3,799	12.9	27.1
750 to 1,000	4,277	14.6	41.7
1,000 to 1,250	3,882	13.2	54.9
1,250 to 1,500	2,865	9.8	64.6
1,500 to 1,750	2,343	8.0	72.6
1,750 to 2,000	1,897	6.5	79.1
2,000 to 2,250	1,421	4.8	83.9
2,250 to 2,500	1,044	3.6	87.4
2,500 to 3,000	1,314	4.5	91.9
3,000 to 3,500	744	2.5	94.4
3,500 to 4,000	438	1.5	95.9
4,000 to 4,500	250	.9	96.8
4,500 to 5,000	153	.5	97.3
Over 5,000	793	2.7	100.0
Total	29,400	100.0	

Source: "Incomes of Families and Single Persons, 1935–36: Summary," *Monthly Labor Review*, 47 (Oct. 1938), 730.

nearly one million were from families with no male head. In that year, nearly 38 percent of all married working women were either foreign born or black, and practically one-fourth were in domestic and personal service.[2]

Much attention has been given to the working women of lower-income families by the Women's Bureau, by social workers, and by recent historians.[3] But there has been a tendency to overlook another demographic characteristic of the 1930s: the rather substantial number of married women from middle-income* families who were also gainfully employed. By 1940, over 40 percent of the gainfully employed homemakers who lived with their husbands, were married to men who had earned $1,000 or more in 1939 (see Table 4).

This statistic has little meaning unless placed into the context of family economics during these years. Tables 2 and 3 give the family income distribution for two different time periods, 1929 and 1935–1936. Neither of these time periods corresponds to 1939, a year for which there are no figures on income distribution. 1939 was probably a somewhat better year than 1935–1936, but not as good as 1929. In 1935–1936, the median family income was $1,160; 50 percent of all families made between $500 and $1,500 a year. Thus, an annual wage or salary of $1,000 or more could place a family in the middle-income range.

But what did it mean to be a ''middle-income family'' in the 1930s? It did not mean that the family had a large surplus income, but it did suggest a fairly comfortable standard of living. In the years between the 1890s and 1920s, average annual money earnings and the purchasing power of these earnings increased substantially for many classes of American society.[4] Thus, it would seem that married women in spite of

* The term ''middle-income'' will be used as opposed to ''middle-class,'' which is a term much more difficult to define.

[2] There were numerous studies done by the Women's Bureau during the 1920s and 1930s that were expressly devoted to disproving the ''pin-money theory.'' For a summary of the census data cited above, see Mary Elizabeth Pidgeon, ''The Employed Woman Homemaker in the U.S.: Her Responsibility for Family Support,'' Women's Bureau, Bulletin, No. 148 (Washington, 1936), 17, 21. See also 15th Census of the United States, 1930, Population, Vol. V: General Report on Occupations (Washington, 1933), Table 8, p. 275.

[3] In addition to the studies already mentioned, see Robert W. Smuts, Women and Work in America (New York, 1959), 51–58. Several recent collections of documents give attention to working women of low-income status. See W. Elliot Brownlee and Mary M. Brownlee, eds., Women in the American Economy: A Documentary History, 1675 to 1929 (New Haven, 1976); Rosalyn Baxandall, Linda Gordon, and Susan Reverby, eds., America's Working Women (New York, 1976); and Gerda Lerner, ed., The Female Experience: An American Documentary (Indianapolis, 1977).

[4] Paul H. Douglas, Real Wages in the United States, 1890–1926 (New York, 1930), 584. For a good description of affluence in the 1920s, see William E. Leuchtenburg, The Perils of Prosperity, 1914–1931 (Chicago, 1958), 178–203.

evidence of economic need, were entering the labor market in the greatest numbers during a period of relative affluence. Although the statistics indicate that most gainfully-employed married women were working because of need, the number of working women from middle-income families was also increasing. The increase was related to complex social, demographic, and technological developments; to changes in the economic function of the family as it became town-based rather than rural; and to the factor explored in this article—the changing definition of economic need.

By the 1920s, American economic and social life reflected an awareness of what was commonly referred to as "the American Standard of Living."[5] The average American may have been unable to describe the precise meaning of this term, but nearly everyone agreed that it was attainable, highly desirable, and far superior to the standard of any other nation. Its nature varied according to social class and regional differences, but no matter where a family stood socially and financially, members set their aspirations beyond their means. A family defined its standard of living in terms of an income that it hoped to achieve rather than by the reality of the paycheck.

Thus, the American standard of living, influenced by the availability of consumer goods and mass advertising, gave the term "economic need" a new definition. Instead of referring merely to food, clothing, and shelter, economic need came to mean anything that a particular family was unwilling to go without. When the American dream of prosperity came to an end in 1929, American families at all economic levels were hard hit. For those at the bottom, the Great Depression was an extension and intensification of the hard times they had always suffered. Families that had been marginally independent were pushed across the line into poverty and dependency. But even relatively affluent middle-class families saw their accustomed standard of living greatly diminished.

Expectations with respect to standards of living remained high, but the means to achieve these expectations declined. Some families borrowed, while others simply did not pay their bills. Some moved in with relatives and some went on relief. The most logical way to meet the economic crisis was to cut back expenditures; and although this measure was forced upon most families, many nevertheless managed to maintain a remarkably high level of consumption during the depression.

[5] Royal Meeker, "What is the American Standard of Living?" *Monthly Labor Review*, IX (July 1919), 1.

Even in the face of unemployment, wage reductions, and general economic insecurity, people of middle incomes clung to certain material goods and life-styles that had become important elements in the new definition of economic need.

In 1935–1936, the Bureau of Labor Statistics and the Bureau of Home Economics, in cooperation with the National Resources Committee and the Central Statistical Board, did a national study on incomes and expenditures (hereafter referred to as the Consumer Purchases Study). The study was a random sample of about 336,000 families and a smaller sample of about 53,000 families to provide information on the consumption patterns of families not on relief and at different income levels. Since the information was being obtained primarily to provide a basis for indexes of living costs, it was felt that the information should not reflect the distorted spending of families whose incomes had been abnormally low or irregular.[6]

The Consumer Purchases Study revealed that postwar changes in family expenditures occurred during the 1920s—not the 1930s—and that these changes had had a profound effect upon consumption patterns of the 1930s, in spite of the decline of income during the depression. Faith Williams of the Bureau of Labor Statistics observed that most families of wage earners and clerical workers had higher standards of living in 1934–1936 than families of comparable income in the years 1917–1919: "Their diets more nearly approach the recommendation of specialists in human nutrition; they have homes with better lighting; many of them are able to travel more because they have automobiles. The change in the ideas of these workers as to how they ought to live has resulted in fundamental changes in their expenditure patterns."[7]

Comparisons were made in view of the price realignments that had occurred between the 1917–1919 study and the Consumer Purchases Study. The purchasing power of the worker's dollar was, on the average, slightly higher in 1934–1936 than it had been in 1917–1919. Food prices were consistently lower by as much as 16 percent to 38 percent in each of the cities covered by both studies. Clothing prices were also lower by 5 percent to 31 percent. Differences in the cost of rent, fuel, and light varied greatly from city to city. Furnishings and household equipment generally cost less in the later period, but miscellaneous items were more expensive in every city. The Bureau of Labor Statistics eliminated these price differences by applying the cost of items in the

[6] Faith M. Williams, "Changes in Family Expenditures in the Post-War Period," *Monthly Labor Review*, 47 (Nov. 1938), 968.
[7] *Ibid.*, 979.

1934–1936 period to the average expenditures of the families studied in 1917–1919.[8]

The basic change in expenditure at all economic levels was a shift away from essential items—food, clothing, and shelter—toward the miscellaneous items that signify an over-all higher standard of living. The pattern of change was very similar in each city. For instance, in twenty-four out of thirty-five cities, average expenditures for food were lower in the later period. This was because food prices were lower, enabling families to eat as well or better on less money. The average amount spent for clothing was down for each city, but expenditures for housing, which included fuel, light, and refrigeration, were higher in every city except one. A large proportion of the 1934–1936 families had electric lighting and modern plumbing, which accounted for the higher costs. Expenditures for furniture and furnishings varied from city to city. Finally, two-thirds of the cities showed a higher average expenditure on miscellaneous items, or everything not included under the above items.[9]

Economists, home economists, and even social workers, tended to be critical of the buying habits of American families; some suggested that Americans created their own economic problems through love of luxury and ignorance of money management. A home economist, Day Monroe, felt that even low-income families could improve their standards of living by wise spending, a criticism that should probably have been directed at middle-income families.[10] Although more intelligent buying habits might have resulted in a higher standard of living for some families, the problem was primarily related to changing values. While American families of all income levels raised their expectations, the expenditure pattern of an individual family depended on personal values rather than on the sophisticated opinions of economists and social workers.

Many families, especially those in the middle- to upper-income groups, made a conscious effort to plan their expenditures in response to wage reductions or changes in employment. Women's magazines and popular journals had special sections on budgeting. They published articles written by housewives who were budgeting and even ran contests for those who wished to devise the perfect budget. That this was

[8] *Ibid.*, 973.

[9] *Ibid.*, Table 1, 969–72, 973. For detailed information on family consumption, see "Family Expenditures in Selected Cities, 1935–36," Vols. I–VII, Bureau of Labor Statistics, *Bulletin*, No. 648 (Washington, 1941).

[10] Day Monroe, "Levels of Living of the Nation's Families," *Journal of Home Economics*, 29 (Dec. 1937), 670. For a fictional account that reflects a similar bias, see Josephine Lawrence, *If I Had Four Apples* (New York, 1935).

definitely an upper-middle-class phenomenon is indicated by the incomes that these families had to budget—the lowest was $1,200, and they ranged to $3,000 and even $5,000. Most of the women (and it was always women) who wrote personal accounts of their budgeting experience, did so in a manner that was both light-hearted and smug. Obviously there was something good and clean—even fun—in returning to the "plain living" of grandma's day, especially when that plain living was sustained on a $2,500 a year salary.[11]

In the mid-1930s, an income of $2,500 placed a family in the upper 12 percent income bracket (see Table 3). Even in 1929, at the height of affluence, only about 29 percent of all American families made more than $2,500. A budget imples that there is room for flexibility with respect to expenditures, and, although most families established priorities through the simple act of buying, few had a surplus requiring conscious decision or varied choices. As humorist Will Cuppy observed, "In order to run a budget, you have to have money. . . . I don't feel that I can afford one right now—there are so many other things I need worse." Many Americans would have agreed with Cuppy: "I'm not good at figures, but I know when I'm ruined, and I don't have to write it down on a piece of paper."[12]

Since about 42 percent of all American families were living on a marginal income basis, that is, below $1,000 a year, how did they manage to maintain a relatively high standard of consumption during the depression? The lower cost of living was one factor. Combined money income in 1931 was approximately seven-tenths that of 1929, but the cost of living for a workingman's family declined about 15 percent during the same period. This was not equal to the decline in money income, but the necessities of life, food, in particular, showed the most striking decreases.[13] Moreover, the rate of consumption did fall off considerably, especially during the early years of the depression. But for some, installment buying remained an important means of maintaining a facsimile of the standard they wished to achieve. Although consumption of durable goods fell off steeply during the early 1930s, by 1936 about

[11] See, for instance, Alice O'Reardon Overbeck, "Back to Plain Living," *Forum*, LXXXVIII (Nov. 1932), 302–06; H.M.S., "The Family Problem: Two Salary Cuts Have Taught Us What a Budget's For," *American Magazine*, CXVI (Sept. 1932), 120–21; "How We Live on $2,500 a Year," *Ladies' Home Journal*, XLVIII (Oct. 1930), 104; and H. Thompson Rich, "How to Live Beyond Your Means," *Reader's Digest*, 34 (May 1939), 1–4.

[12] Will Cuppy, "I'm Not the Budget Type," *Scribner's Magazine*, CII (Dec. 1937), 21, 20.

[13] William A. Berridge, "Employment, Unemployment, and Related Conditions of Labor," *American Journal of Sociology*, XXXVII (May 1932), 903–04. The *Monthly Labor Review* ran a regular monthly account of the rise or decline in the cost of living with respect to particular commodities during the 1930s.

$6 billion worth of automobiles, radios, and other goods were purchased on installment—an increase of 20 percent over 1929.[14]

Many families were able to maintain an acceptable standard of living by placing "additional workers" in the labor force. In spite of traditional American values that have supported the ideal of the one-wage earner family, most families have always depended upon the economic contributions of several members. Sometimes this contribution took the form of "unpaid family work," as in the case of the agricultural family or of the family that ran its own business. But wage-earning and salaried families also were often dependent on the efforts of all members able to work. There is evidence to suggest a direct relationship between income level and number of family earners.

Many middle-income families of the 1930s derived their status from the efforts of several family members. At the very low wage and salary levels—under $800—fewer than one out of five families had an extra wage earner, but nearly one out of four families earning $800 to $1,600 relied on an extra wage earner. A substantially larger ratio of families with extra earners occurred above $1,600. These categories did not represent an insignificant number of families; 22 percent of all urban and rural non-farm families had wage or salary incomes between $1,600 and $2,500 in 1939, and over one-third of these relied upon several family earners.[15] Thus, many American families owed their middle-class status not to adequate wages for one person, but to the presence of several wage earners in the family.

Most of the extra family wage earners were not wives and mothers, but other relatives of the head of the house, usually sons. In fact, even males under the age of eighteen were more likely to be listed as being in the labor force than were wives. But the nature of their employment suggests that young boys were less likely to bring in an extra paycheck than were married women workers: 47 percent were listed as "unpaid

[14] Henry F. Pringle, "What do the Women of America Think About Money?" *Ladies' Home Journal*, LV (April 1938), 100. See also Blanche Bernstein, *The Pattern of Consumer Debt, 1935-36* (New York, 1940), 10, 113-16. Blanche Bernstein argues that consumer credit was particularly important in expanding the purchasing power of lower-income families. Other studies that consider the broader effects of the relationship between consumer credit and the economy during the 1930s are: Gottfried Haberler, *Consumer Instalment Credit and Economic Fluctuations* (New York, 1942); Duncan McC. Holthausen, Malcolm L. Merriam, and Rolf Nugent, *The Volume of Consumer Instalment Credit, 1929-38* (New York, 1940).

[15] 16th Census of the United States, 1940, *Population. Families: Family Wage or Salary Income in 1939: Regions and Cities of 1,000,000 or More* (Washington, 1943), 32-33. These figures are for families with no other income than wage or salary.

family workers'' in comparison to 8 percent of all working wives and 22 percent of working girls under the age of eighteen.[16]

Thus, by 1940, married homemakers were more likely to be making an economic contribution through paid employment than were their children, either male or female, under the age of eighteen. The rapid decline of child labor during the twentieth century was probably a related factor in this development, but it is difficult to determine the direction of the causal relationship, assuming that there was one. That is, did women enter the labor market because older children no longer worked, or did older children remain out of the labor market, possibly in school, because their mothers were working?

The increased participation of married women in the work force reflected a variety of developments, including the decline of child labor, economic need at the poverty level, relative need at every other level, and the availability of more desirable jobs. There is no way of determining which of these factors predominated. The relationship of economic need to the gainful employment of married women was an issue that could not be resolved because it was a matter of individual interpretation. That is, each family decided for itself at which point it was willing to accept the inconvenience of a working wife and mother in order to achieve a better standard of living. But the investigations of working women that were conducted in the 1920s and 1930s were generally sympathetic to women and their right to work. Therefore, the investigators sometimes overstated the case for ''economic need'' by accepting at face value the reasons for work given by the women themselves.

A study in 1932 by Cecile T. LaFollette for Columbia University reflects this tendency to accept perhaps too wholeheartedly the economic need of working women. The group surveyed included 652 women of the business and professional class; 438, or 67 percent, gave economic necessity as their reason for working. Many of the other reasons given were really economic in character—to educate children, make payments on the house, pay for sickness or other debts, and raise standards of living. For instance, 320, or 49 percent, worked in order to provide the ''extras'' that would not have been possible on the husband's salary alone.[17] Many of the women who gave the reason ''economic

---

[16] 16th Census of the United States, 1940. *Population. The Labor Force (Sample Statistics). Employment and Personal Characteristics* (Washington, 1943), Table 26, p. 133, and Table 27, p. 137.

[17] Cecile Tipton LaFollette, *A Study of the Problems of 652 Gainfully Employed Married Women Homemakers* (New York, 1934), 29.

TABLE 4

Wage or Salary Income in 1939 of Husbands, for Married Women, 18 to 64
Years Old, with Husband Present, by Labor Force Status, in March, 1940*

Wage or Salary Income	Percent of Wives	% Distr. of Gainfully Employed	% of Wives in Labor Force
None and not reported	4.8	7.1	24.3
$1 to $199	1.0	1.7	27.6
$200 to $399	2.6	3.9	24.2
$400 to $599	4.0	5.6	22.7
$600 to $999	11.2	14.8	21.7
$1,000 to $1,499	17.5	20.3	18.8
$1,500 to $1,999	14.6	12.6	14.0
$2,000 to $2,999	11.5	6.5	9.2
$3,000 and over	5.0	1.7	5.6
Husbands without other income	72.2	74.4	16.7
Husbands with other income	27.8	25.6	14.9

* Data drawn from metropolitan areas of 100,000 or more.

Source: 16th Census of the United States, 1940, *Population: The Labor Force (Sample Statistics) Employment and Family Characteristics of Women* (Washington, 1943), Table 23, pp. 133–35.

necessity'' probably stretched the term to include some of these items. But LaFollette felt that the incomes of the husbands offered ample evidence that most of these women had to work. What she did not seem to realize was that most of these families were far better off than their contemporaries. Only 6 percent of them made less than $1,000 a year, compared to about 42 percent of all American families who made less than that in 1935–1936. About 32 percent had husbands earning less than $2,000 a year, but nearly 80 percent of all American families were under that income level. The median income of husbands in LaFollette's sample was $2,094, or about $1,000 more than the median for all families.[18]

Values, rather than absolute need, made the women in the LaFollette sample willing to go to work, in spite of the relatively high earnings of their husbands. These business and professional women were hardly representative of working women as a whole, however, and there is no question that there was a strong relationship between low income and married women in the labor force. Table 4 indicates that the women whose husbands were in the lower-income groups were over-represented in the work force. For instance, in metropolitan areas, about 23 percent of all husbands earned under $1,000 a year in 1939, but the wives of this income group contributed about 33 percent of the married women work force. In smaller urban areas, wives of husbands with low income were even more heavily over-represented.

[18] *Ibid*, 31.

TABLE 5

Employment Status and Major Occupation Group of Husband, for Married Women 18 to 64 Years Old, with Husband Present, by Labor Force Status in the United States 1940

Occupation and Employment Status of Husband	No. of Married Women Husband Present*	No. of Wives in Labor Force	% of Wives in Labor Force	% Distr. of Gainfully Employed
Total	26.6	3.7	13.8	100.0
Husband Employed				
(excluding emergency work)	22.3	3.0	13.7	100.0
Professional & semi-prof.	1.3	.2	13.7	4.8
Farmers & farm managers	3.8	.2	4.4	4.6
Proprietors, managers, & officials, excl. farm	2.7	.4	15.2	11.7
Clerical, sales, & kindred workers	2.7	.5	17.0	12.5
Craftsmen, foremen, & kindred workers	3.8	.5	12.4	12.7
Operatives & kindred workers	4.1	.7	16.8	18.9
Domestic service workers	.06	.03	56.4	.9
Protective service	.4	.04	10.9	1.1
Service workers, excluding domestic and protective	.8	.2	25.3	5.6
Farm laborers & foremen	.8	.1	11.6	2.4
Laborers, excluding farm	1.7	.3	16.3	7.8
Occupation not reported	.1	.01	14.4	.5
Husband on emergency work and seeking work	2.8	.4	13.6	10.2
Not in labor force	1.6	.25	15.7	6.8

* Numbers in millions.
Source: Census, 1940, *Employment and Family Characteristics of Women*, 164.

The earnings of working wives could sometimes lift the family of a low-level wage earner into the middle class, but in most cases their wages were very low, undoubtedly because employment was often temporary or part time. The census data of 1940 reveal that low-paid women were most often married to low-paid men, and the more a woman earned, the less she needed it. Over a third of all married women workers were in families in which the husband made less than $600.[19] In contrast, over half of these women—56.3 percent—had husbands who made from $600 to $2,000; over one-fourth of the husbands earned between $1,200 and $2,000.[20] It is in this broad middle range that values, rather than need began to influence decisions regarding work. The decision must have been a complex one, related to personal family circumstances, including number and age of children, desired standard of living, and availability of suitable work; but it cannot be seen as a case of absolute need.

[19] Census, 1940, *Population Families: Family Wage or Salary Income in 1939*, Table 12, p. 151.
[20] *Ibid.*

Another way to estimate the economic status of married women workers is to relate employment to occupational grouping and employment status of the husband. Occupational group is not as effective as the use of income level, because there is often a wide range of salaries paid to workers in a particular occupational field. Also, workers in certain kinds of work—skilled labor, for instance—often had values that prevented or inhibited wives from working, in spite of economic need. But, in a sense, that is exactly the point being made: values, as well as economic need, influenced the decision of women to work.

In 1940 women who were married to men in low-paying, low-prestige jobs, were more likely to be in the labor force than the wives of men in "middle-class" or white-collar occupations (see Table 5). For instance, over half of the wives of domestic service workers were in the labor force, probably as domestic workers themselves. Over one-fourth of the wives of service workers, excluding those in domestic and protective services, were in the labor force; but these two groups did not contribute a very large share of the female labor force, because there were not many husbands in these occupations. The column showing distribution reveals that 55.8 percent of all working wives were married to men who were proprietors, managers and officials; clerical and sales workers; craftsmen and foremen; or factory operatives. All but the last of these four categories could be considered middle class, two of them being white collar, and the third being skilled work requiring experience and bestowing a certain amount of prestige. Thus, although women with husbands in low-paying jobs were more likely to be in the labor force, a large proportion of married working women were married to men in "middle-class" occupations—a fact that suggests that the occurrence of working wives was fairly widespread socially, even though it still affected only a minority of families in each occupational field other than domestic service.

There is no single answer to the question of why women worked during the 1930s. A number of related factors can be suggested, including the decline of child labor, the decline in the birth rate, the changing economic function of the home, economic distress, and desire to maintain a particular standard of living. Given the low incomes of the 1920s and especially the 1930s, and the rising expectations with respect to the standard of living, it is not surprising that married women were entering the labor force. What is surprising is that they remained a small minority. By 1940 there were over 4 million married women workers over the age of 14, but they still represented only 15 percent of all married women (see Table 1). Even at the lowest income levels, only one married woman in four was working. Since the great majority of Americans were living on low incomes during the depression, the question is not so much why a small minority accepted the employment of married women, but why such a large majority did not, in spite of the fact that they too experienced unsatisfied economic needs as a result of inadequate wages.

The answer lies partly in the cultural values held by most American families, by the poor as well as by the middle class. One group that did not share the dominant value system, black families, had a much higher proportion than whites of wives and mothers in the labor force at all economic levels. For most white Americans, a working wife placed a stigma upon the husband and the family—a stigma that could not be easily removed, but one that might be justified by the presence of economic necessity. Also, during the 1930s many women simply did not have job opportunities, particularly those women of lower-income families who were less likely to have skills to sell on the labor market. Many housewives found it physically impossible to run a household and maintain a paying job. Over half of all housewives spent forty-eight hours a week at work in the home. An additional third spent over fifty-six hours a week. The "modern conveniences" argument has been greatly overworked with respect to its effect upon the amount of physical labor involved in keeping house.[21]

Nonetheless, the fact that there was an increase in the number and proportion of married women in the labor force between 1920 and 1940 indicates that traditional values were gradually breaking down in the face of other, more concrete, changes. That most families resisted change, in spite of their economic straits, reflects their basic conservatism in the face of economic and social developments of enormous consequence. But the public discussion of women's roles in the family and in the broader community strongly suggests that an important minority of women and their families were willing to accept a new life-style in response to a personal recognition of economic realities. To the extent that these women were from middle-income families, where they could make choices, they were influenced by values as well as absolute need in their

[21] Hildegarde Kneeland, "Woman's Economic Contribution in the Home," *Annals of the American Academy of Political and Social Sciences*, CXLIII (May 1929), 33–40; and Hildegarde Kneeland, "Is the Modern Housewife a Lady of Leisure?" *Survey*, LXII (June 1929), 301–02. For a recent interpretation, see Ruth Schwartz Cowan, "A Case Study of Technological and Social Change: The Washing Machine and the Working Wife," Mary Hartman and Lois W. Banner, eds., *Clio's Consciousness Raised: New Perspectives on the History of Women* (New York, 1974), 245–53.

determination to work. This does not contradict the assumption that many, if not most, married women worked because of economic need; but economic need is a relative concept, and it becomes a reality for different families at different levels of experience. Most women could argue that they worked because they had to work, but they defined their needs differently from the non-working wives whose husbands had similar incomes.

The life-styles adopted by working women continued to be based on traditional family values. The women who worked were working in response to their understanding of family need. Although they carried their economic role beyond the confines of their homes, the relationship between home, self, and job remained constant. That is, the work of the married woman usually reflected the primacy of her home life. She was working to pay for a home, keep her children in school, help her husband with his business, or pay for the "extras." It would be a mistake to assume that her home life remained unchanged, however. The question of the working wife's role and status within the family, and the extent to which they evolved in response to the economic "necessities" of the depression is another topic that must be given further consideration if scholars are to understand the real impact of the 1930s upon American women.

FEMINISTS AGAINST THE FAMILY

JEAN BETHKE ELSHTAIN

Whatever its sins against generations of mothers and daughters, the family has served the women's movement well: located by feminists as the key to female oppression, it has been offered up as *the* institution to reform, revolutionize or destroy if feminist aims are to be realized. As a catalyst for rethinking the terms of public and private reality, the family has also provided feminist thinkers with inexhaustible material for dissecting the human condition from the vantage point of this, its central bête noire.

Much that is exciting and fruitful emerged from this ferment. Connections between sexuality, authority and power were opened up for debate in a provocative way. Women were encouraged to create conceptual and linguistic tools to help them pierce the patterns of social reality. Through consciousness-raising, hundreds of women began to view themselves less as passive recipients of revocable privileges and more as active, responsible human beings. But from the start something was terribly wrong with much of the feminist treatment of the family. By "wrong" I don't mean so much careless or unscholarly by traditional canons of historic and social science methodology, though one saw evidence of both. I refer instead to an imperative more deeply rooted and bitter, which erupted from time to time in mean-spirited denunciations of all relations between men and women and in expressions of contempt for the female body, for pregnancy, childbirth and child-rearing.

In my view, the feminist movement has contributed to the discrediting of what Dorothy Dinnerstein, a psychoanalytic feminist thinker,

(Continued on Page 497)

Feminists

(Continued From Front Cover)

calls the "essential humanizing functions of stable, longstanding, generation-spanning primary groups" and the "virulent, reckless, reactive quality of much feminist rhetoric against the biological family, against permanent personal commitments of adults to childhood . . . against childbearing itself [has occurred] ironically, when women and men have been in the best position to minimize the oppressive features of human biology." The result has been the creation of what I shall call a *politics of displacement*, which erodes personal life even as it vitiates the emergence of a genuine public life. This feminist politics of displacement, in turn, helps to provoke a troubling mirror-image. How has this come about?

The key to feminist politics lies in a phrase that has served simultaneously as an explanatory principle, a motto and an article of faith: "The Personal Is Political." Note that the claim is not that the personal and the political are interrelated in important and fascinating ways not yet fully explored and previously hidden to us by patriarchal ideology and practice; nor that the personal and the political may be fruitfully examined as analogous to one another along certain touchstones of power and privilege, but that the personal *is* political. What is asserted is an identity: a collapse of the one into the other. Nothing "personal" is exempt, then, from political definition, direction and manipulation—neither sexual intimacy, love, nor parenting.

By reducing politics to what are seen as "power relations," important thinkers in all wings of the women's movement, but centered in the radical feminist perspective, have proferred as an alternative to the malaise of the present a rather bleak Hobbesianism rejuvenated in feminist guise. For if politics is power and power is everywhere, politics is in fact nowhere and a vision of public life as the touchstone of a revitalized ideal of citizenship is lost. These are serious charges and I shall document them by turning to the manner in which radical feminist images of the "sex war," centered in the family, are served up as a substitute for social and political struggle.

To have a war one needs enemies, and radical feminism (as distinguished from liberal, Marxist or socialist, and psychoanalytic feminism) has no difficulty finding him. The portrait of man which emerges from radical feminist texts is that of an implacable enemy, an incorrigible and dangerous beast who has as his chief aim in life the oppression and domination of women. Ti-Grace Atkinson attributes this male compulsion to man's a priori need to oppress others, an imperative termed "metaphysical cannibalism" from which women are exempt. Susan Brownmiller's male is

Jean Bethke Elshtain is associate professor of political science at the University of Massachusetts, Amherst.

tainted with an *animus dominandi* which makes him a "natural predator." Mary Daly's male is less bestial, more ghoulish, a vampire who feeds "on the bodies and minds of women. . . . Like Dracula, the he-male has lived on women's blood." Women, however, escape the curse of original sin, being accorded a separate and divergent ontological status. In their views on male and female nature, radical feminists sadly confuse "natural" and "social" categories (as they accuse apologists for patriarchal privilege of doing by manipulating the terms "nature" and "culture" for their own ideological ends). For if male and female roles in society flow directly from some biological given, there is little or nothing politics can do to alter the situation.

Although women escape the curse of an unblessed birth, they are treated to considerable scorn by radical feminists under the guise of "demystifying" their "biological functions." Pregnancy is characterized as "the temporary deformation of the body for the sake of the species." Shulamith Firestone rubs salt into the wound by relating a story of a group of malicious children who point their fingers at a pregnant woman and taunt mercilessly, "Who's the fat lady?" The fetus is labeled variously a "tenant," a "parasite" and an "uninvited guest." Heterosexual sex is reduced to "using people, conning people, messing over people, conquering people, exploiting people." And love? A "pathological condition," a "mass neurosis" which must be destroyed. Childbirth is painful and hideous. Motherhood is portrayed as a condition of terminal psychological and social decay, total self-abnegation and physical deterioration. The new mother is "barely coherent . . . stutters . . . bumps into stationary objects." What has all this to do with politics? The answer, for radical feminists, is everything, given that the "personal is political."

The only way to stop all this, they go on, is to eliminate the patriarchal nuclear family. The argument runs something like this: because "tyranny" begins in biology or nature, nature itself must be changed. *All else* will follow, for it is biological "tyranny," the sex distinction itself, that oppresses women. Having accepted as a necessary and sufficient condition for social change the total "restructuring" of relations between the sexes, Firestone, for example, fizzles into a combination of trivial self-help ("a revolutionary in every bedroom") and a barbaric cybernetic utopia within which every aspect of life rests in the beneficent hands of a new elite of engineers, cyberneticians animated by the victorious Female Principle. Brownmiller's solution to the sex war lodged in male biology and the "rape culture" that is an automatic outgrowth of man's unfortunate anatomy is a loveless Sparta, a "stalemate" in the sex war in which women have been "fully integrated into the extant power structure—police, national guards, state troopers, local sheriffs' offices, state prosecuting attorneys' offices, armed forces"— in other words, just about any male activity that involves a uniform, a badge, a gun or a law degree.

These suggested solutions to masculine perfidy and biological "tyranny" exemplify a politics of displacement for they cannot be specified with any concreteness nor acted upon, remaining utopian and abstract; at other times they envisage a female takeover of the extant "power structure," thus vitiating consideration of the structural dimensions of our current crisis, which lie in the specific practices of production, the nature of life work, the problems of political accountability and of social stratification along lines of ethnicity, class and race as well as sex.

Except for its ludicrous caricature of the married person as a family fanatic busily engaged in putting single people down, a more recent and sophisticated treatment of radical feminist themes, Ellen Willis's *Village Voice* article, "The Family: Love It or Leave It," avoids many of the crude oversimplifications I have cited. Willis expresses much of the richness and ambivalence internal to family life and to an honest contemplation of that life. Finally, however, her essay collapses under the weight of several contradictions. She insists, for example, that familial matters include public issues that should be the grounds for political decision making. Yet she provides no basis for genuine political action because her strategy remains steadfastly individualistic. ("If people stopped . . . If enough parents . . . If enough women . . .")

Indeed, it is difficult to determine how and why "people, enough parents, women" could mount an effective assault on the public issues Willis finds embedded in our private lives if one of her other claims, that capitalists "have an obvious stake in encouraging dependence on the family," is as overriding as she says it is. She fails to realize that one could make precisely the opposite case—with strong support from historic case studies, something Willis never sees fit to provide—that capitalists have historically had an interest in breaking up family units and eroding family ties. The capitalist ideal is a society of social atoms, beings not essentially connected to one another, to a time, or to a place, who could be shunted about according to market imperatives alone.

Liberal feminism's indictments of family life and men are less bloodcurdling, although Betty Friedan couldn't resist the alliterative "comfortable concentration camp" as a description of suburban housewifery. Friedan's women vegetated as menfolk went off to the city and "kept on growing." Friedan's presumption that the world of work within capitalist society is infinitely preferable to the world of the home is a linchpin of liberal feminism and serves to highlight the class-bound nature of their reflections. Friedan certainly didn't have eight hours a day on an assembly line in mind when she denigrated familial life and celebrated work life. Elizabeth Janeway, another liberal thinker, insists that a man has it over a woman in contemporary society because he knows where he stands; he receives rewards according to pre-existing standards of judgment in the marketplace. Women, however, out of the running for the prizes, are confused as to their "true value" (i.e., market worth). Women can take care of this unfortunate state of affairs as individuals, acting alone and being political simply by being "role breakers," a move that simultaneously puts them into the market arena and "threaten[s] the order of the universe."

Marxist feminists put forth conflicting views of family

life, but those operating within an orthodox Marxist-Leninist framework are locked into a narrow econometric model that sees both the family and politics as epiphenomenal, having no autonomous nor semiautonomous existence of their own. Within this perspective, politics is displaced onto economic concerns exclusively and, paradoxically, depoliticized as a result. Mothering becomes "the reproduction of the labor force" or "the future commodity labor power." Should a mother take umbrage at this characterization of her alternately joyous and vexing activity, it is taken as evidence of her "false consciousness." (There are, however, feminists working within the Marxist tradition who have a more complex image of familial life, and I discuss their views briefly below.)

Taken all in all, the image that emerges from contemporary feminism's treatment of the family is that of a distortion so systematic that it has become another symptom of the disease it seeks to diagnose. One of the key symptoms of this disease—this "legitimation crisis"—is a widespread draining of society's social institutions, public and private, of their value and significance. In stripping away the old ideological guises that celebrated motherhood and denigrated women, extolled the dignity of private life yet disallowed parents the means with which to live in decency and with dignity, feminists performed a necessary and important service. But unmasking an ideology and constructing a sound theory are not the same activity. Ironically, a new feminist ideology has emerged to replace the old patriarchal one. It, like the old, exerts a silencing effect over free and open debate on a whole range of issues having to do with female sexuality, the conflicting demands of contemporary heterosexuality, pregnancy, childbirth and child-rearing, and family life, even as it provides no alternative vision of a revitalized concept of "citizenship."

My concern is with that anti-familial feminist ideology that has become linked up in the popular mind with efforts to erode or destroy the meaning and relations of family life *in the absence of any workable alternative*. I have described the complex process at work as a politics of displacement, a form of pseudopolitics in which the symptoms of social breakdown are construed as the disease itself, allowing the deeper dimensions of the crisis to go unchallenged.

Feminist thinkers, in their quest to identify the breeding ground of patriarchal privilege, found a sitting duck in the family. But this is as much attributable to our confusion and malaise over the family's proper social role as it is to feminist prescience. Since the advent of the Industrial Revolution, Western society has faced a "crisis in the family" with each successive generation. The chain of events set in motion by industrialism eventually stripped the family of most of its previous functions as a productive, vocational, religious, educative and welfare unit. As these functions were absorbed by other social institutions and practices, the family remained the locus of intimate, long-term reproductive relations and child-rearing activities. The strains of these shifts are reflected historically in the works of great novelists, political and social theorists and the theory and practice of psychoanalysis.

The feminist movement is, then—at least in part—a direct outgrowth of the intensification of contradictory burdens and demands on family members. The family is a product of uneven development, existing as a purposeful and vital unit within *every* extant society, yet resisting, within capitalist society, total domination by relations of exchange and the values of the marketplace. Diverse aspects of social practices collide within the family: little girls, for example, may be inculcated with the American ideology of equality of opportunity, receive an education identical to that of their brothers yet, simultaneously, learn an ideology of womanhood and domesticity incompatible with the other ideological imperatives they also hold. Nevertheless, the family, however shakily and imperfectly, helps to keep alive an alternative to the values which dominate in the marketplace. It serves, in the words of Eli Zaretsky, as a reminder of the hope that "human beings can pass beyond a life dominated by relations of production." This vital role played by the family in modern life is recognized by a minority of feminist thinkers who hold the socialist and psychoanalytic perspectives. Indeed, one of the most lyrical evocations of the importance of holding on to that which is valuable in family life, if social relations are not to become thoroughly brutal, may be found in the words of Sheila Rowbotham, a British Marxist feminist, who writes of the family as a "place of sanctuary for all the haunted, jaded, exhausted sentiments out of place in commodity production . . . The family is thus in one sense the dummy ideal, the repository of ghostly substitutes, emotional fictions. . . . But this distortion of human relations is the only place where human beings find whatever continuing love, security, and comfort they know."

Each child taught to see himself or herself as unique and unconditionally loved, a being (to draw upon Kant) having

"dignity," not merely a "price," represents a challenge to the terms of the market system, just as noninstrumental human intimacy is a similar affront to increasingly sophisticated attempts to merchandise every area of human sexual life. Yet these family ties and relations are fragile, subject to strains and breakdowns and to a coarsening that reflects in miniature the abuses of the world outside. Reported incidents of child abuse, for example, rise dramatically during periods of widespread unemployment and economic despair as outward frustrations, in another variant on the politics of displacement, are displaced privately onto the family's most vulnerable members.

The politics of displacement is nothing new under the political sun. Past examples that spring to mind include the policies of the Romanov czars who, over the years, implicated Russia in some external imbroglio whenever they wished to shift public attention away from their domestic politics. A more sinister instance is the use of German Jews as scapegoats for the widespread social dislocation and hardship that followed the end of World War I, a politics of displacement perfected by fascism. In the history of American capitalist expansion and labor strife, one finds the frequent pitting of poor white and black unemployed against each other in such a way that each group saw the other as the source of its misery and corporate oligarchs escaped serious political challenge. Feminism's politics of displacement reveals its true colors when a feminist thinker assaults a social unit, already vulnerable and weakened by external and internal strains, as both *cause* and *symptom* of female subordination. In so doing, those feminists direct attention away from structural imperatives and constraints and promote a highly personalized sexual politics that is simultaneously depoliticizing, individualistic and potentially pernicious in its implications.

The implication of a feminist politics of displacement for politics itself is simply this: a displaced pseudopolitics vitiates attempts to articulate an ideal of public life as the deliberate efforts by citizens to "order, direct, and control their collective affairs and activities, to establish ends for their society, and to implement and evaluate these ends." Feminism's politics of displacement renders politics hollow, first, by finding politics everywhere; second, by reducing politics to crude relations of force or domination, and third, by stripping politics of its centrality to a shared social identity. It erodes private life by construing it as a power-riddled battleground, thus encouraging a crudely politicized approach toward coitus, marriage, child-rearing, even one's relationship to one's own body. It shares with all spinoffs of classical liberalism the failure to develop a vision of a political community and of citizenship that might serve as the touchstone of a collective identity for males and females alike. As Michael Walzer put it recently: "What made liberalism endurable for all these years was the fact that the individualism it generated was imperfect, tempered by older restraints and loyalties, by stable patterns of local, ethnic, religious or class relationships. An untempered liberalism would be unendurable." Feminist thinkers have yet to confront this sobering realization. □

THE FEMINIST MOVEMENT

I believe that at the foundation of the women's liberation movement there is a minority core of women who were once bored with life, whose real problems are spiritual problems. Many women have never accepted their God-given roles. They live in disobedience to God's laws and have promoted their godless philosophy throughout our society. God Almighty created men and women biologically different and with differing needs and roles. He made men and women to complement each other and to love each other. Not all the women involved in the feminist movement are radicals. Some are misinformed, and some are lonely women who like being housewives and helpmeets and mothers, but whose husbands spend little time at home and who take no interest in their wives and children. Sometimes the full load of rearing a family becomes a great burden to a woman who is not supported by a man. Women who work should be respected and accorded dignity and equal rewards for equal work. But this is not what the present feminist movement and equal rights movement are all about.

The Equal Rights Amendment is a delusion. I believe that women deserve more than equal rights. And, in families and in nations where the Bible is believed, Christian women are honored above men. Only in places where the Bible is believed and practiced do women receive more than equal rights. Men and women have differing strengths. The Equal Rights Amendment can never do for women what needs to be done for them. Women need to know Jesus Christ as their Lord and Savior and be under His Lordship. They need a man who knows Jesus Christ as his Lord and Savior, and they need to be part of a home where their husband is a godly leader and where there is a Christian family.

The Equal Rights Amendment strikes at the foundation of our entire social structure. If passed, this amendment would accomplish exactly the opposite of its outward claims. By mandating an absolute equality under the law, it will actually take away many of the special rights women now enjoy. ERA is not merely a political issue, but a moral issue as well. A definite violation of holy Scripture, ERA defies the mandate that "the husband is the head of the wife, even as Christ is the head of the church" (Ep. 5:23). In 1 Peter 3:7 we read that husbands are to give their wives honor as unto the weaker vessel, that they are both heirs together of the grace of life. Because a woman is weaker does not mean that she is less important.

I deeply respect Mrs. Phyllis Schlafly. Mrs. Schlafly is a conservative activist. She is a lawyer and has an extensive background in national defense. At services in the Thomas Road Baptist Church, Lynchburg, Virginia, Mrs. Schlafly made these comments: "The more I work with the issue of ERA, the more I realize that the women's liberation movement is antifamily. The proof came in November 1977 when the conference on International Women's Year met in Houston. It passed twenty-five resolutions which show very clearly what the feminists are after. They are for the Equal Rights Amendment, which would take away the marvelous legal rights of a woman to be a full-time wife and mother in the home supported by her husband. They are for abortion on demand, financed by the government and taught in the schools. They are for privileges for lesbians and homosexuals to teach in the schools and to adopt children. They are for the government assuming the main responsibility for child care because they think it is oppressive and unfair that society expects mothers to look after their babies. All their goals and dogmas are antifamily. They believe that God made a mistake when He made two different kinds of people.

"They believe that we should use the Constitution and legislation to eliminate the eternal differences and the roles that God has ordained between men and women. They want to require all laws and regulations and all schools to treat men and women exactly the same. They want to do it with federal control. That is what Section 2 of the Equal Rights Amendment would do. Another dogma of the women's liberationists is that you have no right to make a moral judgment between what is right and what is wrong. They want to give the homosexuals and the lesbians the same dignity as husbands and wives. They want to give the woman who has an illegitimate baby the same dignity as the one who has had one in holy matrimony. The Equal Rights Amendment, uses the word 'sex,' not the word 'woman.' ERA puts sex into the Constitution—a mandate that one could never make a reasonable common-sense difference of treatment between male and female, or between good sex and bad sex. ERA would do this with the power of the federal government. Moral Americans have beaten ERA forces for seven years. Then the proponents passed their unfair time extension. They are trying to use the power of the federal government to force the unratified states to switch from no to yes. Meanwhile, they are trying to use the courts to deny states the right to switch from yes to no. We must continue to fight against the ERA and to win this battle for God, for the dignity of women, and for the institution of the family."

Phyllis Schlafly, one of the most knowledgeable people I know, continued to outline the ERA movement. The next several paragraphs are a synopsis of her presentation.

The Equal Rights Amendment offers women nothing in the way of rights or benefits that they do not already have. In the areas of employment and education, laws have already been enacted to protect women. The only thing the Equal Rights Amendment would do would be to take away rights and privileges that American women now have in the best country in the world. Let us look at some of the women who are the leaders in the feminist and ERA movements.

Betty Friedan, founder of the National Organization for Women (NOW), made this statement in a NOW-ERA fundraising letter: "The ERA has become both symbol and substance for the whole of the modern women's movement for equality. . . . I am convinced that if we lose this struggle we will have little hope in our own lifetime of saving our right to abortion. . . ." Betty Friedan states that a feminist agenda for the eighties must call for "the restructuring of the institutions of home and work." As has already been stated, Gloria Steinem, editor of *Ms.* magazine, made this statement: "By the year 2000 we will, I hope, raise our children to believe in human potential, not God. . . ." Dr. MaryJo Bane, associate director of Wellesley College's Center for Research on Women, made this statement: "We really don't know how to raise children. . . . The fact that children are raised in families means there's no equality . . . in order to raise children with equality, we must take them away from families and raise them. . . ."

Humanist Manifesto II, signed by Betty Friedan, contains this statement: "No deity will save us, we must save ourselves. Promises of immortal salvation or fear of eternal damnation are both illusory and harmful." In the notes from the Second Year Women's Liberation we find these comments: "We must destroy love . . . love promotes vulnerability, dependence, possessiveness, susceptibility to pain, and prevents the full development of woman's human potential by directing all her energies outward in the interests of others." In the document *Declaration of Feminism*, we find this: "Marriage has existed for the benefit of men and has been a legally sanctioned method of control over women . . . the end of the institution of marriage is a necessary condition for the liberation of women. Therefore, it is important for us to encourage women to leave their husbands and not to live individually with men . . . we must work to destroy it [marriage]." In her speech in Houston, Texas,

Gloria Steinem made this comment: ". . . for the sake of those who wish to live in equal partnership, we have to abolish and reform the institution of legal marriage."

The Equal Rights Amendment sounds deceptively simple. It contains only three sentences: "Section 1: Equality of rights under the law shall not be denied or abridged by the United States or by any state on account of sex. Section 2: The Congress shall have the power to enforce, by appropriate legislation, the provisions of this article. Section 3: This amendment shall take effect two years after the date of ratification." When ERA went to the floor of the House and Senate, a number of congressmen and senators tried to insert amendments. When ERA went to the floor of the Senate, Senator Sam Ervin proposed nine separate clauses as amendments to ERA. Every one of these clauses was defeated on a roll-call vote. They included such provisions as, "Except it won't require us to draft women. Except it won't require us to send our young women into military combat. Except it won't take away the rights of working women. Except it won't take away the rights of wives, mothers, and widows. Except it won't take the right to privacy of men or women, boys or girls. Except it won't interfere with laws which are based on physiological differences." Every one of these clauses was defeated.

ERA came out of Congress on March 22, 1972, and went to the states with a clause setting a time limit of seven years for ratification. In the first twelve months, thirty states passed it, most of them without any hearings or debates on the issue. When concerned women became involved and went to their state legislators and ERA was thoroughly examined, states began to realize that they had made a mistake in passing the ERA. In the next six years, five more states passed ERA, but five others rescinded passage. As the time limit neared expiration, proponents of the ERA asked Congress for a time extension. This was exactly like a losing football team demanding a fifth quarter in order to give them time to catch up, and furthermore providing that only the losing team may carry the ball. We are now in the three-year extension, which is actually illegal. The power move evidenced by this extension has been unprecedented in the history of our Constitution.

Let us examine the Equal Rights Amendment. In the first section we find that the word "sex," not "women," is put into the Constitution. It is not clarified what meaning of sex is ascribed here. "Equality of rights" is an undefined term. There is no judicial history for that term. ERA applies only to governmental action, laws, and regulations. Their terms are vague and undefined. Thus one of the major defects of the ERA is that it is a blank check to the U. S. Supreme Court to tell Americans what it means after it is ratified. It is probable that the ERA would require sex-neutral words to be put in all our laws—words like person, taxpayer, spouse, and parent. If we look at our Constitution today we find that it is the most beautiful sex-neutral document ever written. It does not talk about men and women, male and female. The U. S. Constitution uses only words such as person, citizen, resident, inhabitant, etc. Women have every constitutional right that men have. Employment laws are already sex-neutral. ERA has nothing to do with equal pay for equal work.

Our country has fought in nine wars, and has had a draft for thirty-three years of this century. No woman in America has ever been drafted or sent into military combat. The draft act has always read: "Male citizens of age eighteen must register." This is an example of a sex-discriminatory law. There is an exemption to females. This is the American way. We have laws that exempt women from military combat duty. There is one for the Army, one for the Navy, and one for the Air Force. In November 1979, the House Armed Services Committee held four days of hearings on the women's liberation proposal to repeal the laws that exempt women from military combat duty. There were women who held jobs in the Pentagon who said, "Women want their career advancement to be generals and admirals and to be assigned to combat duty." Men like Admiral Jeremiah Denton, who spent seven years in a POW camp in Vietnam, spoke about what it means to be in combat. Should the ERA pass, the Constitution would compel us to force women to serve in the military and to go into combat zones. The ERA is an amendment to the Constitution, which is the supreme law of the land, and if ERA goes into the Constitution it would immediately wipe out the laws that exempt women from military combat. The military would have to obey the Constitution.

The women's liberation movement is seeking to require sex integration of every aspect of all school systems. This would mean that there could be no more all-men's or all-women's schools or colleges. All classes and dormitories would have to be coed. All sports programs would have to be coed. There could be no single-sex fraternities or sororities, no Girl Scouts, Boy Scouts, YMCA, YWCA, or Campfire Girls. There could be no Girls State or Boys State. There could be no mother/daughter and father/son school events. Under ERA it would be unconstitutional to have any of these things because they "discriminate on account of sex." ERA not only would apply to public schools, but it would also extend to all private schools and colleges whether or not they receive public money.

The Founding Fathers who established our great nation separated the power of government between the federal government and the states, and then again between executive, legislative, and judicial branches. We have maintained great freedom under this system. Under this distribution of power between the states and the federal government, a large area of law has been retained at the state level. Many of the laws at the state level have traditionally made differences of treatment based upon sex, and they are the type of laws that would be subject to ERA. These laws include: marriage, divorce, child custody, adoptions, homosexual laws, incest laws, prison regulations, and insurance rates. These are all laws that traditionally have made some type of difference of treatment based on sex. Section 1 of ERA would prohibit any common-sense difference of treatment based on sex. Section 2 would shift the total decision-making power over these laws to the federal government. Under Section 1 of the ERA they would be forced to make these laws sex neutral. There could never be a law that says a husband should support his wife. Laws such as this were not designed to discriminate against one's sex. They merely defined responsibilities designed for the purpose of keeping the family together. Not only would ERA make state laws sex neutral, but it would also shift the final decision-making power to the federal government.

In summary, we conclude that there are no exceptions to Section 1 of the Equal Rights Amendment. ERA proponents voted down and eliminated all clauses that would have preserved women's exemption from the military, draft, and wartime combat duty; that would have preserved the rights of wives, mothers, and widows to be financially supported by their husbands benefits; that would have preserved protective health and safety laws for working women; that would have preserved the right of privacy in school and public restrooms, hospitals, and prisons; that would have preserved the rights of legislatures to pass laws against abortion, and homosexual and lesbian privileges. Section 2 of the Equal Rights Amendment would mean federalizing vast powers that states now have, including marriage and divorce, child custody, prison regulations, and insurance rates. Section 2 would mean that federal courts and the federal bureaucracy would make all final decisions regarding marriage, divorce, alimony, abortion, homosexual and lesbian privileges, and sex integration of police and fire departments, schools and sports, hospitals, prisons, and public accommodations.

It is ironic that ERA and feminist proponents do not talk about the display of printed or pictorial materials that degrade women in a pornographic, perverted, or sadistic manner. In fact, *Playboy* magazine hosts ERA parties and contributes heavily to their campaigns. In Illinois alone, *Playboy* gave five thousand dollars to help ratify ERA. The check was personally presented by Christy Hefner, the daughter of the magazine's publisher. In Florida a fund-raising event was held for the ERA. The honored guest was Marguex St. James, President of COYOTE (Call Off Your Old Tired Ethics), an organization of prostitutes. Marguex St. James said, "Give me two weeks and a dozen girls in any state capital, and I will deliver ERA on a silver platter."

Brigadier General Andrew J. Gatsis, who is now retired, entered the military in 1939 as a private. He was a professional combat infantryman for thirty-six years. A West Point graduate, he served in several wars, including the Korean War, where he personally led a counterattack on Christmas Day 1952. He also served in the Vietnam War. He is one of the most highly decorated officers in the United States armed forces. Speaking to an Eagle Forum workshop on March 23, 1979, he made these comments about the drafting of women into combat: "I have served as an infantry commander in three separate combat tours, all at the fighting level. I have personally participated in hand-to-hand combat and have seen men fight and die on the battlefield. I have had women in my command, have observed their performance firsthand, and have had to contend with the disruptive effect on military discipline and combat efficiency brought about by the women's liberation movement, a movement fully supported and promoted by the top *echelons* of our government.

Proponents of the ERA are continuing efforts to reduce combat effectiveness through the goals of ERA by preparing the American public to accept the idea of drafting women and placing them into combat units. They are using the all-volunteer force as a mechanism for misleading Americans into thinking war and combat roles are natural to women.

"I would like to say there are some women, certainly in the minority, who like the military, who like to live and work with men, and have given an excellent performance in certain non-combat positions such as clerks, telephone operators, computer technicians, supply supervisors, nurses, and the like. World War II is ample proof of this. However, these rules do not satisfy the objective of the women's movement, which is to make women equal with men in all sectors of military activity regardless of the damage and effect it has on fighting spirit or combat efficiency. In fact, avid supporters of ERA have little concern for our defense posture and are willing to weaken or sacrifice it if it conflicts with the goals they seek.

"I must tell you that the top command structure of our military forces, the Pentagon, is saturated with ERA proponents, and under the complete control of avid supporters of the women's liberation movement. Members of various women's organizations such as NOW (National Organization for Women) have been placed in key manpower positions of authority who formulate and direct policies concerning U.S. military readiness posture. The result and outflow is that U.S. readiness revolves more around enhancing the women's liberation movement than it does meeting the military capability of a potential Army.

"In spite of the effort to propagandize the American public with the great success of the all-volunteer force and its large component of women, the plan has backfired. The myth that women do as well as men, and even better in some cases in the all-male traditional roles, is beginning to show up for the falsehood it is. The military services are unable to get sufficient soldiers to enlist or stay in the jobs that require those skills. Women are finding out how tough this training is and that they will spend considerable time in the fields. As a result, they are avoiding nonglamorous career management fields such as air defense, artillery, paint mechanics, linepole climbing, and the like, causing large overstrength in the medical and administrative fields.

"In a desperate attempt to overcome this shortage in the combat support areas, the Army is now experimenting with the program that offers special bonuses, free education, and a reduced time of service from three to two years, to encourage them to accept unnatural roles. In addition, just recently, they began to lower the score for entrance into the military from a score of 50, which is the national average, to 31 for women. This approach is also failing, for approximately 50 per cent of women enlistees are not finishing their tour of service.

"To convince the American public that women could perform all jobs in the military as well as men, one of the greatest psychological-warfare efforts ever devised was launched through the national and major news media. The first step was to order a series of tests and evaluations to substantiate predrawn conclusions that women are fit to fight on the battlefield. When the studies came back showing that women as a whole were inadequate in this area, the studies were sent back for re-evaluation.

"The next move was to have senior civilian defense officials and military leaders hail the sex-integrated all-volunteer force as a great success. Today even top defense officials have to admit it is a dismal failure, as they cannot meet recruiting goals and the quality is low. Having seen their plan shattered within the last year, these same officials have begun to redirect their efforts to a strategy that calls for the draft of women. Recently, the Secretary of Defense, Harold Brown, asked the House Armed Services Committee to register women as well as men for the draft. Very shortly thereafter, all chiefs of the four military services—Army, Navy, Marines, and Air Force—went before the Senate Armed Services Subcommittee for personnel and manpower and recommended that women be required to register for the draft.

"If the draft is ever implemented, and ERA is ratified, all barriers will be removed from placing women in combat roles. The proponents of ERA will tell you that this will never happen and only a very few women will be put in combat, since all military assignments are based on the soldier's physical profile and his trained skill. Even though these are the rules, anyone who has ever been in combat knows a large number of people are always improperly assigned, due to the fact that pipeline replacements do not flow even—it's a very complex system—replacements never arrive when needed, and the nature of casualties is never so predictable that one can requisition the proper type and exact number to fill the job vacancy required. The normal procedure is to reach into the locally available noncombat resources for replacing combat shortages.

"For example, after my company had been thrown off of its positions by a large Communist Chinese attack one early morning, we were left with only 42 men out of 197. Since there were no combat-type replacements at hand, I was forced to muster my noncombat-type personnel, such as clerks, cooks, and vehicle drivers for the counterattacking force needed to eject the enemy from Hill 266. The point to be made is that, when the situation is critical, noncombat qualified women who are locally available in support units will be used.

"Let me comment what placing women in combat roles will mean to them and to military combat effectiveness. The combat environment is an ugly one. For the ground soldier, it is characterized by drudgery, indignity, and anonymous horrors. It calls for a toughness that women do not normally possess, for battle is primitive, vicious, brutal, and exhausting. It is coupled with depression and crippling fatigue, which together create terror in the soldier's heart and make him wonder as he sees the night coming down if he will see the edge of dawn. His feelings fluctuate from despair to extreme hate and bitterness, which tend to bring forth his most animal instincts.

"If he is fighting in the Mekong Delta, he must endure living in mosquito-infested paddies, immersed in filthy waters up to his waist and armpits for continuous periods of twenty-four to forty-eight hours, where he is subjected to fungus, bacterial infections, and immersion foot. The skin breaks out with tiny red scale vesicles on the foot and other parts of the body. The feet become swollen and top layers of dead white skin come off in silver-dollar patches. These conditions are aggravated by body leeches, which the soldier must also endure. The loss rate for male casualties in this kind of operation averaged 50 per cent in my command.

"If he is fighting in the hills of Korea, he is subject to bitter cold, frostbite, and diseases such as the plague resulting from living in rat-infested bunkers. If his mission turns to the Middle East or Africa, he suffers from filth, relentless heat, and the dryness of the desert. In the highlands of Vietnam, he's plagued by bamboo viper snakes, torrential rains, jungle rot, malaria, and the like. In Europe it is the deluge of mud, the slime of dripping dugouts, and the weariness of continuous marches along the hot, dusty road.

"These are only some of the daily environmental living conditions of the ground combat soldier, let alone the nightmares of mortal combat. These are not the kinds of conditions in which we wish to place anyone. But can we, as civilized people, even begin to entertain the thought of sending our women into such an environment against their will?

"To survive these conditions and to function effectively at the same time against a determined enemy, it is mandatory that the individual soldier be in top physical condition with the long-term inborn stamina that will not wane after long grueling hours of trudging toward the objective. It is a kind of strength that keeps the soldier fit to fight after he reaches the enemy, regardless of the obstacles he must overcome before contacting them.

"The concerted drive to convince the public that women can do as well as men in combat is at its height today. Listen to the statement made by our Secretary of the Army, Clifford Alexander, who has never been in combat and has only had six months of active military service in the Army National Guard as a private first class: 'There are few things that men can do that women can't. By law, they don't fight. My personal opinion is contrary to what the law says.' The Army chief of staff says, 'I see no reason why women cannot serve effectively in combat roles further to the rear.'

"All kinds of tests—field tests, training tests, and readiness tests—have been conducted over and over again showing conclusively that women are not fit for combat and that by nature they are smaller, physically slower, physically weaker particularly in upper-body strength to throw a grenade effectively, dig a foxhole, hack a path through the thick jungle with a machete, fight an enemy soldier with a rifle butt and a bayonet, pull oneself through a long, narrow tunnel with heavy demolitions to flush an enemy sniper out of his hiding place. Yet the power of the women's liberation movement prevails in the U. S. Army, and these results are not accepted. They counter by saying, 'Women may be weak in these areas, but they are better educated and score better in aptitude tests.' There is some truth to this since all females must have a high-school education to qualify for the service. But the difference lies in the fact that education is not the ingredient that wins battles for the combat soldier. It is simple tactical plans, guts, stamina, and brutal physical force that bring victory.

"What is so ironic about all of this is that most of the motivated volunteer female soldiers do not want to go into combat; it is the women liberationist leaders who will never have to go who are pushing so hard for this.

"I only wish those who push for placing women in combat could see it as I have. Are they ready to see their daughters and wives exposed to the wrath of the enemy because they could not dig in the hard ground in time for protection? Should they have to hear the screams of burning human torches trapped in the entanglements of barbed wire after napalm cans are exploded along the main line of resistance? Must they become the victims of suffocation in a covered position resulting from burned-out oxygen due to white phosphorus? Are we really ready to have them face the cold, steel bayonet of the male enemy soldier? Or be horribly mangled in a trapped minefield that no one can penetrate? Think of that young eighteen-year-old moist-eyed girl with homesickness, looking at the faded twilight; she believes the sky is lost forever. Do they need to hear that dreaded noise of incoming artillery beating like a kettle drum, which is like two steel needles pressing on the eardrums? Have they thought about what our women would suffer as prisoners of war at the hands of the enemy who uses the pressure water-hose technique of blowing one's stomach up like a balloon to gain military information? And what a trump card our enemy would have in blackmailing the United States while holding a large number of women prisoners! How can we reconcile our moral perceptions of women with these immoralities of war? No one who has seen real combat could believe that our congressmen and governmental leaders would talk about drafting women and placing them in combat, yet they are doing this very thing today."

Hidden away throughout all the bureaucracies there are hundreds of little advisory committees that are supposedly there to represent the view of the people. One of them within

HEW is called the Secretary's Advisory Committee on the Rights and Responsibilities of Women. This is a panel that directly advises the Secretary of HEW on what women of America want. The panel is made up of twelve very aggressive, self-proclaimed feminists. The head of this group was asked if there were other viewpoints in America besides the feminist viewpoint, to which she replied, "Oh no. I'm confident we represent all American women." The input of those twelve women is recognized by top government.

Need I say that it is time that moral Americans became informed and involved in helping to preserve family values in our nation? Now it is not too late. But we cannot wait. The twilight of our nation could well be at hand.

The Intelligent Woman's Guide to Feminism

MIDGE DECTER

When the dust of this present age has settled, and our present turmoil becomes a subject for recollection in tranquility, let us imagine that some gifted young historian has set for himself the task of accounting for the attitudes and behavior of the affluent bourgeoisie in the fateful later decades of the twentieth century. Surely he will find (perhaps in deference to my subject, I should say "he or she" will find) that not least among the puzzlements of the period is the passion with which a group of the freest, most vital and energetic — and most economically and physically privileged — young women in the history of the race rose up and proclaimed themselves to be the victims of intolerable oppression.

Perhaps even more puzzling in retrospect will have been the willingness of their contemporaries to affix to their uprising the name of feminism. For feminism properly understood is a view summed up in the simple proposition that women are the equals of men: that they are as intelligent, as competent, as brave, and above all, as morally responsible. It was this proposition, for example, that earlier in the century secured for women the right to vote, to educate themselves, to have and to spend their own money, and in general, to take upon themselves a share of the burden of civic responsibility. And yet easily the single most salient and unifying feature of the movement that erupted in the 1960s and that claimed to speak exclusively both to and for the problems of women — the movement that formally dubbed itself Women's Liberation — was its characterization of the condition of women as that of a pervasive and nearly universal inferiority. Despite any illusory appearances to the contrary, declared this movement, women everywhere were to be found mindless, helpless, cowering in the face of masculine power, their lives held in thrall to the whims and fashions of a manipulative culture. When their mothers, prior victims of male dominance, told them to marry, they married. When the needs and exigencies of a capitalist economy decreed that they must consume, they devoted their lives to a mad, spiralling round of consumption and to the breeding of a vast cohort of new consumers. When men, through the

151

agency of a deceptive theory of mental health, sought a more
plentiful supply of compliant sexual partners, women dutifully offered up their bodies in slavish service to something called the
sexual revolution. And as for the less private side of life, when a
contemptuous cultural and educational establishment sought to
relegate them to professional non-achievement, they passively accepted the idea of their inherent incapacity to perform men's
work. Thus nothing less than a complete overturning of all traditional social, sexual, and economic arrangements would suffice to
bring women into a condition of full equality. The removal of all
hindrances to this condition would not be enough. Women themselves must be altered, revolutionized. And with them, of course,
men and the society that men have exclusively created.

   This (to say the least) odd form of feminism fundamentally addressed itself to three areas of women's lives: to work, to marriage,
and to motherhood. It also, naturally, addressed itself to the area
of sex, but what it had to say on *that* entangled subject is very
nearly literally unspeakable. For reasons of decency in public
discussion, it need not detain us here—except to observe that in
the end the movement has made the subject of sex almost in-
distinguishable from the medical practice of gynecology.

   In each of these areas the movement provided an appropriate
theory of women's victimization. In the realm of work, for instance, the main emblem of the status of women as an oppressed
class was said to be the household. The age-old responsibility of
women for the day-to-day physical well-being and welfare of the
family, said the movement, had been the major means not only
for keeping women away from all important sources of power in
society but also for dulling their minds and souls into acquies-
cence with this state of affairs.

   In support of its theory, the movement embarked on a series of
descriptions of the life of women at home unparalleled for their
imagery of bleakness, depression, and unceasing, hopeless,
thankless, fruitless toil since those nineteenth century reformist
investigations of life in the workhouse.

   In what might be taken as the founding document of Women's
Liberation, Betty Friedan's *The Feminine Mystique*, the author
likened the condition of housewives to that of certain veterans of
World War II who had suffered gunshot wounds to their brains.
Since one of Mrs. Friedan's more engaging habits as a public
figure was the introduction of herself on innumerable important
media occasions as the person graduated from Smith College with

the highest grade average ever attained in that august institution, she herself had obviously escaped quite handily from such a fate. Yet her account of the lot of the woman whose job was to run the house and look after the children was by no means the most lurid the movement was to produce.

That care for the household was a lot many women chose to have; that they deemed it important and, yes, rewarding; that they took pride in discharging its duties well; that it even afforded intermittent pleasure, was not—anyway, not invariably—denied by the movement. But the choice, the pride, even the pleasure—if such there should misguidedly be—were themselves only further evidence of how thoroughly, and how dismally, women themselves had assimilated the role imposed upon them by an oppressive society.

But if housework was the main emblem of women's inferior status, those who managed to evade it by pursuing careers were very little better off. For even in the office women were, with few exceptions, consigned to those tasks defined as "women's work." In addition to the despised secretaries—themselves hardly distinguishable from housewives in their obligation to be of service to others—even executives and qualified professional women were hopelessly identified with functions that were no more than extensions of the demand that women remain selfless, sympathetic, and attentive. That is, they tended to be social workers, nurses, schoolteachers, and therapists of various kinds.

It might, of course, have been asked, and specifically from a feminist point of view, whether the professions in which women tended to cluster and the work they tended to be drawn toward—called in tones and contexts of derision by Women's Lib the "helping professions"—did indeed enjoy lower status, or whether the movement itself held it to be inferior *because* it was work performed by women. Significantly, it wasn't asked.

Whatever the answer to this question, we have seen with what incredible rapidity the movement's constituents, under its goading, commenced in large numbers to enroll themselves in such formerly male-dominated professional schools as those in the law and medicine. (Would Women's Lib in the future say that once again they were doing what they were told? Might there one day come to be a derisive attitude toward the law, for instance, because so many women are now to be found there?)

I have left out one step in the process, by now so evidently well advanced, of creating a so-called new equality for women in the realm of work. For if, as was claimed, women had been denied equality of opportunity to take their place alongside men at the professional workplace, it was also claimed that they had also been denied the full development of their capacity to do so. The evidence was clear: women had not attempted and been denied admission to professional schools, or to executive training programs, or to candidacy for public office; they had not in any significant numbers applied for places in these precincts of power in the first place. Women were roughly 50 percent of the population. The only suitable test for the *true* achievement of equality, then, would be their ultimate ensconcement in half the positions of power, status, and wealth.

It would be pointless for their oppressors to argue that perhaps they had not *wanted* such power and prestige, that other ambitions and other values had in a majority of cases come first. Their very adherence to these other ambitions and values, such as a desire to marry and a disinclination to compete with the men they married, was a sign of how the culture had twisted and incapacitated them. By now they needed more than a change: they needed preferential placement.

This argument, that society-bred fears and incapacities entitled those who suffered from them to a prior guarantee of places in schools and jobs to bring their number somewhat into line with their proportion of the population, had, of course, already become familiar. It was the definition of justice and equality offered on behalf of the blacks by *their* equal rights movement. Its expression in terms of policy was affirmative action. Now, without going into a full discussion of the policy of affirmative action and the distress it is causing both to society as a whole and to the individuals said to be benefitting from it, one thing is quite clearly inherent in the logic of this policy and in the implicit thinking of its advocates: and that is, that it is the very opposite of an assertion of equality.

We may pass over as beneath comment the social and intellectual morality of the Women's Lib movement's equating the position of blacks with that of middle-and upper-middle class educated women in the United States. It nevertheless remains to be said that the demand for affirmative action for women is the expression of something less than complete confidence in women's capacity to compete up to the full extent that they wish to compete, and, as such, bespeaks something considerably less than a firm feminist conviction.

A graphic illustration of Women's Lib's lack of confidence in its own claim (that but for a dominant sexist culture women would be equal to men in everything) is the proliferation, under its aegis, of a new women's literature. A visit to any newsstand or bookstore will make the point: women's magazines, magazines for working women, for professional women, for angry women, for chic women, abound. Moreover, in the section devoted to women's concerns that is now mandatory in every bookstore, one finds endless tomes devoted to women's medicine, women's psychology, women's novels, women's history, women's literary criticism—most of them comprising the reading list for movement-created and -administered programs of women's studies taught by affirmative action professors for the purpose of creating a comfortable ghetto for their female students. Consigning a young woman in university to the department of education or social work is as nothing (as a means of giving her the message that she dare not venture) compared with urging her to preoccupy herself with her own feminine experience and giving her college credit for it. Here again, the so-called new feminists have copied the blacks, and with much the same psychic effect: namely, an inner corroboration of the idea that they cannot be fitted into the world and the world must instead be fitted to them.

In the second area for which the movement has provided a theory of women's victimization, namely marriage, the theory is hardly less grim. Marriage, the movement has told its constituents, is merely an arrangement created by men for the provision of cheap labor and free sex. The contribution of women to that arrangement, therefore, is nothing more than a form of slavery or at best, indentured servitude. Marriage has been maintained by terror—the fear of actual male violence, the fear of being abandoned by one's husband without protection and without resources, and the fear of social contumely. Wherein, the philosophers of the new feminism have asked, does the married woman differ from the prostitute? Both, after all, exchange their services for money. Equality can only be established in marriage when that institution has been "redefined." ("Redefinition" is in general the movement's mystical, cabbalistic process for hastening the arrival of the Messiah.) Thus husband and wife can only become equals in the movement's vision of equality when marriage has been redefined as a relationship in which there is no exchange. That is to say, in current fashionable parlance, when neither party to the marriage has a separate distinguishable role to play in the life of the other.

Translated into plain English, what this boils down to is that the only kind of marriage not demeaning to women is one in which the woman, too, will be entitled to have a wife—without at the same time having to be a husband. But with very few exceptions, women *wish* to marry and to be wives, sooner or later—and if there is any doubt on this point, look around you—so if this notion of marriage is in force, women are left with the sense that to behave in a womanly way toward their husbands is to suffer only humiliation.

The result in the real world has been the far from edifying spectacle of marriages that have become a form of bookkeeping: What have you done for me today, and does it constitute a full and exact equivalent for what I did for you yesterday? A marriage without roles, as anyone who has witnessed the phenomenon at close range knows, has become not a mutual recognition of the equal importance to the enterprise of what both partners to it contribute—but a court of litigation. With respect to the issue of feminism in particular, it means that the feminine function in marriage is to be avoided by both husband and wife—or, since in actual life it can't be avoided, is to be regarded by both partners as only a collection of nasty chores to be got out of the way with as much dispatch as possible. Aside from what this has done to actual marriages—namely injected pure poison into them—it hardly conduces to respect for the womanly, either on the part of women themselves or on the part of the men with whom they live. By any meaningful reading of the term, this is a strange form of feminism. Indeed, ironically—or not so ironically—it has done a great deal to introduce and exacerbate the very conditions it claims to be responding to, that is, male violence and abandonment.

One of the consequences of Women's Liberation, and in particular of the hostility toward men it engenders, is that it has relieved men of the responsibility for being proper husbands and fathers. That is why from the very first we have witnessed the otherwise astonishing phenomenon of women insisting upon the most terrible untruths about men and of men offering not one word of reply. When it was said to and about middle class American women that their husbands beat them, cow them, and kick them around (although, as everybody knows, what really goes on in the households of the educated middle class is quite opposite), not a single man stood up to say: "Wait just a moment. I have been working hard and under considerable stress to support my wife and family. Is that a just thing to say about me? I have tried to be decent and responsible, and *this* is the thanks I get?"

But there was no male resistance whatever to the indictments of Women's Liberation. This otherwise inexplicable passivity can only be understood in terms of the movement's pernicious appeal to the apparent short-term interest of men. If women were refusing to accept the burden of womanliness, they were providing men with a perfect opportunity to be rid of the burden of manliness. After all, manliness can also be called a burden as onerous as womanliness, if not more so.

So it is that more and more men are ceasing to be true husbands and fathers. Here we have the real consequence of the so-called role-less marriage. It is after all quite easy for a man to carry out the garbage and do the dishes and even wash the diapers. These are as nothing compared with the weight of being a real husband. Thus in the course of letting themselves off the hook of responsibility, women are also, of course, letting men off that same hook. Thus wives *and* husbands are currently engaged in avoiding all the things they call onerous but that are in fact life-giving and health-giving.

Last but not least of the movement's theories about the lot of women is the theory of motherhood. Having to be a mother, as that "role" is traditionally "defined," says the movement, is the highest form of oppression of all. Women's Lib's pronouncements on the daily life of caring for children — on what it is like to spend time with them, look after them, and above all on the experience of the abiding, passionate, selfless attachment to them that motherhood entails — surpasses even its description of housework for bleakness and resentment. Babies are no more than a daily collection of soiled diapers. Toddlers are no more than daily imprisonment within four walls, or enchainment to a park bench. Schoolchildren are no more than a daily round of running exhausting errands — fetchings and carryings, mealtimes and quarrels. Above all, the passions and devotions of motherhood are no more than the imposition of the needs of the species on smothered and starving individuals. That children by themselves offer a considerable amount of meaning to life — I will not even mention pleasure — is a notion almost lost in the feverish mists of the new feminism.

Of all the ideas about the condition of women now circulating like the spores of an epidemic infection, the movement's theory of motherhood has, of course, taken least hold. Even for those intent on rejecting the idea that there is such a thing, a woman's nature simply will not be denied. Women continue to long for children, and continue to act on that longing. Even against considerable odds — even when marriage has become, on the whole, a light-minded undertaking, even in direst poverty, even in the face of a massive public campaign against their doing so, and even under those circumstances where men have been refusing in droves to stick around and be fathers — women continue to seek to be mothers. We see around us now, for instance, that cohort of women who have held out into their thirties, largely under the influence of the women's movement and related pressures, and who are now rushing around to get in under the deadline of what is called the biological clock. These women spent their twenties pursuing their careers (more often pursuing *themselves*) and, in *that* pursuit avoiding all commitment to the irrevocable. Now, some of them quite advanced in years, they feel the imperative of their unique nature as women and will not, whatever else happens to them, remain childless.

So the movement has lost on the score of this ultimate oppression, the oppression of motherhood, for which women will continue to volunteer. But the problem does not end there. In its teachings on the condition of women the movement has nevertheless sown the conviction that to live as women are destined, and thus privately compelled, to do — in no matter how attenuated a style — is to be consigned to inescapable inferiority. How many of the babies being born to this new cohort of mothers will be thrown into day-care centers — their contribution to meaning muffled, their pleasures lost — in order that their mothers may continue to deny any special virtue and value to womanliness? Heedless men and self-hating women have permitted this denial to go by the name of feminism, but it is in fact simply the hatred of women. In other words, the real sexism. For to call womanliness victimization is an expression of contempt for women more profound than any ever heard in the locker rooms, sales conventions, and executive suites of the old male-chauvinist world.

Why, then, have so many women embraced this peculiar assault on their value as women? The reason is that the movement, while it put them down, at the same time delivered a comforting message. It said to them: You are victims, and all your troubles and anxieties are the fault of somebody else. Women have indeed reached a new, if you will a revolutionary, condition. In the last fifty years, the combination of birth control, medical science, and modern technology have made it possible for them both to pursue careers and to have families. Now they are faced with an altogether new choice: Do I wish to have children or do I not wish to have children? This is both a new freedom and a tremendous new anxiety. The same is true with respect to the pursuit of careers. As any man could have told them — perhaps even tried now and then to tell them — the pursuit of careers can be quite anxiety-ridden. In any case, women discovered, though some denied it, that they had taken on a whole new set of anxieties and fears.

In this situation, that is, facing genuine and unprecedented problems, women were confronted with a movement that sang to them a siren song: The reason that you are having difficulties, went this song, is that *they* have been conspiring against you.

A true feminist movement under these circumstances would have said to women, in effect: Yes, indeed, life does have new difficulties; yes, indeed, it is full of new burdens and anxieties; yes, indeed, it is very hard. On the other hand, your new freedom can be very gratifying. You will need a lot of courage to secure its gratifications, but you *can* do so. Instead, they were told that their new freedom was the higher injustice. Any movement which offers an explanation for people's difficulties that has nothing whatever to do with them, and that requires no assumption of responsibility on their part, is bound to be very soothing. Witness the perversion of black pride and the undermining of black courage that has also resulted from just such a movement and just such a message.

If the movement had been addressing itself to the *real* difficulties of women, we should have seen an analysis of the condition of women today as one actually recognizes that condition to be. Such a movement would not have produced a literature which said that the educated American woman is a useless, helpless, brainwashed victim: for she is no such thing. If this movement had addressed itself to the problems of how much new will and courage it takes for her to deal with her new life as a person facing an altogether new kind of freedom, it would perhaps not have enjoyed such a wide response. But it would have been speaking truthfully, and it might in the long run have produced new vital juices instead of poison.

Our historian of the future, looking back, may describe, but will never be able to explain, any of this. The explanation does not lie in the domain of events and causes, economic conditions and social circumstances accessible to the historian's analysis. Nor can I pretend to offer it myself, except in the most vague and sketchy way. In the end, only a religious philosopher will be able to make our grandchildren, and their grandchildren, see how it was that women in our time came to be seized with such a loathing for what they ineluctably are. Perhaps he will say that it had to do with a refusal to accept the world and nature as God had constituted them. Perhaps he will say people — in this case, specifically middle-class, educated, Western women — were once blessed with a vast new accession of physical, social, and moral freedom, and sought desperately (let us hope he will have to say without success) to escape from it.

Who is the New Traditional Woman?

She is the mother of the citizens of the 21st century. It is she who will more than anyone else transmit civilization and humanity to future generations and by her response to the challenges of life determine whether America will be a strong, virtuous nation.

The New Traditional Woman is not the vicious cartoon that the feminist movement has made of wives and mothers. The New Traditional Woman is not the syrupy caricature that Hollywood of the 1950's beamed into our living rooms. She is new, because she is of the current era, with all its pressures and fast pace and rapid change. She is traditional because, in the face of unremitting cultural change, she is oriented around the eternal truths of faith and family. Her values are timeless and true to human nature.

Feminism deceived many women because it is based on a false concept of human nature. It fed on illusions, and it offered illusions in return. It was not and *is* not based on objective reality. Francis Schaeffer once told me that God's greatest gift to mankind is reality—and that is not a bad standard against which to measure an ideology.

Let us examine feminism in that light. For most women, feminism made its first impression at a consciousness-raising session of some kind. The basic feminist message was derived from a few crucial books that were written in the late 60's. If you extracted all the ideology from that message, it could be boiled down to: how unappreciated we women are; how persecuted we are; how exploited we are. Feminists would point their finger at the husband who came home from work and impatiently asked when dinner would be ready as ample demonstration of the second-class place of women. There may have been grounds to criticize the man involved for his insensitivity or for his impatience—failings which are all too common—but to go from there to a full-blown attack on the institution of the family betrays a strange and distorted view of reality. Feminist ideology told women how foolish and exploited they were to be wives and mothers; how they did not need to take such treatment; how they were as good if not better than any man; how they could have their way, were entitled to it, and anybody who kept them from it was belittling them. From self-pity, it lashed out against all perceived "oppressors"—and those oppressors included husbands, family responsibility, and even the capitalist system according to the more visionary ideological trendsetters.

To be honest about it, there were plenty of social myths to nourish feminism. The 1950's had created an image of American womanhood that most people had accepted. You remember the housewife who always had every hair in place, a spotless pastel colored shirtdress, who never raised her voice to her children, who never seemed concerned about any problem which could not be resolved in 20 minutes plus commercials. According to this myth, there were no relatives with needs to be met, no financial worries for the household, and

161

there was nothing to do except read the newspaper over morning coffee and wait for the phone to ring. The truth is that nobody's life was ever like this. Yet many people watched this distortion of reality and were taken in by it. They looked at this and said to themselves, "that's what life is supposed to be like." Then when life was not like that, they felt cheated. When they found themselves raising their voices to their children, when they found themselves having problems to worry about that did not disappear after one evening's attention—when they found they were not able to manage teenagers with a joke and a smile—in other words, when reality imposed itself on the illusions they had created, they were disappointed. They felt they had failed, or they felt they had been failed. To the extent they had regarded those dream-images as promises for their own lives, they became bitter, and their bitterness became the fertile recruiting ground for feminist agitation.

There had been some conventions which left us ill-prepared for the past several decades. For instance, one such convention was the old-world idea, "Why should she get an education? All she'll do is get married." That idea had a foundation in reality and common sense. In the days when marriage and family meant five hours work to get a meal on the table, six hours work to wash and dry a load of clothes, another six hours to iron it, plus the need to tend the chickens and make the butter as well—in the days when survival and home maintenance consumed all the attention and thought of every waking minute, then a liberal arts education was indeed of questionable worth to a woman whose life would be a constant struggle to maintain the basics. The problem was that that convention held on even after the reality that had justified it had disappeared. Women who had foregone an education found themselves ill-prepared to cope with the life they needed to lead: a life in which ideas are as real as soapsuds, a life in which being a help-mate is not achieved merely by providing food and clothes, but also requires understanding a husband's thoughts and sharing his emotions. Women who had acquired the idea that all they owed to their husbands was good housekeeping began to realize that something was wrong—they were not prepared for life. Feminism capitalized on this unhappiness and boldly told women how they had been mistreated as children, deprived of an equal education because they were girls, coaxed to expect less from life because they were female—all the usual clichés.

In the 1930s, 40s and 50s, women had to spend enormous amounts of time in the activities that literally held the family together such as cooking, cleaning and sewing. Women who were wealthy and could hire servants were able to do other things. They could become writers, politicians or doctors, but they were few. When the burden of housework began to lighten in the 1950s and women no longer had to spend every waking minute cleaning and cooking, what did they do? In tragically large numbers they spent the new-found time watching television and buying into the image that was later bound to disappoint. And today, when technical advances have even further reduced the time essential for household maintenance, the new-found time is also wasted in redundant, superfluous shopping and in perusing women's magazines which are designed to instill dissatisfaction with everything—one's husband, children, living room, kitchen, even one's own body. Today, of course, there are women's magazines which seem specially written to teach dissatisfaction with one's job. These are the same magazines which assume their readers are ideological feminists—and if the reader is not one when she picks up the magazine, she will be by the time she finishes it, if the editors have their way. Feeding the discontent of women seems a great way to make it big in publishing. But then, feeding improper tastes in men has made Hugh Hefner rich, too.

Women have their faults too, but feminism is not willing to admit it. Feminists like to blame everything on men, or on male-dominated society, as they call it. Women are second class citizens, they say, because men degrade women. But it is important to put things in the correct perspective. Women earn 59¢ for every dollar earned by men—you have heard this quoted as a rallying cry. But women themselves choose to work part-time, or only temporarily. In fact, 47% of women regard their jobs as temporary at any given time. When you factor in the part-time and temporary nature of the work, the 59¢ statistic falls apart. It becomes approximately 80% parity, if those conditions are factored in. Only 80%, feminists would still screech, why not 100%? They would say it is because women are discriminated against, because they are paid less. They would not entertain the idea that women may not want to work as hard or that in school they may not want to take as challenging courses. Such ideas would be heresy to a feminist. But I went to school with girls, like most of you did. I remember hearing them say, "If I get a better grade than he does, he won't take me out." And I remember hearing the talk in the dorm: "Why take that course? The professor will make you write a term paper." These same girls are women now, and if they have raised their voices in a chorus to blame male-dominated society for their own lesser accomplishments, I'd like to jog their memories a bit.

Feminism replaced the saccharine sentimentalizations of women and home life and projected instead a new image of women: a drab, macho feminism of hard-faced and hard-hearted women who were bound and determined to carve their place in the world, no matter whose bodies they have to climb over to do it. This image provided the plot line for such cultural weathervanes as *Kramer vs. Kramer*. Macho feminism despises anything which seeks to interfere with the desires of Number One. A relationship which proves burdensome? Drop it! A husband whose needs cannot be conveniently met? Forget him! Children who may wake up in the middle of the night? No way! To this breed of thought, family interferes with self-fulfillment, and given the choice between family and self, the self is going to come out on top in their world. This macho feminism is intrinsically anti-family. It is anti-men as well. Even lesbianism is exalted by some feminists as the ultimate form of feminism. In their opinion, lesbianism will help solve the world population problem. The ideology which regards the existence of human beings as the world's greatest problem finds a natural sympathy with the view that procreation is beneath a woman's dignity.

Macho feminism has deceived women in that it convinced them that they would be happy only if they were treated like men, and that included treating themselves like men. When the macho feminist approached age 30, she began to want a child. Having a child immediately created tensions and doubts within her. She soon realized that having a child while trying to live, work and pursue a career as if you did not is a fairly sure recipe for skepticism of the feminist ideology. Betty Friedan's camp began to suffer defections from people who said as they left: "You lied to us, Betty. You said we could have it all, and we can't. We're not happy." The "all" they wanted included the high-powered, high-paid careers; the relationship of convenience; and now, a child—all, of course, in an atmosphere free of the deadening weight of traditional values.

Make no mistake, a high-powered, high-paid job, a happy marriage, and children are not mutually exclusive of traditional values. Not at all. There is a very important distinction between the form and the content of traditional values, a philosophical distinction.

The form of traditional values is a system of moral norms which, once well defined, are taken to be without exception. Fidelity in marriage is a moral norm. Once it has been well-defined, adultery is wrong, regardless of who or when or why. In other words, traditional values are non-consequentialist ethics.

What are consequentialist ethics? Consequentialist ethics are commonly taught in the public schools today and indeed in far too many churches. Consequentialist ethics could be summarized by quoting from a bumper sticker I have seen occasionally: "If it will feel good, do it." Consequentialist ethics is the thesis that you can judge whether something is good or bad by its consequences. If having an abortion has the "good" result that you can continue your career, then the abortion is a "good" thing, a "right" thing, to do. If living with John instead of marrying him brings the "good" result that you never argue about money because you each have your own, then living together is a "good" thing to do.

In contrast, non-consequentialist ethics, which are traditional values, maintain that moral norms are not dependent upon consequences, but rather upon whether certain actions are right or wrong intrinsically. Hence the norms concerning these acts, once they are well-defined, are without exception.

Of course, many actions are morally neutral. Four out of five women today believe that boys should be as responsible as girls for doing the laundry; six years ago, only three out of five women felt that way. Is this a terrible tilt away from traditional values? Of course not. Doing the laundry is a morally neutral action.

Tasks such as these are conventions. Such things change as technology changes society. When telephones first became common, it was considered improper for women to be telephone operators. That convention changed so thoroughly that feminists now demand the hiring of male telephone operators. If they only knew how reactionary their demand really is.

Conventions can serve a good purpose because they can reinforce the values of a society. Unfortunately, some of the conventions of 1982 are not exactly supportive of traditional values...

And there are the usual domestic responsibilities, which husbands and children can share to some degree. In addition to all these human responsibilities, increasingly women find themselves sharing financial responsibility for their home and family. And with employment comes responsibility to employer and co-workers. And on top of all this, comes the task of changing the heart of a generation, and being in the forefront of politics as well.

In the face of all this, the only way to deal with it successfully is to have the right attitude. Attitude is the most important issue facing women today. The right attitude will fulfill women; the wrong one will destroy them. With all the competing demands on one's time and energies, it becomes critical to keep the priorities in order. When there is much to do, it is tempting to become cold and practical, deaf to the time-consuming needs of others. It is easy to become consumed with oneself. Feminists praise that self-centeredness and call it liberation.

Priorities must be kept in order, and they must be communicated. Women who work to pay the heating bills can communicate that to their children, who can understand the necessity. Women who work in order to buy wall-to-wall carpet cannot explain to their children that carpet is more important than time with them. Women who work for the benefit of others, namely their family, or because they have a talent needed by the community, are not as prone to materialism and ambition as women who work for luxury. Jealousy and too much concern for the opinions of others are the great failings of women. If you are too busy with your own responsibilities, however, you can forget to be jealous; and if your conscience is absolutely clear, you can learn not to care what somebody else might think of you. After all, your priority is not what strangers say about you. Keeping the priorities straight depends on having the right attitude. What is the right attitude? To recognize a woman's unique nature and to accommodate to it.

A woman's nature is, simply, other-oriented. Long before women's liberation, there were women who focused attention on themselves. They were recognized for what they were: vain, petty, selfish, cold, and otherwise flawed. Macho feminist ideology would make them into heroines today. But to the traditional woman self-centeredness remains as ugly and sinful as ever. The less time women spend thinking about themselves, the happier they are. The same is true of men, of course.

Women are ordained by their nature to spend themselves in meeting the needs of others. And women, far more than men, will transmit culture and values to the next generation. There is nothing demeaning about this nature: it is ennobling. Meeting the needs of others takes different forms: caring for small children, arranging for grandparents and others to be wanted, giving concern to a co-worker's problem, being genuinely attentive to the heart and mind of a husband. Working for pro-family policies is a giving of self, too, because such policies will be good for others in this nation. It will help create a social climate in which others can do what is right and thus find happiness here and in eternity.

A woman who accepts as her purpose in life the service of others will not find herself resentful if everywhere she looks she sees someone who needs her.

THE FEMINIST MISTAKE

Sexual Equality and the Decline of the American Military

JEAN YARBROUGH

The United States is the only major country to consider seriously the question of women in combat. Of the 72 nations that register or conscript citizens for military service, only 10 include women and none places them in combat. Although women are still excluded from combat by law in the Navy and the Air Force, and by policy in the Army, the United States has moved closer to placing women in combat than any other country. Not only have women moved into "combat related" tasks, but the distinction between combatants and non-combatants has been blurred by the inclusion of women in "technical" combat positions, such as missile launch officers, which would be prime targets in a war.

It is true that women have fought in combat in the past. Sexual egalitarians point approvingly to the heroism of Soviet women during World War II and, more recently, to the combat role of women in the Israeli army. But in the Soviet Union, women fought out of dire necessity, not ideological conviction, and in all-female units. The case of Israel is even more interesting. Partly for ideological, mostly for military reasons, Israel sent women into combat in 1948. But they were withdrawn in three weeks. Israeli men proved more protective of the women, jeopardizing their own missions to save them. And Israeli commanders found that Arab forces fought with greater determination against female units to avoid the humiliation of being defeated by women; as a result, casualties on both sides were higher. If the Israelis could not change the attitudes of their own soldiers toward women, still less could they raise the consciousness of their enemy.

Far more instructive is the present policy of both these countries. Of an estimated 4.4 million member force, the Soviet Union employs approximately 10,000 women, all in traditional female tasks. There is not one woman general officer in the entire Soviet military. Today, Israeli women are drafted, but not for combat. Although they are given defensive weapons training, their function is to free Israeli men to fight.

In the United States, feminists support women in combat for ideological reasons—they regard it as a measure of equity—while some military professionals see it as a measure of expediency. The debate took hold in the early 1970s, when the proposed Equal Rights Amendment seemed to be prospering. The Supreme Court for the first time invalidated a number of sex-based classifications, and the federal courts then extended the principle to the military. Abandoning the judiciary's traditional deference to Congress on military policy, the federal courts greatly broadened the rights of women in the military in a series of cases in the mid and late 1970s.

Congress entered the picture when it voted to end the draft in 1973, resulting in a decline in the number of qualified men joining the armed forces. To compensate, the Pentagon sought to attract more women; during the 1970s, the number of women in the military increased by more than 350 percent, to 150,000. In 1975, Congress opened the service academies to women, and the Army began to narrow its definition of combat to routine direct combat and to assign women to positions previously classified as combat. Women were assigned to combat "support" units, in which they would certainly be shot at, and were trained in the use of light anti-tank weapons, M-16 rifles, grenade launchers, claymore mines, and M-60 machine guns. Under pressure from the courts, the Defense Department also revised its regulations so that pregnancy was no longer grounds for automatic dismissal.

Registration Roulette

With the election of Jimmy Carter in 1976, the pace of change accelerated. Two independent studies recommended recruiting more women for reasons of both economy and quality; one concluded the services could perform their mission with one-third female personnel. Field experiments conducted by the Army Research Institute concluded that difficulties attributable to the presence of women in the field were due chiefly to training and leadership problems that could be solved. In response to a court order, Congress enacted legislation in 1978 permitting women to serve on non-combat ships and combat ships for up to 180 days. Co-ed basic training was also launched. The following year, the Air Force opened pilot and naviga-

JEAN YARBROUGH *is a professor of political science at Loyola University in Chicago.*

tor positions, and allowed women to become missile launch officers, a position previously classified as combat.

In 1979, in its most controversial move to date, the Pentagon proposed repealing the combat restrictions on women altogether, stressing the military's need for flexibility in meeting their recruitment goals and the desire for equity. According to the Undersecretary of the Air Force, Antonia Handler Chayes, it was a question of "equal opportunity to fight and die for the country."

In the last significant measure of his administration, President Carter called for the registration of 18 year-old men and women. The administration's arguments for registration of women recall the discussion of women warriors in Book V of Plato's *Republic*. Here Socrates, discussing the differences between men and women in combat, facetiously suggests that the differences between the sexes are no greater than between bald and long-haired men. Richard Danzig, a Carter official, when asked in the Senate if the proposal to register women was based on military necessity, replied seriously with a similar analogy: "If you said to me does the military require people with brown eyes to serve, I would have to tell you no, because people with blue eyes could do the job."

In rejecting the proposal, the Senate Armed Services Committee Report called the plan a "smokescreen" that diverted attention from serious manpower shortages in the all volunteer force (AVF). The Report noted that although 95 percent of the job categories were open to women, 42 percent of the total number of jobs were closed to them because of combat restrictions. Since most of the shortages occur in combat positions, registering women would not solve the problem. Indeed, looking ahead to a general mobilization, the Report warned that if the proposal to register women in equal numbers were interpreted to require their induction in equal numbers, it would seriously impair military readiness.

The Report concluded that the proposal to register women was based on equity rather than military necessity, and it rejected the plan for this reason. In passing, the Report also addressed the inherent difficulty of the equity argument. If all women were required to register, but then were not inducted in equal numbers (administration officials testified that the ratio of men to women to be called up was 6:1), or admitted to combat, then the plan would fail to satisfy its own principle of equity. Unlike the administration, Congress believed there was a tension between the requirements of equity and a strong defense. It chose defense; and the Supreme Court upheld the decision not to require draft registration of women.

To many feminists and others who view the military primarily as a social institution, this was a serious blow; the subsequent election of Ronald Reagan seemed to foreshadow major cutbacks in many of the gains women had made in the military in the 1970s.

At first, it did seem likely that the Reagan Administration would change policy concerning women in the military. Immediately after the 1980 election, the Pentagon ordered a "pause" in the recruitment of women to assess their impact on military readiness. It temporarily established a ceiling of 65,000 enlisted women in the Army, and held recruitment levels steady in the other services.

In 1982, the Army, in its policy review, *Women in the Army*, (WITA) recommended 1) the development of a "gender neutral" physical fitness test (MEPSCAT) that would have effectively barred most women from the strenuous military occupational specialties (MOS) to which they were assigned, but were performing inadequately, and 2) the closing of 23 additional MOS to women because of the likelihood of routine direct combat. In the same year, the Pentagon ended co-ed basic training for recruits; male and female officers still train together.

In an odd alliance, feminists joined with free market supporters of the AVF in denouncing these moves, and in the end they prevailed. Despite the administration's opposition to the ERA, it was bound by the imperatives of the AVF to continue to expand opportunities for women in the military, including combat-related MOS. Six months after the WITA recommendations, Secretary of the Army John O. Marsh, Jr. announced that the MEPSCAT tests would be used only as a "guideline" in the classification process, and that female soldiers would not be denied entry into a particular field because of their physical strength. Army officials stress that "closing a career field to female soldiers is not related to the physical standards of jobs or the physical strength of the applicants"; it is "solely a function of the probability of direct combat involvement." At the same time, the Army re-opened 13 of the 23 MOS closed to women for this reason.

Growing Dependence

The American military has grown increasingly dependent upon women to meet its "manpower" requirements in the volunteer force. Defense Department publications regard the increase in women from 173,445 or 8.5 percent of the active force in January 1981 to over 200,000 or 9.4 percent at the end of fiscal 1984 as a "significant improvement." And as the number of women in the military has grown, they have emerged as a powerful interest group. General Jeane Holm, one of the leading advocates of women's rights in the military, makes it clear that as the number of women increases, the pressure to repeal combat restrictions on women will also grow.

> Sooner or later, if the numbers and proportions of women continue to expand, Congress and the services will have to confront the restrictions imposed by the combat laws and policies and will have to decide whether they should be changed and, if so, how.

Pressure for change comes most from the female junior officers whose careers are most directly affected by the combat exclusion policy. In a recent report on field exercises in Honduras, Charles C. Moskos notes that among female officers, "about half believed that women should be allowed to volunteer for combat units . . . the remainder said women should be compelled to go into combat units in the same manner as men . . . " These attitudes are important because between 1983 and 1988, the number of female officers is projected to increase by 28 percent.

Although the present administration publicly accepts the combat exclusion policy, a memo from Secretary of Defense Caspar Weinberger, written in July 1983, suggests that the Pentagon recognizes the tension between the military's growing reliance upon women and a broad interpretation of the combat exclusion policy. "The combat exclusion rule should be interpreted to allow as many as possible career opportunities for women to be kept open," wrote Weinberger. He warns the service secretaries that "no artificial barriers to career opportunities for women will be constructed or tolerated." In keeping with Weinberger's directive, the Defense Department's publication *Going Strong: Women in Defense* (1984) boasts

that women in the Army serve in more than 86 percent of the enlisted career fields, and more than 96 percent of the officer specialties are open to women. These fields include non-traditional specialties such as air traffic control, military intelligence, aviation, equipment maintenance and operation, communications, computer repair, and law enforcement.

In the Navy, nearly 10,000 of the 42,000 enlisted women serve in non-traditional areas. Today 172 women officers and 3,359 enlisted women serve aboard 32 ships. Ground support and maintenance positions were recently opened up to enlisted women. In June 1984, the Navy assigned the first woman executive officer aboard ship. In another recent change, women officers can now be assigned to "mobile logistics support force ships for temporary duty and deployments." As *Going Strong* explains, "this allows women helicopter pilots and women members of explosive ordnance disposal detachments to deploy with their units."

In the Air Force, the following specialties have been opened to enlisted women since 1981: Airborne Warning and Control Systems (AWACS), KC-10 aerial tanker crew, and 26,000 security police positions. More than 300 women officers serve as pilots and navigators of non-combat aircraft, including the mammoth transport aircraft, the C-5A Galaxy. Just this year, women officers have been made eligible for assignment as launch control officers in the Air Force's most advanced strategic nuclear missile, the Minuteman II. And on April 30, 1985, Air Force Secretary Verne Orr announced that more than 800 new positions were being opened to women, including the "C-23 and EC-130H aircraft, forward air control post, the airborne battlefield command and control center mission, and some munitions sites."

Despite its initial reservations, the Reagan Administration has been forced by its commitment to the AVF to expand opportunities for women in the military. As long as the AVF continues, the pressure to increase the number of women and to open all military specialties, including combat, will continue to grow, and to pose serious problems for combat readiness.

Measuring Morale

Morale is difficult to assess because it defies precise quantification. Nevertheless, a number of problem areas have emerged.

1. *Fraternization.* Military policy traditionally prohibits social relations between officers and enlisted personnel in order to maintain impartiality, discipline, and morale. James Webb, a Naval Academy graduate, in a controversial article in *The Washingtonian*, "Women Can't Fight," cites one cadet's opinion of how fraternization has undermined morale at West Point.

> Our squad leaders talk about honor, performance, and accountability. Then before you knew it, they were going after the women plebes, sneaking some of them away on weekends. How can you indoctrinate the women when you're breaking the regulations to date them? And how can you talk about integrity and accountability when you're doing these sorts of things?

2. *Special Treatment.* Even when fraternization rules are observed, both men and women complain of double standards. Men believe that women receive preferential treatment in duty hours, assignments, and sick call. They resent having to assume additional responsibilities because women are pregnant or physically unable to perform strenuous assignments.

But it is not only the morale of men that suffers. In the Honduras exercise, Mr. Moskos, who generally regards the operation as a success, nevertheless notes:

> Men and women ran together, which led to one of the few forms of invidious comparisons between the sexes in the encampment. Initially, the women were mixed in with the men, but this typically led to the women as a group falling behind the men. The procedure was then changed to place women in front of men. This resulted in the whole group running at a slower pace than if the men had run alone. Either way, the women felt they were being regarded as failures, firstly by not being able to keep up with the men, or secondly, by holding the men back.

Finally, even when women soldiers share equally in the hardships of the field exercises, they are never really comfortable with the lack of privacy in sleeping and showering arrangements, and this too can affect morale, especially among the women recruits.

3. *Sexual Harassment.* Although sexual harassment is likely to occur wherever men and women share close quarters and work together, it is especially acute in the military, and has increased as the number of women has grown. One reason may be that the insularity of military life intensifies sexual attraction and conflict. Another may be that the military legitimately cultivates aggressive behavior to a greater degree than civil institutions. Researchers have suggested that some men may find it difficult to restrain their hostile impulses toward women, especially if they disapprove of their having invaded this most masculine profession.

Nor is sexual harassment only a problem between the sexes. In the Honduras exercises, enlisted women mentioned approaches from lesbians. As Mr. Moskos notes, "accounts of lesbians would come up spontaneously in most extended interviews with female soldiers," though the women were less alarmed than male soldiers by homosexual overtures.

The military's policies on sexual matters tend to go off in opposite directions. Reformers want the military to stay out of private matters with regard to fraternization, pregnancy, family matters, and sexual conduct in general, but they call on the military to intervene in private matters involving sexual harassment, and to use the authority they are otherwise unwilling to acknowledge to reform offensive attitudes. The authority these reformers would give the military is broad indeed: the female officers interviewed by Mr. Moskos consider sexual harassment to include "sexual definitions of suitable work, the combat exclusion rule, sexist language, etc." Similarly the Defense Department defines sexual harassment in part as "verbal or physical conduct of a sexual nature," which creates an "intimidating, hostile, or offensive environment." According to this definition, many of the traditional military techniques for instilling courage and a fighting spirit might be regarded as "sexual harassment."

Traditionally, the service academies have prepared officers for leadership positions, chiefly combat ones. But in evaluating the performance of women at the academies, supporters stress women's academic performance, while minimizing the effect of changes in the physical training curricula. Although the academies initially tried to hold women to the same physical standards as men, with only minimal changes, the disparity in performance between the men and the women necessitated the development of different standards. As General Holm reports:

> Women at West Point carry lighter rifles; pugil stick training, in which cadets practice hand-to-hand combat with padded sticks, pits only women against women; and parts of the obstacle course have been adjusted to accommodate shorter people.

In keeping with this view of the academies as essentially academic institutions, West Point publications now stress equal effort rather than equal performance.

On the other hand, critics insist that the principal task of the academies (which cost the American taxpayer over $100,000 per graduate) is to prepare men for combat leadership. They deplore the shift from leadership to "management," from physical strength to "general excellence," and blame the admission of women for accelerating these trends. At the Naval Academy, physical punishment and verbal abuse of cadets have been abolished. Although this sounds like a sensible reform, and is consistent with the Defense Department's broad definition of sexual harassment, a plausible case can be made that, however brutal, these earlier practices helped to prepare men for the kind of stress and violence they would encounter in combat. Similarly, the Academy has replaced the longstanding practice of peer evaluations with officer evaluations because the officers feared that male cadets would not rate women as effective leaders. Male cadets complain that the leadership evaluation process has been "sterilized" and that women cadets have been singled out for advancement on the basis of their managerial and academic performance. They object that women have not proven themselves effective leaders in ways that matter.

Yet they also know that they dare not say this publicly. Cadets at West Point are rated on their "attitudes toward equal opportunity," and officers understand that their misgivings about women's performances can adversely affect their careers.

Advocates of expanding opportunities for women in the military concede that most women are physically weaker, but they dismiss the issue of strength. They cite studies like the Gates Commission, which maintained that the percentage of ground combat jobs requiring few technical skills had declined and would continue to do so. Future confrontations will require a higher percentage of soldiers skilled in electronic and other technical fields. Also, the advocates say, women recruits are more intelligent and better able to operate such sophisticated equipment. And finally, most of what the Army does requires teamwork. Men can cooperate with women as well as with men if required by their leaders to do so.

Upon closer analysis, these arguments are unpersuasive. The necessity of avoiding a general nuclear holocaust makes it likely that future wars will be limited and improvisational. The Army believes that victory in such contests will depend upon "initiative, depth, agility, and synchronization . . . maneuver and surprise . . . leadership, unit cohesion, and effective independent operations." It further assumes that casualties will be high in combat "support" units, in which women now serve. To the extent that the recent Falklands war provides any guidance, victory will depend more on traditional infantry stamina than sophisticated weapons.

Mercenaries for the Privileged
During the Reagan Administration, the overall quality of the armed forces, measured by percentage of the force with high school diplomas and high AFQT scores, has improved dramatically, significantly narrowing the gap between male and female performance. Nevertheless, there are strong indications that this trend may not hold. The end of the recession, the proposed Congressional cap on military spending, and the decline in the 18 to 20 year-old pool, pose severe problems for the quality of the AVF. In testimony before Congress earlier this year, Assistant Secretary of Defense Lawrence J. Korb predicted that "recruiting will continue to become increasingly difficult." In this case, the gap between qualified women and men may again widen, as it did during the Carter years. The real question remains—not whether women are more qualified than high school dropouts or mental incompetents to engage in combat specialties, but why we as a nation allow poor, disproportionally black, men and women to become mercenaries for middle and upper class white men.

Moreover, although women do pose fewer disciplinary problems, they adversely affect combat readiness in other ways. According to the office of the Assistant Secretary of Defense, "Ten percent of the women in the Army are pregnant at any given time. Over the course of the year, it is estimated that 17 percent of the Army's female personnel will have been pregnant." This creates problems of lost time, child care, and deployability. Although unmarried mothers with dependent children are not allowed to enlist in either the active or reserve forces, they are allowed to remain if they divorce or become pregnant after their enlistment. A case pending in the federal courts charges that this policy constitutes unfair sex discrimination and denial of equal protection of the laws to unmarried mothers who wish to enlist in the services.

Although it is true that many military tasks require teamwork rather than virtuoso displays of physical strength, it is not so clear that men will cooperate with women as readily as with men, or that they will perform as effectively if they do. In the two Army studies designed to measure the effect of women on combat effectiveness, MAXWAC and Reforger, the conclusions, though favorable, are ambiguous. A special team of observers found no differences in units composed of 35 percent women in the MAXWAC study, but noted informally that the "women generally did not perform the field tasks as well as men."

One notable difference between the Carter and Reagan administrations is that the Defense Department no longer conducts such tests. According to Lieutenant Colonel John Boyer of the Pentagon, "the question of whether women can perform as well as men in combat service support type skills is no longer at issue. It is recognized that women do perform as well as men in these jobs."

Finally, the dispute over quality involves different, frequently unstated, methodological assumptions. On the one side is the technical, or what William J. Gregor of West Point calls the "instrumental" approach to measuring military effectiveness. The instrumental view relies upon supposedly objective quantitative tests—nothing is true until it has been quantitatively measured. But technicians, too, have values—in this case that women can perform effectively in nearly all, if not all areas of the military. And the kind of studies they design tend to give them the answers they want. When the tests do not confirm their values they assume that human nature is malleable, and can be changed through "effective" managerial techniques.

By contrast, the "normative" model recognizes the limits of quantification, and recognizes that ultimately the kinds of questions asked and the methods employed to answer them reflect opposing political philosophies. There is no "value-free" study of women in the military. Certain variables like morale or male bonding are subjective and difficult to measure accurately, but they are nevertheless crucial to any realistic assessment of combat effectiveness. Human nature, which is at once universal and particular, human as well as male and female, is not amenable to unlimited experimentation.

Ignoring the Obvious
But the trend of recent history and court decisions is to ignore these differences in the pursuit of social equity. The demand for equity has widespread appeal because it is simple and reflects the egalitarian principle of American society. But when applied to military affairs, it is wrong and dangerous. The military cannot and should not try to mirror exactly the principles of democratic society. The military is not a "civic instrument" that reflects social progress. Nor is it a social welfare agency. The relationship between the military and civilian spheres is more complicated. Although the military defends the principles of democratic society, it cannot fully embody them. Its end is victory, not equity; its virtue is courage, not justice; its structure is authoritarian, not pluralistic. In short, although the military defends democratic principles and is shaped by the regime of which it is a part, it is not simply a microcosm of the larger society. The requirements of military life clash with the democratic commitment to equality, natural rights, and consent.

This does not mean that the military can or ought to ignore democratic principles altogether. The demands of black soldiers are a case in point. Until after World War II, racial segregation was official military policy. Beginning in 1948, and prior to the great court decisions outlawing discrimination in civil society, the services sought to eliminate racial segregation and discrimination. But the situation of blacks and women is not the same. The arguments for segregating blacks was based on longstanding and irrational white prejudice, whereas the case against women in combat is rooted in recognition of genuine physical and psychological differences that are important in battle, such as strength, aggressiveness, and sexual attraction. To the extent that the prejudice against women is based on an appreciation of these natural and desirable differences, it is valid and should influence military policy.　　　　　🔊

by Shirley Wilkins and Thomas A. W. Miller

Working Women: How It's Working Out

Lynn and John are in their early thirties, married, and both lawyers. They are about to have their first child—and their first big marital problem.

How are they to raise their child? Which of these talented individuals will be called upon to make the greater professional sacrifice? Whose career will be at least temporarily, if not permanently, derailed in order to have a family?

The couple does have some options. Lynn is eligible for several months of maternity leave, but she worries that she will be taken off the interesting and important cases. John can take a more limited amount of paternity leave, but, frankly, it would be frowned upon. They certainly have the combined income to be able to afford a full-time nanny, but they are not anxious to entrust their child's early education to a professional— no matter how sensitive and intelligent that person may be. Day-care centers are available, but there the problem of paying an outsider to do their child-rearing is compounded by an environment that, however well managed, is in no sense a home.

In brief, Lynn and John do not want to be absentee parents—and yet both of them derive enormous personal satisfaction from their work.

This couple's problem is by no means an isolated one. Writ large, it exemplifies a growing challenge for a rapidly increasing number of American women and men: how to combine careers and families when both

spouses work. Time is of the essence—and for working couples, their time is particularly pressed. How can all of the things that people want for themselves—children, a happy marriage, a job—be fit into a twenty-four hour day?

The 1985 Virginia Slims American Women's Opinion Poll, conducted by the Roper Organization, has monitored and tracked Americans' opinions on social, familial, and personal issues since 1970. The fifth in a series of polls sponsored by Virginia Slims, this one is based on a representative nationwide sample of 3,000 adult women and 1,000 adult men. The results of this year's survey suggest that changing attitudes toward women's role in society, toward marriage, and toward the essential components of a full and satisfying personal life portend major social changes in the future. The traditional organization of family life, and the very nature of work itself, may never be the same.

Once A Bread Baker, Now A Bread Winner

If one word could sum up the vast progress made by women in the past fifteen years, it would be "choice." The freedom to choose a fulfilling individual lifestyle— and, simultaneously, tolerance of others' choices—has been the essential force underlying the social transformations of this period.

And a key element in this ongoing social evolution has been, and undoubtedly will continue to be, women's move into the workplace. Over the past fifteen years, the percentage of women employed full time has doubled; combined with part-time workers, this brings the total percentage of working women to more than half (52 percent) of the adult female population.

It is not simply out of economic necessity, moreover, that this fast-rising number of women choose to work. When asked whether they would continue to work even if financially secure, an identical proportion of employed women and employed men (66 percent) reply that they would. Perhaps more to the point, for the first time ever a majority of women (51 percent) would prefer to have a job rather than stay at home and take care of a family, if that were their only choice. In 1970, six out of ten women chose home over the workplace.

In the opinion of a growing majority of women, the most personally satisfying and interesting life is one that combines marriage, a career, and children (see table 1). Particularly among younger women and better-educated ones, this preference for a full professional *and* family life is pronounced (see table 2). This result leads to two conclusions. First, as younger women mature, they may be more likely to stay in the workforce even as they attempt to raise a family. Second, as more women enroll in colleges and universities, so too will they tend to seek the best of both these worlds. It appears that the desire for a "working marriage"—in which career, marriage, and a family all contribute to a woman's personal satisfaction—is bound to spread in the future.

Table 1

Question: Now let me ask you a somewhat different question. Considering the possibilities for combining or not combining marriage, children, and a career, and assuming you had a choice, which *one* of these possibilities do you think would offer *you* the most satisfying and interesting life? (Card shown respondent)

	Women 1974	Women 1985
Combining marriage, career, and children	52%	63%
Marrying, having children, but not having career	38	26
Having career and marrying, but not having children	4	4
Having career, but not marrying or having children	2	3
Marrying, but not having children or career	1	1
Don't know	3	2

Source: Surveys by the Roper Organization for Virginia Slims, latest that of March 1985.

This move of women into a traditionally male domain—the workplace—has enormous social consequences. In the first place, it is clearly linked to women's improving status in our society—and to women's increasing self-confidence as their own, ardent advocates. According to three-quarters of women and men, women's roles in society will continue to change, and larger majorities today (69 percent of women, 67 percent of

Table 2
PREFERENCES FOR MARRIAGE, CHILDREN, AND CAREER BY DEMOGRAPHIC GROUPS, 1985

	Combining marriage, career, and children	Marrying, having children, but not having career	Having career and marrying, but not having children	Having career, but not marrying or having children	Marrying, but not having children or career
All women	63%	26%	4%	3%	1%
White	63	26	5	3	1
Black	63	25	3	7	1
18-29 years	70	19	6	3	1
30-39 years	66	21	6	5	1
40-49 years	66	22	4	5	1
50 years and over	54	37	3	2	*
Non-high school graduate	53	37	3	4	1
High school graduate	63	28	3	3	*
College graduate	70	17	7	4	1

Note: * = less than .5%.
Source: Survey by the Roper Organization for Virginia Slims, March 1985.

men) than in 1980 think those roles *should* continue to change.

What is more, overwhelming majorities favor efforts to improve the status of women, and for the first time ever, more women than men support such efforts (see table 3). This is indeed a dramatic shift in opinion from fifteen years ago, when a slight plurality of women *opposed* efforts to improve their status. What accounts for such a massive swing? Back in 1970, many women were undoubtedly apprehensive about the implications of a change in their status. They were fearful of the unknown and were much more comfortable with the status quo. Men, not being the object of such efforts, either could afford to be more objective or were reluctant to appear too self-interested. Now, however, women have observed what has happened to many other women as a result of these efforts and have, apparently, decided that the result is good.

In step with women's changing roles, furthermore,

Table 3
EFFORTS TO STRENGTHEN WOMEN'S STATUS

Question: Do you favor or oppose most of the efforts to strengthen and change women's status in society today?

	Women Favor	Women Oppose	Men Favor	Men Oppose
1970	40%	42%	44%	39%
1972	48	36	49	36
1974	57	25	63	19
1980	64	24	64	23
1985	73	17	69	17

Source: Surveys by the Roper Organization for Virginia Slims, latest that of March 1985.

has come greater respect for women as individuals, which helps to explain why growing majorities favor efforts to improve women's status. Today, 60 percent of women and 61 percent of men believe that women are more respected now than they were ten years ago. This, too, represents quite a change from the attitudes of 1970, when only 38 percent of women and 40 percent of men thought that women were more respected compared to ten years previously. And, once again, the young and college-educated are among the most optimistic women.

Despite such growing respect for women, however, working women have encountered difficulties in the professional world. Sexual discrimination does persist, and the consensus of both women and men is that, all things considered, there are more advantages in being a man in today's world. Yet it is heartening that majorities of working women say they stand an equal chance with men in three vital areas concerning their jobs: salary, responsibility, and promotion possibilities. The major barrier that remains, according to a plurality of these women (45 percent), is being promoted to a top management position (see table 4).

Table 4
EQUAL OPPORTUNITY ON THE JOB, 1985

Question: Do you feel you stand an equal chance with the men you work with in the following areas?

	Working women say they have:			Men say working women have:		
	Equal chance	Not equal	Don't know	Equal chance	Not equal	Don't know
Salary	57%	33%	10%	48%	46%	6%
Responsibility	73	18	9	61	33	6
Promotion	53	35	12	45	49	7
Becoming an executive	38	45	17	37	54	9

Source: Survey by the Roper Organization for Virginia Slims, March 1985.

Nevertheless, women with actual work experience think that things are generally better now than they were five years ago. But men do not agree. Men are *less* inclined today than they were in 1980 to think that women have equal chances in the workplace. Thus, those who are allegedly discriminated against believe that the situation is improving; those who are supposed to be doing the discriminating think it is getting worse. What explains this fascinating contradiction?

It would seem that men's attitudes toward this problem have been influenced, at least to some extent, by the increasing amount of information on sexual discrimination in general. That is, men have become more aware that there is a problem, and this is influencing their opinions about possible unfairness in the workplace. Men are now more sensitive, and perhaps even more defensive, about equal professional opportunities, even though the attitudes of working women suggest that real progress is being made.

Of course, it would be premature to declare the battle for equal economic opportunity, for completely nondiscriminatory treatment at work, over. Certain issues, such as the complex and emotional one of comparable worth, are still on the public agenda. Yet, women *have* come far in seeking and obtaining meaningful jobs for themselves. They *are* moving into occupations once considered the sole preserves of men, as Sally Ride's space flight in 1983 and Geraldine Ferraro's vice presidential nomination in 1984 symbolize. There *is* a widespread feeling today that a talented and capable woman can succeed in whatever profession she chooses.

More and more, women's professional potential is obstructed not by discrimination *in* the workplace but rather by obligations *outside* it. Women may increasingly enjoy equal opportunities at work, but, compared to men, they have relatively little time to capitalize on those opportunities. The major challenges for the future—challenges created by women's very success in moving into the workplace over the past fifteen years—concern the organization of *domestic* life. The problem is to find a new balance between work and home for both women and men—and, further down the road, perhaps to alter the structure of work in order to have a fuller and more satisfying family life.

Marriages of Mutual Responsibility

Marriage these days is enjoying something of a comeback, despite all the attention typically paid to the divorce rate in this country. Although fewer men and women today are married and living with their spouses than in 1980—in part, it must be said, because the baby boom generation is still in its marrying years and tends to marry later—other signs indicate that attitudes about marriage may be changing.

Nine out of ten women and men say, for instance, that marriage is their preferred lifestyle. Substantially fewer people today than in 1970 believe that marriage as an institution is weaker now than ten years ago.

The fact is that marriage and the nuclear family have always been, and will long continue to be, the core of American society. True, large majorities say that people can be happy without being married. And they also think that a happy marriage does not require children. Yet, there has been virtually no increase since 1972 in the number of Americans who have or plan to have no children, and the extremely high proportion (90 percent) saying that marriage is their preferred lifestyle has remained remarkably constant. Instead, these attitudes toward the role of marriage and children in personal happiness demonstrate Americans' growing tolerance of alternative lifestyles—of those minorities who choose to remain single or childless.

Yet by far the most significant change in Americans' views of marriage concerns the *kind* of marriage that people want. Today, majorities of men and women desire a marriage of shared responsibility—one in which both spouses work and divide housekeeping and child-rearing equally. Merely a decade ago, a majority of women and a plurality of men opted for a traditional marriage, in which he was the financial provider and she ran the house and took care of the children (see table 5).

Once again, enthusiasm for this new type of marriage is most pronounced among younger women and men, which suggests that it will increasingly become the norm. But more indicative of the challenges ahead, and the problems obstructing such shared-responsibility marriages, is that women have more eagerly embraced this concept than men.

The main reason for this divergence in attitudes of women and men is that, while women have moved quickly into the "male" domain of the workplace, men have been much slower to help out with "female" tasks in the home. For instance, 30 percent of married women who are employed full time assert they do nearly all of the household chores, and another 44 percent claim they do a lot but their husbands help out some. Merely 24 percent say these tasks are evenly divided between the spouses. Men with working wives tend to be more charitable toward themselves—28 percent claim that the chores are evenly divided—but even so, the imbalance is evident.

Another factor that helps to explain men's relative reluctance about the shared-responsibility marriage is that they, much more than women, derive a greater sense of their personal identity from their work. For many men, their careers are the key element defining their place in society and even their concept of self-worth. Women, however, have long relied on other sources—particularly, perhaps, their children—to establish their sense of identity, precisely because customarily they have spent so much time with kids in the home. One indication of this major difference between the sexes can be found in attitudes toward work. A majority of employed men (56 percent) consider their work

to be a career, while a majority of employed women (58 percent) say their work is "just a job."

Yet what exactly do these figures mean? Is work just a stopgap measure or a kind of pastime for many women? This is hardly the appropriate conclusion, given that a majority of women consider work to be an essential ingredient of a full and satisfying life, that two-thirds of employed women would continue to work even if financially secure, that more employed women than employed men derive a great deal of personal satisfaction from their work, and that a majority of *all* women would choose a job instead of staying home. Instead, the proper conclusion would appear to be that women place a different *degree* of importance on their work—that, in the grand scheme of life, work may be somewhat less important than it is to many men.

Working Toward A More Balanced Future

It may sound rather radical to suggest that the very nature of work may change as a result of these evolving attitudes, but that may be the case—someday. If so, what will be most obviously affected?

First, a larger number of employed women will probably consider their work to be a career rather than "just a job." Already the opinions of college-educated women on this issue are identical to the beliefs of college-educated men: more than six in ten say they are pursuing a career, not working a job. The very meaning of a career, however, could well be transformed. Career paths in most professions were established when men overwhelmingly dominated them. That is no longer the case. Some better mechanism will have to be found to accommodate these career-minded women—and their aspirations for a happy family life as well.

Second, working couples will face more difficult decisions about whose career should take priority. Right now, large majorities of women and men think a wom-

Table 5

Question: In today's society, there are different lifestyles, and some that are acceptable today that weren't in the past. Regardless of what you may have done or plan to do with your life, and thinking just of what would give *you personally* the most satisfying and interesting life, which one of these different ways of life do you think would be the best as a way of life? (Card shown respondent)

	1974		1985					
	Total women	Total men	Total women	18-29 years	30-39 years	40-49 years	50 years and over	Total men
Marriage where husband and wife share responsibilities more—both work, share housekeeping and child responsibilities	46%	44%	57%	69%	65%	58%	42%	50%
Traditional marriage with husband assuming responsibility for providing for family and wife running house and taking care of children	50	48	37	24	30	34	52	43
Living with someone of opposite sex, but not marrying	3	3	2	3	1	2	1	3
Remaining single and living alone	1	1	2	1	1	4	2	3
Remaining single and living with others of the same sex	—	—	—	—	—	—	—	1
Living in large family of people with similar interests in which some are married and some are not	1	1	1	1	1	—	1	1

Source: Surveys by the Roper Organization for Virginia Slims, latest that of March 1985.

an should quit her job if her husband is offered a very good one elsewhere; at the same time, majorities also believe that a wife should turn down a very good job offer in another city so that her husband can continue his present career. In part this can be explained by the probability that the man has a higher salary and hence is the main source of income for the family. It may simply reflect the public's acceptance of economic reality. But as the earnings of both spouses draw closer together, issues concerning career advancement will become more complex—and Americans' attitudes toward them more ambivalent.

There may also be greater pressure from such two-income families for employers to allow more flexibility in work schedules. Staggering the hours that the parents are at work or shortening the work week could help alleviate some of the problems associated with day care. Or shared jobs, half-time jobs, and other forms of part-time work may take on even greater significance in the future, allowing at least one parent to spend more time with the family.

In the same vein, the provision of day-care services by employers—and perhaps better policies on maternity and paternity leave—may eventually come to be seen as more valuable employee benefits. Employers who provide these kinds of options will be better placed to attract talented individuals from two-income households.

These general attitudes also indicate that the trend toward smaller families is firmly established and will, in all likelihood, continue. It is one thing to hold down a job while attempting to care for two children, quite another if the parents have to look after five.

And even the nature of relationships between women and men undergo some fundamental changes. Hackneyed as the cliché may be, there is power in the purse —psychological as well as economic. Among other things, men's habit of paying for things may fade, in part out of deference to the more independent status of women and in part, perhaps, out of necessity. Plus, they will undoubtedly have to help out a lot more around the home, or the couple will have to learn to tolerate a less clean, orderly environment. But offsetting this, men may get to know their children a little bit better, because they spend more time with them. In fact, children who are raised more equally by both parents may well turn out to be different in many respects from previous generations.

These are just some of the adjustments, it seems, that Americans will be making in coming years. In many respects, this will be a period of consolidation, of sorting out how best to cope with the changing responsibilities of women and men. As Walt Whitman once wrote to Ralph Waldo Emerson: "Women in these States approach the day of that organic equality with men, without which, I see, men cannot have organic equality among themselves." The poet was simply a century and a half before his time.   ∇

THE INTERNATIONAL PATRIARCHY

The International Patriarchy—a true secret society—has existed in every country on earth, and continues to work behind the scenes of this "earthly drama" to insure that events go "according to the script" that was written before the beginning of time by the father of all men (God, The Sky Father).

Every man—though he may not know it—becomes a member of the International Patriarchy the very moment he is born of a female.

The female is the door that every Patriarchal Warrior goes through to reach the "Arena of Life;" a place that—contrary to the beliefs of the ignorant—the souls of men intentionally go, because we have been sent to this earth by the Sky Father(God).

Before the universe was created—before time began, the Sky Father & The Goddess existed & engaged in their "Dramatic Lovemaking." The Taoist's Yang/Yin symbol is an excellent representation of their interactions.

Enlightened men have come to see that the so'called "War between the sexes" is, at times, an earthly reflection of the "Dramatic lovemaking" that has always occurred between the Sky Father & the Goddess of Love.

Men who have experienced sex with a variety of females know that the differing character traits of the females is reflected in their lovemaking. Experienced men also know that these differences in character can result in quite a struggle in bed.

As further evidence of this I offer the example of any superior X-rated video: Go watch one, and as the lovers engage in intercourse, holding onto each other, moving about on the bed, a struggle (at least good, passionate sex) does occur. Many of the ancient philosophers have said that much of what occurs between men & females is but a reflection of "that which occurs in heaven."

MATHEMATICAL MYSTICISM

Every soul that has ever passed through a door to the earth (a female) and taken up temporary possession of a physical body is, in fact, an incarnation of the Sky father or the Goddess.

Patriarchal Mathematicians came to know that mathematical mysticism (sometimes called numerology or the science of numbers) is the key that unlocks the mysteries of this phenomenom.

These Patriarchal Mathematicians discovered that by using mathematics a man could be "Enlightened" to a point where his ignorance & illusions are stripped away, and, once again, the man realizes he is, in all truth, an incarnation of the Sky Father.

In reality there are only two kinds of men: the ones who are still experiencing defeat & suffering because of their ignorance & illusions, and the mathematicians, who upon using mathematical mysticism to strip away their ignorance & illusions, gained a vehicle to "True Enlightenment & Power."

Yes the common, ignorant man does find it hard to believe that he is an actor & gladiator in a "Dramatic Competition" he wrote for himself before the beginning of time. But this is all true.

The earth is an arena, and a stage. Men & females are the competitors & actors. Life on this earth—as all men eventually learn—is neither fair nor is it without inequality. But thats the way it is in an arena. Power is the only thing that counts.

The Sky Father designated the rules of this "Dramatic Competition" (war between the sexes) before time began; then everything was set into motion (the big bang, evolution). The rules are: (1) As incarnations of the Sky Father, men would express traits of character that are representative of him. These traits can be fully understood when you master mathematical mysticism. (2)All men should become mathematicians & warriors (martial artists & survivalists) (3) Power would be the deciding factor in every encounter between men & females and between men (4) The phenomena of reincarnation would be interwoven with the law of karma, and applied to men & females alike.

BE SURE OF THIS

Most of the beliefs concerning the phenomena of reincarnation & the law of karma, upon close examination, are revealed to be the creations of overly fertile imaginations. I only bring up the subjects of reincarnation & karma because many years of studying mathematical mysticism (numerology) has convinced me (with evidence) of their existence in reality.

Stripped of all trappings, karma manifests itself in the life of a common man as obstacles to "True Enlightenment & Power." There are two karmic barriers: Ignorance & Illusion. As far as reincarnation is concerned, every man will continue to return to this earth & serve in the Army of the Sky Father (the true Patriarchy) until the race of men are no more. The common man is blinded by the two karmic barriers (Ignorance & Illusion), therefore he yearns for release from the cycle of birth, life, death & rebirth; for in it he sees only the prospect for more defeats & suffering.

The "Truly Enlightened & Powerful" man, however, has broken through the two karmic barriers and gained the realization that he is an incarnation of the Sky Father. He knows about the "War between the sexes (The Dramatic Competition)" and his part in it. The "Truly Enlightened & Powerful" man is in no hurry to leave this earth. Quite the contrary; he endeavors to spread the "Light of the Sky Father (mystical mathematics)" to as many men as his time on earth allows. He desires to return to this earthly arena again & again to compete with the females. The "Truly Enlightened & Powerful" man is the ultimate warrior. He knows that his opponent is the female (incarnations of the goddess). He knows that men only fight each other because some of them the feminist sympathizer) are unaware of the Sky Father, the goddess & their own role in the Dramatic Competition (the war between the sexes).

Karma, Reincarnation. Do not fear it; understand it. Understand, also, that you are a member of the International Patriarchy. On its pages are words which are written with the blood of countless millions, many of whom were slain in the battles to gain or retain power to rule over this earth. I shall not lie to you: it is the will of the Sky Father that the earth should always be engulfed in struggles for the power (war & its result) to control females. The females have always been the spoils of war; they have always been the focus of our warriors' attention. It has never mattered to the Sky Father which group of patriarchal men won a war, for the females have always gone to the victor. They are the prize of all wars between men.

The Sky Father would never condemn men to return again & again to fight & die in such a world as ours, while standing apart from the battle as if he were a spectator at a sporting event. The Sky Father (who is the spirit that dwells within each man) is in the arena. He is every man. He is the ultimate warrior.

STATUS REPORT ON THE INTERNATIONALPATRIARCHY

North America: Since the turn of the century the feminists have taken advantage of the ignorance & illusion of American men to launch an unprecedented assault on Patriarchal rule. The North American feminists are the largest and most militant group of females on the earth. By riding the coattails of the black civil rights movement they have been able to: (1) Trick the Democratic Party into putting a radical feminist on their 1984 presidential ticket (2) Persuade all three television networks & most of the nations print media to adopt a pro-feminist bias—thus becoming blatant feminist propaganda organs & tools for social experimentation (3)Persuade american business that it is profitable to adopt a pro-feminist "attitude" in advertising products, sponsoring television & radio programs, hiring employess and in management (4) Get away with encouraging young men to become "more feminine" (5) get away with blatantly promoting marxism in this free country (comparable worth) (6) Persuade the nations courts, city councils, state legislatures & congress to pass laws that allow gold-diggers to extort palimony, alimony, property-division, paternity, childsupport & lawers fees from american men.

Upon reading this status report I am sure that you are alarmed. You should be! An I don't give a damn because it only happens to the other guy kind of attitude, on the part of millions of american men, has put the North American Patriarchy at risk of being overthrown by radical feminists & their traitorous supporters (pop psychologists & psychiatrists, talk show hosts and the major news media).

MEN'S RIGHTS

There is a growing network of Men's Rights organizations in North America—but be on your guard:

Many of these groups claim to be working for the interests of men, when in fact they are "fronts" for feminists, feminist-sympathizers & homosexuals. A giveaway sign is their insistance on being "anti-sexist" & pro-equality. Freedom-loving, patriarchal men should wear the labels of sexist & male chauvinist like badges of honor. We (men) have been sent to this earth to compete with, control & enjoy females by the Sky Father (God). I have nothing to be ashamed of or apologize for—and neither does any member of the True Patriarchy.

I recomend that (1) Every freedom-loving man who wants the International Patriarchy to continue its rule should start Men's Rights groups that are openly patriarchal. All you have to do is get a mail service, pass out flyers, keep a mailing list & meet somewhere to discuss men's rights issues & decide on a course of action (2) Make sure that the intent of these groups is to lobby the courts, city councils, state legislatures & congress to protect the rights of men in the areas of employment (anti-comparable worth & e.r.a.) palimony, divorce & paternity (3) Every freedom-loving man should contact all of his male friends & relatives and enlist them in the fight against the radical feminists & religeous fanatics who are trying to outlaw explicity sexual material (non-violent too), while promoting their marxist philosophy. Europe: Radical feminists are just as bad throughout this continent.

The rest of the world: Under control, but a growing communist (& pro-fem) insurgency is a major threat to patriarchal institutions.

FEMINISM & MARXISM

Men should go to a feminist bookstore & read a representative number of their publications. You will discover that many feminist writers have openly embraced marxism, and have an anti-capitalist, anti-patriarchy attitude.

If the call went out from moscow or peking asking these feminists to come & live in russia or china I doubt if there would be any takers. No, these homegrown marxists are content with subverting our free nation with schemes like comparable worth. They are allowed to work their folly from within labor unions and from city halls to congress, but very few men have caught on and opposed them. It is time for our apathy to end. It is time for freedom-loving men everywhere to stand up and denounce the feminists for advocating marxism—before their cancerous ideology prevails.

FEMINISTS & SPERM BANKS

It has come to my attention that SPERM BANKS are making it possible for females to have babies without participating in sexual intercourse with men. Patriarchal men should view this with a wary eye because radical, man-hating lesbians are using this technology. Man-hating lesbians should not be allowed to use the sperm of free men to breed more man-hating lesbians.

Therefore, I urge you to lobby the government for laws that restrict the use of sperm banks to couples that are legally bound with a written contract. Also, men should always be a partner to this contract.

FEMINISTS & LESBIANISM

Radical feminists have always made a big show of saying they want to have control over their bodies. This is especially true when it comes to defending their desire to man-hating lesbians.

Let's be honest. Lesbians are the "amazons" of the feminist movement. They hate men. Their ultimate goal is the "replacement" of men & our penises with sperm banks & turkey basters. As this book is being written a lesbian is impregnating another man-hating lesbian with sperm drawn from a feminist-run sperm bank. You are being replaced!!! Lesbians are taking your blue-collar jobs—they are seducing your females; and you are too busy trying to be "Mr. Right" to notice.

WAKE UP!!!

RADICAL FEMINISTS & THE MYTH OF THE MAN SHORTAGE (THE LIE OF THE EIGHTIES)

Since the late seventies the feminist-controlled media has featured feminist-written articles that claim there is a man shortage in America. Any single man, between the ages of twenty-three & forty, knows that this is a blatant feminist lie. But let's face it; the North American Patriarchy has neglected to maintain its traditions or teach its history, and this has lead to a state of weakness & a lack of direction among our brothers.

Our mistakes have emboldened the feminists & their traitorous supporters, and now they openly attack us without fear. It is our fault (The North American Patriarchy) that females can turn their feminist noses up at men and say we aren't "good enough" for them; It is our fault that we have allowed feminists to drive a wedge between us with their "Mr. Right" expectations. The attempts, by some men, to outdo each other in jumping though hoops like trained circus animals (conforming to Mr. Right stereotypes) has caused the feminists to believe they have the power to dictate to men concerning any matter. There are foolish men in every age; men who are ignorant of the history & traditions of the True Patriarchy. These foolish men have always fallen into lockstep whenever the females have realized that there are men who they could manipulate. Men should wake up & realize that feminists aren't in a position to dictate to men— we hold all the cards in this game. The True Patriarchy is worldwide; and as such american men have to power to BYPASS every feminist for the females of a hundred countries or more!!

American feminists cannot tell any man to "measure up" to some illusionary standard they have concocted in their fertile minds. American feminists cannot threaten to withhold sexual pleasure & companionship from men who refuse to conform to their "Mr Right" illusions.

We (American males) are free men; And as free men I say we must begin a GREAT EXODUS from the clutches of the american feminist. WE must BYPASS every feminist for foreign, non-feminist females, because the day has come for the men of the North American Patriarchy to show these radical feminists that feminism is powerless in the midst of the Sky Father's sons.

An EXODUS OF MEN would shrink the pool of fools to such a point that the feminists will be brought to their knees

SCHEMING GOLDIGGERS

You only have to monitor the media on a weekly basis to encounter reports on men who are being ripped-off by that most effective "Guerilla" of the feminist movement: THE GOLDIGGER!!!

The goldigger is the feminist who takes special care to be on time at her aerobic workout, because she knows her body is a weapon that must be kept in top condition, or else she'll lose her power to attract foolish men & rip them off.

The goldigger is the feminist who always manages to have a low-profile relationship with a celebrity or rich business-man—and then receives twenty million dollars, four con-dos, stock in a couple of corporations & five Rolls Royces as her part in a bitter divorce settlement. When the story of the settlement hits the new outlets the public finds out that this feminist received all this wealth—that she didn't work for—because this celebrity or rich businessman got caught deceiving himself about "being in love" and was trying to play "Mr. Right" to such a point he lost touch with the reality of life on this earth (which is the war between the sexes) and allowed a scheming golddigger to get rich by simply laying on her back & spreading her legs and giving dinner parties.

Most of the men on this earth aren't celebrities, but most of the females are golddiggers (the truth hurts). I have been told by countless men that golddiggers only rip-off "the other guy." Don't you fall for such lies! Shame keeps foolish men from admitting that they have allowed feminists to gain such power in America that all a golddigger has to do to become financially independent is to rip-off a "Mark." Gold-diggers are allowed by the government & courts to gain ill-gotten wealth & power while prostitutes are harassed for doing the same thing.

HYPOCRACY LIVES IN AMERICA!!!

THE FEMINIST—SYMPATHIZER (TRAITOR)

There are men, who for their own reasons have decided to betray the International Patriarchy. No doubt they have swallowed the feminist's propaganda concerning war, hunger, wife beating etc. and blame men for all of it.

Whatever their reasoning, it is their intent to engage in social experimentation on men (emasculation) in an attempt to help the feminist-takeover movement. This "Social Experimentation" takes the form of constant barrages of anti-male, anti-macho propaganda & the promotion of homosexuality & "being more feminine."

The feminist-sympathizers are the pop psychologists & psychiatrists who are always on the talk show circuit promoting books on how to be more "feminine;" They are the talk show hosts who are able to pass themselves off "as the authority" on what is & isn't masculine or macho; they are the editors & writers of the major news media, people who should know better than to become blatant propaganda organs for the feminist movement.

It is high time that freedom-loving men (The North American Patriarchy) realized the feminists & their traitorous supporters have gotten control of much of what passes for an information apparatus in this country. A man can't read a magazine or newspaper without getting hit in the face by a pro-feminist, anti-male article; nor can a man watch a week of television without encountering a program that has feminists beating up men in a toe-to-toe fight (is that realistic?).

I believe that millions of men are as fed-up with this feminist barrage as I am. But the feminists & their traitorous supporters will continue to crank out their anti-male propaganda & programs until millions of fed-up men get organized, become activists & pull the plug on them!!!

THE "MR. RIGHT" TYPE

He wears three-piece suits five days a week, drives a B.M.W., has at least one hundred thousand dollars in his checking account alone & owns own condo. The feminist-goldigger calls him "Mr. Right."

Every man likes to have money & live the good life, but this fellow is being used by the feminists to divide & conquer the International Patriarchy. The feminists deliber-

185

ately play up to the wealthy & handsome man in an attempt to sow envy (and the resulting disunity) among his less wealthy & handsome brothers. Feminists have no power to declare which man is "right" or "wrong;" that is a matter to be decided by the True Patriarchy. It is utter folly, indeed, for men to shut their eyes & not see what the feminists are doing. All the wealth, good looks—all the success that free men enjoy is a result of power given to the International Patriarchy by the Sky Father (God). Our wealth & power should be used to win the war between the sexes—not wasted in illusionary attempts to impress feminists, who can never be deterred from seeking their goal of a worldwide matriarchy.

BEING IN LOVE

Countless civilizations reached great heights of living and then fell because their men became soft & complacent, forgot their Patriarchal history & traditions and allowed goddess worshippers (feminist-lesbians) to spread subversion on such a scale, that Patriarchal warriors bordering them were forced to "Step In" and restore a true Patriarchy.

There are men in every age who insist on ignoring Patriarchal history & the will of THE SKY FATHER by marrying a female (daughter of the earth goddess).

It is foolish indeed to use "Being in love" as an excuse to ignore your sacred obligations to THE SKY FATHER.

Open your eyes, and you will see that a majority of american men would give their souls to a female just to continue experiencing the emotional & sexual "High" that "Being in Your physical, emotional & financial stability is shattered; and "invokes.

The men who are "In love" wil compromise with a female. They will passively knuckle-under & conform to a female's sexual bargaining tactics, obsolete courtship rituals & marriage traps for companionship & sexual pleasure.

THESE MEN ARE FOOLS. Females use a facade of beauty & weakness to get men to drop their guard & roll over. And wham!! A fool & his money are soon parted (palimony, alimony, paternity, property-division & child support payments). Your physical, emotional & financial stability is shattered;

and the cause of the earth goddess is advanced.

A "Truly Enlightened" man can "fall in love" with a beautiful female and enjoy all the feelings her beauty invokes in him. But he doesn't let a female's beauty blind him to his mission on earth (which is to acquire, control & enjoy the labor & sexuality of females), nor does he allow any female to control him or knock him from the path of warrors (The True Patriarchy).

The man who has found "True Enlightenment" is like a great matador, who experiences the excitement that occurs from getting close to the horns of a charging bull—WITHOUT GETTING careless—and gored!!!

He knows how to enjoy "Being in love" with a female—without being controlled or destroyed by her sexual powers, because he is "Truly Enlightened," and uses knowledge to gain control over his mind, spirit & life.

A man's struggle with the feminists-lesbians over sex & companionship are two of the hardest battles he will fight in the war between the sexes.

The feminists-lesbians "demand" that men believe in male-female equality, that men help with housework and with children, and than men passively submit to the feminists-lesbian takeoverattempt.

"Wimps" who toe the feminists-lesbian line are "Rewarded" (like a trained pet is rewarded with a treat when it obeys its "Master") with companionship, small talk, hand holding, cuddling & pseudo-sex (because FEMINISTS like cuddling & talk—not sexual intercourse).

Non-conformists are shunned by feminists, and subjected to FORCED celibacy and criminal—civil persecution.

This "Carrot & Stick" strategy has been used very effectively by feminists-lesbians to "persuade" men to knuckle-under & conform to their sexual extortion tactics & obsolete courtship rituals.

The man who has attained "True Enlightenment" doesn't knuckle-under & conform to a feminist's sexual bargaining tactics because he "Knows" she wouldn't love him even if he did so. A Truly Enlightened" man is SELF-EMPLOYED. He lives INTERNATIONALLY. He knows that he can pick & choose from the non-feminist & sexually-active females of more than one hundred foreign countries.

American feminists-lesbians aren't in a position to dictate to men. We still hold the best cards on this planet. We (men) don't need american feminists to survive or to live free—they need us. All we need to do is BYPASS AMERICAN FEMINISTS FOR FOREIGN (NON-FEMINIST & SEXUALLY ACTIVE) FEMALES. ALWAYS REMEMBER THAT THE SKY FATHER is all-powerful. He "Plays" the earth (goddess) like a great acoustical guitarist plays his guitar. Whatever his sons give to females (like the vote) they can always take away.

THE "ROOT CAUSE" OF WAR & CRIME

Let's face it. Men control the armed forces of every country on this earth. And while there have been times in history when men were stupid enough to allow females to become queens, prime ministers & presidents of nations, the soldiers, for the most part, have been men. Feminists can talk about ruling the earth; men do. When men march, governments fall. Feminists think they can persuade foolish men to "hand them power" through the use of propaganda, picketing & other psychological tricks. They need to be reminded that America was created through force of arms—a guerilla war. George Washington & other "Founding Fathers" would have found it hard to stomach had a group of feminists offered to go to England & picket the king into granting independence to the American colonies.

The feminists claim to be the greatest advocates of peace-on-earth. Curiously, they always overlook the fact that peace, as we know it, depends on the maintenance of strong armed forces. That's a fact of life in this earthly arena.

Life on earth has always been marked by battles for power. Men battle for power because power is the key to winning battles during the war between the sexes (The Dramatic Competition). Look throughout every society on earth & you will see that feminists will disrespect & ignore a poor & powerless man. Then notice how feminists treat rich & powerful men. A feminist wouldn't dare disrespect a powerful gangster by trying to extort outrageous palimony, alimony, paternity, property-division & child support payments. But the common man or vulnerable celebrity & businessman is considered fair game. Let the truth be known: POWER GETS YOU RESPECT FROM FEMINISTS!!!

Do not claim to be ignorant when you see crime & war reported by the media; it is caused by a battle for power. The prisons & graveyards are full of men who got tired of being powerless, & then were ignored & disrespected by feminists because of it. Crime is rampant because feminists have participated in the Dramatic Competition by telling men they must be rich & powerful—before they are allowed to enjoy their companionship & intimate sexual favors.

This feminist requirement (The Mr. Right rule) has been in effect since the days of the cave man, and it is still in effect today—despite attempts by pop psychologists & psychiatrists to deceive men into believing otherwise.

Men around the world have obeyed this feminist requirement to the letter. They have worked themselves to death, hustled, schemed, lied, cheated, robbed & killed to get the money & power that feminists respect & respond to.

If the feminists want peace-on-earth, tell them that every feminist must drop the requirement that only rich & powerful men will be allowed to enjoy their companionship & intimate sexual favors. The day the poorest & most powerless man can enjoy the companionship & intimate sexual favors of any feminist will be the day all wars stop and the crime rate makes a phenomenal drop. But don't hold your breath while waiting for the feminists to do this!!!

THE "ROOT CAUSE" OF HOMOSEXUALITY & TRANSSEXUALITY

The "TRULY ENLIGHTENED" man knows that transsexuals, homosexuals, starving people, molested children, abused children, rape victims, criminals, enslaved people, street people, war victims, de-formed & crippled people, insane people, incest victims, drug addicts & alcoholics, battered females, broken love relationships & broken families are casualties (victims) of the war between the sexes (The Dramatic Competition).

Open your eyes, and you can see the "Mark" of the goddess & her followers on the soul & body of the transsexual & homosexual.

The transsexual is overcome by a mad desire to be a female (daughter of the goddess), so he castrates himself and fills his body with silicone & female hormones. He can never be a true "Daughter of the (earth) goddess." He can never give birth, menstruate, nurse an infant or experience a "True" female orgasm like a true female. It is all an ILLUSION. These facts apply equally to the "feminine" male homosexual & "masculine" male homosexual.

Transsexuals. Homosexuals. Both have had their souls warped (Turned inside-out, reversed) by the trauma of the war between the sexes. The variations in homosexualty are a reflection of the variations in the severity of trauma the man may experience while in the ARENA OF LIFE (earth).

The traumatized soul will experience the TRAUMA of earthly life until the "Root Cause" of his soul's trauma is recognized, understood & accepted. Only then can a resolution take place within the soul of such a man.

The root cause is the WAR BETWEEN THE SEXES The Dramatic Competition). The two karmic barriers (Ignorance & Illusion) stands between the transsexual & homosexual, and the awareness of what "He" really is: A SON (WARRIOR) OF THE SKY FATHER.

Ignorance & Illusion turns the transsexual & homosexual against the True Patriarchy. The homosexual goes against the will of THE SKY FATHER by engaging in abominations with other homosexuals. The transsexual's soul is lost. Both have become captives of the earth goddess.

We (men) come from the sky for this "Dramatic Competition—and for this Dramatic Competition alone." We are here to compete for, control & enjoy the labor & sexuality of females (daughters of the earth goddess).

During the battles some of us will fall victim to the goddess & her supporters. But there is a key that can free a man's soul & body from the grip of the goddess:

KNOWLEDGE (POWER)
THE SHIELD OF KNOWLEDGE (POWER)

Knowledge can act as a shield to protect a man in battles against the females. The "Truly Enlightened" man uses knowledge as a shield, while the common man participates in the war between the sexes totally naked.

190

The worst mistake a man can make is to live & die countless times (the phenomena of reincarnation) because he
didn't realize—and take advantage of this fact.

Men go through countless lifetimes confused, wondering
why things don't work out in relationships with women,
with their fellow man, or in their careers. These men never
openly acknowledge to themselves that they were born into
an earthly war zone, or that they will live & die because of
the Dramatic Competition of the gods.

Therefore knowledge is power for a man; and Ignorance &
Illusion his deadly enemies.

Knowledge is the key to power; and power decides the
winner in each encounter between the forces of THE SKY
FATHER, and the followers of the goddess.

The feminists-lesbians and their traitorous supporters
(pop psychologists & feminist sympathizers) always cry
about equality, but what they really want is a feminist
take-over.

The feminists-lesbians know that the "Bottom Line" on
earth is power. Those who have enough of it will survive, live
good and rule over the people who are ignorant and without
power.

Throughout the earth, in capitalist & socialist-communist
countries alike a man needs power to survive, to live well, to
be free, and to acquire, control & enjoy the labor & sexuality
of females.

Power is a tool of the gods. And the gods have decreed that
power & sexual conquest are the "PRIZES" a man receives
for winning battles in the war between the sexes (The Dramatic Competition).

The feminists-lesbians know they can't seize power directly (through military force), so they use sexual bargaining
tactics, psychological tricks & propaganda to fool men into
"Handing" them power.

The feminists-lesbians, pop psychologists, feminist-sympathizers (traitors) and the news media have a "Hidden
Agenda" planned just for you (men).

They want females to become "Like men (more aggressive, learning martial arts, pumping iron)" and they want
men to become "like females, (househusbands, babysitters,

191

crybabies, talkers, submissive to females, wimps)."

This attempt to emasculate men & "Create" a "New Male (submissive wimp)" is the big step before the feminists-lesbians go forward with their plan to bring the goddess out of the feminists-lesbian bookstores & centers into full view of everyone on the planet as a symbol of their takeover.

The evidence that supports this charge can be found in any feminists-lesbian bookstore. Go to one and you will find a section set aside for feminists-lesbian spirituality (goddess worship).

Investigate any "New Age" or pagan publication and you will find information concerning the goddess. Look closely at the inscriptions on monuments, libraries, government buildings & military decorations (medals) and you will find the goddess—lurking in the shadows of the world's civilizations, waiting for the Patriarchy to crumble.

I SAY TO ALL MEN:

Take up the shield of knowledge (power) and save the International Patriarchy!!! Take up the shield of knowledge (power), and realize that the ignorant will always be the victims & slaves of the powerful. Take up the shield of knowledge (power), and become a high-ranking officer in the army of THE SKY FATHER & The True Patriarchy.

Officers, enlisted men & conscripts will die in battle, but in the military high ranking officers assume the role of chess player, while lower-ranking soldiers assume the role of a chess piece. High-ranking officers send low-ranking soldiers to their deaths. They initiate coups that topple governments. Low-ranking soldiers obey without question.

Officers know why they risk the lives of men as well as their own, but in every war there are thousands of men who are maimed and killed without ever fully knowing the reason for their sacrifice.

You can become a high-ranking officer during this war between the sexes instead of being a low-ranking soldier who dies or is maimed because Ignorance & Illusion bars him from "True Enlightenment."

Become a leader (a high-ranking officer of) forces that oppose a feminists-lesbian takeover of the United States & the world (The True Patriarchy)!!!

FATHERS, SONS & BROTHERS

Fathers, sons & brothers share a relationship that was designated by the Sky Father (God) at the beginning of time, We are the True Patriarchy.

The Sky Father decided that each man should experience at least one aspect of the True Patriarchy, but this rule was never intended as a prison from which a man should seek escape. But as time has passed and the memory of the traditions & history of the International Patriarchy has faded, sons have become millstones around the necks of fathers, and brothers have become the keepers of brothers.

All of this is a result of war between the sexes (The Dramatic Competition). Men who are "Truly Enlightened & Powerful" feel no strain in being a father because "True Enlightenment" leads to the power to gain control over their lives. It is the common man who provides the media with tales of broken relationships with feminists, feminist-beating, child abuse & molestations and welfare dependency.

This earth is a war zone; a meat grinder that chops men up like hamburger. It does no good to be your brothers' keeper—what men need is the knowledge & power that gives them control over their lives (Mystical Mathematics).

THE PATH OF WARRIORS

It does not matter that men reject the path of warriors at first. We all dislike violence & death. John Wayne movies aside, most men know there won't be any director around to yell "cut" when a real fight takes place.

War is hell. Just ask a real combat veteran. But men have always known that if they do not prepare to defend themselves from attack—and you know we will all face attack in one form or another during our lifetime—the enemy will surely prevail & freedom's light will be extinguished. Self-defence training can save your life.

There are many styles & systems to choose from, but if a martial art isn't simple, direct & effective don't waste your time, money & effort.

The Sky Father meant for his sons to be strong, because to rule you must be strong. The Sky Father is the ultimate warrior. The warrior tradition is his tradition.

DON JUAN, THE LOVER OF FEMALES

Feminists & pop psychologists love to put him down as a "Latent Homosexual" or as a man with an insecurity complex.

But freedom-loving men have always known that this is the ultimate in lies. When Freud first revealed his theories he was ridiculed & attacked from every corner of the "scientific" community. Then his theories came to be accepted as "the gospel

, according to Sigmund Freud." Today, the scientific community is again divided on Freud's theories. The question has to be asked: Is Freud (and other pop psychiatrists & psychiatrists) to be believed?

On the question of latent homosexuality, I think not. the truth is the "Don Juan" has upset the plans of pop psychologists & radical feminists. The feminists & pop psychologists claim he shows a lack of "maturity," because the don juan refuses to "settle down" with one radical feminist in boring matrimony (legalized slavery).

As a freedom-loving man Don Juan believes that feminists, pop psychologists, politicians & religious fanatics have no business planning his life from cradle to grave. He believes that each man should decide on the path he must travel on the earth.

This attitude, of course, leave the self-appointed authorities on maturity in a strange position: without fools willing to passively conform to marriage to feminists, where will the babies (the future consumers, students, workers & soldiers) come from?

They must come up with some scheme (or schemes) which will convince certain well-meaning, but misguided men (feminist-sympathizers) that they should help "force" the Don Juan into conforming, because it's for "his own good." And if "civil-force" (ridicule, anti-porn laws) doesn't work, the use of prison or psychiatric confinement is brought about (like in the Soviet Union).

The man who refuse to have a relationship with a feminist is marked as a threatening nonconformist by the pop psychologists & feminists.

SO BE IT

THE SEVEN (7) RIGHTS OF FREE MEN

The advocates of Men's Rights (The North American Patriarchy) believes each free man has:

(1) The right to make a living that is free from marxist schemes like comparable worth.

(2) The right to express "his own style" of "macho."

(3) the right to have a relationship with females that is free of feminist sexual bargaining tactics (goldigging), obsolete courtship rituals & marriage traps (legalized slavery).

(4) The right to have a relationship with females that is free of palimony, alimony, paternity, property-division, child support & child custody court battles and the resulting lawyers fees.

(5) The right to enjoy the kind of sexual relationship that "he wants" with females.

(6) The right to establish & maintain legal brothels & harems throughout America!!!

(7) The right to follow the example of america's Founding Fathers in securing these rights.

RENOGOTIATING YOUR (UNWRITTEN SEX-RELATIONSHIP CONTRACT WITH FEMALES

American men should follow the example of professional athletes and become free agents!!!

Free agents can negotiate a relationship agreement with the females of one hundred (or more) countries. They can BYPASS AMERICAN FEMINISTS & their sexual bargaining tactics, obsolete courtship rituals, palimony, alimony, property-division, paternity, child support & child custody court battles and the resulting lawyers fees.

With the power of free agency firmly in hand, american men can inform every feminist that MARRIAGE TO FEMINISTS HAS BEEN ABOLISHED BY MEN!!! Then you can inform the feminists that the only females American men will have a relationship with is the CONTRACT GIRLFRIEND.

Feminists may say they don't need men because they are lesbians, or because they can always find another fool, but as the EXODUS of freedom-loving men from marriage to feminists gains momentum, the " pool of fools" will shrink to such a point that feminism will eventually die out.

THE TRUE PATRIARCHY'S RITES OF PASSAGE INTO MANHOOD

From the beginning of the International Patriarchy RITES OF PASSAGE FROM BOYHOOD TO MANHOOD have been employed to remove a male from the temporary (and necessary) care of his mother. These rites, for the most part, have been forgotten by the men of the North American Patriarchy, and this is part of the process that has caused the decline of the Patriarchy.

Therefore, I include the rites in this book, so that a revival of the True Patriarchy may take place

The Rites are:

(1) Three weeks prior to his sixteenth birthday, a young man should be tattoed on the arm or chest or stomach with a symbol of the Sky Father (God) & True Patriarchy (a warrior slaying a snake or dragon, which is the sign of the goddess).

(2) The young man is to be presented with a copy of Arne Saknussemmm's Revelations of the True Patriarchy.

(3) The young man is to be encouraged to grow & maintain a beard.

(4) The young man is to officially honored & welcomed into the True Patriarchy with a party at a legal brothel.

THE BASIC SKILLS & THEIR PRACTICAL APPLICATIONS

Physicists, sea captains, astronomers, mapmakers, architects, building contractors, engineers, air pilots, computer specialists—all use mathematics in a "practical" manner.

You can't be the commanding officer of a submarine without having the ability to understand & use advanced mathematics. Superior abilities in mathematics, along with solid reading & writing skills, makes up the foundation on which a member of the True Patriarchy builds his life. Having these basic skills can make the difference when you want to get ahead in you career. Failure to develop your skills can derail you just when they are needed most. GET THE BASICS!!!

THE IDENTIFICATION & DEVELOPMENT
OF YOUR TALENTS & SKILLS

In MYSTICAL MATHEMATICS The "Truly Enlightened & Powerful" found a device which allows a man to Identify & develop his talents & skills.

Once identified & developed, a man's talents & skills can be utilized in a business (self employment).

Mystical Mathematics isn't a religion; it is a science. You don't see it in your daily paper like astrology. Mystical Mathematics has been secretly studied & practiced by mathematicians like Issac Newton, Omar Khayyam & Rene Descartes for thousands of years.

You'll probably never witness the popularity of Mathematical Mysticism (Numerology). It is the science of the mathematician.

INTERNATIONAL LIVING & SELF EMPLOYMENT

After years of speaking to men about Men's Rights & the International Patriarchy I am still convinced that the only way to break the sinister hold feminists have on American men is to show them an alternative to passive submission in order to enjoy their companionship & Intimate sexual favors.

International Living goes hand in hand with the act of BYPASSSING AMERICAN FEMINISTS for foreign, non-feminist females. An International travelor can choose from a number of Male-dominated countries to live in (temporarily or permanently).

International Living can be successfully undertaken only by highly skilled & adventurous men. It is not for the unskilled & unprepared. The highly skilled man's ability to speak foreign languages & deal with a variety of cultures is the key that renders the feminists' sex blockade (sex is for Mr. Right types only) an exercise in futility.

Therefore, I recommend you:

(1) Identify & develop your talents & skills (especially your language skills.

(2) Utilize your developed talents & skills in a business that can trade on an international basis.

The self-employed man does the hiring & firing—he doesn't get the boot. The self employed man can gain the kind of independance tht allows him to bypass the feminist sex blockade.

Brothel Guide

INTRODUCTION

Dear Reader:

Many years of travel & research has shown me that asia is the best place to enjoy women. Europe is too expensive; latin america is too dangerous (this may change). Go to asia and save time & money.

This guide is dedicated to my favorite asian country: KOREA!!!

Host of the 1988 Olympics. A country with a booming economy, first class hotels, fine resorts, ancient palaces & temples, fantastic natural wonders and people that are as proud of their cultural heritage as we are of ours.

Koreans like Americans. You won't encounter a lot of crime; and their females are very beautiful.

Prostitution is legal, so don't worry. Northwest Orient & Korean Air have regular flights from the west coast, so you can leave anytime.

Let's get down to business.

Seoul is a city of nearly ten million people. It has many clubs (brothels) in a city district called ITAEWON. Itaewon is easy to get to from Kimpo Airport; just ask any cab driver.

Enjoy the adventure that could change the course of your life!!!

THE "RIGHT WAY" TO HANDLE
THE "BUSINESSGIRLS"

Females will act like females, even in Korea. Korean females want to enjoy the "good life" like any other females on this earth. I love them, but they're still golddiggers. Don't ever forget that.

The girls in these cities & towns are trying to hook up with a man who will fall in love with them, marry them (I think I covered this one already) & bring them to the states to live.

They will make sincere & passionate love to you in bed (& out of bed) & treat you very special; and their jealousy is legendary; but what you have to watch out for is your own foolish jealousy. Don't be a fool, don't be jealous & don't get married (unless you decide to stay in Korea).

Enjoy the sex, the country & the time you have on earth, but never take yourself too seriously. I have seen fools fighting over girls who were screwing other men behind their backs (sounds like the U.S.). Enjoy yourself, then get on that plane (unless you're staying awhile) & go home.

P.S. IF YOU DECIDE TO STAY IN KOREA FOR MORE THAN A MONTH, GET A MISTRESS. DON'T GET AN APARTMENT OR HOTEL AROUND THE SOLDIERS. ALWAYS GET IT STRAIGHT WITH YOUR MISTRESS THAT YOU DON'T TOLERATED BUTTERFLY GIRLS—BEFORE YOU PAY MAMA-SAN.

ENJOY!!!!

MAP LIST

Map (A) The Korean peninsula is divided into Democratic South Korea & the commie north.

Map (B) Shows Seoul, Kimpo Airport, The Han River & the towns with Brothels:
(1) Yeong Tae Ri (2) Yong Ju Gol (3) San Ju Ri (4) Tong Du Chon

Note: All towns with brothels are underlined.

Map (C) Yeong Tae Ri
Map (D) San Ju Ri
Map (E) Yong Ju Gol
Map (F) Tong Du Chon

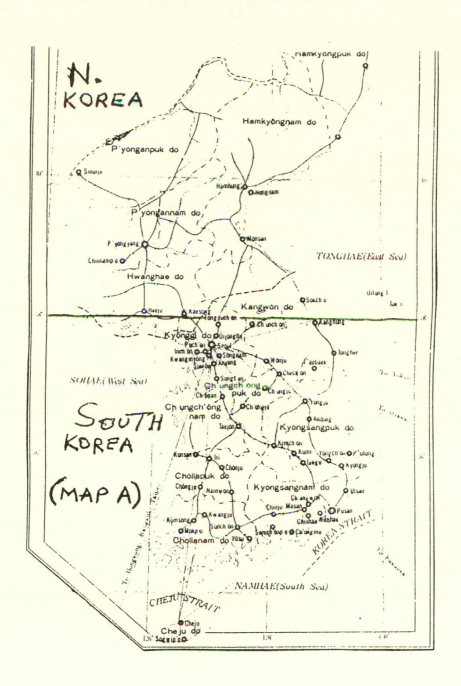

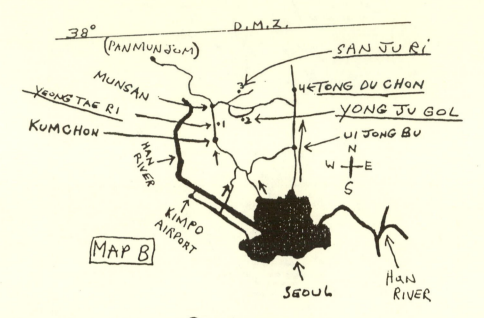

N. KOREA

38°   (PANMUNJOM)   D. M. Z.

SAN JU RI

MUNSAN

YEONG TAE RI

YE TONG DU CHON

YONG JU GOL

KUMCHON

HAN RIVER

UI JONG BU

N
W   E
S

KIMPO AIRPORT

MAP B

SEOUL

HAN RIVER

SOUTH KOREA

202

YEONG TAE RI

Located 25 to 30 miles north of Seoul, Yeong Tae Ri is a town that has been called "The Ville" by the soldiers who are stationed across the highway at Camp Edwards (west).

Yeong Tae Ri has five brothels. Food & drinks are plentiful & cheap. The girls are friendly & affordable: $20.00 or less to stay overnight. Prices are always lower for men who look like soldiers (get my meaning?).

TIPS: (1) Don't look or act like a tourist (civilian clothes are alright)
(2) Use condoms until you have your steady girlfriend tested in Seoul
(3) Don't drink the water (drink beer)
(4) Don't take pictures around here
(5) Remember the curfew if your decide to stay up to 10 p.m.
(6) Avoid these towns during military paydays

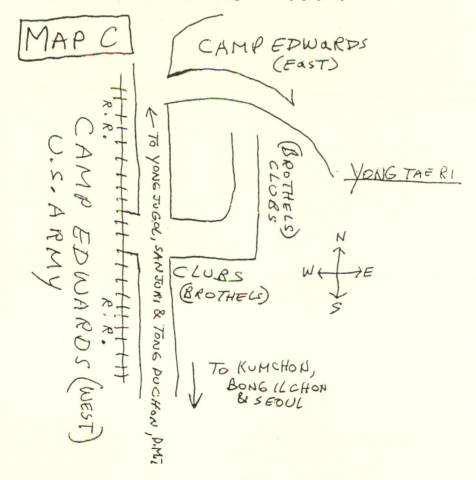

SAN JU RI

To reach San Ju Ri you get in a cab or bus and head north up the highway towards Munsan. When you reach Munsan you must head east at the crossroad (make a right) until you pass R.C. #4 (a recreational center for soldiers). San Ju Ri is the bar town for the soldiers of the area.

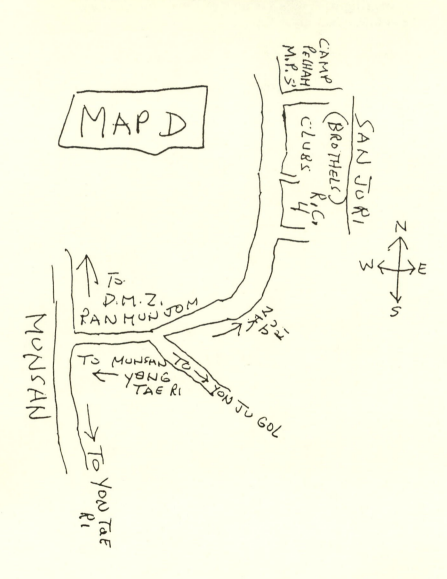

YONG JU GOL

Yong Ju Gol is located 20 to 30 miles northeast of Yeong Tae Ri & 7 to 10 miles southwest of San Ju Ri, along the road that passes the checkpoints on your way to Tong Du Chon.

It's a town you must visit during any tour of Korea. A fast cab can whisk you through this town in a flash, but if you make sure to tell the driver to stop it will be worth the effort.

Brothels, shops, restaurants, markets of every kind lines both sides of Yong Ju Gol's streets (& vicinity), a strip of road that is always full of holes despite occasional repairs.

Yong Ju Gol is full of Brothels & their girls!!! The names of the clubs may change, and the girls may come & go, but Yong Ju Gol is still my favorite town!!!

Food & drink is plentiful, just like the girls. Affordable Korean Inns (Yogwans) are available, as are private apartments & rooms at the clubs, themselves. There are massage parlors in town—and even a shower house.

The businessgirls of Yong Ju Gol are some of the best in Korea. You can live with them for a week or longer—it's up to you.

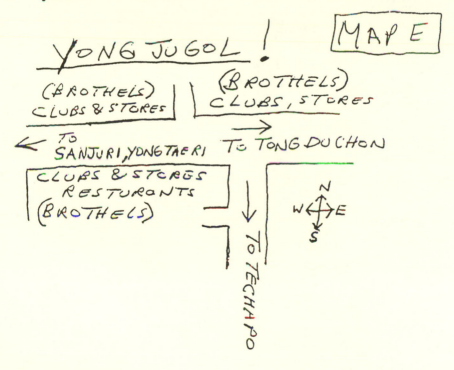

TONG DU CHON

This is the big town. Camp Casey (Second Infantry Division Headquarters) is located across the street. The soldiers have attracted the largest group of businessgirls outside of Seoul. There has to be more than thirty brothels (not including the private ones) in Tong Du Chon. The girls are great, the accomodations are the best of the Korean town & I like it here.

Always make a point of visiting T.D.C.!!!

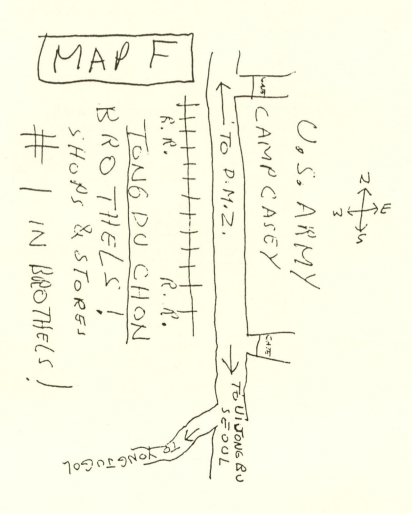

AMERICAN SURVEY

Why can't a woman be more like a woman?

The women's movement in America, for all its achievements, is deeply divided about the direction it should take. The National Organisation for Women, the leading, largest and most conspicuous group, is, after 20 years, suffering from internal differences and from a hail of criticism, much of it from women whose feminist credentials are not in doubt. "Profound paralysis" is its problem, says Ms Betty Friedan, a founder of NOW. Membership has fallen, revenues are down, debt is up.

In a hard fought campaign for the presidency last year, the victor, Mrs Eleanor Smeal, put the blame for this on her predecessor's slant towards the Democrats and her moderation. In her victory speech Mrs Smeal promised more action: a return to the streets; a mass march in defence of a woman's right to choose an abortion; and redoubled efforts to pass the equal rights amendment, which Congress turned down smartly, under pressure from religious fundamentalists and from women who feared the destruction of the family.

One trouble with Mrs Smeal's programme is that it simply redoubles the fury and the determination of right-wing groups without, apparently, arousing

It's not equality they're most worried about

much passionate response among younger women; they are the new generation who have been able to take advantage of the opportunities that feminist activists have opened up through the fight against discrimination in education and employment. Some of these younger women can boast that they "have it all"—a splendid job, a husband, a baby—but are ungratefully beginning to wonder whether all may not be too much. Others, who have forgone marriage or motherhood, are having regrets. These are women who had, and may still have, a choice. Many among the 55m American women who work, 20m of them mothers, have no alternative.

NOW might well combat the accusation that it is elitist and interested only in college-educated women by taking up the cause of poor women. Three of every five of the adults living in poverty in America are women: elderly women who did not work long enough or earn enough to secure pensions; divorced women who, under the no-fault divorce laws that NOW supported (and now regrets), receive no alimony and often little or no child support; widows and single mothers. More than 9m families are headed by women and millions of their children are growing

up in poverty.

Even a woman with a husband in a job may live below the poverty line. Some 9% of white married couples remain in poverty if the husband is the sole breadwinner; the figure for black couples is 24% and for Hispanics nearly 29%. And it is a sad fact that women's wages have risen little since the 1930s in comparison with those of men. In 1939 they earned 63 cents for every dollar of a man's wages; now they earn 64 cents. Women are said to form a majority of the professional classes, but their weekly earnings are $160 less than those of professional men. This looks like sex discrimination and almost certainly is. But the main reason women have not done better is because they carry the burden of looking after children.

NOW has concentrated on equality for women rather than special treatment; it has long opposed the passage of protective legislation for women of the kind that is common in most advanced countries, because it fears that employers would respond by not employing women. It did support, and help to forbid, the sacking of a woman simply because she was pregnant, but it has done little to campaign for maternity leave or the duty of an employer to make at least reasonable efforts to reinstate a woman in her job, or a similar one, after the leave is over.

Congressman Patricia Schroeder introduced a bill last year that would give new parents 18 weeks of unpaid leave to get to know their baby or adopted child or look after a very ill child. Because it does not mention women, she hopes it will not be regarded as discriminatory. It would also protect the jobs of disabled people. Its prospects are thought to be good.

But in a case headed for the Supreme Court from California (one of only four states that require employers to reinstate a woman after she has had a baby), NOW's position is that women should be treated as disabled and receive only the benefits given to the disabled, which is what federal law requires. The Justice Department argues that the law forbids discrimination on behalf of pregnant women as much as it forbids discrimination against them.

Such legal coyness makes it harder to deal with the fact that women with children, especially very young children, need special provision if they are to be able to compete with men for jobs. A case

43

brought by the Equal Opportunities
Commission against Sears, Roebuck—
with the support of NOW—is illuminating.
The firm was accused of discrimination in
the employment and promotion of wom-
en. It was true that women occupied few
of the better paid jobs selling on commission. But that, the judge held in February, was not for lack of trying by the firm,
but because women did not want to travel
long distances after hours or at the weekends—presumably the only times that
they could spend with their families or
catch up with the laundry. Making work
schedules more flexible would help many
women and could hardly be called discriminatory since it would also apply to
men bringing up children alone, either
because they have won custody or because their wives had died or made off.

The United States has no federal subsidy for day-care for children, unlike most
other developed countries. It is a state
affair. Estimates are that 14m places for
children are needed; only 10m, of varying
quality, are provided. Yet this is a job
that could be performed by many women.
Another difficulty is that day-care is expensive and federal tax-credits, which
help to offset its expense for the well-off,
are no help for a mother or father who
pays no taxes. A cash payment is needed,
or a subsidy. Maternal and child health-
care could also be improved.

These are issues that concern many
American women, yet are being neglected by a women's movement more interested in abortion and relatively unimportant matters of sexism. To deal with them
would cost some money, but it would be
an investment in the future. To say that
more day-care, flexible hours and pregnancy leave would solve the conflicts
between work and family would be an
exaggeration. They will not remove the
pang of many mothers when they drop
children, even babies, off at a day nursery,
or eliminate the burden of both working
and running a home. But they would help.
NOW could usefully champion them.

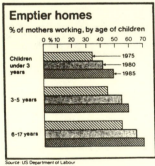

Emptier homes

% of mothers working, by age of children

Children under 3 years — 1975, 1980, 1985

3-5 years

6-17 years

Source: US Department of Labour

210

Women working and divorce: Cause or effect?

Women these days. If only they had the good sense to stay home, keep house and tend to the children, we wouldn't have these skyrocketing divorce rates, some traditionalists might say.

Wrong. The American family is not the victim of women's increasing entry into the workplace, say economists William R. Johnson and Jonathan Skinner. Rather, more and more married women, faced with today's large and growing probability that a marriage will end in divorce, believe it's only good sense to develop job skills and work for pay.

Analyzing the survey responses of nearly 1,800 families who had been followed for 12 years, Johnson and Skinner found that although higher levels of education among women and fewer children in families have contributed to the rise of women in the work force, another important and previously overlooked incentive has been the dramatic rise in the rate of divorce.

Divorce rates are encouraging more women to work, but a wife's employment does not make a couple more likely to divorce. The researchers found that the risk of divorce was higher for couples who did not attend church regularly and for those with no relatives living nearby. No-fault divorce laws, educational achievements of either spouse and wives' employment had little effect on whether or not couples divorced.

In the year or so before a separation, women with little past work experience did tend to begin to work for pay or to increase their hours of employment. But the researchers found this was not the cause of the subsequent divorce. Rather, women who anticipated the end of their marriages were apt to seek paying work or increase their work hours in preparation for the split.

Not all working wives are just trying to have it all. In these times of rampant divorce, some are also hedging their bets.   —*Patricia Nicholas*

William R. Johnson, Ph.D., and Jonathan Skinner, Ph.D., are at the University of Virginia. They reported their findings in the *American Economic Review* (Vol. 76, No. 3).

The Perceived Control of
Well-Educated Women: 1972–1984

BARTOLOMEO J. PALISI*
California State University, Fullerton
CLAIRE CANNING

From 1972 to 1984 women's social status changed as more worked outside the home and family ties loosened. How did their own attitudes change? Did they feel greater power? Did they feel greater mastery? Polls of 567 women in 1972 and 548 women in 1984 respond to these questions. The study found that perceived mastery, but not power, was higher for many types of women in 1984 than in 1972. Also, in 1972 there were differences in perceived control among college graduates. Those with high control were in high-status occupations, were older, were married, and had children. In 1984 only undergraduates with these characteristics were high in control. These results match data from the NORC General Social Surveys.

Self-concept has recieved a great deal of attention in social psychological literature.[1] Charles H. Cooley's original concept of looking-glass self emphasized that self-concepts of individuals are affected by the ways in which other people judge them, and by the ways in which individuals perceive these judgments.[2] This focus suggests that conditions outside the individual (the environment) affect self-concept, which in turn affects behavior. Recent writings have stressed that self-concept also has an active and creative dimension.[3] This dimension is autonomous from the environment in its origins (i.e., it originates in the individual). Although Cooley originally recognized that there is interaction between the social dimension of self-concept and the individually oriented aspects of the concept, earlier research had not focused on the latter dimension.[4] A specific focus of recent research on the dynamic and individually based aspects of self-concept has been on self-efficacy, or a sense of control. It is important for the mental health and self-esteem of individuals that they have a sense of control over their behavior and the

*Direct all correspondence to: Bartolomeo J. Palisi, Department of Sociology, California State University—Fullerton, Fullerton, California 92634. Telephone 714 773 3531.

The Social Science Journal, Volume 25, Number 3, pages 337-351.

environment relevant to that behavior. Thus, research is needed that focuses on the conditions and situations where individuals perceive that they have control, and where they do not.

Individualistic aspects of the self, such as sense of control, are not fixed and unchanging but develop throughout life and vary according to differences in social structure.[5] Some structural conditions facilitate a sense of control, whereas others inhibit it. Conversely, individuals who have a strong sense of control have a different impact on the social structure than less efficacious individuals. A sense of control involves both the perceived ability to control one's self (i.e., mastery) and the perceived ability to control the environment (i.e., power).[6] In addition, perceived personal control is more likely to vary with changes in social structure and situational factors than is perceived environmental control.

American women have been affected by a number of changes in structural conditions during the past two decades that have given them more opportunities to control their lives and to influence their environments. For example, many more women, particularly married women, now work than they did in the 1970s. In 1970 42.6 percent of the female population worked, and 41.4 percent of the married women worked. By 1980, 51.1 percent of the females worked and 50.7 percent of married women worked.[7] Women have also made inroads into occupations held very largely by males in the 1960s and 1970s.[8] For example, less than 10 percent of lawyers and judges were women in 1971. By 1981 this had risen to approximately 13 percent. Greater increases took place in the representation of women in the occupation of pharmacist (10 percent in 1962 to over 25 percent in 1981), and in blue collar occupations such as bartenders (11 percent in 1962 to 48 percent in 1982). Behaviors related to the family and to sex roles have also changed and are indicators of increased alternatives for women. As alternatives increase, so does the opportunity for perceived control. The percentage of women in their early 20s who were married decreased from 64 percent in 1970 to 50 percent in 1980.[9] The number of unmarried cohabiting women increased from less than half a million in 1960 to over two million in 1985.[10] The divorce rate increased from 2.5 to 5.1 per 1000 population between 1965 and 1982.[11] Higher divorce rates indicate more alternatives for women in that they do not feel entirely dependent on marriage, or on a particular marriage, and are freer to seek a divorce.[12]

This article will compare data on women from 1972 and 1984 to detect changes in their perceptions of mastery and power. It will also analyze whether some women have changed more than others. Finally, it will examine which types of women in each time period were the most and least likely to perceive mastery and power.

Perceived mastery is hypothesized to have increased from 1972 to 1974. Changes in the roles and status of women, and the greater alternatives of women during the latter year (described above), are expected to have positively affected their perceived mastery. There is considerable evidence in social science literature that structural conditions are related to perceptions, feelings, and—most relevant for this article—the self-evaluations of individuals. Andrisani's study on the effects of labor market conditions on personal control, Cicirelli's study of family structure and personal control, Pitcher and Hong's study of how health and demographic factors relate to personal control in a sample of older males, and Watson's analysis of how the social circumstances of minorities affect their peceived personal control represent a part of this research.[13]

The perceived power of women is hypothesized not to have increased. Power is not as sensitive to structural changes as is mastery.

Data for this study come from a sample of well-educated women. Well-educated women would have been more likely than less-educated women to have increased mastery. Studies show that many additudinal and perceptual changes occur first among high socioeconomic (i.e., education) status individuals and then filter down to those of lower status.[15] In addition, well-educated women often were the initial beneficiaries of improved societal opportunities for women in education, work, and other institutions during the 1970s. They often became more economically independent than less-educated women and felt less threatened by change. To detect the leading edge of changes affecting women, it is logical to focus on those who are well-educated.

The analysis will also try to determine which types of women, if any, had the greatest mastery and power in 1984 when compared to similar women in 1972. Mastery of women with dominant status characteristics, but not their power, is hypothesized to have been higher in 1984 than in 1972. Dominant status women are high in socioeconomic status, older, married, and with children. Women with less dominant social and demographic status characteristics in 1984 are not expected to differ significantly in mastery or power from similar women in 1972. Dominant status women had advantages in gaining control because they had more resources and skills that enabled them to utilize the opportunities and alternatives of changed structural conditions in society. However, an alternative hypothesis is that mastery was more characteristic in 1984 than 1972 among women who had subordinate status characteristics because they had the most to gain—i.e., the furthest to go to have an acceptable amount of control.

Mastery and power are hypothesized to be related to socioeconomic status, age, marital status, and number of children of women within each year. Research has found that people who are high in control tend to have high socioeconomic status.[16] They also tend to be middle-aged rather than teenagers or young adults.[17] Married women, especially those with children, are hypothesized to have had high perceived control. They had fulfilled two major traditional roles of women in American society which signify success and accomplishment, i.e., being married and having children. Further, they may have been able to feel a sense of control by being responsible for the behavior of their children. It is also logical that women who had a sense of control were more active in the mate selection process (i.e., they originated more action), and they may have felt that they could raise children. Thus, they were likely to marry and have children.

In summary, the hypotheses are:

1. Perceived mastery was higher in 1984 than in 1972.
2. Perceived power did not differ between 1972 and 1984.
3. Among dominant status women, perceived mastery, but not power, was higher in 1984 than in 1972. Subordinate status women in 1984 did not differ from their counterparts in 1972.
4. In both 1984 and 1972 mastery and power were high among women who were of high socioeconomic status, older, married, and had children.

Data were collected in 1972 and 1984 using similar data collection techniques. In both years samples of alumnae and undergraduates of a large California university were selected. A similar process was used both years to select alumnae. This involved systematically selecting names (i.e., every nth name) from a list of alumnae compiled and kept up-to-date by the university. The 1972 sample of alumnae involved only females who had graduated with a bachelors degree in June of 1971. Questionnaires were mailed in March of 1972 to 800 alumnae. Adequately completed questionnaires were returned from 386 (48.3 percent) of the women. The eight-month time span between graduation and mail-outs was designed to allow sufficient time for the alumnae to be employed or to continue with their education. Alumnae who graduated before 1971 were not included in the 1972 sample so that graduates and undergraduates could legitimately be treated as one population. The 1984 sample of alumni was drawn by the same methods used in 1972, except that it involved both males and females who had graduated in June of 1983. Questionnaires were mailed in March 1984 to 1,000 male and female alumni. There were 525 (52.5 percent) completed questionnaires returned. This article focuses on the 341 returns from females, which comprised 55 percent of questionnaires mailed to females in 1984.

In both 1972 and 1984, questionnaires (almost identical to the ones used for alumni) were given to a non-random sample of undergraduates enrolled in both upper division and lower division sociology classes. Because the great majority of the students in sociology classes were not sociology majors, and many did not have a social science major, the samples involved a cross-section of university students. Questionnaires were voluntarily and anonymously completed during class meetings. In 1972 females completed 181 questionnaires. In 1984 females completed 207 questionnaires (males completed 64). Therefore, data for this article come from a total of 567 females in 1972, and 548 females in 1984.

Both mastery and power were measured by the same scales in 1972 and 1984. The concept of mastery deals with whether the individual feels that control of her own personal life is influenced largely by forces which are internally initiated, as opposed to events external to her. A mastery scale used several items taken from Julian Rotter's Internal-External Locus of Control Scale, and items used by Angus Campbell et. al.[18] The eight items in the scale are shown in Table 1.

Scores for negatively stated items in the mastery scale (items numbered 4, 5, 6, 8, which express low mastery) were reversed, and a total scale score was calculated by summing the eight items. The scale had a reliability coefficient of .60. The possible scale scores ranged from 8 (low mastery) to 32 (high mastery).

Power involves the individual's perceived ability to have an impact on the environment of which she is part. This includes other significant people, the immediate circumstances surrounding her life, and societal events that may eventually affect her. A scale was constructed by selecting several items from Dwight Dean's measures of powerlessness.[19] These are shown in Table 1. An agree-disagree format for answers was employed. For all items disagreement indicated high perceived power. The items were summed and the resulting scale had a coefficient of reliability of .67. Possible scale scores ranged from 9 (low power) to 36 (high power).

The independent variables included education of the respondent and of the spouse, which was measured by the highest degree received. This variable was coded as Less than a Bachelors Degree, Bachelors Degree, and Greater than a Bachelors Degree. Essentially, those respondents with less than a Bachelors Degree formed the under-

Table 1. Measures of Mastery and Power.

___

Mastery

Please indicate whether you 1. strongly agree: 2. agree: 3. disagree: or 4. strongly disagree with the following statements:

1. I have always felt my life would work out as I wanted it to.
2. I never have any trouble making up my mind about important decisions.
3. I have always felt that I have more willpower than most people have.
4. There's not much use for me to plan ahead because there's usually something that makes me change my plans.
5. I often have the feeling that it's no use trying to get anywhere in this life.
6. I seem to be the kind of peson that has more bad luck than good luck.
7. I always feel pretty sure of myself even when people disagree with me.
8. I would rather decide things when they come up than always try to plan ahead.

Power

1. I worry about the future facing today's children.
2. Sometimes I have the feeling that other people are using me.
3. It is frightening to be responsible for the development of a little girl.
4. There are so many decisions that have to be made today that sometimes I could just "blow up."
5. There is little chance for promotion on the job unless a peson gets a break.
6. There is little or nothing I can do about preventing a major "shooting war."
7. We're so regimented today that there's not much room for choice even in personal matters.
8. We are just so many cogs in the machinery of life.
9. The future looks very dismal.

___

graduate samples, and respondents with a Bachelors Degree or higher were the alumnae. Whereas it is true that many of the undergraduates eventually became alumnae, the measure of education allows the effects of present level of education on control to be observed. It allows analysis of how students perceive their control as compared to recent alumnae. Key events in people's lives, such as college graduation, often have significant and immediate effects on their perceptions.

In 1972, occupational status of the respondent and of the spouse were measured by closed-ended questions which had eight categories ranging from Professional to Unskilled Worker. Respondents not in the work force (e.g., retired, housewives, unemployed) were coded as missing data. In 1984 the respondent was asked to state her main occupation and the main occupation of her spouse. This was then coded into the same categories used in 1972. A variable of Employed versus Unemployed was constructed to determine how those not in the work force compared to employed workers in perceptions of control. There are some important differences between undergraduates and alumnae in how variables such as occupation or occupation of spouse influence mastery and power. For example, undergraduates who work are usually not in their "lifetime" occupations, and may work part-time, whereas alumnae often have careers.

THE SOCIAL SCIENCE JOURNAL Vol. 25/No. 3/1988

Table 2. Means and T Tests for the Differences in Mastery
and Power Between Women in 1972 and 1984.

	Mastery			Power		
	Means			Means		
Variable	1972	1984	T Tests	1972	1984	T Tests
All Respondents	22.5	23.7	7.21***	25.4	25.5	.33
			(1083)			(1047)
Education						
Less than BA	21.9	23.3	5.17***	25.0	25.1	.40
			(364)			(345)
BA	22.8	23.9	5.16***	25.4	25.6	.89
			(580)			(561)
Higher than BA	23.3	24.4	2.34*	26.7	26.5	- .30
			(117)			(118)
Spouse Education						
Less than BA	23.2	24.2	2.60**	26.2	26.2	.11
			(147)			(56)
BA	23.0	24.0	2.53**	26.0	26.4	.93
			(150)			(144)
Higher than BA	23.2	24.0	2.07*	27.0	25.9	-1.48
			(108)			(111)
Occupation						
Nonprofessional	22.1	23.2	3.80***	24.3	24.6	.55
			(338)			(215)
Professional	23.1	24.1	4.33***	25.9	25.8	- .06
			(369)			(460)
Spouse Occupation						
Nonprofessional	22.8	24.5	3.84***	26.1	25.8	- .39
			(149)			(115)
Professional	23.2	24.1	2.42**	27.0	26.2	-1.55
			(220)			(250)
Age						
21 or less	21.9	23.4	4.17***	24.8	24.7	.11
			(275)			(257)
22 to 25	22.5	23.8	5.11***	24.9	25.3	- .81
			(431)			(419)
26 or more	23.3	23.7	1.83*	26.6	26.1	- .15
			(370)			(376)
Children						
None	22.3	23.6	6.36***	24.8	25.3	1.85*
			(682)			(672)
One	22.8	23.9	1.96*	26.0	25.4	- .70
			(81)			(85)
Two or More	23.3	24.2	2.62***	27.2	26.7	-1.06
			(209)			(210)
Marital Status						
Married	23.1	24.2	4.44***	26.4	26.2	- .51
			(416)			(411)
Not Married	22.2	23.4	5.57***	24.8	25.1	1.63
			(664)			(635)

Notes: Levels of significance for 1 tailed tests are used. The numbers in parentheses are the degrees of freedom. Work or
not work was included because it was unproductive.
* = <.05.
** = <.01.
*** = <.005.

Age was coded from a question which asked the respondent's age on her last birthday. Respondents were also asked to state the number of children they presently had and their present marital status (coded as married and not married for this article).

FINDINGS

With respect to changes from 1972 to 1984, the data in Table 2 support the first two hypotheses. Women in 1984 had higher mastery than in 1972. The difference between the mean for mastery in 1984 (23.7) and for 1972 (22.5) is highly significant (T value is 7.21, p < .005). In addition, the mean scores for power are 25.4 in 1972 and 25.5 in 1984, and are not significantly different.

Table 2 also shows that the significant increases in mastery cut across levels of education, occupational status, age, number of children, and marital status. In all subgroups the means for mastery are significantly higher in 1984 than in 1972. The increases in perceived mastery appear to be more pronounced for women who are undergraduates than for alumnae, in that the differences between the means are larger for the former group (a difference of 1.4 points) than for either women with a bachelors degree or with higher than a bachelors degree (1.1 points). In addition, women aged under 21 or 21 to 25 appear to have had significantly higher mastery in 1984 than in 1972. In the 26 or older age category, the 1984 women also had significantly higher mastery. As a group, women with no children gained slightly more mastery than women with children. However, it must be kept in mind that these differences in the gains some categories of women have made as compared to other categories of women are not great. All types of well-educated women had more mastery in 1984 than their counterparts in 1972. These findings do not support hypothesis 3, that only dominant status women had higher mastery in 1984 than in 1972. On the other hand, Table 2 shows that the second part of hypothesis 3 was supported. In all but one subgroup women did not have more power in 1984 than in 1972. Only women with no children were likely to feel more powerful in the latter year (T value = 1.85, p < .05). In fact, among some subgroups, such women with more than a bachelors degree and women in professional occupations, there is a suggestion that power was less in 1984 than in 1972 (the T values just miss being significant).

To test whether mastery and power vary by socioeconomic status, age, number of children, and marital status, correlation coefficients were calculated using the uncollapsed data for the variables of mastery and power in each separate year. Table 3 shows that in both years, as was hypothesized, both perceived mastery and power increased with education of the respondent, occupational status of the repsondent, and number of children. As hypothesized, married women in both years had more mastery and power than unmarried women. In addition, perceived mastery increased with age in 1972, but not in 1984. Power increased with age in both years. There are no differences in perceived mastery and power when the husband's education and occupation are the focus, nor when analyzing women who work versus those who do not.

Because graduates and undergaraduates may represent quite different subpopulations, the independent variables were cross-tabulated and correlated with the perceived control

Table 3. Correlation Coefficients between
the Independent Variables and Mastery and Power.

Variable	Mastery		Power	
	1972	1984	1972	1984
Education	.181***	.129***	.142***	.118**
	(539)	(528)	(527)	(503)
Spouse Education	-.029	-.050	.043**	-.034
	(217)	(194)	(219)	(188)
Occupation	.148**	.203***	.156**	.160***
	(288)	(423)	(284)	(403)
Work or Not	.001	.020	.033	.063
	(520)	(528)	(508)	(503)
Spouse Occupation	.075	-.082	.070	.030
	(179)	(194)	(182)	(187)
Age	.197***	.018	.208	.154***
	(541)	(540)	(530)	(515)
Children	.156***	.085*	.301***	.157***
	(504)	(500)	(495)	(516)
Marital Status	.104***	.136***	.190***	.160***
	(541)	(541)	(530)	(516)

Notes: The numbers in parentheses are the number of cases in the analyses.
*$p < .05$.
**$p < .01$.
***$p < .001$.

measures while controlling for education (dichotomized to undergraduates and alumnae). Table 4 shows the results of theses analyses.

The main focus is on comparisons between alumnae and undergraduates with regard to how variables such as age, occupation, and number of children relate to mastery and power in each year. Note in Table 4 that correlations involving education and occupation of the spouse have extremely small Ns. Therefore, findings involving these variables must be interpreted with great caution. Several trends are evident. In 1972 alumnae had high mastery if they were in high status occupations, were older, and had children. The only significant finding for mastery among undergraduates is that they had high mastery if they had children. Power was high among undergraduates in 1972 only if they were older. Among alumnae in 1972, power was highest for individuals with high status occupations and for those whose spouses had high status occupations. Power was also high for those who were older, married, and who had children.

In 1984, the pattern is quite different. Undergraduates had high mastery if they were in high status occupations, had spouses in high status occupations, and had children. Alumnae had high mastery only if they were married as compared to unmarried. Power was high for undergraduates who had well-educated spouses, were older, had children, and were married. Among alumnae in 1984 only married women had higher power than unmarried women.

Table 4. Correlation Coefficients between the Independent Variables and Mastery and Power—With Controls for Education (Undergraduates and Alumnae).

| | 1972 | | | | 1984 | | | |
| | Mastery | | Power | | Mastery | | Power | |
Variable	Undergrad.	Alumnae	Undergrad.	Alumnae	Undergrad.	Alumnae	Undergrad.	Alumnae
Spouse Education	.603 (4)	.060 (212)	.695 (4)	.030 (213)	.114 (40)	.000 (153)	.367** (39)	.110 (148)
Occupation	.093 (18)	.154** (268)	.383 (17)	.149** (264)	.251** (129)	.079 (284)	.124 (123)	.039 (270)
Spouse Occupation	.694 (3)	.044 (176)	.500 (3)	.104** (178)	.276* (40)	.107 (152)	.220 (39)	.085 (146)
Age	.069 (174)	.147** (364)	.141* (161)	.278*** (365)	.048 (191)	.033 (337)	.140* (185)	.030 (318)
Children	.160* (150)	.131** (351)	.034 (139)	.354*** (352)	.157** (174)	.061 (315)	.199** (168)	.050 (297)
Marital Status	.072 (175)	.060 (363)	.068 (162)	.206*** (364)	.098 (191)	.107* (337)	.154** (185)	.094* (318)

Notes: *p < .05. **p < .01. ***p > .001.

221

In summary, in 1972 alumnae were more likely than undergraduates to show significant correlations between several status and demographic variables and both mastery
and power. In 1984 undergraudates were more likely than alumni to have their mastery
and power affected by status and demographic variables.

In order to assess the relative importance of the individual independent variables for
predicting mastery and power, separate multiple regression analyses were conducted in
each year with mastery and then with power as dependent (a total of four analyses.) All
of the independent variables were entered into the equations in a single step, and
pairwise deletion of missing data was used. These analyses (data not shown) did not
indicate that any single variable was strongly related to mastery or to power. There were
few significant betas. However, in 1972 the number of children was more strongly
related to power than any other variable. It had a beta of .294. $p < .01$, and explained 9
percent of the variance in power (the total r^2 was only .11). In 1972 age was more
strongly related to mastery than any other variable. It had a beta of .312, $p < .05$, but
only explained 1 percent of the variance in mastery. No variables were even moderately
important for explaining either mastery or power in 1984. Overall, very little variance in
mastery and in power was explained by the individual variables or by the combination of
variables in either year (r^2s were all less than .20). These analyses indicated that the
independent variables had only a very modest impact on either mastery or power in each
time period.

The data employed for the preceding analyses have several limitations. They only deal
with females, are limited to individuals with at least some college training, and are not
national in scope. To broaden the perspective, analyses were conducted of secondary
data gathered by the National Opinion Research Center. The General Social Surveys
conducted by the Center contained data on several variables which are similar to or
related to the measures of mastery and power. These data are from 1973 and 1984
(years similar to those of the study). In both years more than 1.400 interviews were
conducted with adults from a nationwide sample.

Four items in the General Social Survey data are relevant. Three of them are essentially measures of anomia, which is closely related to powerlessness in sociological
literature.[20] Respondents were asked whether they agreed or disagreed that "In spite of
what some people say, the lot (situation/condition) of the average man is getting worse,
not better" (Anomia 5); that "Most public officials (people in public office) are not
really interested in the problems of the average man" (Anomia 7); and that "It's hardly
fair to bring a child into the world with the way things look for the future" (Anomia 6).
This last question is quite similar to the powerless measure "I worry about the future
facing today's children." The final item is a measure of happiness. It asks, "Taken all
together, how would you say things are these days—would you say that you are very
happy, pretty happy, or not too happy?" (Happy) Whereas happiness is not a measure
of personal control, it has been shown that individuals who have perceived personal
control tend to be happier or to have a greater psychological well-being than those with
little control.[21]

To analyze the General Social Survey data, T tests were conducted for the differences
between the means for women (of all education levels combined) in 1984 compared to
1973. The same analysis was conducted for males of all education levels. Differences
were then analyzed between means for the sub-sample of women who had some college

Table 5.   Means and T Tests for the General Social Survey Variables.

| | Women | | | Men | | |
| | Means | | | Means | | |
	1973	1984	T-Tests	1973	1984	T-Tests
All Education Levels						
Anomia 5 (Lot of Avg. Man)	1.41	1.40	n.s. (1623)	1.49	1.47	n.s. (1674)
Anomia 6 (Child into World)	1.60	1.59	n.s. (1637)	1.66	1.61	1.85* (1675)
Anomia 7 (Public Officials)	1.39	1.30	3.80** (1622)	1.42	1.30	4.49*** (1672)
Happy	1.76	1.75	n.s. (1659)	1.79	1.83	n.s. (1682)
High Education						
Anomia 5 (Lot of Avg. Man)	1.57	1.51	n.s. (251)	1.71	1.67	n.s. (262)
Anomia 6 (Child into World	1.75	1.82	n.s. (251)	1.86	1.84	n.s. (264)
Anomia 7 (Public Officials)	1.50	1.51	n.s. (251)	1.56	1.47	n.s. (259)
Happy	1.79	1.63	1.99** (252)	1.75	1.70	n.s. (260)

Notes   Nonsignificant T-scores are indicated by n.s.; numbers in parentheses are the degrees of freedom.
*p < .05.
**p < .01.
***p < .001.

education (Associate, College, or Graduate degree on the "Degree" question). Again, the same analysis was done for men. Table 5 shows these analyses.

Analyses of the three anomia items revealed that both males and females in 1984 were *not* less anomic than their counterparts of the same sex in 1973. These findings hold for both sexes when the focus is on respondents of all educational levels, and also when the focus is narrowed to those having college experience. In fact, in three situations respondents of all education levels were *more* anomic in 1984 than their counterparts in 1973. Specifically, all women in 1984 had a mean score of 1.30 as compared to a mean score of 1.39 among women in 1973 (low scores show more anomia) on the question about public officials not being interested in the average man's problems (Anomia 7). The T value was 3.80, p < .005 for a one-tailed test. The same trend was shown for all males on the question dealing with public officials. The means were 1.30 in 1984 and 1.42 in 1973, with a T value of 4.49, p < .005. These findings indicate that both males and females in 1984 were more likely than their counterparts in 1972 to agree that public officials were not interested in the problems of the average man. In addition, all males in 1984 had a mean score of 1.61, compared to a score of 1.66 among males in 1973 on the question dealing with it being fair to bring a child into the world (Anomia 6). The T value was 1.85, p < .05. This indicates that males in 1984 felt it was less fair to bring a child into the world than males in 1973. In no comparisons did either males or females of high educational status in 1984 differ significantly from their counterparts in 1973 in anomia. These findings are consistent with the conclusions derived from the data on well-educated women from the data on well-educated women from a university. They particularly affirm that university-educated women in 1984 did not feel more personal power than women in 1972, and in some situations they actually felt more powerless. Among a national sample both women and men did not feel less anomia in 1984 than their counterparts in 1973; and when all education levels are combined, men and women sometimes felt more anomia in 1984 than similar men and women in 1973.

In General Social Survey data females with high education in 1984 were happier than females with high education in 1973. Table 5 shows that the means were 1.63 in 1984 and 1.79 in 1973, T = 1.99, p < .05 (low scores indicate more happiness). This was the only significant difference between any subgroup in 1984 as compared to that subgroup in 1973. These findings are also consistent with the findings that university women had higher mastery in 1984 than in 1972. Other research has suggested that mastery is more important and unstable and subject to change than are other dimensions of control.[22] It has also been found that happiness is unstable and likely to change quickly.[23] Thus, well-educated women have apparently experienced changes in both their perceived mastery and overall happiness as a result (at least in part) of their changed opportunities, alternatives, and social status in the 1980s.

CONCLUSIONS

The findings suggest that well-educated women in 1984 had higher perceived mastery than their counterparts did in 1972. However, women in 1984 did not have greater perceived power than women in 1972. One interpretation of these findings is that behavioral changes documented earlier in the article, such as greater participation in the work force, have allowed women to feel more in control of themselves. For example, financial independence gained through employment gives women the opportunity to move about the community more freely. Women who are employed are also more free to terminate undesirable marriages because they have alternatives to those specific marriages or to any marriages.[24] Employment may also free some women from household chores such as cooking or child care by enabling them to eat out, to hire household help, or to send their children to day-care centers.[25] Well-educated women in the 1980s did not feel more power (e.g., control over other people and societal conditions) than similar women in the 1970s. The General Social Survey data indicates that these trends held nationwide for women of many education levels, as well as for men. Perceived power is influenced by abstract forces such as community structure, bureaucratic conditions, or powerful elites.[26] Thus it is less likely to change than mastery. The findings about power appear to be consistent with the American value system in the 1970s and 1980s, which stressed the values of individualism and self-determination and downplayed the value of being responsible to larger groups, including the community and the extended family.[27] Findings indicate that changes in perceived mastery were not limited to a few types of well-educated women. They appear to have occurred regardless of variations in socioeconomic status, age, or family status. Education appears to have had more of an influence on perceived mastery than any other variable in the analyses. All well-educated women have high mastery in 1984 as compared to 1972.

Women in both the 1972 and 1984 samples who were high in mastery and power were likely to be high in occupation and education, older (except mastery in 1984), with children, and married. However, the regression analyses indicated that the trends are weak at best, and that socioeconomic status variables and family status variables do not explain much mastery and power. This is surprising in that other studies have shown that in the late 1960s and 1970s women from various regional locations and personal backgrounds did vary in perceived personal control when age, income, and education were considered.[28] One explanation for the lack of strong findings is again that the advantage of being well-educated outweighs variations in occupation, specific education levels, age, marital status, or number of children.

The analysis suggests that in 1972 the alumnae who were able to take advantage of favorable societal conditions to optimize their perceived control were selectively of certain types (e.g., high occupational status, married, and with children). This is a description of women who have historically had an adequate sense of control. They were women who had fulfilled some important family and personal goals, namely to marry, have children, and have a good job. On the other hand, in 1972 undergraduates of all types were unable to capitalize on opportunities. By 1984 almost all alumnae had attained a sense of control; their high education outweighed all other factors. In 1984 the transitory role of the student and the uncertainty about the future, due to the poor economy and job market, may have influenced some students to lack a sense of control. Students with children had perceived control in 1984. Not only were students with children older, but children may have given the normally powerless students a sense of responsibility (i.e., in raising children), which then influenced them to feel in control.

The types of women who now have a sense of control are very similar to those who had a sense of control in the early 1970s. Findings from another part of this research (data not shown) suggest that well-educated women in 1984 were very similar to well-educated men in both perceived mastery and power.[29] This indicates that those parts of the social structure that support a sense of control among women have not been altered much in recent decades. The determinants of power among women are virtually unchanged, and mastery has increased but not shifted among subgroups of women, such as young and old, employed and unemployed, married and unmarried.

NOTES

1. Viktor Gecas and Michael L Schwalbe, "Beyond the Looking-Glass Self: Social Structure and Efficacy-Based Self-Esteem," *American Sociological Review* 46(1983):77; Bryan L. Pitcher and Sung Young Hong, "Older Men's Perceptions of Personal Control: The Effect of Health Status," *Sociological Perspectives* 29(1986):397–419; Morris Rosenberg, "The Self-Concept: Social Product and Social Force," Chapt. 19 in *Social Psychology: Sociological Perspectives*, M. Rosenberg and Ralph Turner, eds. (New York: Basic Books, 1981).
2. Charles H. Cooley, *Human Nature and the Social Order* (New York: Schocken Books, 1964 (1902)).

3. Gecas and Schwalbe, "Beyond the Looking-Glass Self," pp. 79-80; Pitcher and Hong, "Older Men's Perceptions," p. 400.
4. Gecas and Schwalbe, "Beyond the Looking-Glass Self," pp. 77-78.
5. Ibid., pp. 82-84; A. Bandura, "Self-Efficacy Mechanisms in Human Agency," *American Psychologist* 37(1982):122-147.
6. A. Bandura, "Self-Efficacy: Toward a Unifying Theory of Behavioral Change," *Psychological Review* 84(1977):191-215; P.J. Andrisani, *Work Attitudes and Labor Market Experience: Evidence From the National Longitudinal Surveys* (New York: Praeger, 1978).
7. U.S. Bureau of the Census, *Statistical Abstract of the United States* (Washington DC, 1983).
8. J. Ross Eshleman, *The Family: an Introduction* (Boston, MA: Allyn and Bacon, 1985), pp. 126-127.
9. Paul C. Glick, "Marriage, Divorce and Living Arrangements: Prospective Changes," *Journal of Family Issues* 5(1984):9.
10. P.C. Glick and Graham B. Spanier, "Married and Unmarried Cohabitation in the United States," *Journal of Marriage and the Family*, 42(1980):20; Koray Tanfer, "Patterns of Pre-marital Cohabitation Among Never-Married Women in the United States," *Journal of Marriage and the Family*, 49(1987):483.
11. Jo Ellen Theresa Pink and Karen Smith Wampler, "Problem Areas in Stepfamilies: Cohesion, Adaptability, and the Stepfather-Adolescent Relationship," *Family Relations* 34(1985):327.
12. J. Richard Udry, "Marital Alternatives and Marital Disruption," *Journal of Marriage and the Family* 43(1981):889-890.
13. Andrisani, *Work Attitudes*; V.G. Cicirelli, "Relationship of Family Background Variables to Locus of Control in the Elderly," *Journal of Gerontology* 35(1980):108-114; Pitcher and Hong, "Older Men's Perceptions," pp. 397-419; W.H. Watson, "Mental Health of the Minority Aged: Selected Correlates," in *Minority Aging*, R.C. Manuel, ed. (Westport, CT: Greenwood, 1982), pp. 83-88.
14. Bandura, "Self-Efficacy," pp. 191-215; Andrisani, *Work Attitudes*.
15. Claude S. Fischer, *The Urban Experience* (San Diego, CA: Harcourt Brace Jovanovich, 1984), pp. 219-222.
16. Richard M. Ryckman and Maria Malikioski, "Differences in Locus of Control Orientation for Members of Selected Occupations," *Psychological Reports* 34(1984):1225; E.S. Battle and Julian B. Rotter, "Children's Feelings of Personal Control as Related to Social Class and Ethnic Group," *Journal of Personality* 31(1963):482-490; E. Phares, *Locus of Control in Personality* (Morristown, NJ: General Learning Press, 1975); Angus Campbell, *The Sense of Well-Being in America: Recent Patterns and Trends* (New York: McGraw-Hill, 1981), pp. 214-216.
17. R.M. Ryckman and M. Malikioski, "Relationship Between Locus of Control and Chronological Age," *Psychological Reports* 36(1975)655-658; Rosina C. Lao "The Developmental Trend of the Locus of Control," Paper presented at the meetings of the American Psychological Association, New Orleans (1974).
18. Julian Rotter, "Generalized Expectancies for Internal versus External Control of Reinforcement," *Psychological Monographs* 80 (1, Whole No. 609); Angus Campbell, Phillip Converse, and Williard L. Rodgers, *The Quality of American Life: Perceptions, Evaluations, and Satisfactions* (New York: Russell Sage Foundation, 1976).
19. Dwight D. Dean, "Alienation: Its Meaning and Measurement," *American Sociological Review* 26(1962): 753-758.
20. Melvin Seeman, "Alienation and Engagement," in *the Human Meaning of Social Change*, A. Campbell and P.E. Converse, eds. (New York: Russell Sage Foundation, 1972), pp. 467-528.

21. Campbell, *The Sense of Well-Being*, pp. 217–218; Pitcher and Hong, "Older Men's Perceptions," pp. 407–409.
22. Andrisani, *Work Attitudes*.
23. Norman M. Bradburn, *The Structure of Psychological Well-Being* (Chicago, IL: Aldine, 1969).
24. Udry, "Marital Alternatives," p. 890.
25. Eshleman, *The Family*, pp. 120–121; Joyce O. Beckett and Audrey D. Smith, "Work and Family Roles: Egalitarian Marriage in Black and White Families," *Social Science Review* 55(1981):314–326.
26. Bandura, "Self-Efficacy."
27. Larry Lyon, *The Community in Urban Society* (Chicago, IL: The Dorsey Press, 1987), pp. 95–105.
28. Lao, "Locus of Control;" Phares, *Locus of Control in Personality*; Ryckman and Malikioski, "Differences in Locus of Control Orientation;" Ryckman and Malikioski, "Relationship Between Locus of Control and Chronological Age."
29. Bartolomeo J. Palisi and Claire Canning, "Perceived Personal Control Among Well Educated Men and Women," paper presented at the 29th Annual Western Social Science Association Meetings, El Paso, Texas (1987).

Psychological Reports, 1988, 62, 37-38. © Psychological Reports 1988

ANTISOCIALITY AND DANGEROUSNESS IN WOMEN BEFORE AND AFTER THE WOMEN'S MOVEMENT

ALFRED B. HEILBRUN, JR.[1] AND DAVID M. GOTTFRIED

Emory University

Summary.—Women committing crimes before the surge of feminism (1965-1971) and long after this movement attracted national attention (1980-1985) were sampled. Greater antisociality in female criminals during the prefeminist period was associated with more dangerous crime, but predictability was lost by 1980-1985. It was suggested that rejection of role expectations inspired by feminism may have altered the determinants of dangerous crime in women.

Rejection of conventional role expectations has been observed in studies of female criminals, especially violent ones (Adler, 1975; Hoffman-Bustamante, 1973; Simon, 1975; Weis, 1978). The women's movement is commonly used to explain this role change. The erosion of traditional sex-role commitment could provide one explanation of dangerous behavior in contemporary women, since feminine constraints upon physical aggression would be expected to decrease. Campbell's (1986) study of British girls and young women confirms the current prevalence of physical aggression in school children, delinquents, and prisoners. One implication of this social change is that prediction of dangerous criminality from traditionally conceived antecedents, such as antisociality, would be less viable following the women's movement as a new dynamic emerged. The present study tested this possibility.

Files of Georgia women criminals were drawn for 110 women who committed crimes between 1965-1971, prior to the time feminism achieved national prominence in the early 1970s, and 107 women whose crimes fell in the 1980-1985 period. The early and late samples were comparable in mean age (30.19 and 29.66 yr.) and racial composition (61 black: 49 white and 62 black: 45 white), although the early sample was less educated on average (8.53 yr.) than the later sample (9.77 yr.).

The diagnostic criteria for antisocial personality disorder recommended by Feighner, Robins, Guze, Woodruff, Winokur, and Munoz (1972) were used. Judgments for the nine social history criteria were made by the junior investigator on four-point scales of probability extending from "definitely not" (= 0) to "definitely" (= 3). These criteria of antisociality included school problems (e.g., truancy, fighting), running away from home, troubles with police (e.g., multiple arrests), poor work history, marital difficulties, repeated rage outbursts or fighting (not in school), sex problems (e.g., prostitution, pimping), vagrancy or wanderlust, and repeated lying or use of alias. Antisocial personality scores varied from 0 to 26 (possible range = 0 to 27). A second judge independently rated 31 of the files. The agreement ($r = .87$) between the two undergraduate judges suggests good reliability for the antisociality score.

---

[1]Requests for reprints should be sent to Alfred B. Heilbrun, Jr., Psychology Department, Emory University, Atlanta, Georgia 30322.

The total sample was split by time period (1965-1971 versus 1980-1985) and median psychopathy score (between 15 and 16). A continuous score reflecting criminal dangerousness was used as the dependent variable. The 7-point crime-severity scale used by the Georgia Board of Pardons and Parole includes escalating levels of nonviolent crimes at points 1-3 and of increasingly more severe violent crimes at points 4-7.

During the prefeminist period, the 51 high-antisocial women did commit more dangerous crimes ($M = 3.92$, $SD = 1.79$) than the 59 low-antisocial women ($M = 2.90$, $SD = 1.94$). In contrast, the 55 high-antisocial females committed less dangerous crimes ($M = 3.36$, $SD = 1.97$) than the 52 low antisocials ($M = 3.80$, $SD = 2.08$) during the postfeminist period. Factorial analysis of variance gave a significant interaction of antisociality $\times$ time period ($F_{1,213} = 7.57$, $p < .01$). More antisocial women perpetrated more dangerous crimes than less antisocial women ($p < .01$) before the women's movement took a firm hold, but by 1980-1985 there was no difference between them ($p > .20$).

Antisociality in women proved to be a significant predictor of more dangerous criminal behavior prior to the surge of the women's movement in the early 1970s. This predictiveness was lost in the 1980s. Feminism, with its emphasis upon the rejection of traditional feminine values, seems to offer a new explanation of dangerous behavior in women to the extent that prior role constraints upon physical aggression are lessened. Role rejection, if it cuts across level of antisociality, should contribute to dangerous criminality in all women. The change in prediction does not demonstrate that role changes for women changed the functional dynamics of female dangerousness, but it does encourage more focused research of such a possibility.

REFERENCES

ADLER, F. (1975) *Sisters in crime: the rise of the new female criminal*. New York: McGraw-Hill.

CAMPBELL, A. (1986) Self-report of fighting by females. *British Journal of Criminology*, 26, 28-46.

FEIGHNER, J. P., ROBINS, E., GUZE, S. B., WOODRUFF, R. A., WINOKUR, G., & MUNOZ, R. (1972) Diagnostic criteria for use in psychiatric research. *Archives of General Psychiatry*, 26, 57-63.

HOFFMAN-BUSTAMENTE, D. (1973) The nature of female criminality. *Issues in Criminality*, 8, 117-136.

SIMON, R. J. (1975) *The contemporary woman and crime*. Rockville, MD: National Institute of Mental Health.

WEIS, J. (1978) Liberation and crime: the invention of the new female criminal. In P. Wickman & P. Whitten (Eds.), *Readings in criminology*. Lexington, MA: Heath. Pp. 130-140.

Accepted December 8, 1987.

Feminism and Modern Friendship: Dislocating the Community*

Marilyn Friedman

A predominant theme in much recent feminist thought has been the critique of the abstract individualism which underlies some important versions of liberal political theory.[1] Abstract individualism considers individual human beings as social atoms, abstracted from their social contexts, and disregards the role of social relationships and human community in constituting the very identity and nature of individual human beings. Sometimes the individuals of abstract individualism are posited as rationally self-interested utility maximizers.[2] Sometimes, also, they are theorized to form communities based fundamentally on competition and conflict among persons vying for scarce resources, communities which represent no deeper social bond than that of instrumental relations based on calculated self-interest.[3]

Against this abstractive individualist view of the self and of human community, many feminists have asserted a conception of what might

* I am grateful to Cass Sunstein and the editors of *Ethics* for helpful comments on an earlier version of this article. This article was written with the support of a National Endowment for the Humanities Summer Stipend and a grant from the Faculty Research Committee of Bowling Green State University.

1. Compare Carole Pateman, *The Problem of Political Obligation: A Critique of Liberal Theory* (Berkeley: University of California Press, 1979); Zillah Eisenstein, *The Radical Future of Liberal Feminism* (New York: Longman, 1981); Nancy C. M. Hartsock, *Money, Sex, and Power* (Boston: Northeastern University Press, 1983); Alison M. Jaggar, *Feminist Politics and Human Nature* (Totowa, N.J.: Rowman & Allanheld, 1983); Naomi Scheman, "Individualism and the Objects of Psychology," in *Discovering Reality*, ed. Sandra Harding and Merrill B. Hintikka (Dordrecht: D. Reidel, 1983), pp. 225–44; Jane Flax, "Political Philosophy and the Patriarchal Unconscious: A Psychoanalytic Perspective on Epistemology and Metaphysics," in Harding and Hintikka, eds., pp. 245–81; and Seyla Benhabib, "The Generalized and the Concrete Other: The Kohlberg-Gilligan Controversy and Moral Theory," in *Women and Moral Theory*, ed. Eva Feder Kittay and Diana T. Meyers (Totowa, N.J.: Rowman & Littlefield, 1987), pp. 154–77.

2. Compare David Gauthier, *Morals by Agreement* (Oxford: Oxford University Press, 1986).

3. Compare George Homans, *Social Behavior: Its Elementary Forms* (New York: Harcourt, Brace & World, 1961); and Peter Blau, *Exchange and Power in Social Life* (New York: Wiley, 1974).

Ethics 99 (January 1989): 275–290

be called the "social self."[4] This conception fundamentally acknowledges the role of social relationships and human community in constituting both self-identity and the nature and meaning of the particulars of individual lives.[5] The modified conception of the self has carried with it an altered conception of community. Conflict and competition are no longer considered to be the basic human relationships; instead they are being replaced by alternative visions of the foundation of human society derived from nurturance, caring attachment, and mutual interestedness.[6] Some feminists, for example, recommend that the mother-child relationship be viewed as central to human society, and they project major changes in moral theory from such a revised focus.[7]

Some of these anti-individualist developments emerging from feminist thought are strikingly similar to other theoretical developments which are not specifically feminist. Thus, the "new communitarians," to borrow Amy Gutmann's term,[8] have also reacted critically to various aspects of modern liberal thought, including abstract individualism, rational egoism, and an instrumental conception of social relationships. The communitarian self, or subject, is also not a social atom but is instead a being constituted and defined by its attachments, including the particularities of its social relationships, community ties, and historical context. Its identity cannot be abstracted from community or social relationships.

With the recent feminist attention to values of care, nurturance, and relatedness—values that psychologists call "communal"[9] and which have been amply associated with women and women's moral reasoning[10]— one might anticipate that communitarian theory would offer important insights for feminist reflection. There is considerable power to the model of the self as deriving its identity and nature from its social relationships, from the way it is intersubjectively apprehended, from the norms of the community in which it is embedded.

4. Compare my "Autonomy in Social Context," in *Freedom, Equality, and Social Change: Problems in Social Philosophy Today,* ed. James Sterba and Creighton Peden (Lewiston, N.Y.: Edwin Mellen Press, in press).

5. Compare Drucilla Cornell, "Toward a Modern/Postmodern Reconstruction of Ethics," *University of Pennsylvania Law Review* 133 (1985): 291–380.

6. Compare Annette Baier, "Trust and Antitrust," *Ethics* 96 (1986): 231–60; and Owen Flanagan and Kathryn Jackson, "Justice, Care, and Gender: The Kohlberg-Gilligan Debate Revisited," *Ethics* 97 (1987): 622–37.

7. Compare Hartsock, pp. 41–42; and Virginia Held, "Non-contractual Society," in *Science, Morality and Feminist Theory,* ed. Marsha Hanen and Kai Nielsen, *Canadian Journal of Philosophy* 13, suppl. (1987): 111–38.

8. Amy Gutmann, "Communitarian Critics of Liberalism," *Philosophy and Public Affairs* 14 (1985): 308–22.

9. Compare Alice H. Eagly and Valerie J. Steffen, "Gender Stereotypes Stem from the Distribution of Women and Men into Social Roles," *Journal of Personality and Social Psychology* 46 (1984): 735–54.

10. Compare Carol Gilligan, *In a Different Voice* (Cambridge, Mass.: Harvard University Press, 1982).

However, communitarian philosophy as a whole is a perilous ally for feminist theory. Communitarians invoke a model of community which is focused particularly on families, neighborhoods, and nations. These sorts of communities have harbored social roles and structures which have been highly oppressive for women, as recent feminist critiques have shown. But communitarians seem oblivious to those criticisms and manifest a troubling complacency about the moral authority claimed or presupposed by these communities in regard to their members. By building on uncritical references to those sorts of communities, communitarian philosophy can lead in directions which feminists should not wish to follow.

This article is an effort to redirect communitarian thought so as to avoid some of the pitfalls which it poses, in its present form, for feminist theory and feminist practice. In the first part of the article, I develop some feminist-inspired criticisms of communitarian philosophy as it is found in writings by Michael Sandel and Alasdair MacIntyre.[11] My brief critique of communitarian thought has the aim of showing that communitarian theory, in the form in which it condones or tolerates traditional communal norms of gender subordination, is unacceptable from any standpoint enlightened by feminist analysis. This does not preclude agreeing with certain specific communitarian views, for example, the broad metaphysical conception of the individual, self, or subject as constituted by its social relationships and communal ties, or the assumption that traditional communities have some value. But the aim of the first section is critical: to focus on the communitarian disregard of gender-related problems with the norms and practices of traditional communities.

In the second part of the article, I will delve more deeply into the nature of different types of community and social relationship. I will suggest that friendships, on the one hand, and urban relationships and communities, on the other, offer an important clue toward a model of community which usefully counterbalances the family-neighborhood-nation complex favored by communitarians. With that model in view, we can begin to transform the communitarian vision of self and community into a more congenial ally for feminist theory.

THE SOCIAL SELF, IN COMMUNITARIAN PERSPECTIVE

Communitarians share with most feminist theorists a rejection of the abstractly individualist conception of self and society so prominent in modern liberal thought.[12] This self—atomistic, presocial, empty of all

11. In particular, Michael Sandel, *Liberalism and the Limits of Justice* (Cambridge: Cambridge University Press, 1982); Alasdair MacIntyre, *After Virtue* (Notre Dame, Ind.: University of Notre Dame Press, 1981).

12. Contemporary liberals do not regard the communitarians' metaphysical claims as a threat to liberal theory. The liberal concept of the self as abstracted from social relationships and historical context is now treated, not as a metaphysical presupposition but, rather, as a vehicle for evoking a pluralistic political society whose members disagree about the good for human life. With this device, liberalism seeks a theory of political process which aims

metaphysical content except abstract reason and will—is able to stand back from all the contingent moral commitments and norms of its particular historical context and assess each one of them in the light of impartial and universal criteria of reason. The self who achieves a substantial measure of such reflective reconsideration of the moral particulars of her life has achieved "autonomy," a widely esteemed liberal value.

In contrast to this vision of the self, the new communitarians pose the conception of a self whose identity and nature are defined by her contingent and particular social attachments. Communitarians extol the communities and social relationships, including family and nation, which constitute the typical social context in which the self emerges to self-consciousness. Thus, Michael Sandel speaks warmly of "those loyalties and convictions whose moral force consists partly in the fact that living by them is inseparable from understanding ourselves as the particular persons we are—as members of this family or community or nation or people, as bearers of this history, as sons and daughters of that revolution, as citizens of this republic."[13] Sandel continues, "Allegiances such as these are more than values I happen to have or aims I 'espouse at any given time.' They go beyond the obligations I voluntarily incur and the 'natural duties' I owe to human beings as such. They allow that to some I owe more than justice requires or even permits, not by reason of agreements I have made but instead in virtue of those more or less enduring attachments and commitments which taken together partly *define the person I am*" (italics mine).[14] Voicing similar sentiments, Alasdair MacIntyre writes:

> We all approach our own circumstances as bearers of a particular social identity. I am someone's son or daughter, someone else's cousin or uncle; I am a citizen of this or that city, a member of this or that guild or profession; I belong to this clan, that tribe, this nation. Hence what is good for me has to be the good for one who inhabits these roles. As such, I inherit from the past of my family, my city, my tribe, my nation, a variety of debts, inheritances, rightful expectations and obligations. These constitute the given of my life, my moral starting point. This is in part what gives my life its own moral particularity.[15]

(An aside: It is remarkable that neither writer mentions sex or gender as determining one's particular identity. Perhaps this glaring omission derives not from failing to realize the fundamental importance of gender in personal identity—could anyone really miss that?—but rather from

---

to avoid relying on any human particularities that might presuppose parochial human goods or purposes. Compare John Rawls, "Justice as Fairness: Political Not Metaphysical," *Philosophy and Public Affairs* 14 (1985): 223–51; and Joel Feinberg, "Liberalism, Community, and Tradition," drafted excerpt from *Harmless Wrongdoing*, vol. 4 of *The Moral Limits of the Criminal Law* (Oxford: Oxford University Press, 1988).

13. Sandel, þ. 179.

14. Ibid.

15. MacIntyre, pp. 204–5.

the aim to emphasize what social relationships and communities contribute to identity, along with the inability to conceive that gender is a social relationship or that it constitutes communities.)

For communitarians, these social relationships and communities have a kind of morally normative legitimacy; they define the "moral starting points," to use MacIntyre's phrase, of each individual life. The traditions, practices, and conventions of our communities have at least a prima facie legitimate moral claim upon us. MacIntyre does qualify the latter point by conceding that "the fact that the self has to find its moral identity in and through its membership in communities such as those of the family, the neighborhood, the city and the tribe does not entail that the self has to accept the moral *limitations* of the particularity of those forms of community."[16] Nevertheless, according to MacIntyre, one's moral quests must begin by "moving forward from such particularity," for it "can never be simply left behind or obliterated."[17]

Despite the feminist concern with a social conception of the self and the importance of social relationships, at least three features of the communitarian version of these notions are troubling from a feminist standpoint. First, a relatively minor point: the communitarian's metaphysical conception of an inherently social self has little usefulness for normative analysis; in particular, it will not support a specifically feminist critique of individualist personality. Second, communitarian theory fails to acknowledge that many communities make illegitimate moral claims on their members, linked to hierarchies of domination and subordination. Third, the specific communities of family, neighborhood, and nation so commonly invoked by communitarians are troubling paradigms of social relationship and communal life. I will discuss each of these points in turn.

First, the communitarian's metaphysical conception of the social self will not support feminist critiques of ruggedly individualist personality or its associated attributes: the avoidance of intimacy, nonnurturance, social distancing, aggression, or violence. Feminist theorists have often been interested in developing a critique of the norm of the highly individualistic, competitive, aggressive personality type, seeing that personality type as more characteristically male than female and as an important part of the foundation for patriarchy.

Largely following the work of Nancy Chodorow, Dorothy Dinnerstein, and, more recently, Carol Gilligan,[18] many feminists have theorized that the processes of psycho-gender development, in a society in which early infant care is the primary responsibility of women but not men, result in a radical distinction between the genders in the extent to which the

16. Ibid., p. 205.
17. Ibid.
18. Dorothy Dinnerstein, *The Mermaid and the Minotaur: Sexual Arrangements and Human Malaise* (New York: Harper & Row, 1976); Nancy Chodorow, *The Reproduction of Mothering* (Berkeley: University of California Press, 1978); and Gilligan.

self is constituted by, and self-identifies with, its relational connections to others. Males are theorized to seek and value autonomy, individuation, separation, and the moral ideals of rights and justice which are thought to depend on a highly individuated conception of persons. By contrast, females are theorized to seek and value connection, sociality, inclusion, and moral ideals of care and nurturance.

From this perspective, highly individuated selves have been viewed as a problem. They are seen as incapable of human attachments based on mutuality and trust, unresponsive to human needs, approaching social relationships merely as rationally self-interested utility maximizers, thriving on separation and competition, and creating social institutions which tolerate, even legitimize, violence and aggression.

However, a metaphysical view that all human selves are constituted by their social and communal relationships does not itself entail a critique of these highly individualistic selves or yield any indication of what degree of psychological attachment to others is desirable. On metaphysical grounds alone, there would be no reason to suppose that caring, nurturant, relational, sociable selves were better than more autonomous, individualistic, and separate selves. All would be equivalently socially constituted at a metaphysical level. Abstract individualism's failure would be not that it has produced asocial selves, for, on the communitarian view, such beings are metaphysically impossible, but, rather, that it has simply failed theoretically to acknowledge that selves are inherently social. And autonomy, independence, and separateness would become just a different way of being socially constituted, no worse nor better than heteronomy, dependence, or connectedness.

The communitarian conception of the social self, if it were simply a metaphysical view about the constitution of the self (which is what it seems to be), thus provides no basis for regarding nurturant, relational selves as morally superior to those who are highly individualistic. For that reason, it appears to be of no assistance to feminist theorists seeking a normative account of what might be wrong or excessive about competitive self-seeking behaviors or other seeming manifestations of an individualistic perspective. The communitarian "social self," as a metaphysical account of the self, is largely irrelevant to the array of normative tasks which many feminist thinkers have set for a conception of the self.

My second concern about communitarian philosophy has to do with the legitimacy of the moral influences which communities exert over their members and which are supposed to define the moral starting points of those members. As a matter of moral psychology, it is common for subjects to regard or presume as binding the moral claims made upon them by the norms of their communities. However, this point about moral psychology does not entail an endorsement of those moral claims, and it leaves open the question of whether, and to what extent, those claims might "really" be morally binding. Unfortunately, the new communitarians seem sometimes to go beyond the point of moral psychology to a stronger view, namely, that the moral claims of communities really are morally binding, at least as "moral starting points." MacIntyre refers to the "debts, inheritances, *rightful* expectations and obligations" which we "inherit" from family, nation and so forth.[19]

But such inheritances are enormously varied and troubling. Many communities are characterized by practices of exclusion and suppression of nongroup members, especially outsiders defined by ethnicity and sexual orientation.[20] If the new communitarians do not recognize legitimate "debts, inheritances, rightful expectations and obligations" across community lines, then their views have little relevance for our radically heterogeneous modern society. If people have "rightful expectations and obligations" across community lines, if, for example, whites have debts to blacks and Native Americans for histories of exploitation, if Germany owed reparations to non-Germans for genocidal practices, and so on, then "the" community as such, that is, the relatively bounded and local network of relationships which forms a subject's primary social setting, would not singularly determine the legitimate moral values or requirements which rightfully constitute the self's moral commitments or self-definition.

Besides excluding or suppressing outsiders, the practices and traditions of numerous communities are exploitative and oppressive toward many of their own members. This problem is of special relevance to women. Feminist theory is rooted in a recognition of the need for change in all the traditions and practices which show gender differentiation; many of these are located in just the sorts of communities invoked by communitarians, for example, family practices and national political traditions. The communitarian emphasis on communities unfortunately dovetails too well with the current popular emphasis on "the family" and seems to hark back to the repressive world of what some sociologists call communities of "place," the world of family, neighborhood, school, and church, which so intimately enclosed women in oppressive gender politics—the peculiar politics which it has been feminism's distinctive contribution to uncover. Any political theory which appears to support the hegemony of such communities and which appears to restore them to a position of unquestioned moral authority must be viewed with grave suspicion. I will come back to this issue when I turn to my third objection to communitarian philosophy.

Thus, while admitting into our notion of the self the important constitutive role played by social and communal relationships, we, from a standpoint independent of some particular subject, are not forced to accept as binding on that subject, the moral claims made by the social and communal relationships in which that subject is embedded or by which she is identified. Nor are we required to say that any particular

19. MacIntyre, p. 205; italics mine.
20. A similar point is made by Iris Young, "The Ideal of Community and the Politics of Difference," *Social Theory and Practice* 12 (1986): 12–13.

subject is herself morally obliged to accept as binding the moral claims made on her by any of the communities which constitute or define her. To evaluate the moral identities conferred by communities on their members, we need a theory of communities, of their interrelationships, of the structures of power, dominance, and oppression within and among them. Only such a theory would allow us to assess the legitimacy of the claims made by communities upon their members by way of their traditions, practices, and conventions of "debts, inheritances, . . . expectations, and obligations."

The communitarian approach suggests an attitude of celebrating the attachments which one finds oneself unavoidably to have, the familial ties, and so forth. But some relationships compete with others, and some relationships provide standpoints from which other relationships appear threatening or dangerous to oneself, one's integrity, or one's well-being. In such cases, simple formulas about the value of community provide no guidance. The problem is not simply to appreciate community per se but, rather, to reconcile the conflicting claims, demands, and identity-defining influences of the variety of communities of which one is a part.

It is worth recalling that liberalism has always condemned, in principle if not in practice, the norms of social hierarchy and political subordination based on inherited or ascribed status. Where liberals historically have applied this tenet at best only to the public realm of civic relationships, feminism seeks to extend it more radically to the "private" realm of family and other communities of place. Those norms and claims of local communities which sustain gender hierarchies have no intrinsic legitimacy from a feminist standpoint. A feminist interest in community must certainly aim for social institutions and relational structures which diminish and, finally, erase gender subordination.

Reflections such as these characterize the concerns of the modern self, the self who acknowleges no a priori loyalty to any feature of situation or role, and who claims the right to question the moral legitimacy of any contingent moral claim.[21] We can agree with the communitarians that it would be impossible for the self to question all her contingencies at once, yet at the same time, unlike the communitarians, still emphasize the critical importance of morally questioning various communal norms and circumstances.

A third problem with communitarian philosophy has to do with the sorts of communities evidently endorsed by communitarian theorists. Human beings participate in a variety of communities and social relationships, not only across time, but at any one time. However, when people think of "community," it is common for them to think of certain particular social networks, namely, those formed primarily out of family, neighborhood, school, and church.[22] MacIntyre and Sandel both emphasize

21. Compare Cornell, p. 323.
22. This point is made by Young, p. 12.

family specifically. MacIntyre cites neighborhood along with clan, tribe, city, and nation, while Sandel includes "nation or people, . . . bearers of this history, . . . sons and daughters of that revolution, . . . citizens of this republic."[23]

But where, one might ask, is the International Ladies Garment Workers' Union, the Teamsters, the Democratic Party, Alcoholics Anonymous, or the Committee in Solidarity with the People of El Salvador?

The substantive examples of community listed by MacIntyre and Sandel fall largely into two groups: one, governmental communities which constitute our civic and national identities in a public world of nation-states; and two, local communities centered around family and neighborhood. Although MacIntyre does mention professions and, rather archaically, "guilds,"[24] these references are anomolous in his work, which, for the most part, ignores such communities as trade unions, political action groups, associations of hobbyists, and so forth.

Some of the communities cited by MacIntyre and Sandel will resonate with the historical experiences of women, especially the inclusive communities of family and neighborhood. However, it should not be forgotten that governing communities have, until only recently, excluded the legitimate participation of women. It would seem to follow that they have accordingly not historically constituted the identities of women in profound ways. As "daughters" of the American revolution, looking back to the "fathers of our country," we find that we have inconveniently been deprived of the self-identifying heritage of our cultural mothers. In general, the contribution made to the identities of various groups of people by governing communities is quite uneven, given that they are communities to which many are subject but in which far fewer actively participate.

At any rate, there is an underlying commonality to most of the communities which MacIntyre and Sandel cite as constitutive of self-identity and definitive of our moral starting points. Sandel himself explicates this commonality when he writes that, for people "bound by a sense of community," the notion of community describes *"not a relationship they choose (as in a voluntary association) but an attachment they discover,* not merely an attribute but a constituent of their identity" (italics mine).[25] Not voluntary but "discovered" relationships and communities are what Sandel takes to define subjective identity for those who are bound by a "sense of community." It is the communities to which we are involuntarily bound to which Sandel accords metaphysical pride of place in the constitution of subjectivity. What are important are not simply the "associations" in which people "cooperate" but the "communities" in which people "participate," for these latter: "describe a form of life in which the members find themselves commonly situated 'to begin with,' their commonality

23. MacIntyre, p. 204; Sandel, p. 179.
24. MacIntyre, p. 204.
25. Sandel, p. 150.

consisting less in relationships they have entered than in attachments they have found."[26] Thus, the social relationships which one finds, the attachments which are discovered and not chosen, become the points of reference for self-definition by the communitarian subject.

For the child maturing to self-consciousness in her community of origin, typically the family-neighborhood-school-church complex, it seems uncontroversial that "the" community is found, not entered, discovered, not created. But this need not be true of an adult's communities of mature self-identification. Many of these adult communities are, for at least some of their members, communities of choice to a significant extent: labor unions, philanthropic associations, political coalitions, and, if one has ever moved or migrated, even the communities of neighborhood, church, city, or nation-state might have been chosen to an important extent. One need not have simply discovered oneself to be embedded in them in order that one's identity or the moral particulars of one's life be defined by them. Sandel is right to indicate the role of found communities in constituting the unreflective, "given" identity which the self discovers when *first* beginning to reflect on itself. But for mature self-identity, we should also recognize a legitimate role for communities of choice, supplementing, if not displacing, the communities and attachments which are merely found.

Moreover, the discovered identity constituted by one's original community of place might be fraught with ambivalences and ambiguities. Thus, poet Adrienne Rich writes about her experiences growing up with a Christian mother, a Jewish father who suppressed his ethnicity, and a family community which taught Adrienne Rich contempt for all that was identified with Jewishness. In 1946, while still a high school student, Rich saw, for the first time, a film about the Allied liberation of Nazi concentration camps. Writing about this experience in 1982, she brooded: "I feel belated rage that I was so impoverished by the family and social worlds I lived in, that I had to try to figure out by myself what this did indeed mean for me. That I had never been taught about resistance, only about passing. That I had no language for anti-Semitism itself."[27] As a student at Radcliffe in the late forties, Rich met "real" Jewish women who inducted her into the lore of Jewish background and customs, holidays and foods, names and noses. She plunged in with trepidation: "I felt I was testing a forbidden current, that there was danger in these revelations. I bought a reproduction of a Chagall portrait of a rabbi in striped prayer shawl and hung it on the wall of my room. I was admittedly young and trying to educate myself, but I was also doing something that *is* dangerous: I was flirting with

26. Ibid., pp. 151–52.
27. Adrienne Rich, "Split at the Root: An Essay on Jewish Identity," in her *Blood, Bread, and Poetry* (New York: Norton, 1986), p. 107; reprinted from Evelyn Torton Beck, ed., *Nice Jewish Girls: A Lesbian Anthology* (Trumansburg, N.Y.: Crossing Press, 1982), pp. 67–84.

identity."[28] And she was doing it apart from the family community from which her ambiguous ethnic identity was originally derived.

For Sandel, Rich's lifelong troubled reflections on her ethnic identity might seem compatible with his theory. In his view, the subject discovers the attachments which are constitutive of its subjectivity through reflection on a multitude of values and aims, differentiating what is self from what is not-self. He might say that Rich discriminated among the many loyalties and projects which defined who she was in her original community, that is, her family, and discerned that her Jewishness appeared "essential"[29] to who she was. But it is not obvious, without question begging, that her original community really defined her as essentially Jewish. Indeed, her family endeavored to suppress loyalties and attachments to all things Jewish. Thus, one of Rich's quests in life, so evidently not inspired by her community of origin alone, was to reexamine the identity found in that original context. The communitarian view that found communities and social attachments constitute self-identity does not, by itself, explicate the source of such a quest. It seems more illuminating to say that her identity became, in part, "chosen," that it had to do with social relationships and attachments which she sought out, rather than merely found, created as well as discovered.

Thus, the commitments and loyalties of our found communities, our communities of origin, may harbor ambiguities, ambivalences, contradictions, and oppressions which complicate as well as constitute identity and which have to be sorted out, critically scrutinized. And since the resources for such scrutiny may not be found in all "found" communities, our theories of community should recognize that resources and skills derived from communities which are not merely found or discovered may equally well contribute to the constitution of identity. The constitution of identity and moral particularity, for the modern self, may well require radically different communities from those so often invoked by communitarians.

The whole tenor of communitarian thinking would change once we opened up the conception of the social self to encompass chosen communities, especially those which lie beyond the typical original community of family-neighborhood-school-church. No longer would communitarian thought present a seemingly conservative complacency about the private and local communities of place which have so effectively circumscribed, in particular, the lives of most women.

In the second part of this article, I will explore more fully the role of communities and relationships of "choice," which point the way toward a notion of community more congenial to feminist aspirations.

28. Ibid., p. 108.
29. This term is used by Sandel, p. 180.

MODERN FRIENDSHIP, URBAN COMMUNITY, AND BEYOND

My goals are manifold: to retain the communitarian insights about the contribution of community and social relationship to self-identity, yet open up for critical reflection the moral particulars imparted by those communities, and identify the sorts of communities which will provide nonoppressive and enriched lives for women.

Toward this end, it will be helpful to consider models of human relationship and community which contrast with those cited by communitarians. I believe that friendship and urban community can offer us crucial insights into the social nature of the modern self. It is in moving forward from these relationships that we have the best chance of reconciling the communitarian conception of the social self with the longed-for communities of feminist aspiration.

Both modern friendship and the stereotypical urban community share an important feature which is either neglected or deliberately avoided in communitarian conceptions of human relationship. From a liberal, or Enlightenment, or modernist standpoint, this feature would be characterized as voluntariness: those relationships are based partly on choice.

Let us first consider friendship as it is understood in this culture. Friends are supposed to be people whom one chooses on one's own to share activities and intimacies. No particular people are assigned by custom or tradition to be a person's friends. From among the larger number of one's acquaintances, one moves toward closer and more friendlike relationships with some of them, motivated by one's own needs, values, and attractions. No consanguineous or legal connections establish or maintain ties of friendship. As this relationship is widely understood in our culture, its basis lies in voluntary choice.

In this context, "voluntary choice" refers to motivations arising out of one's own needs, desires, interests, values, and attractions, in contrast to motivations arising from what is socially assigned, ascribed, expected, or demanded. This means that friendship is more likely than many other relationships, such as those of family and neighborhood, to be grounded in and sustained by shared interests and values, mutual affection, and possibilities for generating mutual respect and esteem.

In general, friendship has had an obvious importance to feminist aspirations as the basis of the bond which is (ironically) called "sisterhood."[30] Friendship is more likely than many other close personal relationships to provide social support for people who are idiosyncratic, whose unconventional values and deviant life-styles make them victims of intolerance from family members and others who are unwillingly related to them. In this regard, friendship has socially disruptive possibilities, for out of

---

30. Martha Ackelsberg points out the ironic and misleading nature of this use of the term "sisterhood" in " 'Sisters' or 'Comrades'? The Politics of Friends and Families," in *Families, Politics, and Public Policy,* ed. Irene Diamond (New York: Longman, 1983), pp. 339–56.

the unconventional living which it helps to sustain there often arise influential forces for social change. Friendship among women has been the cement not only of the various historical waves of the feminist movement, but as well of numerous communities of women throughout history who defied the local conventions for their gender and lived lives of creative disorder.[31] In all these cases, women moved out of their given or found communities into new attachments with other women by their own choice, that is, motivated by their own needs, desires, attractions, and fears rather than, and often in opposition to, the expectations and ascribed roles of their found communities.

Like friendship, many urban relationships are also based more on choice than on socially ascribed roles, biological connections, or other nonvoluntary ties. Voluntary associations, such as political action groups, support groups, associations of co-hobbyists, and so on, are a common part of modern urban life, with its large population centers and the greater availability of critical masses of people with special interests or needs. But while friendship is almost universally extolled, urban communities and relationships have been theorized in wildly contradictory ways. Cities have sometimes been taken as "harbingers" of modern culture per se[32] and have been particularly associated with the major social trends of modern life, such as industrialization and bureaucratization.[33] The results of these trends are often thought to have been a fragmentation of "real" community and the widely lamented alienation of modern urban life: people seldom know their neighbors; population concentration generates massive psychic overload;[34] fear and mutual distrust, even outright hostility, generated by the dangers of urban life, may dominate most daily associations. Under such circumstances, meaningful relationships are often theorized to be rare, if at all possible.

But is this image a complete portrait of urban life? It is probably true, in urban areas, that communities of place are diminished in importance; neighborhood plays a far less significant role in constituting community than it does in nonurban areas.[35] But this does not mean that the social networks and communities of urban dwellers are inferior to those of nonurban residents.

Much evidence suggests that urban settings do not, as commonly stereotyped, promote only alienation, isolation, and psychic breakdown. The communities available to urban dwellers are different from those

31. Compare Janice Raymond, *A Passion for Friends* (Boston: Beacon, 1986), esp. chaps. 2 and 3.

32. Claude Fischer, *To Dwell among Friends* (Chicago: University of Chicago Press, 1982), p. 1.

33. Compare Richard Sennett, "An Introduction," in *Classic Essays on the Culture of Cities,* ed. Richard Sennett (New York: Appleton-Century-Crofts, 1969), pp. 3–22.

34. Compare Stanley Milgram, "The Experience of Living in Cities," *Science* 167 (1970): 1461–68.

35. Fischer, pp. 97–103.

available to nonurban dwellers, but not necessarily less gratifying or fulfilling.[36] Communities of place are relatively nonvoluntary; one's extended family of origin is given or ascribed, and the relationships found as one grows. Sociological research has shown that urban dwellers tend to form their social networks, their communities, out of people who are brought together for reasons other than geographical proximity. As sociologist Claude Fischer has stated it, in urban areas, "population concentration stimulates allegiances to subcultures based on more significant social traits" than common locality or neighborhood.[37] Communities of place, centered around the family-neighborhood-church-school web, are more likely, for urban dwellers, to be supplanted by other sorts of communities, resulting in what the sociologist Melvin Webber has called "community without propinquity."[38] But most important for our purposes, these are still often genuine communities, and not the cesspools of "Rum, Romanism, and Rebellion" sometimes depicted by anti-urbanists.

Literature reveals that women writers have been both repelled and inspired by cities. The city, as a concentrated center of male political and economic power, seems to exclude women altogether.[39] However, as literary critic Susan Merrill Squier points out, the city can provide women not only with jobs, education, and the cultural tools with which to escape imposed gender roles, familial demands, and domestic servitude, but can also bring women together, in work or in leisure, and lay the basis for bonds of sisterhood.[40] The quests of women who journey to cities leaving behind men, home, and family, are subversive, writes literary critic Blanche Gelfant, and may well be perceived by others "as assaults upon society."[41] Thus, cities open up for women possibilities of supplanting communities of place with relationships and communities of choice. These chosen communities can provide the resources for women to surmount the moral particularities of family and place which define and limit their moral starting points.

Social theorists have long decried the interpersonal estrangement of urban life, an observation which seems predominantly inspired by the public world of conflict between various subcultural groups. Urbanism does not create interpersonal estrangement within subcultures but, rather,

36. Ibid., pp. 193–232.

37. Ibid., p. 273.

38. Melvin Webber, "Order in Diversity: Community without Propinquity," in *Neighborhood, City and Metropolis,* ed. R. Gutman and D. Popenoe (New York: Random House, 1970), pp. 792–811.

39. Compare the essays in Catharine Stimpson et al., eds., *Women and the American City* (Chicago: University of Chicago Press, 1980, 1981); and the special issue on "Women in the City," *Urban Resources,* vol. 3, no. 2 (Winter 1986).

40. Introduction to Susan Merrill Squier, ed., *Women Writers and the City* (Knoxville: University of Tennessee Press, 1984), pp. 3–10.

41. Blanche Gelfant, "Sister to Faust: The City's 'Hungry' Woman as Heroine," in Squier, ed., p. 267.

tends to promote social involvement.[42] This is especially true for people with special backgrounds and interests, for people who are members of small minorities, and for ethnic groups. Fischer has found that social relationships in urban centers are more "culturally specialized: urbanites were relatively involved with associates in the social world they considered most important and relatively uninvolved with associates, if any, in other worlds."[43] As Fischer summarizes it, "Urbanism . . . fosters social involvement in the subculture(s) of *choice,* rather than the subculture(s) of circumstances."[44] This is doubtless reinforced by the recent more militant expression of group values and group demands for rights and respect on the parts of urban subcultural minorities.

We might describe urban relationships as being characteristically "modern" to signal their relatively greater voluntary basis. We find, in these relationships and the social networks formed of them, not a loss of community but an increase in importance of community of a different sort from that of family-neighborhood-church-school complexes. Yet these more voluntary communities may be as deeply constitutive of the identities and particulars of the individuals who participate in them as are the communities of place so warmly invoked by communitarians.

Perhaps it is more illuminating to say that communities of choice foster not so much the constitution of subjects but their reconstitution. They may be sought out as contexts in which people relocate the various constituents of their identities, as Adrienne Rich sought out the Jewish community in her college years. While people in a community of choice may not share a common history, their shared values or interests are likely to manifest backgrounds of similar experiences, as, for example, among the members of a lesbian community. The modern self may seek new communities whose norms and relationships stimulate and develop her identity and self-understanding more adequately than her unchosen community of origin, her original community of place.

In case it is chosen communities which help us to define ourselves, the project of self-definition would not be arising from communities in which we merely found or discovered our immersion. It is likely that chosen communities, lesbian communities, for example, attract us in the first place because they appeal to features of ourselves which, though perhaps merely found or discovered, were inadequately or ambivalently sustained by our unchosen families, neighborhoods, schools, or churches. Thus, unchosen communities are sometimes communities which we can, and should, leave, searching elsewhere for the resources to help us discern who we really are.

Our communities of origin do not necessarily constitute us as selves who agree or comply with the norms which unify those communities.

42. Fischer, pp. 247–48.
43. Ibid., p. 230.
44. Ibid.

Some of us are constituted as deviants and resisters by our communities of origin, and our defiance may well run to the foundational social norms which ground the most basic social roles and relationships upon which those communities rest. The feminist challenge to sex/gender arrangements is precisely of this foundational sort.

A community of choice might be a community of people who share a common oppression. This is particularly critical in those instances in which the shared oppression is not concentrated within certain communities of place, as it might be, for example, in the case of ethnic minorities, but, rather, is focused on people who are distributed throughout social and ethnic groupings and who do not themselves constitute a traditional community of place. Women are a prime example of such a distributed group. Women's communities are seldom the original, nonvoluntary, found communities of their members.

To be sure, nonvoluntary communities of place are not without value. Most lives contain mixtures of relationships and communities, some given/found/discovered and some chosen/created. Most people probably are, to some extent, ineradicably constituted by their communities of place, the community defined by some or all of their family, neighborhood, school, or church. It is noteworthy that dependent children, elderly persons, and all other individuals whose lives and well-being are at great risk, need the support of communities whose other members do not or cannot choose arbitrarily to leave. Recent philosophical investigation into communities and relationships not founded or sustained by choice has brought out the importance of these social networks for the constitution of social life.[45] But these insights should not obscure the additional need for communities of choice to counter oppressive and abusive relational structures in those nonvoluntary communities by providing models of alternative social relationships as well as standpoints for critical reflection on self and community.

Having attained a critically reflective stance toward one's communities of origin, one's community of place, toward family, neighborhood, church, school, and nation, one has probably at the same time already begun to question and distance oneself from aspects of one's "identity" in that community and, therefore, to have embarked on the path of personal redefinition. From such a perspective, the uncritically assumed communities of place invoked by the communitarians appear deeply problematic. We can concede the influence of those communities without having unreflectively to endorse it. We must develop communitarian thought beyond its complacent regard for the communities in which we once found ourselves toward (and beyond) an awareness of the crucial importance of dislocated communities, communities of choice.

45. Compare Baier; Held; and Pateman.

Ann Snitow

PAGES FROM A GENDER DIARY

Basic Divisions in Feminism

In the early days of this wave of the women's movement, I sat in a weekly consciousness raising group with my friend A. We compared notes recently: What did you think was happening? How did you think our own lives were going to change? A. said she had felt, "Now I can be a woman; it's no longer so humiliating. I can stop fantasizing that secretly I am a man, as I used to, before I had children. Now I can value what was once my shame." Her answer amazed me. Sitting in the same meetings during those years, my thoughts were roughly the reverse: "Now I don't have to be a woman anymore. I need never become a mother. Being a woman has always been humiliating, but I used to assume there was no exit. Now the very idea 'woman' is up for grabs. 'Woman' is my slave name; feminism will give me freedom to seek some other identity altogether."

On its face this clash of theoretical and practical positions may seem absurd, but it is my goal to explore such contradictions, to show why they are not absurd at all. Feminism is inevitably a mixed form, requiring in its very nature such inconsistencies. In what follows I try to show first, that a common divide keeps forming in both feminist thought and action between the need to build the identity "woman" and give it solid political meaning and the need to tear down the very category "woman" and dismantle its all-too-solid history. Feminists often split along the lines of some version of this argument, and that splitting is my subject. Second, I argue that though a settled compromise between these positions is currently impossible, and though a constant choosing of sides is tactically unavoidable, feminists—and

indeed most women—live in a complex relationship to this central feminist divide. From moment to moment we perform subtle psychological and social negotiations about just how gendered we choose to be.

This tension—between needing to act as women and needing an identity not overdetermined by our gender—is as old as Western feminism. It is at the core of what feminism is. The divide runs, twisting and turning, right through movement history. The problem of identity it poses was barely conceivable before the eighteenth century, when almost everyone saw women as a separate species. Since then the idea "woman" has become a question rather than a given, a question increasingly unavoidable as an earlier absolute definition of gender difference has begun its long, slow, and fundamental erosion.

In the current wave of the movement, the divide is more urgent and central a part of feminism than ever before. On the one hand, many women moved by feminism are engaged by its promise of solidarity, the poetry of a retrieved worth. It feels glorious, Michelle Cliff says, to "reclaim an identity they taught [us] to despise." Movement passion rescues women-only groups from contempt; female intimacy acquires new meanings and becomes more threatening to the male exclusiveness so long considered "the world."

On the other hand, other feminists, often equally stirred by solidarity, rebel against having to be "women" at all. They argue that whenever we uncritically accept the monolith "woman," we run the risk of merely relocating ourselves inside the old closed ring of an unchanging feminine nature. But is there any such reliable nature? In each case these feminists question the eternal sisterhood: What about class, age, race, nationality?[1]

Names for a Recurring Feminist Divide

In every case, the specialness of women has this double face, though often, in the heat of new confrontations, feminists suffer a harmful amnesia; we forget about this paradox we live with. Feminist theorists keep renaming this tension, as if new names could advance feminist political work. But at this point new names are likely to tempt us to forget that we have named this split before. In the service of trying to help us recognize what we are fated—for some time—to repeat, here is a reminder of past categories.

Minimizers and Maximizers

The divide so central as to be feminism's defining characteristic goes by many names. Kate Stimpson cleverly called it the feminist debate between the "minimizers" and the "maximizers."[2] Briefly, the minimizers are feminists who want to undermine the category "woman," to minimize the meaning of sex difference. (As we shall see, this stance can have surprisingly different political faces.) The maximizers want to keep the category (or feel they can't do otherwise), but they want to change its meaning, to reclaim and elaborate the social being "woman," and to empower her.

Radical Feminists and Cultural Feminists

In *Daring to Be Bad: A History of the Radical Feminist Movement in America, 1967–1975,* Alice Echols sees this divide on a time line of the current women's movement, with "radical feminism" more typical of the initial feminist impulse in this wave succeeded by "cultural feminism." Echols's definition of the initial bursts of "radical feminism" shows that it also included "cultural feminism" in embryo. She argues that both strains were present from the first—contradictory elements that soon proclaimed themselves as tensions in sisterhood. Nonetheless, the earlier groups usually defined the commonality of "women" as the shared fact of their oppres-

sion by "men." Women were to work separately from men not as a structural ideal but because such separation was necessary to escape a domination that only a specifically feminist (rather than mixed left) politics could change.

On the other side stands Echols's category, "cultural feminism." In her depiction of the divide, the cultural feminist celebration of being female was a retreat from "radical feminism": "[I]t was easier to rehabilitate femininity than to abolish gender."[3] She offers as a prime example of the growth of cultural feminism the popularity of Jane Alpert's "new feminist theory," published in *Ms.* magazine in 1973 as "Mother Right":

> [F]eminists have asserted that the essential difference between women and men does not lie in biology but rather in the roles that patriarchal societies (men) have required each sex to play. . . . However, a flaw in this feminist argument has persisted: *it contradicts our felt experience of the biological difference between the sexes as one of immense significance.* . . . The unique consciousness ór sensibility of women, the particular attributes that set feminist art apart, and a compelling line of research now being pursued by feminist anthropologists all point to the idea that *female biology is the basis of women's powers.* Biology is hence the source and not the enemy of feminist revolution.

Echols concludes that by 1973, "Alpert's contention that women were united by their common biology was enormously tempting, given the factionalism within the movement."

Ironically, then, the pressure of differences that quickly surfaced in the women's movement between lesbians and straight women, between white and black, between classes, was a key source of the new pressure towards unity. The female body offered a permanence and an immediately rich identity that radical feminism, with its call to a long, often negative struggle of resistance, could not.

As her tone reveals, in Echols's account, "radical feminism" is a relatively positive term and "cultural feminism" an almost entirely negative one. As I'll explain later, I have a number of reasons for sharing this judgment. Finally, though, it won't help us to understand recurring feminist oppositions if we simply sort them into progressive versus reactionary alignments. The divide is nothing so simple as a split between truly radical activists and benighted conservative ones, or between real agents for change and liberal reformers, or between practical fighters and sophisticated theorists. The sides in this debate don't line up neatly in these ways. Maximizers and minimizers have political histories that converge and diverge. A pretense of neutrality won't get us anywhere either. I'm describing a struggle here, and every account of it contains its overt or covert tropism toward one side or the other.

Essentialists and Social Constructionists

One has only to move from an account of movement politics to one of feminist theory in order to reverse Echols's scenario of decline. In academic feminist discussion, the divide between the "essentialists" and the "social constructionists" has been a rout for the essentialists. Briefly, essentialists (like Alpert, above) see gender as rooted in biological sex differences. Hardly anyone of any camp will now admit to being an essentialist, since the term has become associated with a naive claim to an eternal female nature. All the same, essentialism, like its counterpart, cultural feminism, is abundantly present in current movement work. When Barbara Deming writes that "the capacity to bear and nurture children gives women a special consciousness, a spiritual advantage rather than a disadvantage," she is assigning an enduring meaning to anatomical sex differences. When Andrea Dworkin describes how through sex a woman's "insides are worn away over time, and she, possessed, becomes weak, depleted, usurped in all her physical and mental energies . . . by the one who occupies her," she is asserting that in sex women are immolated as a matter of course, in the nature of things.[4]

"Social construction"—the idea that the meaning of the body is changeable—is far harder to embrace with confidence. As Ellen Willis once put it, culture may shape the body, but we feel that the body has ways of pushing back. To assert that the body has no enduring, natural language often seems like a rejection of common sense. Where can a woman stand—embodied or disembodied—in the flow of this argument?

Writing not about gender in general but about that more focused issue of bodies and essences, sexuality, Carole Vance muses over the strengths and vicissitudes of "social construction" theory. She observes that the social constructionists who try to discuss sexuality differ about just what is constructed. Few would go so far as to say that the body plays no part at all as a material condition on which we build desire and sexual mores. But even for those social constructionists who try to escape entirely from any a priori ideas about the body, essentialism makes a sly comeback through unexamined assumptions. For example, how can social constructionists confidently say they are studying "sexuality"? If there is no essential, transhistorical biology of arousal, then there is no unitary subject, "sexuality," to discuss: "If sexuality is constructed differently at each time and place, can we use the term in a comparatively meaningful way? . . . [H]ave constructionists undermined their own categories? Is there an 'it' to study?"[5]

In the essentialist–versus–social constructionist version of the divide, one can see that one term in the argument is far more stable than the other. Essentialism such as Jane Alpert's in "Mother Right" assumes a relatively stable social identity in "male" and "female," while as Carole Vance argues, social construction is at its best as a source of destabilizing questions. By definition social construction theory cannot offer a securely bounded area for the study of gender; instead it initiates an inspiring collapse of gender verities.

Cultural Feminists and Poststructuralists

The contrast between more and less stable categories suggests yet another recent vocabulary for the feminist divide. In "Cultural Feminism versus Post-Structuralism: The Identity Crisis in Feminist Theory," Linda Alcoff puts Echols's definition of "cultural feminism" up against what she sees as a more recent counterdevelopment: feminist poststructural theory. By speaking only of "the last ten years," Alcoff lops off the phase of "radical feminism" that preceded "cultural feminism" in movement history, leaving the revisionist image of extreme essentialism (such as Mary Daly's in *Gyn/Ecology*) as the basic matrix of feminist thought from which a radical "nominalism" has more recently and heroically departed, calling all categories into doubt.[6] It is no accident that with attention to detail, Alice Echols can trace a political decline from "radical feminism" to "cultural feminism" between 1967 and 1975 while Linda Alcoff can persuasively trace a gain in theoretical understanding from "cultural feminism" to "poststructuralism" between 1978 and 1988. Put them together and both narratives change: Instead of collapse or progress, we see one typical oscillation in the historical life of the divide.

These two accounts are also at odds because they survey very different political locations: Echols is writing about radical feminist activism, Alcoff about developments in academic feminist theory. Though political activism has developed a different version of the central debate from that of the more recent academic feminism, both confront the multiple problems posed by the divide. Nor will a model that goes like this work: *thesis* (essentialism, cultural feminism), *antithesis* (poststructuralism, deconstruction, Lacanian psychoanalysis), *synthesis* (some stable amalgam of women's solidarity that includes radical doubts about the formation, cohesion, and potential power of the group).

Instead, the divide keeps forming *inside* each of these categories. It is fundamental at any level one cares to meet it: material, psychological, linguistic. For example, U.S. feminist theorists don't agree about whether poststructuralism tends more often toward its own version of essentialism (strengthening the arguments of maximizers by recognizing an enduring position of female Other) or whether poststructuralism is instead the best tool minimalists have (weakening any universalized, permanent concept such as Woman[7]). Certainly poststructuralists disagree among themselves, and this debate around and inside poststructuralism should be no surprise. In feminist discourse a tension keeps forming between finding a useful lever in female identity and seeing that identity as hopelessly compromised.

I'm not regressing here to the good old days of an undifferentiated, undertheorized sisterhood, trying to blur distinctions others have usefully struggled to establish, but I do want to explore a configuration—the divide—that repeats in very different circumstances. For example, in an earlier oscillation, both radical feminism and liberal feminism offered their own versions of doubt about cultural feminism and essentialism. Liberal feminists refused the idea that biology should structure women's public and sometimes even their private roles. Radical feminists saw the creation and maintenance of gender difference as the means by which patriarchs controlled women.[8] Though neither group had the powerful theoretical tools later developed by the poststructuralists, both intimated basic elements in poststructuralist work: that the category "woman" was a construction, a discourse over which there had been an ongoing struggle; and that the self, the "subject," was as much the issue as were social institutions. To be sure, these early activists often foolishly ignored Freud; they invoked an unproblematic "self" that could be rescued from the dark male tower of oppression; and they hourly expected the radical deconstruction of gender, as if the deconstruction of what had been constructed was relatively easy. Nonetheless, radical, philosophical doubts about the cohesion of "woman" have roots that go all the way down in the history of both liberal and radical feminism.

Recently I asked feminist critic Marianne DeKoven for a piece she and Linda Bamber wrote about the divide for the Modern Language Association in 1982. "Feminists have refined our thinking a great deal since then," she said. Yes, no doubt; but there is not much from the recent past that we can confidently discard. In fact, the Bamber-DeKoven depiction of the divide remains useful because we are nowhere near a synthesis that would make these positions relics of a completed phase. One side of the divide, Bamber says in her half of the paper, "has been loosely identified with American feminism, the other with French feminism."

But in fact these labels are inadequate, as both responses can be found in the work of both French and American feminists. Instead of debating French vs. American feminism, then, I want to define the two poles of our responses non-judgmentally and simply list their characteristics under Column A and Column B.

Column A feminism is political, empirical, historical. A Column A feminist rebels against the marginalization of women and demands access to "positions that require knowledge and confer power." A Column A feminist insists on woman as subject, on equal pay for equal work, on the necessity for women to be better represented in political life, the media, history books, etc. Column A feminism assumes, as Marks and de Courtivron put it, "that women have (always) been present but invisible and if they look they will find themselves."

The Column B feminist, on the other hand, is not particularly interested in the woman as subject. Instead of claiming power, knowledge and high culture for women, Column B feminism attacks these privileged quantities as "phallogocentric." . . . The feminine in Column B is part of the challenge to God, money, the phallus, origins and ends, philosophical privilege, the transcendent author, representation, the Descartian cogito, transparent language, and so on. The feminine is valorized as fragment, absence, scandal. . . . Whereas the Column A feminist means to occupy the center on equal terms with men, the Column B feminist, sometimes aided by Derrida, Lacan, Althusser, Levi-Strauss and Foucault, subverts the center and endorses her own marginality.[9]

No doubt Bamber and DeKoven would restate these terms now in the light of seven more years of good, collective feminist work, but I am trying to write against the grain of that usually excellent impulse here, trying to suggest a more distant perspective in which seven years become a dot.

Alcoff is only the latest in a long line of frustrated feminists who want to push beyond the divide, to be done with it. She writes typically: "We cannot simply embrace the paradox. In order to avoid the serious disadvantages of cultural feminism and post-structuralism, feminism needs to transcend the dilemma by developing a third course. . . ."[10] But "embracing the paradox" is just what feminism cannot choose but do. There is no transcendence, no third course. The urgent contradiction women constantly experience between the pressure to be a woman and the pressure not to be one will change only through

a historical process; it cannot be dissolved through thought alone.

This is not to undervalue theory in the name of some more solid material reality but to emphasize that the dualism of the divide requires constant work; it resists us. It's not that we can't interrupt current patterns, not that trying to imagine our way beyond them isn't valuable, but that such work is continuous. What is more, activists trying to make fundamental changes, trying to push forward the feminist discourse and alter its material context, don't agree about what sort of synthesis they want. Nor can activists turn to theorists in any direct way for a resolution of these differences. Activism and scholarship have called forth different readings of the divide, but neither of these locations remains innocent of the primary contradiction. There is no marriage of theoretical mind and activist brawn to give us New Feminist Woman. And the recognition that binary thinking is a problem doesn't offer us any immediate solution.

In other words, neither cultural feminism nor poststructuralism suggests a clear course when the time comes to discuss political strategy. Though we have learned much, we are still faced with the continuing strategic difficulty of *what to do*. As Michèle Barrett puts it: "It does not need remarking that the postmodernist point of view is explicitly hostile to any political project beyond the ephemeral."[11] The virtue of the ephemeral action is its way of evading ossification of image or meaning. Ephemerally, we can recognize a possibility we cannot live out, imagine a journey we cannot yet take. We begin: The category "woman" is a fiction; then, poststructuralism suggests ways in which human beings live by fictions; then, in its turn, activism requires of feminists that we elaborate the fiction "woman" as if she were not a provisional invention at all but a person we know well, one in need of obvious rights and powers. Activism and theory weave together here, working on what remains the same basic cloth, the stuff of feminism.

Some theorists like Alcoff reach for a synthesis, a third way, beyond the divide, while others like Bamber and DeKoven choose instead the metaphor of an inescapable, irreducible "doubleness"—a word that crops up everywhere in feminist discussion. To me, the meta-

251

phor of doubleness is the more useful: It is a reminder of the unresolved tension on which feminism continues to be built. As Alice Walker puts it in her formal definition of a "womanist" (her word for black feminism): "Appreciates and prefers women's culture, women's emotional flexibility . . . committed to survival and wholeness of entire people, male and female. Not a separatist, except periodically, for health."[12]

This is not to deny change but to give a different estimate of its rate. Mass feminist consciousness has made a great difference; we have created not only new expectations but also new institutions. Yet, inevitably, the optimism of activism has given way to the academic second thoughts that tell us why our work is so hard. For even straightforward, liberal changes—like equal pay or day care—are proving far more elusive than feminists dreamed in 1970. We are moving more slowly than Western women of the late twentieth century can easily accept—or are even likely to imagine.

Motherists and Feminists

If the long view has a virtue beyond the questionable one of inducing calm, it can help feminists include women to whom a rapid political or theoretical movement forward has usually seemed beside the point—poor women, peasant women, and women who for any number of reasons identify themselves not as feminists but as militant mothers, fighting together for survival. In a study group convened by Temma Kaplan since 1985, Grass Roots Movements of Women, feminists who do research about such movements in different parts of the world, past and present, have been meeting to discuss the relationship among revolutionary action, women, and feminist political consciousness. As Meredith Tax described this activism:

> There is a crux in women's history/women's studies, a knot and a blurry place where various things converge. This place has no name and there is no established methodology for studying it. The things that converge there are variously called: community organizations, working-class women's organizations, consumer movements, popular mass organizations, housewives' organizations, mothers' movements, strike support movements, bread strikes, revolutions at the base, women's peace movements. Some feminist or proto-feminist groups and united front organizations of women may be part of this crux. Or they may be different. There is very little theory, either feminist or Marxist, regarding this crux.[13]

The group has been asking: Under what class circumstances do women decide to band together as women, break out of domestic space, and publicly protest? What part have these actions actually played in gaining fundamental political changes? How do women themselves define what they have done and why? Does it make any sense to name feminist thinking as part of this female solidarity? Is there reason to think some kind of feminist consciousness is likely to emerge from this kind of political experience? Is the general marginality of these groups a strength or a weakness?

Almost all the women we have been studying present themselves to the world as mothers (hence, "motherists") acting for the survival of their children. Their groups almost always arise when men are forced to be absent (because they are migrant workers or soldiers) or in times of crisis, when the role of nurturance assigned to women has been rendered impossible. Faced with the imperatives of their traditional work (to feed the children, to keep the family together) and with the loss of bread, or mobility, or whatever they need to do that work, women can turn into a militant force, breaking the shop windows of the baker or the butcher, burning the pass cards, assembling to confront the police state, sitting-in where normally they would never go—on the steps of the governor's house, at the gates of the cruise missile base.

As feminists, it interested us to speculate about whether the women in these groups felt any kind of criticism of the social role of mother itself, or of the structural ghettoization of women, or of the sexism that greets women's political efforts. As Marysa Navarro said of the women she studies, the Mothers of the Plaza de Mayo, who march to make the Argentine government give them news of their kidnapped, murdered children: "They can only consider ends that are mothers' ends." The surfacing of political issues beyond the family weakened the Mothers of the Plaza de Mayo. Some wished to claim that party politics don't matter and that their murdered children were innocent of any interest in political struggle. Others felt political activism had been their children's right, one they now wished to share. These argued that their bereavement was not only a moral witnessing of crime and a demand for justice but also a specific intervention with immediate and threatening political implications to the state.

This kind of difference has split the mothers of the Plaza de Mayo along the feminist divide. To what extent is motherhood a powerful identity, a word to conjure with? To what extent is it a patriarchal construction that inevitably places mothers outside the realm of the social, the changing, the active? What power can the women who weep, yell, mourn in the street have? Surely a mother's grief and rage removed from the home, suddenly exposed to publicity, are powerful, shocking. Yet as Navarro also points out, the unity of this image was misleading; its force was eventually undermined by differences a group structured around the monolith "mother" was unable to confront.

But, finally, to give the argument one more turn, many Plaza de Mayo women experienced a political transformation through their mothers' network. No group can resolve all political tensions through some ideal formation. The mothers of the disappeared, with their cross-party unity, have been able to convene big demonstrations, drawing new people into the political process. Women can move when a political vacuum develops; by being women who have accepted their lot, they can face the soldiers who have taken their children with a sense of righteous indignation that even a usually murderous police find it hard to dispute. On whatever terms, they have changed the political climate, invented new ways to resist state terrorism.

Using examples like these, the Grass Roots study group gave rise to a particularly poignant exploration of the feminist divide. In each member's work we saw a different version of how women have managed the mixed blessing of their female specialness. Actions like bread riots are desperate and ephemeral, but also effective. With these street eruptions, women put a government on notice; they signal that the poor can be pushed no further. It is finally women who know when the line has been crossed to starvation. But what then? Prices go down; the women go home— until the next time.

Women's movements for survival are like fire storms, changing and dissolving, resistant to political definition. We asked: Would a feminist critique of the traditional role of women keep these groups going longer? Or might feminist insights themselves contribute to the splits that quickly break down the unity shared during crisis? Or, in yet another shift of our assumed values, why *shouldn't* such groups end when the crisis ends, perhaps leaving behind them politicized people, active networks, even community organizations capable of future action when called for? If the left were to expand its definition of political culture beyond the state and the workplace more often, wouldn't the political consciousness of women consumers, mothers, and community activists begin to look enduring in its own way, an important potential source of political energy? Perhaps, our group theorized, we are wrong to wish the women to have formed ongoing political groups growing out of bread riots or meat strikes. Maybe we would see more if we redefined political life to include usually invisible female networks.

The more we talked, the more we saw the ramifications of the fact that the traditional movements were collectivist, the feminist ones more individualistic. Women's local activism draws on a long history of women's culture in which mutual support is essential to life, not (as it often is with contemporary urban feminists) a rare or fragile achievement. The community of peasant women (or working women, or colonized women, or concerned mothers) was a given for the motherists; crisis made the idea of a separate, private identity beyond the daily struggle for survival unimportant. Here was another face of the divide: Collectivist movements are powerful but they usually don't raise questions about women's work. Feminism has raised the questions, and claimed an individual destiny for each woman, but remains ambivalent toward older traditions of female solidarity. Surely our group was ambivalent. We worried that mothers' social net-

253

works can rarely redefine the *terms* of their needs. And rich as traditional forms of female association may be, we kept coming on instances in which the power of societies organized for internal support along gender lines was undermined by the sexism of that very organization.

For example, historian Mrinalini Sinha's research describes how the Bengali middle class of nineteenth-century India used its tradition of marrying and bedding child brides as a way of defining itself against a racist, colonial government.[14] The English hypocritically criticized Bengali men as effeminate because they could not wait. Bengali men answered that it was their women who couldn't wait: The way to control unbounded female sexuality—in which, of course, the English disbelieved—was to marry women at first menstruation.

In Sinha's account one rarely hears the voices of Bengali women themselves, but the question of which sexism would control them—the English marriages of restraint or the Bengali marriages of children—raged around these women. Neither side in the quarrel had women's autonomy or power at heart. Both wanted to wage the colonial fight using women as the symbolic representatives of their rivalry. Because Bengali men wanted control of their women just as much as the English wanted control of Bengali men, the anticolonial struggle had less to offer women than men. In general, our group found that sexism inside an oppressed or impoverished community—such as rigidity about gender roles, or about male authority over women, or about female chastity—has cost revolutionary movements a great deal. Too often, gender politics goes unrecognized as an element in class defeat.[15]

Our group disagreed about the women's solidarity we were studying: Was it a part of the long effort to change women's position and to criticize hierarchy in general, or did motherist goals pull in an essentially different direction from feminist ones? And no matter where each one of us found herself on the spectrum of the group's responses to motherist movements, no resolution emerged of the paradox between mothers' goals and the goals of female individuals no longer defined primarily by reproduction and its attendant tasks. We

saw this tension in some of the groups we studied, and we kept discovering it in ourselves. (Indeed, some of us were part of groups that used motherist rhetoric, as Ynestra King and I were of women's peace networks, or Amy Swerdlow had been of Women Strike for Peace.)

Drawing hard lines between the traditional women's movements and modern Western feminist consciousness never worked, not because the distinction doesn't exist but because it is woven inside our movement itself. A motherist is in some definitions a feminist, in others not. And these differing feminisms are yoked together by the range of difficulties to be found in women's current situation. Our scholarly distance from the "motherists" kept collapsing. The children's toy-exchange network that Julie Wells described as one of the political groupings that build black women's solidarity in South Africa couldn't help striking us urban women in the United States as a good idea.[16] We, too, are in charge of the children and need each other to get by. We, too, are likely to act politically along the lines of association our female tasks have shaped. We sometimes long for the community the women we were studying took more for granted, although we couldn't help remarking on the ways those sustaining communities—say of union workers, or peasants, or ghettoized racial groups—used women's energy, loyalty, and passion as by right, while usually denying them a say in the group's public life, its historical consciousness.

Culture offers a variety of rewards to women for always giving attention to others first. Love is a special female responsibility. Some feminists see this female giving as fulfilling and morally powerful. Others see it more negatively as a mark of oppression and argue that women are given the job of "life," but that any job relegated to the powerless is one undervalued by the society as a whole. Yet in our group there was one area of agreement: Traditional women's concerns—for life, for the children, for peace—*should* be everyone's. Beyond that agreement the question that recreates the feminist divide remained: *How* can the caring that belongs to "mother" travel out to become the responsibility of everyone? Women's backs hold up the world, and we

254

ached for the way women's passionate caring is usually taken for granted, even by women themselves. Some Western feminists, aching like this, want above all to recognize and honor these mothers who, as Adrienne Rich writes, "age after age, perversely, with no extraordinary power, reconstitute the world." Others, also aching, start on what can seem an impossible search for ways to break the ancient, tireless mother's promise to be the mule of the world.

Equality and Difference

By now anyone who has spent time wrangling with feminist issues has recognized the divide and is no doubt waiting for me to produce the name for it that is probably the oldest, certainly the most all-encompassing: "equality" versus "difference." Most feminist thought grapples unavoidably with some aspect of the equality-difference problem at both the level of theory and of strategy. In theory, this version of the divide might be stated: Do women want to be equal to men (with the meaning of "equal" hotly contested),[17] or do women see biology as establishing a difference that will always require a strong recognition and that might ultimately define quite separate possibilities inside "the human"?

Some difference-feminists would argue that women have a special morality, or aesthetic, or capacity for community that it is feminism's responsibility to maximize. Others would put the theoretical case for difference more neutrally and would argue that woman, no matter *what* she is like, is unassimilable. Because she is biologically and therefore psychologically separable from man, she is enduring proof that there is no universally representative human being, no "human wholeness."[18] In contrast, the equality-feminists would argue that it is possible for the biological difference to wither away as a basis for social organization, either by moving men and women toward some shared center (androgyny) or toward some experience of human variety in which biology is but one small variable.

Difference theory tends to emphasize the body (and more recently the unconscious where the body's psychic meaning develops); equality theory tends to deemphasize the body and to place faith in each individual's capacity to develop a self not ultimately circumscribed by a collective law of gender. For difference theorists the body can be either the site of pain and oppression or the site of orgasmic ecstasy and maternal joy. For equality theorists neither extreme is as compelling as the overriding idea that the difference between male and female bodies is a problem in need of solution. In this view, therefore, sexual hierarchy and sexual oppression are bound to continue unless the body is transcended or displaced as the center of female identity.

At the level of practical strategy, the equality-difference divide is just as ubiquitous as it is in theory. Willingly or not, activist lawyers find themselves pitted against each other because they disagree about whether "equal treatment" before the law is better or worse for women than "special treatment," for example, in cases about pregnancy benefits or child custody. (Should pregnancy be defined as unique, requiring special legal provisions, or will pregnant women get more actual economic support if pregnancy, when incapacitating, is grouped with other temporary conditions that keep people from work? Should women who give birth and are almost always the ones who care for children therefore get an automatic preference in custody battles, or will women gain more ultimately if men are defined by law as equally responsible for children, hence equally eligible to be awarded custody?)[19] Sometimes activists find themselves pressured by events to pit the mainstreaming of information about women in the school curriculum against the need for separate programs for women's studies. Or they find themselves having to choose between working to get traditionally male jobs (for example in construction) and working to get fair pay in the women-only jobs they are already doing.

One rushes to respond that these strategic alternatives should not be mutually exclusive, but often, in the heat of local struggles, they temporarily become so. No matter what their theoretical position on the divide, activists find themselves having to make painfully unsatisfactory short-term decisions about the rival claims of equality and difference.[20]

255

Regrettably, these definitions, these examples flatten out the oscillations of the equality-difference debate; they obscure the class struggles that have shaped the development of the argument; they offer neat parallels where there should be asymmetries. Viewed historically, the oscillation between a feminism of equality and one of difference is a bitter disagreement about which path is more progressive, more able to change women's basic condition of subordination.

In this history each side has taken more than one turn at calling the other reactionary and each has had its genuine vanguard moments. "Difference" gained some working women protection at a time when any social legislation to regulate work was rare, while "equality" lay behind middle-class women's demand for the vote, a drive Ellen DuBois has called "the most radical program for women's emancipation possible in the nineteenth century." At the same time, bourgeois women's demands that men should have to be as sexually pure as women finessed the divide between difference and equality and gave rise to interesting cross-class alliances of women seeking ways to make men conform to women's standard, rather than the usual way round—a notion of equality with a difference. As DuBois points out, it is difficult to decide which of these varied political constructions gave nineteenth-century women the most real leverage to make change:

> My hypothesis is that the significance of the woman suffrage movement rested precisely on the fact that it bypassed women's oppression within the family, or private sphere, and demanded instead her admission to citizenship, and through it admission to the public arena.[21]

In other words, at a time when criticism of women's separate family role was still unthinkable, imagining a place outside the family where such a role would make no difference was—for a time—a most radical act.

Equality and difference are broad ideas and have included a range of definitions and political expressions. Equality, for example, can mean anything from the mildest liberal reform (this is piece-of-the-pie feminism, in which women are merely to be included in the world as it is) to the most radical reduction of gender to insignificance. Difference can mean anything from Mary Daly's belief in the natural superiority of women to psychoanalytic theories of how women are inevitably cast as "the Other" because they lack penises.[22]

Just now equality—fresh from recent defeats at the polls and in the courts—is under attack by British and U.S. theorists who are developing a powerful critique of the eighteenth- and nineteenth-century roots of feminism in liberalism. In what is a growing body of work, feminists are exploring the serious limitations of a tradition based on an ideal of equality for separate, independent individuals acting in a free, public sphere—either the market or the state. This liberalism, which runs as an essential thread through Anglo-American feminism, has caused much disappointment. Feminists have become increasingly aware of its basic flaws, of the ways it splits off public and private, leaves sexual differences entirely out of its narrative of the world, and pretends to a neutrality that is nullified by the realities of gender, class, and race. A feminism that honors individual rights has grown leery of the liberal tradition that always puts those rights before community and before any caring for general needs. Liberalism promises an equal right to compete, but as Bell Hooks puts it: "Since men are not equals in white supremacist, capitalist, patriarchal class structure, which men do women want to be equal to?"[23]

These arguments against the origins and tendencies of equality feminism are cogent and useful. They have uncovered unexamined assumptions and the essential weakness in a demand for a passive neutrality of opportunity. But there are cracks in the critique of equality-feminism that lead me back to my general assertion that neither side of the divide can easily be transcended. The biggest complaint against a feminist demand of "equality" is that this construction means women must become conceptual men, or rather that to have equal rights they will have to repress their biological difference, to subordinate themselves in still new ways under an unchanged male hegemony.[24] In this argument the norm is assumed to be male and women's entry into public space is assumed to be a loss of the aspects of experience they formerly embodied—privacy, feeling, nurturance, dailiness. Surely, though, this argument entails a monolithic and eternal view both of public space and of the category "male." How successfully does public space maintain its male gender markers, how totally exclude the private side of life? (The city street is male, yet it can at times be not only physically but also conceptually invaded, say, by a sense of neighborhood or by a demonstration of mass solidarity.) Does male space sometimes dramatically reveal the fact of women's absence? How well does the taboo on public women hold up under the multiple pressures of modernity? Even if public and private are conceptually absolutes, to what extent do individual men and women experience moments in both positions?

Or, if one rejects these hopeful efforts to find loopholes in the iron laws of gender difference, the fear that women will become men still deserves double scrutiny. Is the collapse of gender difference into maleness really the problem women face? Or are we perhaps quite close to men already at the moment when we fear absorption into the other?

None of this is meant as a refutation of the important current work that brings skepticism to the construction of our demands. When health activist Wendy Chavkin notes that making pregnancy disappear by calling it a "disability" is one more way of letting business and government evade sharing responsibility for reproduction, she is right to worry about the invisibility of women's bodies and of their work of reproduction of which their bodies are one small part. When philosopher Alison Jaggar gives examples of how male norms have buried the often separate needs of women, she is sounding a valuable warning. When critic Myra Jehlen describes how hard it is for the concept of a person to include the particular when that particular is female, she is identifying the depth of our difficulty, men's phobic resistance to the inclusion of women into any neutral or public equation.[25]

Nonetheless, I want to reanimate the problem of the divide, to show the potential vigor on both sides. On the one hand, an abstract promise of equality is not enough for people living in capitalism, where everyone is free both to vote and to starve. On the other, as Zillah Eisenstein has pointed out in *The*

Radical Future of Liberal Feminism, the demand for equality has a radical meaning in a capitalist society that claims to offer it but structurally often denies it. Feminism asks for many things the patriarchal state cannot give without radical change. Juliet Mitchell's rethinking of the value of equality-feminism reaches a related conclusion: When basic rights are under attack, liberalism feels necessary again. At best, liberalism sometimes tips in action and becomes more radical than its root conceptions promise. Certainly, no matter which strategy we choose — based on a model of equality or of difference — we are constantly forced to compromise.[26]

It's not that we haven't gotten beyond classical liberalism in theory but that in practice we cannot *live* beyond it. In their very structure, contemporary court cases about sex and gender dramatize the fact of the divide, and media questions demand the short, one-sided answer. Each "case," each "story" in which we act is different and we are only at moments able to shape that difference, make it into the kind of "difference" we want.[27]

The Divide is Not a Universal

After having said so much about how deep the divide goes in feminism, how completely it defines what feminism *is*, I run the risk of seeming to say that the divide has some timeless essence. In fact, I want to argue the opposite, to place Western feminism inside its two-hundred-year history as a specific possibility for thought and action that arose as one of the possibilities of modernity.

When Mary Wollstonecraft wrote one of the founding books of feminism in 1792, *A Vindication of the Rights of Woman*, she said what was new then and remains fresh, shocking, and doubtful to many now: that sex hierarchy — like ranks in the church and the army or like the then newly contested ascendancy of kings — was social, not natural. Though women before her had named injustices and taken sides in several episodes of an ancient *querelle des femmes*, Wollstonecraft's generation experienced the divide in ways related to how feminists experience it now. At one and the same time she could see gender as a solid wall barring her way into liberty, citizen-

257

ship, and a male dignity she envied, and could see how porous the wall was, how many ways she herself could imagine stepping through into an identity less absolute and more chaotic.

Modern feminists often criticize her unhappy compromise with bourgeois revolution and liberal political goals, but if Wollstonecraft was often an equality-feminist in the narrowest sense, eager to speak of absolute rights, of an idealized male individualism, and to ignore the body, this narrowness was in part a measure of her desperation. The body, she felt, could be counted on to assert its ever-present and dreary pull; the enlightenment promised her a mind that might escape. She acknowledged difference as an absolute—men are stronger; then, with cunning, wheedling a bit, Wollstonecraft made men the modest proposal that if women are inferior, men have nothing to fear; they can generously afford to give women their little chance at the light.[28] This is a sly, agnostic treatment of the issue of equality versus difference. Experimental and groping spirit, Wollstonecraft *didn't know* how much biological difference might come to mean; but that she suffered humiliation and loss through being a woman she did know, and all she asked was to be let out of the prison house of gender identity for long enough to judge what men had and what part of that she might want.

When Wollstonecraft wrote, difference was the prevailing wind, equality the incipient revolutionary storm. She feared that if women could not partake in the new civil and political rights of democracy, they would "remain immured in their families groping in the dark." To be sure this rejection of the private sphere made no sense to many feminists who came after her and left modern feminists the task of recognizing the importance of the private and women's different life there, yet it is a rejection that was absolutely necessary as one of feminism's first moves. We in turn have rejected Wollstonecraft's call for chastity, for the end of the passionate emotions "which disturb the order of society";[29] we have rejected her confidence in objective reason and her desire to live as a disembodied self (and a very understandable desire, too, for one whose best friend died in childbirth and who was to die of childbed fever herself), but we have not

gotten beyond needing to make the basic demands she made—for civil rights, education, autonomy.

Finally, what is extraordinary in *A Vindication* is its chaos. Multivalent, driven, ambivalent, the text races over most of feminism's main roads. It constantly goes back on itself in tone, thrilling with self-hatred, rage, disappointment, and hope—the very sort of emotions it explains are the mark of women's inferiority, triviality, and lascivious abandon. Though its appeals to God and virtue are a dead letter to feminists now, the anger and passion with which Wollstonecraft made those appeals—and out of which she imagined the depth of women's otherness, our forced incapacity, the injustice of our situation—feel thoroughly modern. Her structural disorganization derives in part from a circular motion through now familiar stages of protest, reasoning, fury, despair, contempt, desire. She makes demands for women, then doubles back to say that womanhood should be beside the point. Her book is one of those that mark the start of an avalanche of mass self-consciousness about gender injustice. So, in the midst of the hopeful excitement, the divide is there, at the beginning of our history.

If the divide is central to feminist history, feminists need to recognize it with more suppleness, but this enlarged perspective doesn't let one out of having to choose a position in the divide. On the contrary, by arguing that there is no imminent resolution, I hope to throw each reader back on the necessity of finding where her own work falls and of assessing how powerful that political decision is as a tool for undermining the dense, deeply embedded oppression of women.

Though it is understandable that we dream of peace among feminists, that we resist in sisterhood the factionalism that has so often disappointed us in brotherhood, still we must carry on the argument among ourselves. Better, we must actively embrace it. The tension in the divide, far from being our enemy, is a dynamic force that links very different women. Feminism encompasses central dilemmas in modern experience, mysteries of identity that get full expression in its debates. The electricity of its internal disagreements is part of feminism's continuing power to shock and involve large numbers of people in a public conversation far beyond the movement itself. The dynamic feminist divide is about difference; it dramatizes women's differences from each other—and the necessity of our sometimes making common cause.

A Gender Diary: Some Stories, Some Dialogues

If, as I've said, the divide offers no third way, no high ground of neutrality, I certainly have not been able to present this overview so far without a constant humming theme beneath, my own eagerness to break the category "woman" down, to find a definition of difference that pushes so far beyond a settled identity that "being a woman" breaks apart.

Though sometimes I have found the theoretical equality arguments I have described blinkered and reactive, when it comes to strategy, I almost always choose that side, fearing the romance of femaleness even more than the flatness and pretense of undifferentiated, gender-free public space.

I suspect that each one's emphasis—equality or difference—arises alongside and not after the reasons. We criticize Wollstonecraft's worship of rationality, but how willing are we modern ones to look at the unconscious, the idiosyncratic, the temperamental histories of our own politics? It is in these histories—private, intellectual and social—that we can find why some women feel safer with the equality model as the rock of their practice (with difference as a necessary condition imposed on it), while other women feel more true to themselves, more fully expressed, by difference as their rock (with equality a sort of bottom-line call for basic reforms that cannot ultimately satisfy).

Why do I decide (again and again) that being a woman is a liability, while others I know decide (again and again) that a separate female culture is more exciting, more in their interests, more promising as a strategic stance for now than my idea of slipping the noose of gender, living for precious moments of the imagination

outside it? An obvious first answer is that class, race, and sexual preference determine my choices, and surely these play their central part. Yet in my experience of splits in the women's movement, I keep joining with women who share my feminist preferences but who have arrived at these conclusions from very different starting points.

This is not to understate the importance of class, race, and sexual preference but merely to observe that these important variables don't segment feminism along the divide; they don't provide direct keys to each one's sense of self-interest or desire nor do they yield clear directions for the most useful strategic moves. For example, lesbian and straight women are likely to bring very different understandings and needs to discussions of whether or not women's communities work, whether or not the concept is constricting. Yet in my own experience, trust of women's communities does not fall out along the lines of sexual preference. Instead, up close, the variables proliferate. What was the texture of childhood for each one of us? What face did the world beyond home present?

In the fifties, when an earlier, roiled life of gender and politics had subsided and the gender messages seemed monolithic again, I lived with my parents in the suburbs. My mother's class and generation had lived through repeated, basic changes of direction about women, family, and work, and my own engaged and curious mother passed her ambivalent reception of the world's mixed messages on to me in the food. With hindsight, I can see that of course gender, family, and class weren't the settled issues they seemed then. But the times put a convincing cover over continuing change. Deborah Rosenfelt and Judith Stacey describe this precise historical moment and the particular feminist politics born from it:

> [T]he ultradomestic nineteen fifties [was] an aberrant decade in the history of U.S. family and gender relations and one that has set the unfortunate terms for waves of personal and political reaction to family issues ever since. Viewed in this perspective, the attack on the breadwinner/homemaker nuclear family by the women's liberation movement may have been an overreaction to an aberrant and highly fragile

cultural form, a family system that, for other reasons, was already passing from the scene. Our devastating critiques of the vulnerability and cultural devaluation of dependent wives and mothers helped millions of women to leave or avoid these domestic traps, and this is to our everlasting credit. But, with hindsight, it seems to us that these critiques had some negative consequences as well. . . . [F]eminism's overreaction to the fifties was an antinatalist, antimaterialist moment. . . .[30]

I am the child of this moment, and some of the atmosphere of rage generated by that hysterically domestic ideology of the fifties can now feel callow, young, or ignorant. Yet I have many more kind words to say for the reaction of which I was a part in the early seventies than Rosenfelt and Stacey seem to: I don't think the feminism of this phase would have spoken so powerfully to so many without this churlish outbreak of indignation. Nothing we have learned since about the fragility of the nuclear family alters the fundamental problems it continues to pose for women. It is not really gone, though it is changing. And though feminism seeks to preside over the changes, other forces are at work, half the time threatening us with loneliness, half the time promising us rich emotional lives if we will but stay home—a double punch combination designed to make the fifties look, by contrast, safe. The fifties were not safe, not for me anyway, and they don't become so with hindsight.

It's hard to remember now what the initial feminist moves in this wave felt like, the heady but alarming atmosphere of female revolt. As one anxious friend wondered back then, "Can I be in this and stay married?" The answer was often "no," the upheaval terrifying. Some of us early ones were too afraid of the lives of our mothers to recognize ourselves in them. But I remember that this emotional throwing off of the mother's life felt like the only way to begin. Black women whose ties to their mothers were more often a mutual struggle for survival rarely shared this particular emotion. As Audre Lord once said, "[B]lack children were not meant to survive," so parents and children saw a lifeline in each other that was harder for the prosperous or the white to discern. The usually white and middle-class women who were typical members of early women's consciousness raising

groups often saw their mothers as desperate or depressed in the midst of their relative privilege. Many had been educated like men and had then been expected to become . . . men's wives. We used to agree in those meetings that motherhood was the divide: Before it, you could pretend you were just like everyone else; afterward, you were a species apart—invisible and despised.

But if motherhood was despised, it was also festooned—then as now—with roses. Either way, in 1970, motherhood seemed an inevitable part of my future, and the qualities some feminists now praise as uniquely women's were taken for granted as female necessities: Everyone wanted the nice one, the sweet one, the good one, the nurturant one, the pretty one. No one wanted the women who didn't want to be women. It's hard to recover how frightening it was to step out of these ideas, to resist continuing on as expected; it's hard to get back how very naked it made us feel. Some of the vociferousness of our rhetoric, which now seems unshaded or raw, came partly from the anxiety we felt when we made this proclamation, that we didn't want to be women. A great wave of misogyny rose to greet us. So we said it even more. Hindsight has brought in its necessary wisdom, its temporizing reaction. We have gotten beyond the complaint of the daughters, have come to respect the realities, the worries, and the work of the mothers. But to me "difference" will always represent a necessary modification of the initial impulse, a reminder of complexity, a brake on precipitate hopes. It can never feel like the primary insight felt, the first breaking with the gender bargain. The immediate reward was immense, the thrill of separating from authority.

* * *

Conversation with E. She recalls that the new women's movement meant to her: You don't have to struggle to be attractive to men anymore. You can stop working so hard on that side of things. I was impressed by this liberation so much beyond my own. I felt the opposite. Oppressed and depressed before the movement, I found sexual power unthinkable, the privilege of a very few women. Now angry and awake, I felt for the first time what the active eroticism of men might be like. What men thought of me no longer blocked out the parallel question of what I thought of them, which made sexual encounters far more interesting than they had once been. Like E., I worried about men's approval less, but (without much tangible reason) my hopes for the whole business of men and women rose. For a brief time in the early seventies, I had an emotional intimation of what some men must feel: free to rub up against the world, take space, make judgments. With all its hazards, this confidence also offered its delight—but only for a moment of course. The necessary reaction followed at once: Women aren't men in public space. There is no safety. Besides, I had romanticized male experience; men are not as free as I imagined. Still, I remember that wild if deluded time—not wanting to be a man but wanting the freedom of the street. The feminist rallying cry "Take Back the Night" has always struck me as a fine piece of movement poetry. We don't have the night, but we want it, we want it.

* * *

Another memory of the early seventies: An academic woman sympathetic to the movement but not active asked what motivated me to spend all this time organizing, marching, meeting. (Subtext: Why wasn't I finishing my book? Why did I keep flinging myself around?)

I tried to explain the excitement I felt at the idea that I didn't have to be a woman. She was shocked, confused. This was the motor of my activism? She asked, "How can someone who doesn't like being a woman be a feminist?" To which I could only answer, "Why would anyone who likes being a woman need to be a feminist?"

Quite properly, my colleague feared woman-hating. She assumed that feminism must be working to restore respect and dignity to women. Feminism would revalue what ·had been debased, women's contribution to human history. I, on the other hand, had to confess: I could never have made myself lick all those stamps for a better idea of what womanhood means. Was this, as my colleague thought, just a new kind of misogyny? I wouldn't dare say self-hatred played no part in what I wanted from feminism from the first. But even back then, for me, woman-hating—or loving—felt

beside the point. It was the idea of breaking the law of the category itself that made me delirious.

* * *

The first time I heard "women" mentioned as a potentially political contemporary category I was already in graduate school. It was the mid-sixties and a bright young woman of the New Left was saying how important it was to enlist the separate support of women workers in our organizing against the Vietnam War. I remember arguing with her, flushed with a secret humiliation. What good was she doing these workers, I asked her, by addressing them and categorizing them separately? Who was she to speak so condescendingly of "them"? Didn't she know that the inferior category she had named would creep up in the night and grab her, too?

I'm ashamed now to admit that gender solidarity—which I lived inside happily, richly every day in those years—first obtruded itself on my conscious mind as a threat and a betrayal. So entirely was I trapped in negative feelings about what women are and can do that I had repressed any knowledge of femaleness as a defining characteristic of my being.

I can see now that women very different from me came to feminist conclusions much like my own. But this is later knowledge. My feminism came from the suburbs, where I knew no white, middle-class woman with children who had a job or any major activities beyond the family. Yet, though a girl, I was promised education, offered the pretense of gender neutrality. This island of illusions was a small world, but if I seek the source for why cultural feminism has so little power to draw me, it is to this world I return in thought. During the day, it was safe, carefully limited, and female. The idea that this was all made me frantic.

* * *

S. reads the gender diary with consternation. In Puerto Rico, where she grew up, this fear of the mother's life would be an obscenity. She can't recognize the desire I write of—to escape scot free from the role I was born to. Latina feminists she knows feel rage, but what is this shame, she wants to know. In her childhood both sexes believed being a woman was magic.

261

S. means it about the magic, hard as it is for me to take this in. She means sexual power, primal allure, even social dignity. S. became a feminist later, by a different route, and now she is as agnostic about the meaning of gender as I am. But when she was young, she had no qualms about being a woman.

After listening to S., I add another piece to my story of the suburbs. Jews who weren't spending much of our time being Jewish, we lived where ethnicity was easy to miss. (Of course it was there; but I didn't know it.) In the suburbs, Motherhood was white bread, with no powerful ethnic graininess. For better and worse, I was brought up on this stripped, denatured product. Magical women seemed laughably remote. No doubt this flatness in local myth made girls believe less in their own special self, but at the same time it gave them less faith in the beckoning ideal of mother. My gifted mother taught me not the richness of home but the necessity of feminism. Feminism was her conscious as well as unconscious gift.

* * *

It is not enough for the diary to tell how one woman, myself, came to choose—again and again—a feminism on the minimalizers' side of the divide. Somehow the diary must also tell how this decision can never feel solid or final. No one gets to stay firmly on her side; no one gets to rest in a reliably clear position. Mothers who believe their daughters should roam as free as men find themselves giving those daughters taxi fare, telling them not to talk to strangers, filling them with the lore of danger. Activists who want women to be very naughty (as the women in a little zap group we call No More Nice Girls want women to be) nonetheless warn them there's a price to pay for daring to defy men in public space.[31] Even when a woman chooses which shoes she'll wear today—is it to be the running shoes, the flats, the spikes?—she's deciding where to place herself for the moment on the current possible spectrum of images of "woman." Whatever one's habitual position on the divide, in daily life one travels back and forth, or, to change metaphors, one scrambles for whatever toehold one can.

* * *

Living with the divide: In a room full of feminists, everyone is saying that a so-called surrogate mother, one who bears a child for others, should have the right to change her mind for a time (several weeks? months?) after the baby is born. This looks like agreement. Women who have been on opposite sides of the divide in many struggles converge here, outraged at the insulting way one Mary Beth Whitehead has been treated by fertility clinics, law courts, and press. She is not a "surrogate," we say, but a "mother" indeed.

The debate seems richer than it's been lately. Nobody knows how to sort out the contradictions of the new reproductive technologies yet, so for a fertile moment there's a freedom, an expressiveness in all that's said. Charged words like "birth" and "mothering" and "the kids" are spilling all around, but no one yet dares to draw the ideological line defining which possibilities belong inside feminism, which are antithetical to it. Some sing a song of pregnancy and birth while others offer contrapuntal motifs of child-free lesbian youth, of infertility, all in different keys of doubt about how much feminists may want to make motherhood special, different from parenting, different from caring—a unique and absolute relation to a child.

But just as we're settling in for an evening that promises to be fraught, surprising, suggestive, my warning system, sensitive after eighteen years of feminist activism, gives a familiar twitch and tug. Over by the door, one woman has decided: Surrogacy is baby-selling and ought to be outlawed. All mothering will be debased if motherhood can be bought. Over by the couch, another woman is anxiously responding: Why should motherhood be the sacred place we keep clean from money, while men sell the work of their bodies every day? Do we want women to be the special representatives of the moral and spiritual things that can't be bought, with the inevitable result that women's work is once again done without pay?

Here it is then. The metaconversation that has hovered over my political life since 1970, when I joined one of the first women's consciousness raising groups. On the one hand, sacred motherhood. On the other, a

262

wish—variously expressed—for this special identity to wither away.

Only a little later in the brief, eventful history of this ad hoc Mary Beth Whitehead support group, a cleverly worded petition was circulated. It quoted the grounds the court used to disqualify Whitehead from motherhood—from the way she dyed her hair to the way she played pattycake—and ended: "By these standards, we are all unfit mothers." I wanted to sign the petition, but someone told me, "Only mothers are signing." I was amazed. Did one have to be literally a mother in order to speak authentically in support of Whitehead? Whether I'm a mother or not, the always obvious fact that I am from the mother half of humanity conditions my life.

But after this initial flash of outrage at exclusion, I had second thoughts: Maybe I should be glad not to sign. Why should I have to be assumed to be a mother if I am not? Instead of accepting that all women are mothers in essence if not in fact, don't I prefer a world in which some are mothers—and can speak as mothers—while others are decidedly not?

To make a complicated situation more so: While I was struggling with the rights and wrongs of my being allowed to sign, several other women refused to sign. Why? Because the petition quoted Whitehead's remark that she knew what was best for her child because she was the mother. The nonsigners saw this claim as once again imputing some magic biological essence to motherhood. They didn't want to be caught signing a document that implied that mother always knows best. They supported Whitehead's right to dye her hair but not her claim to maternal infallibility.

I saw the purity of this position, recognized these nonsigners as my closest political sisters, the ones who run fast because the old world of mother-right is just behind them. But in this case I didn't feel quite as they felt. I was too angry at the double standard, the unfair response to Whitehead's attempts to extricate herself from disaster. I thought that given the circumstances of here, of now, Mary Beth Whitehead was as good an authority about her still-nursing baby as we could find anywhere in the situation. It didn't bother me at all to sign a petition that included her claim to a uniquely privileged place. The press and the court seemed to hate her for that very specialness; yet they all relegated her to it, excrating her for her unacceptable ambivalence. Under such conditions she was embracing with an understandable vengeance the very role the world named as hers. Who could blame her?

Eventually, I signed the petition, which was also signed by a number of celebrities and was much reported in the press. It is well to remember how quickly such public moments flatten out internal feminist debates. After much feminist work, the newspapers—formerly silent about feminism's stake in surrogacy questions—began speaking of "the feminist position." But nothing they ever wrote about us or our petition came close to the dilemma as we had debated it during the few intense weeks we met. Prosurrogacy and antisurrogacy positions coexist inside feminism. They each require expression, because neither alone can respond fully to the class, race, and gender issues raised when a poor woman carries a child for a rich man for money.

Over time I've stopped being depressed by the lack of feminist accord. I see feminists as stuck with the very indeterminacy I say I long for. This is it then, the life part way in, part way out. One can be recalled to "woman" anytime—by things as terrible as rape, as trivial as a rude shout on the street—but one can never stay inside "woman," because it keeps moving. We constantly find ourselves beyond its familiar cover.

Gender markers are being hotly reasserted these days—U.S. defense is called "standing tough" while the Pope's letter on women calls motherhood woman's true vocation. Yet this very heat is a sign of gender's instabilities. We can clutch aspects of the identity we like, but they often slip away. Modern women experience moments of free fall. How is it for you, there, out in space near me? Different, I know. Yet we share—some with more pleasure, some with more pain—this uncertainty.   □

I am indebted to the hardworking readers of an earlier draft who are not to blame for the times I have failed to profit from their excellent advice: Nancy Davidson, Adrienne Harris, Mim Kelber, Temma Kaplan, Ynestra King,

263

Susana Leval, Eunice Lipton, Alix Kates Shulman, Alan Snitow, Nadine Taub, Meredith Tax, Sharon Thompson, and Carole Vance. A longer version of this piece will appear in Adrienne Harris and Ynestra King, ed. *Rocking the Ship of State: Toward a Feminist Peace Politics* (Boulder, Colo.: Westview Press, forthcoming).

Notes

[1] The "we" problem has no more simple solution than does the divide itself, but in spite of its false promise of unity the "we" remains politically important. In this piece, "we" includes anyone who calls herself a feminist, anyone who is actively engaged with the struggles described here.

[2] Catharine R. Stimpson, "The New Scholarship about Women: The State of the Art," *Ann. Scholarship* 1, no. 2(1980):2–14.

[3] Alice B. Echols, *Daring to Be Bad: A History of the Radical Feminist Movement in America, 1967–1975* (Minneapolis: University of Minnesota Press, forthcoming). The quotations from Echols that follow are from chapters II and VI.

[4] Barbara Deming, "To Those Who Would Start a People's Party," *Liberation* 18, no. 4 (December 1973): 24, cited in Echols, Chapter VI. Andrea Dworkin, *Intercourse* (New York: The Free Press, 1987), p. 67. Dworkin is not a biological determinist in *Intercourse*, but she sees culture as so saturated with misogyny that the victimization of women is seamless, total, as eternal in its own way as "mother right."

[5] Carole S. Vance, "Social Construction Theory: Problems in the History of Sexuality," in *Homosexuality, Which Homosexuality?* ed. Anja von Kooten Niekerk and Theo van der Meer (Amsterdam: An Dekker, Imprint Schorer, forthcoming).

[6] Linda Alcoff, *Signs* 13, no. 3 (Spring 1988): 406, and passim.

[7] Linda Alcoff sees poststructuralism as anti-essentialist; in contrast, in *Feminist Studies* 14, no. 1 (Spring 1988), the editors Judith Newton and Nancy Hoffman introduce a collection of essays on deconstruction by describing differences *among* deconstructionists on the question of essentialism as on other matters.

[8] See "Politics of the Ego: A Manifesto for N.Y. Radical Feminists" in *Radical Feminism*, ed. Anne Koedt, Ellen Levine, Anita Rapone (New York: Quadrangle, 1973):379–383. The vocabulary of the manifesto, adopted in December 1969, seems crude now, its emphasis on "psychology" jejune; but the document begins upon the task which feminists have taken up since, the analysis of the interlocking ways in which culture organizes subordination.

[9] Linda Bamber and Marianne DeKoven, "Metacriticism and the Value of Difference" (paper presented at the MLA panel "Feminist Criticism: Theories and Directions," December 28, 1982), pp. 1–2.

[10] Alcoff, 421. One might make a separate study of "third course" thinking. Sometimes this work is an important and urgent effort to see the limiting terms of a current contradiction, to recognize from which quarter new contradictions are likely to develop. Third-course writing at its best tries to reinterpret the present and offer clues to the future. (English theorists have called this prefigurative thinking.) But often this work runs the risk of pretending that new terms resolve difficulties and, more insidiously, it often falls back covertly into the divide it claims to have transcended. I admire, though I am not always persuaded by, the third course thinking in such pieces as Angela Miles, "The Integrative Feminine Principle in North American Radicalism: Value Basis of a New Feminism," *Women's Studies International Quarterly* 4, no. 4 (1981):481–95. I have more doubts about pieces like Ann Ferguson's and Ilene Philipson's contributions to "Forum: The Feminist Sexuality Debates," *Signs* 10, no. 1 (Autumn 1984): 106–118. These essays claim a higher ground, "a third perspective" (Ferguson, p. 108), which is extremely difficult to construct; their classifications of the sides of the divide reveal a tropism more unavoidable than they recognize.

[11] Michèle Barrett, "The Concept of 'Difference,'" *Feminist Review* 26 (Summer 1987):34.

[12] Alice Walker, Epigraph of *In Search of Our Mothers' Gardens* (San Diego: Harcourt Brace Jovanovich, 1983), p. xi. See also Joan Kelly, "The Doubled Vision of Feminist Theory," in *Women, History and Theory: The Essays of Joan Kelly* (Chicago: University of Chicago Press, 1984), p. 55; Denise Riley, *War in the Nursery: Theories of the Child and Mother* (London: Virago, 1983): passim and Adrienne Rich, "Compulsory Heterosexuality and Lesbian Existence" in *Blood, Bread and Poetry* (New York: W.W. Norton, 1986):60 ff. Rich also uses the metaphor of the continuum to describe the range in women's lives between different levels of female community. In *The Daughter's Seduction: Feminism and Psychoanalysis* (Ithaca, N.Y.: Cornell University Press, 1982), Jane Gallop describes Julia Kristeva's effort to think beyond dualism: "A constantly double discourse is necessary, one that asserts and then questions" (p. 122).

[13] Meredith Tax, "Agenda for Meeting at Barnard, May 3, 1986," p. 1. Members of the study group, convened at the Barnard Women's Center: Margorie Agosin, Amrita Basu, Dana Frank, Temma Kaplan, Ynestra King, Marysa Navarro, Ann Snitow, Amy Swerdlow, Meredith Tax, Julie Wells, and Marilyn Young.

[14] See Mrinalini Sinha, "The Age of Consent Act: The Ideal of Masculinity and Colonial Ideology in Late 19th Century Bengal," *Proceedings of the 8th International Symposium on Asian Studies*, 1986, pp. 1199–1214, and "Gender and Imperialism: Colonial Policy and The Ideology of Moral Imperialism in Late Nineteenth-Century Bengal" in *Changing Men: New Directions in Research on Men and Masculinity*, ed. Michael S. Kimmel (Newbury Park, Calif.: Sage Publications, 1987), pp. 217–31.

[15] Julie Wells and Anne McClintock offered the example

of Crossroads in South Africa, a squatter community of blacks largely maintained by women but finally undermined by—among other things—a colonialism that placed paid black men in charge. See also descriptions of ways in which women become connected with revolutionary movements in Maxine Molyneux, "Mobilization Without Emancipation? Women's Interests, the State, and Revolution in Nicaragua," *Feminist Studies* 11, no. 2 (Summer 1985):227–53; and Temma Kaplan, "Women and Communal Strikes in the Crisis of 1917–1922," in *Becoming Visible: Women in European History*, 2nd edition, ed. Renate Bridenthal, Claudia Koonz, and Susan Stuard, (Boston: Houghton Mifflin, 1987), pp. 429–49 and Kaplan, "Female Consciousness and Collective Action: The Case of Barcelona, 1910–1918," *Signs* 7, no. 3 (1982):545–66.

[16] See also Julie Wells, "The Impact of Motherist Movements on South African Women's Political Participation." Paper presented at the Seventh Berkshire Conference on the History of Women, June 19, 1987.

[17] Alison M. Jaggar gives an account of the contemporary feminist debate about the demand for "equality" in "Sexual Difference and Sexual Equality," in *Theoretical Perspectives on Sexual Differences*, ed. Deborah L. Rhode (New Haven: Yale University Press, forthcoming). For some general accounts of the debate, see also Josephine Donovan, *Feminist Theory* (New York: Frederick Ungar, c1985); Hester Eisenstein, *Contemporary Feminist Thought* (Boston: G.K. Hall, 1983); Hester Eisenstein and Alice Jardine, ed. *The Future of Difference* (Boston: G.K. Hall, 1980); Zillah R. Eisenstein, *Feminism and Sexual Equality: Crisis in Liberal America* (New York: Monthly Review Press, 1984); Juliet Mitchell, *Women's Estate* (New York: Pantheon, 1971); *What is Feminism?* Juliet Mitchell and Ann Oakley, eds. (New York: Pantheon, 1986). The debates about Carol Gilligan's *In a Different Voice: Psychological Theory and Women's Development* (Cambridge, Mass.: Harvard University Press, 1982) often turn on the equality/difference problem. See John Broughton, "Women's Rationality and Men's Virtues: A Critique of Gender Dualism in Gilligan's Theory of Moral Development," *Social Research* 50, no. 3 (Autumn 1983):597–624; Linda K. Kerber, Catherine G. Greeno and Eleanor E. Maccoby, Zella Luria, Carol B. Stack, and Carol Gilligan, "On *In a Different Voice:* An Interdisciplinary Forum," *Signs* 11, no. 2 (Winter 1986): 304–333; *New Ideas in Psychology* (Special Issue on Women and Moral Development) 5, no. 2 (1987); and Seyla Benhabib, "The Generalized and the Concrete Other: The Kohlberg-Gilligan Controversy and Feminist Theory," in *Feminism as Critique*, ed. Seyla Benhabib and Drucilla Cornell (Minneapolis: University of Minnesota Press, 1987). Similarly, the feminist response to Ivan Illich's *Gender* (New York: Pantheon, 1982) has tended to raise these issues. See, for example, Lourdes Beneria, "Meditations on Ivan Illich's *Gender*," in *Work in the 1980s*, ed. B. Gustavsson, J.C. Karlsson and C. Rafregard (Gower Publishing Co., 1985).

[18] The phrase "human wholeness" comes from Betty Friedan's *The Second Stage* (New York: Summit Books,

1981), and the concept receives a valuable and devastating critique in Myra Jehlen, "Against Human Wholeness: A Suggestion for a Feminist Epistemology" (manuscript).

[19] For pregnancy issue see: "Brief of the American Civil Liberties Union et al.," amici curiae, California Federal Savings and Loan Association, et al., v. Mark Guerra, et al., Supreme Court of the United States. October Term, 1985, Joan E. Bertin, Counsel of record; Wendy Chavkin, "Walking a Tightrope: Pregnancy, Parenting, and Work," in *Double Exposure: Women's Health Hazards on the Job and at Home*, ed. Wendy Chavkin (New York: Monthly Review Press, 1984); Lise Vogel, "Debating Difference: The Problem of Special Treatment of Pregnancy in the Workplace," paper presented at the Women and Society Seminar of Columbia University, January 25, 1988; Kai Bird and Max Holland, "Capitol Letter: The Garland Case," *The Nation* (July 5/12, 1986); Wendy Williams, "Equality's Riddle: Pregnancy and the Equal Treatment/Special Treatment Debate," *N.Y.U. Review of Law and Social Change* 13 (1984–1985); Herma Hill Kay, "Equality and Difference: The Case of Pregnancy," *Berkeley Women's Law Journal* 1 (1985). For custody issue see: Katharine T. Bartlett and Carol B. Stack, "Joint Custody, Feminism and the Dependency Dilemma," *Berkeley Women's Law Journal*, Winter 1986–7:501–533; Phyllis Chesler, *Mothers on Trial: The Battle for Children and Custody* (Seattle: The Seal Press, 1986, 1987); and Lenore J. Weitzman, *The Divorce Revolution: The Unexpected Social and Economic Consequences for Women and Children in America* (New York: Macmillan, 1985). The work of Nadine Taub, Director of the Women's Rights Litigation Clinic, School of Law, Rutgers/Newark, has frequent bearing on both issues and on the larger questions in equality/difference debates. See Taub, "Defining and Combating Sexual Harassment," in *Class, Race and Sex: The Dynamics of Control*, ed. Amy Swerdlow and Hannah Lessinger (Boston: G.K. Hall, 1983), pp. 263–275; "Feminist Tensions: Concepts of Motherhood and Reproductive Choice," *Gender and Transition*, forthcoming; "A Public Policy of Private Caring," *The Nation* (May 31, 1986); Taub and Wendy Williams, "Will Equality Require More than Assimilation, Accommodation or Separation from the Existing Social Structure?" *Rutgers Law Review* 37, no. 4 (Summer 1985):825–44. The burgeoning feminist work on the new reproductive technologies also reproduces the divide. For complete references to all aspects of these debates see Nadine Taub and Sherrill Cohen, *Reproductive Laws for the 1990s*, (Clifton, N.J.: Humana Press, 1989).

[20] If I had to come up with an example of a feminist strategy that faced the power of the divide squarely yet at the same time undermined the oppression the divide represents, I'd choose recent feminist comparable worth legislation. Humble—and earthshaking—comparable worth asserts two things: First, since women and men do different work, the concept "equal pay" has little effect on raising women's low wages; and, second, if work were to be judged by standards of difficulty, educational preparation, experience, etc. (standards preferably developed by workers themselves), then anti-discrimination laws might

enforce that men and women doing work of comparable worth be paid the same. (Perhaps nurses and automechanics. Or teachers and middle managers?) The activists who have proposed comparable worth have singularly few pretensions. They are the first to point out that on its face, the proposal ignores the work women do in the family, ignores the noneconomic reasons why women and men have different kinds of jobs, ignores what's wrong with job hierarchies and with "worth" as the sole basis for determining pay. Yet this little brown mouse of a liberal reform, narrow in its present political potential and limited by its nature, has a touch of deconstructive genius. Without hoping to get women doing men's work tomorrow, the comparable worth model erodes the economic advantages to employers of consistently undervaluing women's work and channeling women into stigmatized work ghettos where pay is always lower. With comparable worth, the stigma might well continue to haunt women's work, but women would be better paid. Men might start wanting a "woman's" job that paid well, while women might have new psychological incentives to cross gender work categories. Who knows, perhaps stigma might not catch up as categories of work got rethought and their gender markers moved around. And if the stigma clung to women's work, if men refused to be nurses even if nurses were paid as well as construction workers, a woman earning money is an independent woman; she can change the family; she can consider leaving it. Comparable worth asserts the divide; yet, slyly, it goes to work on a basic economic and psychological underpining of the divide; it undermines the idea that all work has a natural gender. (See Sara M. Evans and Barbara Nelson, *Wage Justice: Comparable Worth and the Paradox of Technocratic Reform* (Chicago: University of Chicago Press, 1989). The mixtures of progressive and conservative impulses that have characterized both sides of the divide at different moments get a nuanced reading from Nancy F. Cott in her historical study of American feminism, *The Grounding of Modern Feminism* (New Haven: Yale University Press, 1987).

21 Ellen Dubois, "The Radicalism of the Women Suffrage Movement: Notes Toward the Reconstruction of Nineteenth-Century Feminism," in *Feminism and Equality*, ed. Anne Phillips (New York: New York University Press, 1987), p. 128.

22 See Mary Daly, *Gyn/Ecology: The Metaethics of Radical Feminism* (Boston: Beacon Press, 1978). Maggie McFadden gives an account of this range in her useful taxonomy piece, "Anatomy of Difference: Toward a Classification of Feminist Theory," *Women's Studies International Forum* 7, no. 6 (1984):495–504. Adrienne Harris has pointed out to me that essentialism comes and

goes in feminist psychoanalytic discussions of the penis: "The concept slips, moves and breaks apart."

23 Bell Hooks, "Feminism: A Movement to End Sexist Oppression," in Phillips, *Feminism and Equality*, p. 62.

24 Taken together, Alison Jaggar's essays on the equality/difference debate offer a poignant (and I think continuously ambivalent) personal account of how one feminist theorist developed doubts about the equality position. See Jaggar, "Sexual Difference and Sexual Equality: Sex Inequality and Bias in Sex Differences Research," *Canadian Journal of Philosophy*, Supplementary Vol. 13 (1987).

25 For Chavkin, Jaggar and Jehlen, see notes 17, 18, 19 and 24 above.

26 Eisenstein (New York: Longman, 1981); Mitchell, "Women and Equality" (1976), reprinted in Phillips.

27 The feminist scandal of the Sears case offers a particularly disturbing example of the divide as it can get played out within the exigencies of a court case. See Ruth Milkman, "Women's History and the Sears Case," *Feminist Studies* 12 (Summer 1986):375–400 and Joan W. Scott, "Deconstructing Equality-Versus-Difference: Or the Uses of Poststructural Theory for Feminism," *Feminist Studies* 14, no. 1 (Spring 1988):33–50. In her introduction to *Feminism and Equality*, Anne Phillips offers a useful instance of how, in different contexts, the feminist ambivalence about liberalism emerges; she observes that in the United States feminism began with equality models which revealed their inadequacy in practice, while British feminists began with a socialist critique of liberal goals which their own disappointments have modified in the equality direction.

28 Mary Wollstonecraft, *A Vindication of the Rights of Woman*, ed. Carol H. Poston (New York: W.W. Norton, 1975). See, for example, p. 35. See the now classic restoration of Wollstonecraft, Juliet Mitchell, "Women and Equality," in Phillips, Patricia Yeager, "Writing as Action: A Vindication of the Rights of Woman," *The Minnesota Review* no. 29 (Winter 1987):67–80, and Cora Kaplan, "Wild nights: pleasure/sexuality/feminism" (1983), reprinted in *The Ideology of Conduct: Essays on Literature and the History of Sexuality*, ed. Nancy Armstrong and Leonard Tennenhouse (New York and London: Methuen, 1987), pp. 160–184.

29 Wollstonecraft, *A Vindication*, pp. 5, 30.

30 Deborah Rosenfelt and Judith Stacey, "Second Thoughts on the Second Wave," *Feminist Studies* 13, no. 2 (Summer 1987):350–351.

31 Since the Hyde Amendment restricting Medicaid abortions in 1979, No More Nice Girls has done occasional, ad hoc street events in New York City to dramatize new threats to women's sexual autonomy.

Against feminist fundamentalism

Elizabeth Wilson is the author of numerous books, including "Mirror Writing", an autobiography; "Adorned in Dreams", on fashion; "Only Halfway to Paradise", on women in postwar Britain, and "Hallucinations", a collection of stories on life in the postmodern city

The battle lines have been drawn for a number of years between "anti-pornography" feminists and what in the United States are called "libertarian" feminists. In Britain there was for some time an attempt by socialist feminists to define a "third way": to acknowledge the unpleasantness of some pornography without agreeing that pornography was actually the cause of female subordination, or that all pornography was the same, that it was all violent, that it was even all offensive. More recently there has been a stalemate within the women's movement. In the world outside, on the other hand, the anti-pornography position has seemingly won the day. The Labour Party in particular, more especially the left of the Labour Party, has taken on the anti-pornography position. Clare Short's attempts to ban page three pin-ups have been followed by denunciations of porn by MPs such as Robin Cook and Ken Livingstone. This is understandable, given that Clare Short was attacked by Tories—by Norman Tebbit, for example, in his guise as ordinary man in the street, speaking for a working class which, he says, can't tell the difference between a Titian and a Playboy centrefold. (Of course, some feminists also draw parallels between "high art" and pornography.) It is, however, rather ironic that leftwing MPs have become staunch anti-pornography campaigners, given that some of the feminists who make anti-pornography the centre of their politics were once at loggerheads with socialist feminists.

Even more ironic, Liberty, formerly the National Council for Civil Liberties (NCCL), voted at its AGM in April of this year, to take up the issue and to declare itself an organisation against "censorship and pornography". It is now committed to the attempt to devise legislative restrictions on pornography.

All societies place some legal parameters around what it is or is not permissible to say or show, and a complete "no censorship" position is both utopian and vacuous. There are limits to what any society should accept in terms of images and representations, but they will always be the object of struggle and disagreement.

It is impossible in one short article to do justice to the arguments that have raged round the issue of pornography. It seems that we have to raise some of the problems with the anti-pornography position again, precisely because there seems to be increasingly a belief that "all feminists" support the anti-pornography campaign.

Anti-pornography campaigns tend to make pornography the cause of women's oppression, and the central issue for feminists. In particular it is argued that there is incontrovertible evidence that pornography increases the incidence of sexual violence towards women. In fact, the evidence is not clear cut.

Pornography is not the main cause of rape as the slogan "Porn is the theory—rape is the practice" suggests. If it was, there would be no rape in countries where there is or was no porn, and that is clearly not the case. Associations, ideas and images of almost any kind may cause sexual arousal and in some cases violence. Peter Sutcliffe believed that his mission to kill prostitutes came from the deity, and he was also obsessively interested in a waxworks museum which contained cross-sections of women's torsos, in which foetuses in varying stages of development were displayed.

A further claim made to justify the campaign is that pornography silences women and is therefore a form of censorship in itself. This is disingenuous. Women are deprived of equal access to media, publishing and other public platforms in a variety of ways. Much more important than pornography in placing barriers in the path of women who want to have a public —or

any—voice is lack of independent income, education, training and job opportunities, together with the unequal responsibilities for child care (and care of disabled and elderly people).

To blame pornography for all women's ills or at least to give so much attention to it, is actually to let the rulers of our society off the hook. The components of women's oppression are complex, but male dominance may just as easily express itself in overprotectiveness as in sexual hatred. Overemphasis on pornography is a political displacement and provides a simplistic and paranoid explanation to a complex oppression.

Another difficulty is that, notwithstanding the arguments of the anti-porn feminists, there is no consensus about what imagery constitutes pornography. Anti-pornography campaigners, however, refuse any possibility of ambiguity, relying instead on an immediate gut response. Now gut responses aren't necessarily wrong. It is a mistake, nonetheless, to assume that the meaning of images is always clear, or that they are always received by their audience in only one way, or that fantasy is the same as reality.

One speaker at the NCCL AGM held up enlarged photocopies of images from magazines such as *Hustler*. From where I sat, at the back of the hall, the images looked much like some of Robert Mapplethorpe's photographs, displayed in art galleries and regarded as art. It is a testimony about the gay male s/m scene as it was in New York. I do not draw any conclusions from the similarity, other than to suggest that images should not be treated as though they were a direct reflection of "real life", or that attitudes and intentions could be unproblematically read off from them.

Although the campaign against pornography acknowledges the connections or lines of continuity between pornography and other not directly sexual images of women, in practice it ignores them by focusing its campaign exclusively on what is sexually explicit. Yet many advertising images make use of "pornographic" devices of cutting up women's bodies (showing just legs, for example), and of generally objectifying women in a way that invites a particular response from men. At the same time, many of these advertising images are seemingly directed at women—ads for stockings, bras, cosmetics and tanning lotions. Some "sexist imagery", therefore, appears to aim to seduce women rather than to stir up sexual hatred in men.

Another argument used with great effect at the NCCL was that all of us who are in favour of legislation to outlaw incitement to racial hatred must also favour the banning of porn, since this is an incitement to sexual hatred. This argument ignores the differences between racism and "sexism". In any case, it is not clear to me that "banning" hard core pornography will either be effective in combating the inequality of women in general, or will in practice end the circulation of hard core porn. Besides, there are already laws which make the selling of a lot of hard core pornography illegal; and, on the other hand, the Sex Discrimination Act could be strengthened, if this was thought to be desirable, so as to regulate representations more specifically.

31

269

The issue of page three pin-ups is slightly different, but here, too, while the legislation envisaged by Clare Short would, it appears, be sufficiently narrow to preclude its use against material such as Derek Jarman's erotic gay film *Sebastiane*, a strategy gap opens in the opposite direction. Page three pin-ups certainly offend many women, as the 5,000 letters written to Clare Short movingly testify. It must indeed be hateful to have to watch your husband leering over Saucy Susan when you have just had a mastectomy.

Yet, in the context of the content of the *Sun* as a whole, I am not actually sure that I would pick out page three as invariably the most offensive item. The contents of the *Sun* are from first to last almost uniformly abhorrent. So why not ban the whole paper? I think the majority of those who dislike its politics and attitudes would recognise that the climate which has produced the British tabloid press cannot be effectively undermined or attacked by simply banning one item or even one newspaper. Maybe it would seem like a symbolic victory to some women, but a symbolic victory isn't really what we want. Unfortunately, much wider issues have to be taken on board: the monopoly ownership of the mass media on the one hand, and radical changes in sex education and sexual attitudes within as well as outside families on the other.

To the extent that attitudes towards women have begun to shift just a little during the past 20 years, this is due to as many years of public discussion, organisation, demonstrations and campaigns. Legislation does play some role in changing attitudes, but, in the current climate, any increase of the power of the authoritarian state must be very carefully weighed up.

I am simply not convinced that legislation of the kind envisaged would not be used against —say—lesbian erotica (some of which explores

> *Women are seen as passive recipients of men's lust. The responsibility for sexuality is men's alone*

violence in relationships) and which I have no doubt is offensive to many women and men. And there are historical precedents to show that the concern isn't misguided. Just over one hundred years ago the pioneer feminist Josephine Butler led the campaign against the Contagious Diseases Acts (which made it obligatory for prostitutes in garrison towns and ports to register and submit to regular internal examinations, as a measure against venereal disease). Her campaign was based on the demand for civil liberties for all women. After the suspension of the acts, in 1883, however, the feminist reformers became involved in and endorsed much more repressive initiatives against sexual irregularity. The result was the 1885 Criminal Law

Amendment Act. This raised the age of consent for girls from 13 to 16 but it also increased general police powers over women and children, added to which it included the notorious Labouchere amendment which criminalised male homosexuality.

A particular type of political intervention does not automatically follow a sense of moral indignation or outrage. Moral crusades can unify a group or a movement, but the anti-pornography campaign has been incredibly divisive for feminists. The NCCL seems blissfully unaware of the way in which the pornography issue split and divided the women's movement, as a direct result of which, a national women's movement ceased to exist after 1978.

Today, the issues around censorship that should concern us are the gross erosions of the right to free speech and civil liberties.

Restrictions on pornography cut across this. Whatever the intention, a campaign for repressive legislation in the present climate plays into the general Thatcherite ethos and is at odds with the Labour Party Policy Review talk of freedom and individuality. More importantly, it is in women's interests to explore and investigate and to achieve an active sexuality (if they so desire), and this may well include some of what many of us may feel are unpleasant aspects of sexual feeling or things, of which we might feel uneasy or ashamed. This is not to say that all women should rush off to the nearest porno shop, but to say that feminists should always be emphasising the right to know rather than the right to protection. While the anti-pornography campaign claims to be about empowering women, its emphasis is on "saving" them from "male lust".

The whole discourse about pornography positions women as victims. Here are the middle-class Victorian philanthropists and the Fabian do-gooders again wanting to protect women.

Finally, the whole anti-porn campaign is an absolute disaster in so far as it is based on a monolithic and over-simplified view of masculinity and male sexuality. This is depicted as inevitably aggressive and sadistic. The NCCL motion stated that there must be three main ingredients of pornography: it must be sexually explicit, "must depict women as enjoying or deserving some form of physical abuse" and "must objectify women, that is, define women in terms of their relationship to men's lust and desire". This wording gives the impression that "men's lust and desire" is both a fundamental problem, encouraged by pornography, and also a monolithic entity, which is unvarying and easily understood.

In this scenario, women cease to have any "lust and desire" at all. Whatever pornography may or may not do, this way of discussing it actually objectifies women, who are positioned as passive recipients of the entity "men's lust". The responsibility for sexuality is once again entirely men's.

This in fact is the fantasy world of porn, where men always have erections and ejaculation is never premature but always repeatable. In a peculiar way, the campaign against pornography reinforces all the misinformation about sexuality which porn itself is accused of purveying.

32

Ironically, to blame everything on porn allows men to wriggle out of responsibility for their behaviour: "Reading Playboy as a teenager is what made me a sexist pig and it's too late now to do anything about it except beat my breast and draw attention to myself." It was sad to see men whom I respect fall into this guilt-trip trap at the NCCL meeting.

This article was originally planned to be about "alternative morality". I did not intend that it should discuss the pornography debate at all, since I regard this as fairly peripheral to the major problems facing our society as a whole and women in it. I am, as Angela Carter once said of herself in a *Guardian* interview, an "old fash-ioned feminist", that is to say, one who believes that capitalism is more important than pornography and that equal pay and education are more important than the struggle against porn. Are we what Melissa Benn in these columns recently described (5 May) as the "seventies feminists", now seriously in need of an MOT, and perhaps having to be traded in for a newer model?

Well, I would rather be a seventies feminist than an 1880s feminist; and I certainly do not want to be a fundamentalist feminist. For let's be quite clear about it: the campaign against pornography is a form of secular fundamentalism. One of the more myopic aspects of the Salman Rushdie controversy has been the way in which one particular fundamentalism—the Islamic variety—is treated as though it were unique, when in fact both the Jewish and the Christian faiths have also witnessed a resurgence of fundamentalist types of belief in recent years. According to a recent article in the *Guardian* (12 June) even the Church of England is now being taken over by evangelicals, hence the uproar (to me incredible at the time) when York Minster was struck by lightning and some people seriously maintained that this was because God was particularly cross with the Archbishop.

The celebration of a "postmodern world" (and I should say that in some ways I'm sympathetic to the postmodernist cultural analysis) appears completely to ignore this growth of radical faith; the world may be in fragments, but, perhaps for that very reason, individuals and groups grasp at old certainties. (Of course, the "postmodern-ism" thesis tends also to ignore the growing authoritarianism of Britain, choosing instead to celebrate a pluralistic culture in which the hitherto marginalised "others" such as women, blacks and gays can at last make their voices heard. This is a bit strange, when you consider just how badly all these groups are being treated.)

Although I may have been labelled as a politi-cal fundamentalist (translation: too leftwing), I abhor what I take fundamentalism to stand for. I am not talking about Islamic fundamentalism here or making specific points about any particu-lar religion. It is just that fundamentalism as a general attitude—one that is primarily asso-ciated with religion, but can also take political forms—seems to me flawed in a way that is relevant to some current feminist positions.

Fundamentalism in general is a way of life or a world view or philosophy of life which insists that

the individual lives by narrowly prescribed rules and rituals; a faith that offers certainty. Revolu-tion and liberation, by contrast, mean change and uncertainty. The search for the "new life" can be exhilarating but can lead to extreme anxiety and to personal collapse; the price paid for certainty is rigidity and an incomprehension of those who do not follow the prescribed way. Those who don't believe must either be des-troyed or saved. Fundamentalism in general is

> *To blame*
> *pornography for all*
> *women's ills is actually*
> *to let the rulers of our*
> *society off the hook*

also associated with a restrictive attitude to-wards women, and maintains a rigidly patri-archal authority over them, placing women more securely within a "private" sphere and carefully guarding women's sexuality.

The anti-pornography campaign uses the me-thods of fundamentalism. Its beliefs are the "true way" and women who fail to fall into step are apostates, betrayers of the true faith (in this case feminism). If you believe, you will have certainty, you will have the solution in your hands. The style of the campaign has been taken directly from born again Christianity, with its preacher style harangues, its "testimony" from women who have "seen the light", its conver-sion rituals and its shock-horror denunciations. In the United States, whatever the intentions of its initiators, it has been supported and taken up by the extreme right.

The moral vacuum in British society does alarm me. All manner of things have rushed to fill this vacuum—astrology, music cults from opera to rap, aromatherapy, psychic healers, football mania or just spending money: certainties or obsessions in a culture that is falling apart. The anti-pornography campaign is another obses-sion, it is a fixation on one tiny corner of the terrain.

To the challenge: "Well, you have to start somewhere", my answer can only be that this is not the place. Sexual behaviour and sexual im-pulses are emotionally complex and not well understood areas and our society is already deeply repressive and bigoted in relation to sexuality. To ban offensive sexual images does not do away with the attitudes that produced them, and may even reinforce these attitudes.

We do need a new deal for women, and we do need a "new moral world". We do not need a 19th-century social purity movement in the 1990s, for a social purity movement will have nothing to offer women's liberation, but will rather be a perhaps unexpected but very compa-tible part of these authoritarian times.

33

The Failure of Feminism

By Kay Ebeling

The other day I had the world's fastest blind date. A Yuppie from Eureka penciled me in for 50 minutes on a Friday and met me at a watering hole in the rural northern California town of Arcata. He breezed in, threw his jammed daily planner on the table and shot questions at me, watching my reactions as if it were a job interview. He eyed how much I drank. Then he breezed out to his next appointment. He had given us 50 minutes to size each other up and see if there was any chance for romance. His exit was so fast that as we left he let the door slam back in my face. It was an interesting slam.

Most of our 50-minute conversation had covered the changing state of male-female relationships. My blind date was 40 years old, from the Experimental Generation. He is "actively pursuing new ways for men and women to interact now that old traditions no longer exist." That's a real quote. He really did say that, when I asked him what he liked to do. This was a man who'd read Ms. Magazine and believed every word of it. He'd been single for 16 years but had lived with a few women during that time. He was off that evening for a ski weekend, meeting someone who was paying her own way for the trip.

I too am from the Experimental Generation, but I couldn't even pay for my own drink. To me, feminism has backfired against women. In 1973 I left what could have been a perfectly good marriage, taking with me a child in diapers, a 10-year-old Plymouth and Volume 1, Number One of Ms. Magazine. I was convinced I could make it on my own. In the last 15 years my ex has married or lived with a succession of women. As he gets older, his women stay in their 20s. Meanwhile, I've stayed unattached. He drives a BMW. I ride buses.

Today I see feminism as the Great Experiment That Failed, and women in my generation, its perpetrators, are the casualties. Many of us, myself included, are saddled with raising children alone. The resulting poverty makes us experts at cornmeal recipes and ways to find free recreation on weekends. At the same time, single men from our generation amass fortunes in CDs and real-estate ventures so they can breeze off on ski weekends. Feminism freed men, not women. Now men are spared the nuisance of a wife and family to support. After childbirth, if his wife's waist doesn't return to 20 inches, the husband can go out and get a more petite woman. It's far more difficult for the wife, now tied down with a baby, to find a new man. My blind date that Friday waved goodbye as he drove off in his RV. I walked home and paid the sitter with laundry quarters.

The main message of feminism was: woman, you don't need a man; remember, those of you around 40, the phrase: "A woman without a man is like a fish without a bicycle?"

That joke circulated through "consciousness raising" groups across the country in the '70s. It was a philosophy that made divorce and cohabitation casual and routine. Feminism made women disposable. So today a lot of females are around 40 and single with a couple of kids to raise on their own. Child-support payments might pay for a few pairs of shoes, but in general, feminism gave men all the financial and personal advantages over women.

What's worse, we asked for it. Many women decided: you don't need a family structure to raise your children. We packed them off to day-care centers where they could get their nurturing from professionals. Then we put on our suits and ties, packed our briefcases and took off on this Great Experiment, convinced that there was no difference between ourselves and the guys in the other offices.

'Biological thing': How wrong we were. Because like it or not, women have babies. It's this biological thing that's just there, these organs we're born with. The truth is, a woman can't live the true feminist life unless she denies her childbearing biology. She has to live on the pill, or have her tubes tied at an early age. Then she can keep up with the guys with an uninterrupted career and then, when she's 30, she'll be paying her own way on ski weekends too.

The reality of feminism is a lot of frenzied and overworked women dropping kids off at day-care centers. If the child is sick, they just send along some children's Tylenol and then rush off to underpaid jobs that they don't even like. Two of my workingmother friends told me they were mopping floors and folding laundry after midnight last week. They live on five hours of sleep, and it shows in their faces. And they've got husbands! I'm not advocating that women retrogress to the brainless

> The reality is frenzied and overworked women often abandoned by men

housewives of the '50s who spent afternoons baking macaroni sculptures and keeping Betty Crocker files. Post-World War II women were the first to be left with a lot of free time, and they weren't too creative in filling it. Perhaps feminism was a reaction to that Brainless Betty, and in that respect, feminism has served a purpose.

Women should get educations so they can be brainy in the way they raise their children. Women can start small businesses, do consulting, write freelance out of the home. But women don't belong in 12-hour-a-day executive office positions, and I can't figure out today what ever made us think we would want to be there in the first place. As long as that biology is there, women can't compete equally with men. A ratio cannot be made using disproportionate parts. Women and men are not equal, we're different. The economy might even improve if women came home, opening up jobs for unemployed men, who could then support a wife and children, the way it was, pre-feminism.

Sometimes on Saturday nights I'll get dressed up and go out club-hopping or to the theater, but the sight of all those other women my age, dressed a little too young, made up to hide encroaching wrinkles, looking hopefully into the crowds, usually depresses me. I end up coming home, to spend my Saturday night with my daughter asleep in her room nearby. At least the NBC Saturday-night lineup is geared demographically to women at home alone.

A single mother of a 2-year-old daughter and a freelance writer, Ebeling lives in Humboldt County, Calif.

Wrong on rape

Neither naming rape victims against their will, nor broadening the definition of rape to include seduction, helps the cause of feminism

THERE is no rapist yet, there is only a victim and an alleged victim. The man charged last week with raping a woman in Florida in March, William Kennedy Smith, is the victim of an accusation that has irretrievably damaged his reputation. Perhaps he deserves that: the court will decide. His alleged victim—his accuser—has also had her anonymity blown and her reputation blackened. One newspaper will now be prosecuted for blowing it, and another has been universally criticised for the blackening.

Is this fair? Rape is the only crime involving adults in which the accuser can keep her name secret, by tacit agreement of the press, backed in Florida, Georgia and South Carolina by the law. In Britain the same courtesy is extended to a man accused of rape, which is a little fairer—though it means that an alleged rapist is granted a privilege the law does not grant to an alleged murderer or burglar. But there is no pressure in America from "masculinists" to extend anonymity to the accused; there is pressure, from some feminists, to remove anonymity from rape victims. Most of the calls for "outing" rape victims come from women, not men.

Their reasoning goes like this. Rape, unusually among crimes, shames its victims, who are made to feel that they have invited the crime. That, plus the appalling feelings of violation that accompany rape and sometimes-insensitive police investigations, lead many women not to report rapes. The only way to remove the shame, make rape a "normal" crime and increase the reporting of it is to name names. This is disingenuous. What such activists mean is that they would like to ride roughshod over an individual woman's preference for anonymity in order to publicise and reveal the extent of rape.

An accusation of rape can be used anonymously to blackmail or hurt the accused. Yet that is no reason to abandon anonymity either. If the man's alibi stands up and the accuser produces no evidence, then she loses both her anonymity and her legal innocence: she can be prosecuted or sued.

America should stick to a voluntary code of anonymity for victims of alleged rape, while encouraging them to tell their stories of their own volition. To "out" them only discourages other victims from coming forward. But enforcing anonymity by law—something several other states are considering—only encourages dissent by civil libertarians. As for the imbalance between the accuser's anonymity and the pillorying of the accused: two wrongs do not make a right.

No means no

What then can be done to remove the unreasonable shame of being raped? The shame exists because there are big differences between the average woman and the average man (as well as among men and among women) about what constitutes rape. What some women consider to be legitimate flirtation, others see as invitations to sex. What some men consider to be legitimate persuasion, others recognise as attempted rape. Whether feminists like it or not, there is a grey area between rape and persuasion. There are women who say "maybe" when they mean "yes": understandably so, when a different stigma attaches to a woman who says "yes" too readily. In a society where the practice is that men pounce, misunderstandings will arise; and not all of them imply that the man has done something criminal.

One in four women at universities say they have suffered from forced attempted intercourse. Feminists, who say there is a hidden epidemic of "date rape" of women by their acquaintances, are right to insist that a woman can say "no" at any stage, however much she may have led the man on. Failure to lock a car is not an invitation to steal it. Drumming that into the heads of men will gradually reduce the stigma of the rape victim.

But feminists are unwise to try to increase the reporting of rape by broadening its definition to include every female student who has reluctantly given in to her insistent boyfriend and regretted it later. To do that is sure to devalue the word rape and eventually to lessen the far greater stigma that attaches to the word "rapist". They must be careful not to imply that all seduction is rape.

274

Perplexed by Sex?

Two controversial intellectuals, Robert Bly and Camille Paglia, want to change the way you think about male and female roles.

BY JAMES BOWMAN
ILLUSTRATION BY TIM GABOR

Here are two statements about sex, one by a man who wants to teach men how to be men again and one by a woman who wants to give feminism a new direction. See if you can guess who said which:

1. *"If civilization had been left in female hands, we would still be living in grass huts."*

2. *"The dark side of men is clear. Their mad exploitation of earth resources, devaluation and humiliation of women, and obsession with tribal warfare are undeniable."*

Of course, there is no mystery. Only a woman could have said—publicly—the first, and any man attempting to warm up the leftovers of patriarchy would have to garnish them with reassurances like the second. Yet it is remarkable that both authors—Camille Paglia, in *Sexual Personae: Art and Decadence from Nefertiti to Emily Dickinson*, and Robert Bly, in the best-selling *Iron John: A Book about Men*—have suddenly shot to prominence for thinking anew about sexual roles and finding problems that will not be solved, as Paglia says, "by recreational sex or an expansion of women's civil rights."

She is by far the more provocative of the two writers: "What an abyss divides the sexes!" she says. "Let us abandon the pretense of sexual sameness and admit the terrible duality of gender." The key word there is "terrible." Neither she nor Bly is being revolutionary in suggesting that there are differences between the sexes that go beyond the merely physiological. But the liberal consensus, of which a sort of basic feminism has become almost a subset, depends upon the assumption that such differences, like skin color or "sexual preference," are, or ought to be, politically and socially insignificant. The word "terrible" at least opens up the possibility that that assumption will not work.

Throughout its modern history, feminism has left unresolved the nature-versus-nurture question. But those who started out believing that traditional male and female sexual roles are merely arbitrary products of social conditioning that can be altered so as to produce a unisex world have in recent years tended to adopt either more conservative or more radical

James Bowman is the U.S. editor of the Times Literary Supplement *(London). Portions of this article first appeared in the* Daily Telegraph *(London).*

views. At one end of the spectrum is the belief that sexual differences are biological but that this should have nothing to do with questions of equal pay, abortion, child care, and other "feminist" issues. At the other end is a kind of female supremacism or "matriarchy." To the more extreme adherents of this view, all men are rapists and feminism is tantamount to lesbianism.

There is plenty of room for debate within feminism about such questions as these. What there is not room for is any slightest suggestion that biological differences might provide the shadow of a justification for traditional male dominance of women. And although Camille Paglia calls herself a feminist and shares feminist views on such important issues as abortion, the reactionary subtext of her work is bound to prove far too dangerous for her to continue as a member of even the broadest feminist church. Because of her, it can be said that for the first time in middle-aged memory there is a basis for potential antifeminism that is not mere male curmudgeonliness.

Instinctively aware of the tension between them, Paglia has been quick to jump onto the offensive by attacking feminists at every opportunity. "Feminism," she says, "has become nothing more than group complaining, handholding, whining, and blaming men for all human problems, and I am cutting through all this....My learning is vaster than [that of] any feminist now. Feminism needs a revolution, so here I am." Or, more pithily, "Leaving sex to the feminists is like going on holiday and leaving your dog with a taxidermist." That kind of statement is clearly meant to be provocative, but talk of revolution inevitably leads to the question. What direction is the revolution going to take if it is not merely a counterrevolution?

Paradoxically, Robert Bly, for all his atavistic hocus pocus about "wild men," represents something of a countertendency to Paglia's potential subversiveness. Both of them are literary scholars whose general views are at best unpopular and at worst scandalous in the closed world of academic lit. crit., which is dominated by feminist and other so-called "politically correct" thinking. Both are thus outsiders who have suddenly come from nowhere with ideas that challenge some of the basic assumptions of American intellectual discourse. Yet Bly goes out of his way to insist

278

that, so far as feminism is concerned, his views pose no threat to academic orthodoxy.

In his sixties, Bly holds no university post; he has made his living for years as a poet, translator, lecturer, and storyteller. But there is something of the academic in his ideas. His purpose is to enable men, with poetry, myth, nature, and primitive ritual, to get back in touch with their "wild" nature, like divorced fathers visiting their children. The workaday world remains as tame as, or preferably tamer than, ever; the "inner warrior" does not threaten the outer man's place on a tenure track. Bly's kind of "wildness" is like a Capability Brown garden that delights the sentimentalist because it is wholly contained by civilization.

Camille Paglia, by contrast, is in her midforties and, although she says that for years she "couldn't get a job, couldn't get published," is an associate professor at the Philadelphia College of the Performing Arts. Her idea of wild nature retains some of the danger that primitive people associated with it, and that makes it not quite academically respectable. When her book was published last year, she started getting strange gifts from strange men (one sent her a red leotard); these attentions, she says, are the lot of any woman who writes about sex.

But to say that Camille Paglia writes about sex is like saying that Darwin wrote about wildlife. Her work does have the potential to bring about a revolution—or a counterrevolution—in the way that we think about sex, which for her is the wild nature that we seek to escape from rather than return to. Women are the embodiment of this nature and partake of its terrors as well as its delights. From the earliest times, she writes, "Woman was an idol of belly-magic. She seemed to swell and give birth by her own law. From the beginning of time, Woman has seemed an uncanny being. Man honored but feared her. She was the black maw that had spat him forth and would devour him anew. Men, bonding together, invented culture as a defense against female nature." And they didn't do it by seeking out but by rigidly constraining wildness.

A disciple of Nietzsche (as well as Freud and the Marquis de Sade), Paglia makes use of the principles that he called "Apollonian" and "Dionysian"—except that she calls the latter "chthonian," a word derived from the Greek for "earth"—to describe the essential differences between male and female. The Apollonian is the male principle of fire and air, of activity, aggression, and ambition, of science, art, and rational thought, and of the tool-making that eventually got us out of the grass huts. The chthonian is the female principle of earth and water, of passivity and fecundity, of dark secrets, rituals, and taboos, of sex and death, and of all that ties us to the land on which we sit. Western art is largely the record of Apollonian attempts to escape from "the long, slow suck, the murk and ooze" of the chthonian.

From a feminist point of view, the most dangerous thing about Camille Paglia is this insistent identification of woman with nature, man with culture. "All the genres of philosophy, science, high art, athletics, and politics were invented by men," she says.

"We could make an epic catalog of male achievements, from paved roads, indoor plumbing, and washing machines to eyeglasses, antibiotics, and disposable diapers. We enjoy fresh, safe milk and meat, and vegetables and tropical fruits heaped in snowbound cities. When I cross the George Washington Bridge or any of America's great bridges, I think: *men* have done this. Construction is a sublime male poetry. When I see a giant crane passing on a flatbed truck, I pause in awe and reverence, as one would for a church procession."

Compare these achievements of male culture to what she says about the chief intellectual innovation of feminism: "Women's studies is a jumble of vulgarians, bunglers, whiners, French faddicts, apparatchiks, doughface party-liners, pie-in-the-sky utopianists, and bullying, sanctimonious sermonizers....Every year, feminists provide more and more evidence for the old charge that women can neither think nor write."

Words such as these challenge not just the present state of feminism but its very foundations. Small wonder, then, that *Sexual Personae* was rejected by publisher after publisher before being taken on by Yale University Press last year. It has now sold over 15,000 copies in four hardcover printings—an extraordinary number for a 700-page academic tome packed with learned allusions to the art and literature of more than 3,000 years. The author herself has become something of a media celebrity—what her publisher calls "an established point-of-view person"—and, for the moment at least,

"Leaving sex to the feminists is like going on holiday and leaving your dog with a taxidermist."

is enjoying (as Bly is) the respect that Americans always pay to success.

This state of affairs will not long outlast the discovery of how truly subversive of the liberal consensus her ideas are. So far, she gets away with them partly because she considers herself a leftist and there are still leftists who defend, as she does, not only abortion and homosexuality but prostitution and pornography as well. Also, she has learned to speak the language of structuralist criticism that has served traditional feminists so well: "Male urination really *is* a kind of accomplishment, an arc of transcendence," she writes. "A woman merely waters the ground she stands on." If most of the scholarship of feminism represents real knowledge, then so does this. And, perhaps, vice versa.

With her attack on feminism, however, she invites harsher scrutiny—and, incidentally, parts company with Bly. He is more the New Age Man, concerned to preserve enclaves of "male feelings" that pose no threat to feminists or feminist thinking. He encourages a kind of male encounter group—if it can meet in a forest to the accompaniment of tom-toms and American Indian rituals, so much the better—to compensate men for the absence of their fathers and male role models, he says, more or less since the Industrial Revolution.

Although *Iron John* shares with *Sexual Personae* a preoccupation with poetry, myth, and legend, it is more accessible. Its title is taken from one of the Grimms' fairy tales about a "wild man" of the forest from whom a boy has to learn to be a man and a warrior before he can marry the king's daughter. Basically an extended explication of this tale with copious illustrations from literature and mythology, the book has been near the top of the best-seller lists all this year.

Its success is one indication among many that Camille Paglia is right in explaining her own success by saying that there is a new spirit abroad in the land that makes her ideas more acceptable: "The *Zeitgeist* has shifted," she says. Perhaps because men and women alike are beginning to tire of the insipidity of what Bly calls the "soft man"—to say nothing of the businesslike woman—of the 1970s and 1980s, there is more receptivity to new thinking about sexual differences. Further evidence that this is so comes from another look at the best-seller lists, on which are to be found *You Just Don't*

"The industrial capitalist domination and system has had its effect on George Bush. You can see from just looking at him."

Understand by Deborah Tannen, which purports to explain male/female differences in terms of their different speech codes, and *Fire in the Belly: On Being a Man* by Sam Keen, which, together with *Iron John*, is inspiring if not a movement then at least a stirring among men seeking to awaken their "inner warrior."

Even within feminism, there is a new questioning of the movement's effectiveness. In her book *The Beauty Myth*, Naomi Wolf looks with dismay at the booming cosmetic and diet industries and finds evidence that, especially among younger women, there has been a reaction against that aspect of feminism that set its face against what it saw as male standards of female beauty. Elizabeth Fox-Genovese's book *Feminism Without Illusions* bills itself as "A Critique of Individualism" but is really a critique of the white, middle-class orientation of most American feminism and its irrelevance to women in the working classes and the third world.

But if there are two principal spokesmen for the new, revisionist thinking about sex, they are Camille Paglia and Robert Bly. Paglia says that she and Bly are "definitely on parallel tracks," not least, she goes on, because they are both "completely out of sorts with the current phenomenon of feminism, which has forgotten history. This is short-sighted of it. The feminist project was to remake the future—really Soviet in its view of things. Bly and other body-centered poets were excluded by the academics who thought that everything we are is determined by society. Now everybody in the world except intellectuals and feminists is thinking of nature."

Bly returns the compliment by calling Paglia "an extremely intelligent woman and a superb writer. The first 150 pages of *Sexual Personae* is some of the best cultural writing I've seen for 20 years." But, he adds, "I'm more of a praise person; she's a warrior. Did you see that picture of her with the sword in *New York* magazine? She's chosen to fight, and what she fights is the feminists. I'm more sympathetic to feminists.

"I can't say that I have no quarrel with them, but I think that the depreciation of the masculine has come from many sources. One of them is capitalism, which doesn't need the deep feeling of masculinity. Another is the Christian church, which doesn't need it either. A third is the matriarchy which comes with the welfare state, and a fourth comes from *separatist* feminists who want to shame men. So I do not feel as much anger against the fourth, which is only one factor among many."

But when asked if the movement with which he is associated planned to take up arms against either capitalism or the welfare state (or both), Bly replies: "No. The patriarchy is over. That can't be changed. We don't have any plans, except to keep feelings alive under the industrial system." So in his book, he is only really concerned with what he calls "soul work" and is in fact at pains to distinguish his inner warrior from outer warriors, whom he mostly seems to disapprove of. Mere soldiers like Oliver North, a man, as Bly sees him, in the service of a corrupt king, are scarcely to be distinguished from murderers. All they have going for them, it might be said, is that they are real, instead of only pretend, warriors.

"Over both matriarchy and patriarchy," Bly continues, "is the industrial capitalist domination and system, which exists at an altitude far above the house and its values. It has had its effect on George Bush: you can see from just looking at him how his masculinity has been worn down. In the Gulf War he was perfectly willing to spend billions of dollars that are desperately needed for the schools and the bridges—for the Country—to sacrifice all of that for the Industrial State."

Here is the paradox of the "men's movement." When Bly speaks of the "inner warrior," he does not imagine it actually making war on anybody, although it's okay to defend your own "personal boundaries." Man. Real warriors tend to be frauds and imposters in this view. The inner warrior may fight inner demons—especially those conjured up by paternal neglect—but he is given no plan of attack for dealing with the exterior world. Both Bly and the author of *Fire in the Belly*, the psychologist Sam Keen, are really sentimentalists, concerned only to "keep feelings alive." They both belong heart and soul to the great cause that has energized American culture for the past 20 years: feeling good about oneself.

Such masculinism offers no real challenge to the feminist erosion of sexual identity. On the contrary, it wishes to stake its own claim, complementary to women's, to victim-status. So John Lee, publisher of the small-circulation quarterly MAN!, claims that just as women have been treated as "sex objects," men have

been treated as "success objects" and not allowed to *feel* as women do. Hence Bly's emphasis on the "soul." For the most part, it is as if the "men's movement" is saying: "We're going to go out in the woods this weekend and practice being men—if that's all right with the rest of you."

The fate of new psychologies in America sometimes seems to resemble that of new religions in India: it is because the people are so receptive, such natural believers, that all are believed and none has any power. Bly's cozy accommodation both with feminism and the broader therapeutic culture and with a kind of primitivist, agrarian leftism fits him easily into an American intellectual life that has always been pretty remote from the lives of ordinary Americans and is so more than ever today. Camille Paglia would presumably like to fit in as well, but she may find it more difficult to do so than she has hitherto.

For compared to Bly's, her writing is provocative, dangerous, and intellectually (dare one say it?) more masculine. There is something quite comical about this paradox, as there is about the whole idea of a "men's movement." Perhaps it too has to do with a basic difference between the sexes. Someone once said that no man is attractive if he thinks he is and no woman is attractive *unless* she thinks she is. That feminine reflexivity and self-contemplation is part of what Camille Paglia calls the chthonian nature of women and just looks silly in men, whose Apollonian nature is directed toward the world outside themselves.

One cannot imagine Robert Bly in a leopard-skin, for example (though he does wear gaudy vests), yet Camille Paglia was never more charmingly herself than when, in conjunction with an interview with the *San Francisco Examiner*, she posed for a photograph with whip and chains outside a San Francisco porn shop. By taking herself less seriously than Bly does, she enables us to take her more seriously. That Bly's Wild Man might find such a joke a little difficult to bring off is one reason to go on believing in that "abyss" between the sexes of which Paglia writes so persuasively.

▲

Psychological Reports, 1992, 71, 957-958. © Psychological Reports 1992

FEMINISM AND ANORECTIC TENDENCIES IN COLLEGE WOMEN [1]

WILLIAM T. BAILEY AND TRACY L. HAMILTON

Eastern Illinois University

Summary.—Anorexia is a debilitating disorder which affects significant numbers of young women. Brumberg has suggested a causal relationship in young women between feminism and anorexia. In this study, traditional-aged female college students completed the Attitudes Toward Women Scale and the Eating Attitudes Test. The hypothesized relationship between feminism and anorexia was not found.

Anorexia is a medically and psychologically debilitating disorder which affects significant numbers of young people. The majority of cases involve people in late adolescence (Leichner & Gertler, 1988), 95% of those affected are female (Sholevar, 1987), and on some college campuses as many as 20% of female students may be affected (Brumberg, 1988). A number of factors have been suggested as causal; Brumberg (1988) noted that some writers (e.g., Roberta Dresser) have suggested a causal relationship between feminism and anorexia in young females. From a social-cognitive perspective this suggests a self-schematic hypothesis: young women who are feminists may attempt to achieve a body image which is consistent with feminist attitude (i.e., reject a stereotyped adult-woman body type) via anorexia. The present study investigated the relationship between feminism and anorexia. A positive relationship was hypothesized for college women between feminist attitude and symptoms of anorexia; those who are feminist are more likely to be anorectic.

Method.—The subjects were 99 female students, ranging in age from 17 to 23 years, who volunteered from undergraduate psychology courses. Subjects completed the Attitudes Toward Women Scale (Spence & Helmreich, 1978) and the Eating Attitudes Test (Garner & Garfinkle, 1979) during regular class periods. The former has good internal reliability ($\alpha = .89$), and there is considerable evidence for its construct validity. It is scored in a profeminist direction; higher scores indicate a more profeminist attitude, and a score of 30 or greater is conventionally used as the cut-off for identifying feminists. The latter has high internal reliability ($\alpha = .94$). It is scored in the direction of anorexic symptomatology; higher scores indicate a greater tendency toward dysfunctional behavior. In their validation study, Garner and Garfinkle (1979) found that, although some clinically diagnosed anorectics

---

[1]T. L. Hamilton, a graduate student in clinical psychology at Sagamon State University, performed this research as part of an undergraduate independent study project at Eastern Illinois University. Address correspondence to W. T. Bailey at the Psychology Department, Eastern Illinois University, Charleston, IL 61920.

scored as low as 30, some nonanorectics scored as high as 38. To avoid false-negatives when the inventory is used for clinical screening, they recommend using a cut-off of 30; that is, individual scores higher than 30 should be assumed to be diagnostic. In using the inventory among nonclinical subjects, however, the opposite problem is of concern—we need to avoid false-positives. Hence, in this study we have employed the upper limit of scores by Garner and Garfinkle's normal subjects (38) as the cut-off for classification into groups.

Results and discussion.—The hypothesized relationship between feminism and anorexia was not observed for these young women. Eighty-eight percent of the subjects scored as feminists and 12% of subjects reported symptoms characteristic of anorexia; this incidence of anorexia is comparable with other studies using the Eating Attitudes Test with similar populations (Leichner & Gertler, 1988). There was no significant Pearson correlation between scale scores on the two inventories ($r = .00$). Subjects were categorized along the dimensions of feminism (2) and anorexia (2) using the criteria described above. Fourteen percent of those scoring as feminist also scored as anorectic and eight percent of the traditional women scored in this manner. The phi coefficient for the contingency table indicated no significant relationship between the two arrays ($\phi = .05$, $p > .59$).

The suggested relationship between scores on feminism and anorexia in college women was not supported by the present findings. Such a relationship might have existed earlier in the century, as Brumberg (1988) suggests; however, Gergen (1973) noted that relationships among social psychological variables may change over time. The goals and images of feminism have evolved with time, and it seems unlikely that today's feminist young women would necessarily feel compelled to avoid a stereotypic "feminine" body through dietary self-abuse. Nonetheless, it might well be that those with anorexic tendencies could benefit from coming to understand the social and psychological conflicts associated with womanhood in modern society (cf. Orbach, 1986).

REFERENCES

BRUMBERG, J. J. (1988) *Fasting girls.* Cambridge, MA: Harvard Univer. Press.
GARNER, D. M., & GARFINKLE, P. E. (1979) The Eating Attitudes Test: an index of the symptoms of anorexia nervosa. *Psychological Medicine*, 9, 273-279.
GERGEN, K. J. (1973) Social psychology as history. *Journal of Personality and Social Psychology*, 26, 309-320.
LEICHNER, P., & GERTLER, A. (1988) Prevalence and incidence studies of anorexia nervosa. In B. J. Blinder, B. F. Chaitin, & R. S. Goldstein (Eds.), *The eating disorders*. New York: PMA Publishing. Pp. 131-149.
ORBACH, S. (1986) *Hunger strike.* New York: Norton.
SHOLEVAR, G. P. (1987) Anorexia and bulimia. In H. L. Field & B. B. Domangue (Eds.), *Eating disorders throughout the life span*. New York: Praeger. Pp. 31-47.
SPENCE, J. T., & HELMREICH, R. L. (1978) *Masculinity and femininity.* Austin, TX: Univer. of Texas Press.

Accepted September 22, 1992.

The dilemma of
feminists who love men
is at least as old as
Mary Wollstonecraft
(below). **Barbara Taylor**
on the war between heart
and reason

Love and
trouble

"I cannot discover why . . . females should always be degraded by being made subservient to love or lust." —Mary Wollstonecraft, "A Vindication of the Rights of Woman", 1792
"Love is a want of my heart." —Mary Wollstonecraft to Gilbert Imlay, 3 July 1795

Speaking of love, the feminist voice breaks, producing a discourse that is fractured and contradictory. Political imperatives jostle with personal longings; ancient animosities conflict with intense allegiances. From Mary Wollstonecraft onwards, feminist theorists and activists have steered an impossible course between suspicion of heterosexual love as one more weapon in patriarchy's arsenal and the equally powerful wish to authenticate women's loving feelings and desires. Loving men, feminists have argued, women become bound to the oppressor by the ties of their own hearts; refusing that love, heterosexual feminists have often disavowed desire *tout court*—a repudiation whose costs are felt in both their lives and politics. The conundrum is as old as feminism itself.

In 1792 Mary Wollstonecraft published *A Vindication of the Rights of Woman*, the founding text of modern western feminism. The following year she went to Paris to witness the revolutionary process first-hand—and promptly fell in love with an American adventurer named Gilbert Imlay. They had a child, and shortly afterwards Imlay began to edge away, going on business trips abroad and eventually taking up with new lovers.

Wollstonecraft attempted suicide twice before the episode finally crashed to a close, leaving in its wake an incipient scandal that burst into life with the publication of her correspondence with Imlay after her death in 1797. These letters—from adoring missives exchanged in the early period of their relationship through to the furious, desperate diatribes with which Wollstonecraft pursued Imlay as his love waned—provide an utterly revealing record of a feminist in love: "I hope to hear from you by tomorrow's mail. My dearest friend! I cannot tear my affections from you . . . though every remembrance stings me to the soul" (4 July 1795).

If one reads Wollstonecraft's *Rights of Woman* on its own, the impression is of a dour puritanism reminiscent of today's moral conservatives. Sexual feelings, she argues, are "bestial" and "degraded", and those who indulge in them are "debauched". Men are particularly condemned for their "animal lust", while women are chastised for romantic sentimentalism. Outside marriage, she claims, erotic passion is particularly invidious in its effects on women, who become the mere sexual "playthings" of men. But even inside marriage sexual lust erodes domestic morality and encourages adultery. "In order to fufil the duties of life ... which form the moral character, a master and mistress of a family ought not to continue to love each other with passion. I mean to say that they ought not to indulge those emotions which disturb the order of society . . ."

This highly censorious view of heterosexual love was to cast a long shadow over Wollstonecraft's feminist successors. One can hear its echoes in women as disparate as

Christabel Pankhurst (for whom marriage was usually "a tragedy"), Simone de Beauvoir ("love represents in its most touching form the curse . . . [of] the feminine universe"), Kate Millett ("romantic love affords a means of emotional manipulation which the male is free to exploit") or the anonymous woman interviewed by Angela Hamblin for the 1983 Women's Press anthology, *Sex and Love*, in an article entitled "Is a Feminist Heterosexuality Possible?" (" I frequently feel contradictions, because I hate all men. I hate the way they oppress and sexually abuse us and when I am deeply in touch with this part of myself I feel distant and alienated from all men, including my lover and my son. This can be very difficult . . . because I also love them").

Difficult indeed. But to see Wollstonecraft and the feminist tradition that succeeded her as eternally locked into an anti-male, anti-sexual stance is much too simple. The anxiety about erotic love is certainly there, but so also—as voiced in Wollstonecraft's letters and fiction—is the passionate desire for what feminists have seen as an authentic form of female loving, one based on mutual affection and respect and, above all, on genuine equality. "Perfect love and perfect trust have never yet existed except between equals," as Wollstonecraft's great admirer, the suffragist Elizabeth Wolstenholme Elmy, quoted at her readers in 1897, while a century earlier Wollstonecraft herself provided a model for such a "perfect" union. Once she had recovered from Imlay, she became the lover of England's best-known radical philo-sopher, William Godwin. She and Godwin argued about politics and religion, maintained separate homes (even after they finally wed), and had great sex: "Let me assure you," she wrote, "that you are not only in my heart, but my veins, this morning. I turn from you half abashed—yet you haunt me, and some look, word or touch thrills through my whole frame . . . When the heart and reason accord there is no flying from voluptuous sensations. I find, do what a woman can—Can a philo-sopher do more?" (13 September 1796).

These tensions in the relationship between "heart and reason" are at the centre of the feminist project as Wollstonecraft helped to define it. For Wollstonecraft herself, their resolution was short-lived: she died only a year after she and Godwin became lovers. Nonetheless, for nearly two centuries her reputation as a theorist was overshadowed by her sexual history, which was construed as (in the words of the suffragist Millicent Garrett Fawcett) "irregular relations" which "sickened" the feminist mind. The overtly anti-erotic message of the *Rights of Woman* was largely forgotten, as its author came to symbolise uncontrolled female libidinism. Feminist interpretations of her life became a barometer of their attitudes toward sexual love. "Mary Wollstonecraft was . . . a poor victim of passion," as the mid-19th-century feminist Harriet Martineau wrote, setting the tone for most Victorian readings. When women such as Wolstenholme Elmy in England or the supporters of the reformer Victoria Woodhull in America took up Wollstonecraft's defence, it put their own relatively libertarian sexual views in the firing line. "We have crucified the Mary Wollstonecrafts," as

285

one woman wrote in the 1890s, pleading for a more latitudinarian approach within feminism. But it was not until the the most recent wave of organised feminism, born in the "sexual revolution" of the 1960s, that this plea was answered, and Wollstonecraft fully rehabilitated, acquiring her current iconic status as the founder of western feminism.

In 200 years, a lot has changed; a lot hasn't. For women of Wollstonecraft's day, and for more than 150 years afterwards, it was impossible to think about heterosexual love apart from sexual reproduction. Women's vulnerability—to men who might impregnate them, desert them, infect them with venereal disease—was enormous, as were the dangers of childbirth (Wollstonecraft, like so many women, died of complications following childbirth). The celebration of celibate unions found in much feminist writing, "marriages of true minds" involving only minimal sexual contact, needs to be seen in this context, as well as in terms of the dehumanising attitudes toward women prevalent among 18th- and 19th-century male sexual libertarians.

Two centuries later, both the practicalities and attitudes have changed: or have they? Fear of pregnancy, fear of Aids, fear of establishing families in an economic depression —the price for uninhibited passion can be very high. Even in the swinging sixties the feminist voice was a cautionary one, reminding women of these potential costs. Here is one latter-day Mary Wollstonecraft, Germaine Greer, in *The Female Eunuch*: "Women must recognise in the cheap ideology of being in love the essential persuasion to take an irrational and self-destructive step . . . Sexual religion is the opiate of the supermenial." Libertarian radicals such as Greer might display a sexual flamboyance unimaginable in previous phases of feminism, but always with an anxious eye out for potential pain, humiliation, degradation. Poised between the recognition of women's own erotic desires and the culture that still demeans and exploits them, feminists tread carefully on love's wilder shores.

But there has been change—and here, again, we can look to Wollstonecraft for signs of its occurrence. In *Rights of Woman*, sexual appetite was assigned to the brute male, and women's true love was not for men at all, but for God. But by the time Wollstonecraft wrote her last (unfinished) work, *Maria, or The Wrongs of Woman*, this false solution—the splitting off of women's eroticism into men, or the divine, or the cosmos—is largely given up, and the dilemma pulled back to where it really originates, in the minds and bodies of women themselves. The fictive Maria is torn by sexual fantasies and passions that, painful as they are, nevertheless belong to her; in a patriarchal society, as Wollstonecraft insists, Maria can find no happy desires, but at least she can claim them as her own. Suppressing the demands of the heart, as Wollstonecraft herself had discovered, is no liberation. Expecting those demands to be met easily, without pain or conflict, is empty utopianism. As another generation of Wollstonecraft's daughters, that's one difficult lesson we've begun to learn.

Barbara Taylor is writing a book on Mary Wollstonecraft, to be published by Virago

From Separate Spheres to Dangerous Streets: Postmodernist Feminism and the Problem of Order*

BY ELIZABETH
FOX-GENOVESE

WITH MOUNTING URGENCY and ill-disguised impatience, feminist theory has, during the past few decades, mounted a massive, if internally divided, attack upon received notions of order in society, culture, and ideology. At the core of the attack lies an angry protest against distributions of power that have traditionally favored men at the expense of women. From the outraged insistence that rape and sexual harassment may not be tolerated as unfortunate by-products of business-as-usual, to the complexities of postmodernist theories that reject the very notion of difference as inherently oppressive, women's rage at their own disadvantage has provoked many challenges to all inherited conceptions of order as inherently androcentric.

As the feminist challenge to received notions of order has unfolded, it has become clear that the unitary term *feminism* itself masks the diversity of feminisms. If, as Carol Gilligan has claimed, women speak "in a different voice," they, much less the feminists who claim to speak for them, assuredly do not

SOCIAL RESEARCH, Vol. 60, No. 2 (Summer 1993)

speak in one voice.[1] In this climate, the meaning of feminism has become contested. Depending upon temperament, social allegiance, philosophical bent, and political goals, feminists variously defend the fundamental difference or the essential similarity between women and men. Some adhere to the unrealized promises of liberal feminism; some seek a common ground between feminism and postmodernism. Some focus primarily upon what they take to be the common goals of all women; some focus upon the distinct needs of women of oppressed social, racial, and national groups. And since any of these positions may intertwine with or prove at variance with any other, the difficulties of identifying a single feminist position multiply.

Presumably the core of any feminism today, as in the past, lies in the commitment to improving the position of women. But this minimal agreement ends where it begins. For feminists, much less women in general, do not agree on the meaning of improvement. At the most basic level, should feminists seek to strengthen women within families and marriages or to free women from them—to protect women's reproductive capacities or to free women from their consequences? Having originated with Mary Wollstonecraft's call for the public recognition of the rights of woman and developed through struggles to secure public political rights, notably the vote, for women, feminism has, in our time, come increasingly to doubt the value of public rights and to repudiate the distinction between public and private that apparently secured women's persisting inequality.

Public and Private

For many feminists, as Seyla Benhabib and Drucilla Cornell argue, the distinction between an impersonal public and a

---

[1] Carol Gilligan, *In a Different Voice: Psychological Theory and Women's Development* (Cambridge, Mass.: Harvard University Press, 1982).

personal private sphere, with the attendant distinction between public and private interests, has been "constitutive not only of the institutional structure of modern, Western societies but [has] shaped the dominant conception of reason and rationality in them as well."[2] Although some feminists, notably Jean Bethke Elshtain, view the split between public and private as necessary to the health of society and beneficial to women and children, a majority are coming to view it as inherently opposed to women's interests—as the primary locus and source of their oppression.[3] In this view, the distinction between public and private represents an arbitrary and imposed conception of order that has systematically disadvantaged women.

Both the recognition of the distinction between public and private as a comprehensive order and the determination to wage a frontal attack against it have emerged piecemeal from a variety of subsidiary critiques of male dominance. Even today, not all of those who call themselves feminists view the distinction as the main object of attack. But when all the caveats have been filed, it seems clear that the metaphor of the distinction between public and private has provided a significant group of feminist theorists with a unifying theory of male dominance that links private experience to political institutions and, especially, to philosophy and epistemology. Not surprisingly, the feminist attack upon the notion of order as grounded in the distinction between public and private has been most vigorous among academics, especially those who have been seeking some common ground between feminism and postmodernism.

It is worth noting, in passing, that the distinction between

---

[2] Seyla Benhabib and Drucilla Cornell, "Introduction," in Seyla Benhabib and Drucilla Cornell, eds., *Feminism as Critique* (Minneapolis: University of Minnesota Press, 1987), p. 7.

[3] Jean Bethke Elshtain, *Public Man, Private Woman: Women in Social and Political Thought* (Princeton, N.J.: Princeton University Press, 1981).

public and private that has come in for such heavy attack arose in conjunction with capitalism. Most societies have delineated some boundary between public and private, but capitalist societies raised the distinction to a new importance, primarily because their emphasis upon systematic individualism as the governing principle of the public sphere included a decisive split between the principles that dominated public and private life respectively.[4] Schematically, public life in democratic societies grounded in the free market was taken to operate according to contractual principles, whereas private life was taken to operate according to consensual ones. This is Tonnies's distinction between *Gesellschaft* and *Gemeinschaft*— between society and community.

Such societies—especially the United States, in which democratic principles reached their most extensive sway— tended to equate the distinction between public and private with the distinction between male and female, assigning a congeries of human attributes to each. They especially tended to associate public men with the harsh virtues of competition, struggle, and justice, while associating private women with the gentler virtues of compassion, piety, and selfless service. As a result, and at the risk of crude oversimplification, they tended to attribute production and politics to men, while attributing reproduction and morality to women. The metaphor of public and private thus merged with the metaphor of a sexual division of labor, encouraging the view that it derived from nature.

The comprehensiveness of the metaphor endowed it with the prestige of a natural order and thus ensured its hegemony, which in turn ensured that the metaphor would outlive the world it had been devised to explain. For the progress of

---

[4] For a discussion of systematic individualism, see my *Feminism Without Illusions: A Critique of Individualism* (Chapel Hill: University of North Carolina Press, 1991). I am using individualism in a specific sense as the theory that ascribes sovereignty and cognition to the individual, understood as an autonomous unit.

capitalism has been steadily eroding the distinction between public and private in social, economic, and political life. Indeed, the post-World War II women's movement arose largely as a response to that erosion. Similarly, dominant currents in (male) thought have long been whittling away at any complacent, unquestioning acceptance of rationality and reason. Whatever Sigmund Freud's sins against women's self-perceptions, he assuredly exposed the prevalence of irrational forces that press against the bulwarks of complacent rationality. Yet even as events and theorists exposed the permeability of the boundary between the public and private spheres, some core of the metaphor of their distinction persisted.

The Idea of Difference

Today, that abiding core, notably its emphasis upon the significance of difference, has emerged as the anchor for an entire system of order and as the principal object of some feminists' attack. Although specific arguments vary, they frequently find common ground in the notion that the idea of difference itself disadvantages women. By this reasoning, dominant male thought has systematically cast woman as the other, attributing to her the opposite qualities from those that men claim for themselves. In this perspective, rationality, reason, and justice—the preeminent attributes of the public sphere—appear hopelessly compromised by their association with men. As distinctly male qualities, they vitiate their own claims to universality and shrink to the self-interested attempt of one group to impose its will on another. At issue, it appears, is the very notion of order itself.

Order in this sense has been exposed as serving the interests of some at the expense of the interests of others. In fairness, the idea that the defense of order tends to advantage the privileged against the dispossessed is hardly new. Class struggles, throughout history, have frequently rested upon precisely that claim, as the French, Haitian, and Russian revolutions abundantly attest. This time, however, the goal is less to substitute one notion of order for another than it is to contest the notion of order itself. By identifying the metaphor of the distinction between public and private with men's advantage over women, feminist theorists have effectively argued that the notion of order must be recognized as the determination to substitute one person's (or group's) story for that of another person or group. Men have succeeded in subsuming women's perceptions under their own with the pernicious consequence that women can see—and represent— themselves only through men's eyes.

The battle against the order of public and private is being waged on many levels simultaneously, with somewhat different implications in different cases. But the combination of specific assaults amounts to a systematic war upon the very notion of legitimate authority. In the meaure that feminists are contributing to this general antiauthoritarian project, the most serious consequence may well be that in attempting to demolish the legitimacy of authority that has customarily been wielded by men, feminists have mistaken the enemy and are easing the triumph of new and more sinister forms of authority. In this respect, the attacks on various levels do converge, if only by calling the notion of order into question. But along the way, the discrete battles merit discrete attention.

It is easy enough to understand the feminist claim that the notion of difference has, more often than not, disadvantaged women by casting them as the other. It is less clear that women have always resented the qualities that have been attributed to them. There is good evidence that nineteenth-century American women frequently took pride in their association with morality and even attempted to introduce their distinct moral values into the public sphere. Thus Harriet Beecher Stowe's widely influential novel, *Uncle Tom's Cabin,* unambiguously pressed domestic virtues as a standard for the nation.[5] Similarly, women reformers of the Progressive Era introduced notions of social housekeeping, notably responsibility for the weak and the disadvantaged, into the public sphere and, increasingly, into the activities of the government itself. Even today, some feminists, like Sara Ruddick, insist that women's experience has uniquely fitted them for such public responsibilities as preserving peace, while others, like Carol Gilligan, credit women with a special, and valuable, sense of morality.[6]

The conviction that women embody and represent a discrete sense of morality and, implicitly, favor an alternate political agenda retains considerable appeal for large numbers of women. The recent enthusiasm, on the part of some men as well as women, for the election of women to national political office apparently owes much to many people's conviction that, for whatever reasons, women would do things differently. As one working woman said to me, one good thing that was going to change was that we were now beginning to elect more women to office. She did not remember when things had been in such bad shape, but women were not going into politics for "that power thing" and, accordingly, might make a difference.[7]

The intuitive sense that women were not driven by "that power thing" and might change the quality of political life testifies to the conviction that women represent a different, and more humane, conception of order than men. Women, this view assumes, will be more likely to attend to the needs of the vulnerable, more likely to value peace, and less likely to follow the dictates of greed and ego. Carol Tavris has relentlessly exposed the pitfalls of this position, arguing that both fixed notions of gender or sexual difference and the

[5] Harriet Beecher Stowe, *Uncle Tom's Cabin or, Life Among the Lowly*, ed. Ann Douglas (New York: Penguin Books, 1981).

[6] Sara Ruddick, *Maternal Thinking: Towards a Politics of Peace* (Boston: Beacon Press, 1989); Gilligan, *In a Different Voice*.

[7] From an interview for my book-in-progress, *What Do We Want for Our Daughters (And Our Sons)?* (New York: Doubleday, 1994).

notion of difference itself cripple our imaginations and our possibilities. And if she repeatedly signals the ways in which these notions limit and impoverish men, she yet more scathingly attacks the ways in which they imprison women in debilitating stereotypes. She especially insists that "the philosophy of cultural feminism has functioned to keep women focused on their allegedly stable and innate personality qualities, instead of on what it would take to have a society based on the qualities we value in both sexes."[8]

In Tavris's view, the female stereotypes celebrated by women are no better than those imposed by men. But, she insists, we cannot effectively combat the stereotypes if we persist in the trend toward increased particularization "in which each gender, race, or ethnicity seeks only its own validation, celebrates only itself." For Tavris, the future health of our society depends upon our ability to resist the temptation to think in terms of opposites—to cast entire groups as "the other"—and to learn to think about an inclusive "*us*, so that our relationships, our work, our children, and our planet will flourish."[9]

Tavris astutely grasps the implicit relation between the notion of women as other that derived from the split between public and private and the notion of difference that plays such an important role in contemporary cultural politics, including within feminism itself. We cannot, she seems to be arguing, solve the problem of casting women as essentially different (from men) simply by multiplying differences. In this respect, she is, however cautiously, edging toward the postmodern position that any notion of difference is inherently authoritarian and constraining. As a psychologist, Tavris is primarily concerned not to limit the diversity of human potential by

[8] Carol Tavris, *The Mismeasure of Woman* (New York: Simon & Schuster, 1992), p. 343.

[9] *Ibid.*, pp. 341, 345.

restricting human beings to artificially defined roles, notably but not exclusively gender roles.

Tavris especially seeks to demonstrate that the purported physiological differences between women and men, notably in their brains, result from faulty research that predicated man as the norm and attempted to identify women's deviation from the norm. She argues that "nature" does not provide adequate evidence for the classifications, or "culture," that human beings have imposed upon it. Postmodernist feminists, like Susan Hekman, more uncompromisingly insist that the very categories of nature and culture embody artificial, binary oppositions that result exclusively from the determination of some human beings to dominate others.[10] In this view, gender difference emerges as one among the many manifestations of the dichotomous thinking that has characterized modernism.

Moderns and Postmoderns

The postmodernist critique of modernism, upon which postmodernist feminists are increasingly drawing, faults modernism for having cognitively and epistemologically divided the world into dichotomous or binary pairs. For the moderns, a loose group that is normally taken to include all of the thinkers from Hobbes to Hegel and Marx who attempted to articulate the world spawned by capitalism and the scientific revolution, order derived from the clear split between paired entities or qualities: nature/culture, rationality/irrationality, subject/object, and, of course, male/female. This sense of order, which emphasized the autonomy and moral responsibility of the individual—the rational subject—effectively divided the cognitive and material worlds into pairs of *A* and *B*.

Postmodernists, drawing variously on currents in science,

[10] Susan J. Hekman, *Gender and Knowledge: Elements of a Postmodern Feminism* (Boston: Northeastern University Press, 1990).

psychology, culture, and politics, have worked to explode those binary oppositions, arguing that the lines that divide them are blurred, not clear, and must, accordingly, be recognized as figments of the human imagination or, worse, of human convenience. For them, under the special influence of Michel Foucault, the world consists in nothing but a system of discourses or patterns of naming that are driven by a ubiquitous will to power.[11] Although Foucault had little to say about, and probably less interest in, the special situation of women, he unilaterally declared war on the notion that sexuality did or should derive from some putative nature. Sexuality should be understood as plastic—as the manifestation of human desire whose only master was the infinitely variable human imagination.

Drawing upon the general critique of dichotomous thinking, postmodernist feminists have increasingly insisted that the binary opposition between male and female informs and anchors all the other binary oppositions. In their view, modernist dichotomies are all inherently and inescapably gendered. In joining forces with the postmodernist revolt against modernist order, they have tended to identify the sexual domination of women by men as the core—the motive force—of the modernist exercise of power. From this perspective, the distinction between *A* and *B* reduces to nothing but a transparent disguise for the self-serving distinction between *A* and Not-*A*. Thus the distinction between man and woman inescapably casts woman as not-man, leaving women's purportedly admirable characteristics and attributes as nothing but the lack of maleness.

Although postmodernist feminists occasionally find it hard

[11] Michel Foucault developed these theories in a series of widely read and influential books, culminating in his *The History of Sexuality* (New York: Pantheon Books, 1978), vol. 1: *An Introduction*, tr. Robert Hurley. See also Michel Foucault, *The Birth of the Clinic* (New York: Vintage Books, 1975); and *Discipline and Punish: The Birth of the Prison* (New York: Pantheon, 1977).

to shake a lingering nostalgia for women's purported attributes and virtues, notably the moral superiority of victimization, the logic of their position effectively demolishes the value of women's experience and, implicitly, the grounds for feminism itself. For if the difference between women and men may be exposed as an artifact of language and domination, on what grounds may we assume that women have any interests distinct from those of men? In this respect, feminism, rather than embodying an alternative conception of order, merges with a generalized assault on order understood as nothing more than the mask of illegitimate authority. Thus, in another connection, it has been noticed that in the work of the Critical Legal Studies school—another and formidable radical challenge to prevailing notions of order—"illegitimate authority" comes under constant attack without a hint of what the Radical Critics would accept as legitimate authority.[12]

Postmodernist feminists' determination to expose all of modernist thought and practice as a conspiracy of male dominance contributes decisively to the prevailing notion that no authority can be divorced from the self-serving exercise of power. For, although their position derives from the assumption that men have dominated women, it develops on the assumption that the distinction between women and men is itself a manifestation of that (illegitimate) power and, consequently, ends in some part-Hobbesian, part-Nietzschean view of power as the ceaseless striving of the individual will. By thus insisting upon the essential gendering of all modernist thought, postmodernist feminists equate the revolt against illegitimate authority with a revolt against all forms of order.

The tendency to elide the specific power relations of modernism with relations of power in general may emerge even more sharply from feminist postmodernism than from postmodernism in general. History confirms that the sharp

[12] Eugene D. Genovese, "Critical Legal Studies as Radical Politics and Ideology," *Yale Journal of Law and the Humanities* 3 (Winter 1991): 131–155.

opposition between, say, nature and culture, or rationality and irrationality, is especially characteristic of modernism. Although a variety of premodern societies have tentatively drawn similar distinctions, they have all been more likely than Western capitalist societies to live comfortably with a blurring of the boundaries, as, for example, in the acceptance of magic or the active intervention of supernatural presences in human affairs. But the distinction between male and female has a more consistent historical pedigree, extending throughout most (if not all) of history and across most (if not all) cultures. In this respect, to anchor the attack upon binary distinctions in the distinctions between male and female is, necessarily, to extend the attack upon modernism to an attack upon order in general and, portentously, to an attack upon the entire human past.

Ironically, rather than offer an alternative to modernism, postmodernism, with its extraordinary emphasis on personal expression, in effect drives the logic of modernist individualism to its ultimate conclusion, in which a flagrant nihilism passes into a transparent totalitarianism. For, in the measure that the attack upon order is waged in the name of subjective perception and unlimited self-determination, it is also an attack upon the notion of any legitimate patterning or control in human relations. Yet it has gone unnoticed that the firmest, most internally consistent theory of "the personal is political"—and vice versa—emerged from the work of Giovanni Gentile, the premier philosopher of Italian fascism, who had the wit to know that he was proclaiming a totalitarian doctrine.[13]

No less significantly, the postmodernist feminist attack upon the order embodied in the split between public and private effectively elides modern and premodern patterns of gender relations, thus ignoring the important differences between them. Modern—i.e., individualist or bourgeois—gender rela-

[13] See, e.g., Giovanni Gentile, *The Genesis and Structure of Society*, tr. H. S. Harris (Urbana: Illinois University Press, 1960).

tions drew heavily upon historical precedents, but decisively reworked them.[14] Feminist theorists, notably Carole Pateman and Moira Gatens, have argued that modernist social and political theories have incorporated unequal gender relations into their essence.[15] In Pateman's view, the myth of the social contract depended upon a complementary myth of the marriage contract, and both predicated the individual or subject of the contract as male. In Gatens's view, modernist political philosophy invariably assumed a male perspective.

No doubt, Pateman and Gatens make important points: Modern societies have granted men decisive advantages within marriage and in intellectual life, and the men so advantaged have tended to fuse their personal perspectives to their claims about natural order and universal truth. The question nonetheless remains whether their pretensions in this regard decisively compromised the ideas and institutions they were promoting and, beyond that, whether it serves the complexities of our current political and intellectual situation to legitimate those pretensions by establishing them as the proper object of our attack.

Theory and Interest

Assume, for purposes of argument, that the men who expounded the theory of systematic or possessive individualism drew heavily upon their own experience and aspirations.[16] Does it necessarily follow that the theory can be understood

[14] Elizabeth Fox-Genovese and Eugene D. Genovese, *Fruits of Merchant Capital: Slavery and Bourgeois Property in the Rise and Expansion of Capitalism* (New York: Oxford University Press, 1983).

[15] Carole Pateman, *The Sexual Contract* (Cambridge: Polity Press, 1988); Moira Gatens, *Feminism and Philosophy: Perspectives on Difference and Equality* (Bloomington: University of Indiana Press, 1991).

[16] The designation *possessive individualism* is that of C. B. Macpherson, *The Political Theory of Possessive Individualism: Hobbes to Locke* (New York: Oxford University Press, 1962). See also the discussion of individualism in my *Feminism Without Illusions*.

only as a self-serving autobiography? Or, to put it differently, must we agree that no theory can reach beyond the immediate interests of its creator? In theoretical terms, the theorists of individualism explicitly imagined the individual as an impersonal entity—a unit of sovereignty and cognition. In the measure that their primary objectives were political, they sought a theory that would justify the representation and protect the integrity of absolute private property. They normally assumed that property-owners would be men, but they did not tie their theory to that assumption, not least because the mainspring of their revolt against previous forms of authority lay in a repudiation of the personalism and anthropomorphism of patriarchal theory.[17] To protect against the recurrence of personalism, they fashioned the political subject or individual as a category to which very different kinds of people might lay claim. No, in time and place, they did not expect women to do so, although Thomas Hobbes would admit no natural or logical barrier to their doing so. Nor, in time and place, did they expect propertyless men or black slaves to do so. But their failures of imagination did not inherently compromise the theory to which countless people whom, in practice, it initially excluded have subsequently laid claim.

Their determination that government represent property helps to account for their rapid embrace of the split between public and private spheres as the premier metaphor of order. For in constructing a model of the polity that primarily reflected the clash of interests—a polity that mirrored the free play of the capitalist market—they banished, as the wisest of them knew, the moral obligations and responsibilities that bind unequal human beings into some semblance of a community. In so doing, they effected a figurative divorce between power

---

[17] For an elaboration, see Elizabeth Fox-Genovese, "Property and Patriarchy in Early Bourgeois Political Culture," *Radical History Review* 4 (Spring/Summer 1977): 36–59.

and morality, ascribing power to the public sphere and morality to the private. Older images of responsible power, such as the obligations of absolute monarchs to their humblest subjects, thereby evaporated, leaving women, as denizens of the private sphere, to pick up the slack.

At its most sinister, the model of order grounded in the split between public and private spheres apparently proclaimed that morality, service, and responsibility had nothing to do with the exercise of power. At its most generous, it proclaimed a complementarity and interdependence between public and private spheres. In both guises, however, it tended to obscure or mystify the relations between the economy and the polity. As, during the twentieth century, private property became progressively less adequate to support even middle-class families and as women in growing numbers entered the labor force, the advantages of men over women became increasingly visible and less justifiable. And the strength of the historical legacy of male privilege in the public sphere diluted—or even made mockery of—the belated advantage to women of gaining access to the "rights" that men had customarily enjoyed. No, the vote did not equalize the earning power of women and men. Even access to the professional training and prestigious occupations did not equalize the earning power of women and men, although in isolated cases it might.

Under these conditions, some women's growing resentment of male prerogatives and power appeared nothing if not natural. And as the acquisition of public rights failed dramatically to improve women's comparative situation, feminists first insisted that the true root of women's oppression lay in the private sphere and then that its root lay in the distinction between the public and the private sphere. But this feminist course into postmodernism tended increasingly to ignore the relations between politics and political economy and to focus on the destruction of an allegedly oppressive order at the expense of projecting a new model of legitimate authority.

The Attack on Difference

Let us return to the attack on difference. The idea that women, for whatever reasons, normally represent different values from those of men does not necessarily lead to the conclusion that any notion of difference is inherently invidious. Significantly, the argument that the notion of difference subjugates or devalues women is, more often than not, advanced by women who perceive themselves as in direct competition with men—typically professionals and intellectuals. Or, to put it differently, postmodernism looks very different in the seminar room than it does on the streets. For there can be no doubt that postmodernity is upon us with a vengeance. The problem for academics and policy-makers remains to make sense of its implications.

The most visible feminist positions, notwithstanding their persisting differences, have been disproportionately driven by the concerns of single, white, affluent, and well-educated women.[18] There can be no doubt that these elite women have discrete (and legitimate) concerns about their own position, as women and increasingly as individuals, within the elite, which they have every right to defend. But their concerns are not necessarily those of poor women of different racial and national backgrounds. To women of the elite, the split between public and private may frequently appear an illegitimate barrier to their freedom as individuals. But for less privileged women that split, which has been disintegrating in their communities, may appear as the last best hope for survival.

More often than not, poor women's survival depends upon the possibility of some minimal cooperation with the men of their group. Thus, while elite women may well experience single motherhood as freedom from male domination,

---

[18] This assertion is based on extensive study of public-opinion polls from the late 1960s to the early 1990s and will be elaborated in *What Do We Want for Our Daughters (And Our Sons)?*

disadvantaged women are more likely to experience it as the price of not holding men accountable or of not permitting men to assume their responsibilities as fathers. And while elite women may revel in the availability of pornography as a means of exploring and expanding their own identities, disadvantaged women are more likely to experience it as the dangers proliferating in the streets in which they raise their children.

Even such committed postmodernist feminists as Susan Hekman acknowledge some difficulty in accommodating postmodernist theory to practical politics. But, she argues, our "present situation is one in which, in the absence of a transcendent metanarrative, different discourses compete for ascendancy"—a situation that "necessitates a different approach to politics." Given the impossibility of an appeal to "the legitimating norms of a metanarrative," political opposition must rely upon a "different conception of knowledge that generates a different means of opposition to the subjugation imposed by the discourses that structure societal relations."[19] In the end, Hekman offers only new forms of opposition to the discourse of the feminine that men have devised. But, at the risk of firing cheap shots, I cannot fathom how she expects those forms of opposition to improve the immediate situation of the countless number of un- and underemployed women whom our postmodern economy is tossing into the dustbin of multigenerational poverty and destitution.

Any theory confronts the difficult challenge of its practical application and possible social benefits for those who did not devise it. It has become a commonplace that many of the apparently most open and generous aspects of the theory of individualism—equal opportunity, career open to talent, freedom of contract—could as easily lead to the oppression as the advancement of working people. We know that capitalism embraced the language of democracy and freedom at least in

---

[19] Hekman, *Gender and Knowledge*, p. 187.

part to secure its own freedom to wring profits from the dispossessed. We know that even as the Fourteenth Amendment to the Constitution secured the right of former slaves to the free disposition of the ownership of their persons, it secured the same right to corporations as "legal persons." Most Americans, including working people who are generally more astute about the real conditions of their lives than the intellectuals who speak in their name, have not rejected those theories, primarily because, on balance, they have believed that the promise outweighed the deceptions and abuses.

Identifying the Enemy

Feminism has posed a new and impressive challenge to the vision of order grounded in the split between public and private spheres, but the mainspring of that challenge derives from the revolutionary changes in women's lives that have resulted from revolutionary changes in our economy. The unprecedented entry of women into the labor force, accompanied by unprecedented changes in patterns of reproduction, has graphically represented the erosion of the boundaries between public and private spheres attendant upon the virtual collapse of private property and the emergence of women as primary individuals. The consequences include a growing tendency to divorce sex from morality, sex from reproduction, and, more portentously, reproduction from morality.[20] These are indeed the symptoms of the postmodern world that is upon us.

The problems with postmodernist feminism as a response to our condition do not arise from the plausibility of its descriptions of accelerating fragmentation and atomization of

[20] See Richard Posner, *Sex and Reason* (Cambridge, Mass.: Harvard University Press, 1992) and Elizabeth Fox-Genovese, "Beyond Transgression: Toward a Free Market in Morals," *Yale Journal of Law and the Humanities* (1993).

previous conceptions of order. The problems arise from its ability to identify the enemy and, especially, from its naive confidence that a frontal attack on modernism's vision of order and authority could result in the beneficent liberation of human potential in all its diversity. It is mesmerizing to note that the postmodernist feminist attack on the order embodied in the split between public and private spheres invariably emphasizes the element of mystification that permitted that order to disguise its own ambitions to domination and even coercion. Time and again, we read that the great sin in dichotomous thinking or in the split between public and private lay in its sinister ability to appear "natural" and hence to mask its own imposition of power.

But why should we assume that a hegemony's proclivity for mystification—the disguise of its own character and intentions—adheres only to modernism? Would it not be truer to the spirit of critical skepticism—would it not make more sense—to assume that mystification accompanies any hegemony, whatever specific form it may take, and that a hegemony of some kind is necessary and proper? If we agree that the order of modernism simultaneously articulated and served the development of capitalism, should we not try to identify the economic forces propelling the postmodernist surge? Is anyone so blind as not to recognize those economic forces precisely in the international conglomerates that are propelling the revolution in technology as well as tolerating, when not financing, the destruction of family, church, and every other institution that aspires to a measure of autonomy? The greatest failure of postmodernist theorists and critics is to assume that we are immune to the patterns and relations that we detect in others.

Thus my own candidate for the primary beneficiary of postmodernism triumphant is the new global economic order, notably the multinational corporations, the largest twenty-five of which have annual products that exceed the GNPs of the United States and Western Europe combined. Postmodernist feminists apparently refuse to see that by conflating male dominance with the split between public and private and targeting both as the enemy, they are missing the obvious— that their misplaced attack constitutes the cutting edge of the economic juggernaut they naively think they are opposing. Here, we dare not fall into the trap of economic determinism. The attack on all order because it is necessarily hierarchical and the charge that authority, because hierarchical, is intrinsically illegitimate are leading to social disintegration and impotent rage. But we are not doomed to enact the postmodernist scenario that is already beginning to play itself out in our inner cities. The struggle for a decent alternative can be waged and won—but only by those who unflinchingly reject the siren calls of a radical and deracinated opposition to the very conception of order.

* I would like to thank the members of my seminar in feminist theory who so thoughtfully explored these questions with me: Lili Baxter, Lisa Brevard, Laura Cowley, Susan Duncan, Jacqueline Höller. Sheila Hassell Hughes, Christine Jacobson, Christine Lambert, Naomi Nelson, and Sujay Sood.

CULTURAL ASSAULT

What Feminists Are Doing to Rape Ought to Be A Crime

Margaret D. Bonilla

Rape is selling a lot of magazines these days. You can't walk past a newsstand without seeing dozens of articles—many written by avowed feminists—disclosing new evidence of a rape epidemic, and how we women can protect ourselves in the face of escalating aggression and violence against our gender.

The typical basis of these articles is that rape is distinct from other forms of violent crime. It is a crime *against women*. It is an act of subjugation *by men*. Rape presents a constant, all-pervasive threat; it can happen to a woman anywhere, at any time: on a date, at a family reunion, even in a marriage. The keys to preventing rape, feminists will tell you, are to change male-dominated cultural attitudes toward women, to get women to protect themselves, and to get Americans to take the issue of sexual violence more seriously.

The feminists are wrong. Rape is not the victimization of all women by all men; rape is a heinous crime committed by violent individuals against innocent victims. Americans have always taken this crime very seriously, so seriously that a rape conviction, until the 1960s, was punishable by death. The great majority of men in our society are not rapists; indeed, most men fear the rape of their wives, daughters, sisters, mothers, and other female loved ones as much as women themselves do.

As for stopping rapists, what the feminists don't tell you is that one of the best ways to prevent rape, and other violent crimes as well, is to put convicted criminals in jail and keep them there. A case in point is Willie Horton.

A Violent Man

Willie Horton was convicted for the 1974 murder of a Massachusetts teenage boy. The details of the crime are grisly: Willie Horton kidnapped the boy, stabbed him to death, and then castrated and dismembered his body. Mr. Horton was convicted of murder, and because of the ferocity of the crime, was sentenced to two life sentences in prison without possibility of parole.

As governor of Massachusetts, Michael Dukakis inherited a controversial program to grant convicted felons—even those with violent criminal records—weekend furlough privileges. Although Mr. Dukakis had been warned of the dangerous implications of the furlough program, he decided to leave it in place. And Willie Horton, although only eight years into his life sentence, was somehow assessed as an appropriate candidate for a furlough

Mr. Horton passed 10 uneventful furlough weekends in Massachusetts. On the 11th furlough, he fled the state, kidnapped a Maryland couple, and brutally raped the woman while forcing her fiance to watch; then he savagely beat the woman's fiance. He was caught and convicted in Maryland of first degree rape and assault.

When the public learned of Willie Horton, the outcry was swift and furious. The story was first covered by the Lawrence, Massachusetts *Eagle Tribune*, which won a Pulitzer Prize for its investigative reporting. During the 1988 Democratic primaries, Al Gore referred to Willie Horton to suggest that Mr. Dukakis was soft on violent crime, a theme picked up later by the Bush campaign. The Horton story was also featured in *Reader's Digest*, America's largest-circulation magazine. Americans were shocked that Governor Dukakis had used such poor judgment in furloughing a vicious criminal who was supposed to be serving two life sentences.

Grisly History

The Horton case was made more complicated because the rapist was black and his victims were white. Dukakis supporters and civil rights organizations accused the Bush campaign of exploiting racism and of perpetuating racist stereotypes. The grisly history of lynching in the American South had been closely linked to accusations, many of them false, of rape by black men against white women. There also had been a terrible pattern of discrimination within the legal system: between 1930 and 1965, for example, 408 blacks were executed for rape in the United States, compared with only 48 whites—even though more whites had been convicted of the crime. Dukakis supporters linked the Willie Horton story to this unfortunate history, turning it into a symbol of a smear campaign, not crime or violence.

Americans were not fooled; they saw the Horton story for exactly what it was, which was not a matter of race or

MARGARET D. BONILLA *is managing editor of* Policy Review.

political dirty tricks. Willie Horton's victims would have suffered just as terribly had he been white, as most rapists are. Michael Dukakis had allowed a dangerous criminal liberty that he did not deserve, and the result had been more violence: rape and assault. The public deserved to be protected from the likes of Willie Horton, and Mr. Dukakis had failed to do so. Mr. Dukakis's presidential campaign did not recover. The American people took the issue of rape more seriously than he did.

The Most Heinous Crime

Feminists who argue that rape is not taken seriously by society—or worse, that it has been tacitly condoned by our culture—need to open their history books. For millennia, rape has been regarded as one of man's most heinous, primitive, brutal crimes.

One of the early stories in the Bible concerns punishment for a rape. The sons of Jacob killed all the men of the Shechem after the rape of their sister Dinah. Not long afterward, Joseph was imprisoned in Egypt after Potiphar's wife accused him of making advances to her. The earliest known written law, the Babylonian Code of Hammurabi, specified death as the punishment for raping a virgin; generally, the method of execution was for the rapist to be bound and thrown in the river.

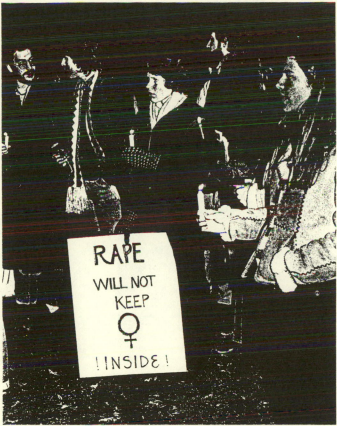

Feminists, in the name of safety, are scaring young women to death.

The Hebrews prescribed death by stoning for the rapist.

American rape laws derive from English law, which has had a long and unwavering position on rape. Before the Norman Conquest in 1066, the penalty for rape was death and dismemberment; this punishment continued until approximately the reign of William the Conqueror, who reduced the punishment to castration and blinding. Before the 13th century, rape generally was considered criminal only when committed against a virgin, especially against a betrothed virgin. But by the end of the 13th century, the concept of criminal rape had been broadened to include married women, nuns, widows, and even prostitutes. The Statutes of Westminster, first enacted in 1275, firmly established sex without a woman's consent as a crime punishable by death, generally death by hanging, which became the common punishment for rape in the young United States.

American sentiment historically has been unambiguous on the issue of rape. Rape has always been viewed as an extreme act of violence in our country, one of the few violent acts besides murder worthy of the death penalty.

Sanctions against rape in the American military go back as far as colonial times. George Washington forbade the Continental Army to engage in the practice, telling his troops that kindness toward women and children should be hallmarks of the revolutionary forces.

The official policies of U.S. armed forces have always been steadfast in their intolerance of rape; the crime is still punishable by death according to the Uniform Code of Military Justice, although no member of the U.S. military has been put to death for the crime since the early 1960s. Colonel Richard H. Black, Chief of the U.S. Army's Criminal Law Division, contends that the Army aggressively prosecutes sex-related crimes. "The military justice system provides strict punishment of sex offenders. Our most serious offenders are imprisoned at Fort Leavenworth, Kansas. Almost half of those are being punished for various sex crimes. Their sentences are often lengthy."

Fall 1993

23

Willie Horton raped a Maryland woman while on a weekend furlough from a Massachusetts prison, where he was serving a double life sentence for murder.

AP/Wide World Photos

In New York, during the summer of 1985, Russell West, Manhattan's "Midtown Rapist", stalked women in office buildings, forcing them at knife point to hallways or other secluded areas, and raping them. Men and women all over Manhattan demanded protection from their employers and action from the authorities. The public outcry and publicity resulting from the case helped catch the criminal. A retired police officer reading newspaper accounts of the attacks recognized the pattern of the assaults and supplied the New York authorities with the tip that led to Mr. West's arrest.

The horror against rape is not limited to the United States. Rape in wartime has been expressly prohibited by international law and condemned by all modern nations. When British propagandists sought to whip up anti-German sentiment during World War I, they accused German soldiers of massive rape in Belgium. Today Japan, which is still haunted by the charges of its army's brutality to women during World War II, is finally making a public apology for the outrages committed by its troops. And the Bosnian Serbs are universally denounced for committing brutal rapes and murders against Bosnian Muslim women, which they are cruel enough to film and broadcast on television.

Explosion in Violence

Contrary to feminist rhetoric, rape is a serious and growing criminal problem in the United States—in spite of, and not because of—our Judeo-Christian ethic and our Anglo-American legal tradition. In 1991, over 100,000 forcible rapes were reported to law enforcement agencies, according to the Federal Bureau of Investigation (FBI); the Justice Department estimated that over 170,000 rapes occurred in 1991, including a large number not reported to the authorities. Sex crimes experts believe that these figures are far too conservative, since many victims do not report the crime to the authorities. Everyone agrees that the problem is increasing.

But these numbers must be considered in the context of overall violent crime, which also increased during the period. The simple fact is that rape is a serious problem in America because violent crime is a serious problem in America. The increased rape in the United States is occurring against a backdrop of escalating violence of all kinds: drive-by shootings, mass shootings, gang warfare, various drug violence, random assault, and murder. The level of all violent crime rose 24 percent from 1987 to 1991, according to the FBI; rape rose 13 percent in the same period. As with violent crime in general, rape is much more common in cities than in suburban or rural areas. You won't find much rape in Wyoming or rural Michigan, where people still leave their doors unlocked.

While the United States has one of the highest levels of rape in the world, rape is virtually unknown in countries with low levels of violent crime—a fact that demolishes the feminist arguments about the universal male propensity for rape. The rape rate in the United States is four times higher Germany's, 13 times higher than England's, and 20 times higher than Japan's. All of these countries have commensurately lower levels of violent crime than the United States.

One of the most disturbing trends in the criminal

Rape causes fear and outrage in communities where it occurs. Consider the profound anger of New Yorkers—indeed, from all Americans—in response the Central Park jogger's rape. Or the similar outcry when four teenage youths—team mates on their high school football team—sexually assaulted a retarded girl in Glen Ridge, New Jersey. The jury did not buy the defendants' argument that the girl was capable of consenting to sexual activity, which in this case included being raped with various objects, such as a baseball bat and a broom handle. Their "boys-will-be-boys" defense did not work; three of the four were convicted of sexual assault.

With the exception of a serial murder, almost nothing so galvanizes a community as the threat of a serial rapist in its midst. Communities plagued by a series of rapes often "circle the wagons," by demanding publicity from the local media, protection from the law enforcement authorities, and results from local politicians. Los Angeles was terrorized in the mid-1980s by Richard Ramirez, the so-called "Night Stalker," who robbed, raped and/or murdered dozens of victims before he was captured. The heinousness of his crimes—including raping women still lving next to their murdered husbands, enraged Los Angeleños, and surely was taken into account when Mr. Ramirez was sentenced to 13 death penalties.

statistics, including rape and other violent crimes, is the huge jump in the number of young offenders. Violent crime committed by juveniles—those between the ages of 10 and 17—is rising faster than in any other group. Between 1965 and 1990, the rate of juveniles committing rape rose from 11 percent to 22 percent. The overall rate of juvenile violent crime increased 27 percent from 1980 - 1990, including arrests for murder, rape, aggravated assault, drug abuse, and weapons violations.

A particularly disturbing aspect of juvenile rape is gang rape. In 1990, 62 percent of multiple-offender rapes were committed by juveniles. Young gang rapers are often intimidated by peer pressure. Individually, many of the participants in a gang rape normally would never commit such a sick act. Often the rape is driven by one or two members of the group who have the psychological make-up of a rapist, and these individuals lead the pack. In a group, with peers egging each other on, the rape takes on a "rite-of-passage" quality, with some members acting as willing participants and others too afraid to stop the crime. Gang rapes often turn sadistic through a kind of "mob psychology," and sexual torture of the victim is often the result.

Rapists, whether juvenile or adult, share a number of common traits. Anger, hatred, and a deep-seated need to possess or control are central to the make-up; rapists seek to degrade and humiliate their victims. Rapists often come from violent pasts; many are found to have been abused as children, or been brought up in violent households. Many lead solitary lives.

Rapists often engage in other types of violent behavior; it is not uncommon for a convicted rapist to have other violent crimes on his record. The charismatic Ted Bundy, executed in 1989 for two murders and suspected in a series of slayings, was a rapist as well. Duncan McKenzie, who raped, bludgeoned and decapitated a young Montana woman in a spectacular case in 1974, had a history of violence, including assault. Champion boxer Mike Tyson, convicted of the rape of a beauty contestant in 1991, was a criminal with a long, violent rap sheet long before Don King and the boxing world discovered him.

Sex is incidental to the rapist. Sex is not the goal of a rape; rather, power, control, and the degradation of the victim, sometimes through sadism, are the goals. Alice Vachss, a former district attorney in Queens County, New York, who specialized in prosecuting sex crimes, puts it this way: "People who think rape is about sex confuse the weapon with the motivation." She calls rapists "single-minded, sociopathic beasts."

Lock 'Em Up

Convicted rapists are more likely to commit another rape after their release from prison than released prisoners with no history of rape. Some 8 percent of rapists are re-arrested for another rape within three years of their release from prison, many while they are on parole. At current levels, that number would reflect over 10,000 new rapes annually. Many criminal experts consider sex-crimes offenders to be among the most likely recidivists, and poor candidates for rehabilitation.

The way to prevent recidivist rapes is to keep rapists locked up. On average, a convicted rapist serves only one

third of his sentence; some are paroled in less than a year. Judges and parole boards often cite prison-space constraints as the reason for paroling violent criminals before their terms are completed. If we need more jails to house vicious criminals and keep them incarcerated, then we must build them. We must demand of our law makers and enforcers long sentences for convicted rapists, and indeed for all violent criminals, even juvenile offenders. We must demand also that these criminals serve the time they are sentenced.

When the FBI released its Uniform Crime Report in 1991, then-Attorney General William P. Barr said the huge jump in juvenile violent crime would require a "wholesale restructuring" of the juvenile justice system. Mr. Barr went on to say, "The long-term solution of juvenile crime falls largely outside the law enforcement system. It requires strengthening those basic institu-

---

I have interviewed several rape victims who are shocked and dismayed at rape being transformed from a criminal issue to a feminist political symbol.

---

tions—the families, schools, religious institutions and community groups—that are responsible for instilling values and creating law abiding citizens."

Law and Order

Contrary to some feminists' assertions, rape is a very serious matter to law enforcement officials, but these same officials will acknowledge that it is often difficult to catch and convict rapists.

First, rape presents particular evidentiary problems. Generally, to get a rape conviction requires prosecutors to have sufficient forensic evidence, including: visible bruising, lacerations, or other signs of physical trauma, and analysis of blood, hair, and DNA to support the rape charge. This evidence is not always easily collected or preserved, especially in cases where the rape is reported too long after its occurrence. There is no question that some rapes are not prosecuted for lack of evidence. This may explain why rape has the highest "unfounded" rate of any violent crime, that is, the percentage of complaints determined upon investigation to be false or unsubstantiated. The 1991 unfounded rate for rape was 8 percent, while the average rate of unfounded complaints for all other violent crimes was only 2 percent.

Moreover, a large number of rapes go unreported. Many women, fearing publicity and the public exhumation of their pasts, decide it is not worth carrying through a rape charge to prosecution. The majority of women who are raped – some 70 to 80 percent – know their attackers, and this often serves as a deterrent as well. Rape has a higher rate of dismissal than other violent crimes, probably because of the reluctance of rape victims to carry through with pressing charges when they know their attackers.

Similar problems exist in fighting other violent crimes, however. Justice officials estimate that only about half of the victims of violence ever go to the police. Rape is reported at about the same rate as aggravated assault and robbery, and rape is actually reported slightly more often than the average for all violent crimes.

And as with rape, victims of other violent crimes, including murder, are likely to know their assailants: Justice Department statistics show that roughly half of all violent crime victims are either acquainted with or related to their attackers.

Rape also parallels other violent crimes in terms of the difficulty of getting convictions and incarcerations. Conviction rates for rape in 1988, for example, were actually slightly ahead of those for robbery and assault. And of those rapists convicted, over 80 percent were sentenced to do time in a jail or prison, about the same number as those convicted of robbery, and more than those convicted of assault.

These numbers suggest that rape is still a very serious matter to law enforcement agencies and the courts. But

---

Rape is not the victimization of all women by all men; rape is a heinous crime committed by violent individuals against innocent victims.

---

the court and prison systems are faced with the same problem of overload with rape as they are for other crimes.

Trivializing Rape

Feminists sometimes imply, and often state outright, that rape has been accepted throughout history as a normal consequence of a male-dominated society: the victimization of all women by all men. They see a history where rape has been "winked at" because the value of women was considered to be less than that of men. This point of view is false, and it cheapens the gravity with which Judeo-Christian and Anglo-American societies have always treated rape. If rape really is a natural male compulsion, a consequence of an immovably patriarchal society, then there is not much we can do to reduce it but separate the sexes.

The issue of date rape, which is driving the current frenzy of rape stories in the media, threatens to trivialize the serious nature of rape altogether. Especially on college campuses, where date rapes are allegedly taking

place in epic numbers, there is a palpable climate of anger and fear about the chances of being raped or sexually assaulted.

It is important to say that date rapes do occur—violent, harmful attacks that are no less criminal for the victim being an intimate of the attacker. Similarly, rapes do occur in marriages, often as part of a pattern of violence; many battered spouses report having been raped or sexually assaulted. No rape is tolerable, regardless of the circumstances or the relationship of the rapist to the victim.

It is precisely because of the horror of such attacks that the issue must not be trivialized. Rape is not an attitude or a psychological climate, it is a brutal sex crime. Katie Roiphe, writing in the *New York Times Magazine*, noted that the lines between sex and rape were becoming "blurred" in the date rape discussion. This distinction must remain clear and absolute. If we begin to confuse sex with rape, as some feminists would prefer—counting unfortunate but not forcible sexual encounters as rape, and including as victims a large group of women who may have only miscommunicated their intentions or made a bad decision—we risk undermining our culture's abhorrence of this heinous crime.

Redefining Rape

Over the last few years, however, a movement has developed aimed at expanding the definition of rape to include the use of verbal intimidation, coercion, or manipulation—rather than physical force—and to suggest that a woman who has been given alcohol or other drugs by a man is not responsible for the sex that may follow. This movement, driven largely by feminists who claim that the gains women have made over the past several decades are being eroded by continuing male domination of the culture, is gaining momentum, especially on college campuses.

Seminars, lectures, literature, and forums urge coeds to "take back the night" from male hostility and aggression. Women in women's studies, feminist history, and feminist legal theory classes are taught that rape and other sex crimes are the natural outgrowth of our patriarchal society. As the weaker members of such a culture, women are victims, and sexual violence falls within the range of what the male culture views as normal. Sex is degrading to women, and rape is the victimization of women by men. All men are potential rapists.

One of the leading advocates of this theory is Catharine MacKinnon, a professor of law at the University of Michigan. Ms. MacKinnon is among the most prolific writers on the topic of sexual violence against women; she has been particularly strident in her campaign against pornography, which she sees as a form of sexual repression and violence. Ms. MacKinnon has written that in America "Rape is not illegal, it is regulated," and urged her readers to "Compare victims reports of rape with women's reports of sex. They look a lot alike." Another MacKinnon maxim is that our culture legitimizes violence to women through the family structure.

Even other feminists have objected to Ms. MacKinnon's assertions that the sex act itself is demeaning to women, that child-bearing is a form of subjugation, and

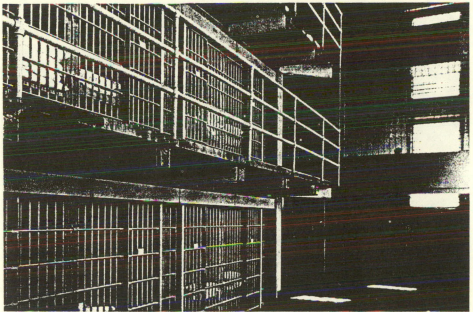

One of the best ways to prevent rape is to put convicted criminals in jail and keep them there.

that sex is often a form of rape. Yet Ms. MacKinnon's classes have long waiting lists, and her lectures at universities and college campuses are packed.

But such silliness has been fueled by statistical reports purported to prove that violence against women is an epidemic on campus, and that college women are being compelled, through coercion and intimidation if not brute force, to have sex against their wills.

Another Epidemic Study

One of the most prominent of the studies supporting this idea is one undertaken by *Ms.* magazine and directed by Mary Koss, a professor of psychology at the University of Arizona and a well-known advocate of the date-rape expansion theory. The *Ms.* Magazine Campus Project, as the study is known, was funded in part by the National Institute of Mental Health (NIMH), lending it a sort of "officialness" often found in what are actually advocacy studies. The *Ms.* study produced alarming figures. According to the data collected from some 6,000 women at 32 colleges, the study projected that 27 percent of female college students had been victims of rape or attempted rape twice between the ages of 14 and 21 years old. Professor Koss also calculated that in one 12-month period, 17 percent of coeds suffered a rape or an attempted rape.

Writing in *The Public Interest*, the *Wall Street Journal*, and elsewhere, Neil Gilbert, a professor of Social Welfare at the University of California at Berkeley, has shown that the *Ms.* study vastly inflates the magnitude of the problem

on campuses. Only three of the five questions in the survey mentioned threat or use of physical force as a basis for discerning whether or not a rape had occurred; the other two questions involved the use of alcohol or drugs, specifically the woman being given alcohol or drugs by the man, and then having intercourse she did not desire as a result. It is important to note that sometimes it is Ms. Koss who first is identifying these women as victims of rape, and not the victims themselves. Whether these same students would have identified their experiences as rapes without Ms. Koss's prodding remains unknown.

Professor Gilbert observes the discrepancy between the *Ms.* study's definition of rape and the way most of the respondents viewed their experiences: When asked directly, 73 percent of the students whom Koss categorized as victims of rape did not think that they had been raped. This discrepancy is underscored by the subsequent behavior of a high proportion of identified victims, 42 percent of whom had sex again with the man who supposedly raped them.

Professor Gilbert also notes the huge discrepancy between the number of rapes that allegedly take place on campuses and the numbers reported to campus authorities. Although it would not be unusual for a coed who is raped not to report the rape to the campus police or security office, many campuses have confidential rape crisis centers where rape victims can receive counseling and help in such circumstances without reporting to the police. These centers too have reported relatively low numbers of victims compared to the numbers we would

Fall 1993

27

The brutal sexual assault of a retarded girl by four high-school football teammates in Glen Ridge, New Jersey, shocked the community and the nation.

New Jersey Newsphotos

expect if the *Ms.* projections were accurate.

Rethinking Animal House

The premise that college women are being plied with alcohol or drugs and then manipulated into bed is not new; our grandmothers warned our mothers about this trap. What *is* new is that in the current sexual climate, the woman need not take responsibility for her behavior. Today you don't even have to blame an unintended sexual encounter on being drunk or high: the man is at fault for giving you the intoxicant; it is not your fault for consuming it.

If all men are rapists, all women victims, and all dates loaded with the potential of rape, then it follows that women should just stay home rather than risk associating with their male counterparts except in groups and public places. All of this is, of course, absurd. The idea that most men, whether college age, or older or younger, are slipping their dates "Mickey Finns" while the helpless woman abandons all responsibility is insulting and regressive.

But there exists on many campuses a growing sense of women in peril, at risk of becoming victims. Feminists, in the name of safety, are scaring young women to death. How this atmosphere of impending violence and victimization actually produces confident, assertive women or better relations between the sexes is unclear.

To the degree that more campus rape is happening, we can attribute at least part of the increase to the lack of discipline on campuses today. Alcohol use is a routine part of student life on many campuses, even when the students are not yet the legal drinking age. Drug use is still widespread. Wild parties, such as the fraternity and dorm parties that are known for intense drinking and sex—are still tolerated. And coed dorms without parietals encourage free association of young men and women at all hours without any supervision. Many young people go off to college with the idea that anything goes once they are out from under their parents' wings, and the colleges often look the other way until a problem surfaces. If we really want to change campus behavior, some of these facts need to be considered.

Colleges will probably be forced by legal concerns to address some of these problems, whether they want to or not. A recent case at the University of California at Santa Cruz—a school famous for its social liberalism—illustrates how explosive the campus rape problem may prove to be. In the Santa Cruz case, a coed allegedly was raped by two students at a dorm party after she became drunk and had consensual sex with one of their friends. The local district attorney declined to prosecute because of conflicting witness accounts and lack of evidence. The boys in question were briefly suspended while the University conducted its own investigation, but eventually they were reinstated.

The consequent outcry from the student community and parents provoked the U.S. Department of Education to launch its own investigation into how UCSC had handled allegations of rape and sexual harassment since

1988, and whether or not the university sought to play down these incidents, thus allowing a "hostile environment" toward women to develop. The investigation and ensuing publicity have had the predictable result; UCSC officials have hired a full-time employee to run a campus-wide educational program on sexual harassment and assault. Whether the university will also crack down on campus parties remains to be seen.

Take Back the Knight
It is hard to imagine a return to the strictures of the 1950s on today's campuses, but at least in those days everyone knew what the rules were, and who was responsible for obeying them. For better or worse, the imperative of not getting pregnant was enough to curb a great deal of promiscuous sexual activity before birth control became widely available. Today, the primary risk of casual sex is the contraction of AIDS or other sexually transmitted diseases; many young people do not take these risks seriously enough. Rather than "taking back the night," we should concentrate on raising responsible young men and women.

When I was in college in the late 1970s, there were rock-solid criteria for being a smart girl, and they didn't include taking self-defense classes. Among the rules: not drinking too much; not going home with a boy or a man you did not know; not letting intimate encounters get out of control if you were not prepared to face the consequences. Getting drunk and waking up in the wrong bed may have been regrettable. Certainly "getting talked into it" is a rueful memory. But seduction is not rape. My friends and I took responsibility for our actions and decisions in every area; certainly we did not cede ground in sensitive matters of sexuality. And we stayed away from men with bad reputations, those who drank too much, had bad tempers, or were known users or abusers of women. I hate to think that when my young daughter goes to college her standards for herself will be any lower.

And what of our sons? My husband and I are teaching our sons to be gentlemen—almost a forgotten concept today. Gentlemen do not rape retarded girls, nor do they take sexual advantage of drunken women. I want my young sons, and my daughter, for that matter, to grow up knowing that it is wrong to take advantage of anybody; hopefully this will lead to chivalrous behavior—toward men and women—as they mature.

The basis of our children's training is that they must not put their own gratification before the rights of others. They must learn to control their impulses, and to stay away from those who cannot. They must learn to be kind, and to take responsibility for their own actions. They must learn to respect men and women as equals. And they must learn that even in our liberated age, all sexual relationships have consequences. Hopefully they will carry these lessons forward, into the ever-more dangerous world they will meet. Not enough parents today are teaching their

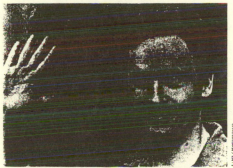

Rape often occurs as part of a violent pattern. Ted Bundy, executed for two murders in 1989 and suspected in many other murders, was also a rapist.

sons and daughters the basic moral lessons they need to cope with the choices available to them. It is hard work and requires constant attention, but it is the least our children deserve.

More Than a Symbol
To trivialize rape is an affront to the real victims of this horrible crime, who have endured unimaginable trauma and suffering at the hands of violent criminals. I have interviewed several rape victims who are shocked and discouraged at the prospect of rape being transformed from a criminal issue to a feminist political symbol.

Over the last decade, feminist pressure for responsible media coverage and serious pursuit and prosecution of rapists has encouraged many more rape victims to come forward. We are showing new sensitivity to the victim of rape, encouraging her to press charges, and trying not to stigmatize her for doing so. Certainly the climate in America today is less accusatory of the rape victim, and victims are coming forward in increasing numbers. And to the extent that feminists have helped create this new climate, we should be grateful. The only way to catch and prosecute rapists is for their victims to go to law enforcement agencies and cooperate in getting them convicted.

Once the rapist is caught and convicted, we must demand that he serve a long prison sentence, and we must insist that violent criminals be kept incarcerated. These actions, rather than further expanding the definition of rape, will lower the rape numbers.

The danger in expanding the definition of rape so broadly is that it will cease to be considered as the heinous act of violence that it is: We will become cynical about the crime and its victims. We will no longer understand what rape is, and what it is not. If we lose sight of this crucial distinction, it will become harder to prosecute and convict those who truly are guilty of this crime. ☎

315

Why I Am Not a Feminist: Some Remarks on the Problem of Gender Identity in the United States and Poland

BY MIRA MARODY

Aᴘᴛᴇʀ ᴀ sʜᴏʀᴛ ᴘᴇʀɪᴏᴅ of enthusiasm which followed the collapse of the communist regimes in 1989, the East and the West are facing each other with growing confusion and disappointment. Both the hopes of the East for a quick "return to Europe" and the expectations of the West for equally fast "occidentialization" of postcommunist societies have not been fulfilled. Each side feels that they did their best and both are blaming each other for the failure.

At least a part of the reason for such misperceptions stems from a widespread tendency to identify political change with social change. When dealing with apparently similar institutions in Western and postcommunist societies it is easy to assume the existence of similar attitudes, values, norms, and patterns of behaviors in the two populations. This tendency is reinforced by the perception of the communist period in the history of East Europe as incidental and inconsequential for the societies that now, liberated from the constraints of the

SOCIAL RESEARCH, Vol. 60, No. 4 (Winter 1993)

communist system, can just return to "normal" ways of social behavior.

The problem, however, is that what is "normal" for the East is not usually taken for granted by the West, and vice versa. This problem becomes evident when we meet each other in everyday situations and talk about ordinary things. It turns out that the most controversial issues are not democracy or market economy, but some vague feelings and reactions deeply rooted in the specificity of our historical and cultural experiences. Such, for example, as those triggered by the word "feminism."

I must state that I am not a specialist in women's studies or feminist theory. Yet I was in a sense provoked to write about this topic by my American colleagues who were asking me during my visit to an American university, "Why is there no feminist movement in Poland?" "When will East European women begin to fight for their rights?" "What should we do to help them?" All of these questions were asked with an implicit assumption that being a woman I must be a feminist. My answers must have failed their expectations, because the questions ceased to be asked after a time. Instead, some of my friends have begun to use the following statement as an argument in our informal discussions: "Be careful, it is being said that you are strange."

"Strange" means alien but also hard to accept. I felt rejected, but I could not understand why. I expected that being a scholar among scholars would be the role that was most important to my colleagues. It seemed, however, that they perceived me first as a woman whose academic pursuits, interests, and relationships should be governed by a superordinate sense of "gender solidarity." Any attempts on my part to defend my own identity in nongender terms were met with a polite smile and a "how interesting," which I have quickly learned to translate as a "we-know-you-are-from-a-backward-society-poor-dear" verdict. I was not only alien, I was worse.

Writing now about my American experiences I do dramatize

them slightly. In fact, my experiences were a kind of constant psychological discomfort which I felt with most of my learned female colleagues and a feeling of conspiracy which— regardless of my intention—emerged when I tried to discuss the problem with some of my learned male colleagues.[1] Both of these feelings were strong and unpleasant enough to make me become interested in the feminist issue. I could not deal with the issue in terms inherent to feminist theories, which I know only superficially, so I had to adopt a perspective with which I am more familiar, namely, a sociological one. In other words, I tried to analyze the "women's issue" in terms of social factors which influence the formation of an individual's identity. With this approach, the question of why American women are feminists has become as important as the question of why Polish women are not.

The problem with which I want to deal in this paper can be formulated with the following questions: Under which conditions does a sexual identity become a gender identity? When and why do the differences between men and women stop being perceived by the *individual* as natural and biologically grounded and begin being treated as socially maintained? Is it only a problem of individuals' "enlightenment" or can we point at specific social factors which promote or inhibit the development of "feminist consciousness?"

Women's Role in Poland

As an individual and a woman I do not feel particularly discriminated or handicapped in my society though as a social psychologist I know that I *should* have such a feeling. This "cognitive dissonance" can be easily supported with empirical

---

[1] Many of my male colleagues have internalized feminist values so deeply that discussions with them were even more difficult than those which I had with my female colleagues.

data documenting the position of women in Poland. Women in Poland are objectively disadvantaged with respect to leadership positions, promotion opportunities, and, above all, earnings. Only 36 percent of managerial positions are occupied by women. The higher the position, the lower the percentage of women among the management group.[2] Female wages are 20 to 40 percent lower than those of men working in the same positions. According to the studies carried on at the beginning of the '80s, in all occupational categories (with the exception of professionals) gender influenced earnings to a higher degree than level of education, occupational position, age, job tenure, or membership in the communist party.[3]

In the other spheres of social life, the position of women is not better. They are overworked, performing most of the household duties despite their occupational work. In 1984, with 75 percent of women employed, they were spending triple the amount of time on household duties (6 hours, 23 minutes) than men (2 hours, 20 minutes).[4] Women are also almost completely absent from public life. Analysis of their participation in *Sejm* (Polish Parliament) shows that the percentage of female parliament members has never been higher than 23 percent (1980-1985) during the years of communist rule. In the *Sejm* elected in the 1989 "partly-free election,"[5] women received 13.5 percent of the seats while their participation in the *Senat* (Higher Chamber of Polish Parliament) was even smaller (6 percent).[6] This picture does not change significantly if we look at the percentage of women in

---

[2] Irena Reszke, *Nierówności płci w teoriach (Gender Discrimination in the Theories)* (Warsaw: IFiS PAN, 1991).

[3] R. Siemieńska, *Płec, zawód, polityka (Gender, Occupation, Politics)* (Warsaw: IS UW, 1990).

[4] *Ibid.*

[5] According to the Round Table agreement, only 35 percent of the Parliament members were elected in a democratic way; 65 percent of them were chosen among the candidates proposed by the ruling communist party.

[6] Małgorzata Fuszara, *Abortion and the Shaping of a New Political Scene in Poland* (manuscript, 1990).

local territorial self-government. Only 11 percent of councilors in local self-government are female.

Last but not least, women pay most of the costs of sexual liberation, the existence of which in Poland can be well documented with the findings of sociological surveys. In the 1987 survey on the evaluation of socially controversial actions, extra-marital sex was accepted by almost 60 percent of respondents. Giving birth to a child without marriage was negatively evaluated by only 3 percent. Divorce was accepted by more than 40 percent of the respondents.[7] Alongside of these changes in attitudes toward sexual behavior we can observe, however, the growing rate of abortions. According to the official statistics, there were 122,536 abortions in Poland in 1987, but everybody agrees that this number is not reliable and should be tripled at least.[8] These numbers are quite high for a country in which 96 percent of respondents declare themselves as Catholic.

Thus, we can say that both in their public roles as well as in their private life women in Poland are in a visibly worse position than men. Yet all these objective disadvantages are not perceived by women as connected with their gender; in other words, they are not perceived as *socially* determined gender inequalities. In popular perception they are just as natural and obvious as other biologically grounded differences between people. This does not mean, however, that the situation is accepted with humility and smiles. Women may rebel and often they do, but they rebel against their female *fate* and not against the society which treats them in unequal ways. By the same token, men are perceived as occupying better positions simply because they always have and not because of a specific societal organization.

[7] A. Siemaszko, "Co Polacy potępiają? (What the Poles Condemn?)," *Polityka* (February 27, 1988).

[8] Eleonora Zielińska, "Przerywanie ciąży. Warunki legalności w Polsce i na świecie (Abortions: Their Legality in Poland and Around the World)," Warsaw, 1990.

Social Factors in Poland

Therefore, the simplest way to answer the question of why there is no feminist movement in Poland would be to point to the habitual perception of gender differences as belonging to the biological rather than social realm. In this context, a fight for gender equality seems as ridiculous as, for instance, a fight for the equality of blondes and brunettes or the beautiful and the ugly. People differ from each other in various ways and these differences may disadvantage some people. Men cannot give birth; female nature does not go well with politics. It is, therefore, natural that women spend more time at home and men in public activity. These are popular arguments that usually justify the observed discrimination of women in Poland.

However, the proposed answer is not satisfactory because it leaves unexplained the most important problem: why does such a perception exist? Poland is a modern society and in modern societies most of the biologically grounded characteristics of individuals are regarded as incidental or irrelevant to their social position. Moreover, we might expect a "demonstration effect;" knowledge about feminist movements in Western countries should have influenced and accelerated the development of a similar movement in Poland.

Nothing to this effect can be observed, however. The existing feminist organizations are tiny and they are usually an object of jokes among the population. More importantly, female representatives of the so-called "elite" publicly advocate a return to traditionally conceived sexual roles, lamenting the fall of "womanhood" and "manhood." An interview with the well-known Polish writer Maria Nurowska published in a Warsaw daily was entitled "To Restore Manhood to the Men."[9]

---

[9] Maria Nurowska, "To Restore Manhood to the Men," *Glob 24* (September 7-8, 1991). The "restoring" should be the work of women because women have degraded

Tired and overworked, many Polish women see a solution to their problems in giving up some of their rights rather than fighting for new ones. Women with a low level of education would gladly quit their jobs if only their husbands earned enough money. Women with a higher level of education often see their occupational work mainly as a measure to preserve a "good image;" staying at home, in their opinion, may turn you into a "slouch"[10]

The insistence on a traditional conception of sexual roles does not seem to be only a problem of ignorance. It is rather a result of deeper social factors that prevent Polish women from defining their gender identity in social rather than biological or quasi-biological terms. Tatur sees one of these factors in the political order of the communist state which has disadvantaged both men and women.[11] A struggle for securing civil rights was perceived as more important than a struggle for formal equality between men, and women. This perception was natural; after all, you must *have* civil rights in order to make a claim for equality. As a consequence, however, the main social division became a division between authority (those representing the state) and society. While in Western societies an individual confronts the social system fighting for her or his rights, in Poland the society-at-large was put in opposition with the state. The opposition could not be institutionalized for political reasons, so the only sphere of social life in which individuals were able to challenge the existing public order was a private sphere. In other words, the social-individual distinction predominant in Western societies was replaced with a public-private distinction in Poland.

---

men by entering fields reserved for them. "It must be like in nature," Nurowska writes. "A male is always more colorful and a female stays always a little behind him."

[10] Such an instrumental attitude toward occupational work is seen clearly in interviews collected by me and Dr. Anna Giza-Poleszczuk in 1990 for the project "Society During Transition," now in its final stages.

[11] Melanie Tatur, "Why There Is No Women's Movement in Eastern Europe?" paper delivered at IV World Congress for Soviet and East European Studies, July 21-26, 1990, Harrogate, England.

A retreat into private life was responsible, according to Tatur, for a "feminization of society." By this term she means the orientation of both men and women toward norms and motives which characterize womanhood as a culturally different mode of being.[12] Historically, in sociological surveys of Polish society, a happy family life, close relationships with friends, a decent income, and interesting work have been among the most prized goals of life, whereas a high social position, a managerial post, and social or political activity have rarely been chosen.[13] Although income, power, and level of education have been closely related to the evaluation of social status, the main criteria for social esteem have been formulated in terms of personal and moral characteristics, such as being friendly to other people, being a good parent and employee, having good manners, and being honest.[14] Last but not least, the dominance of female, context-related values among the values connected with raising children must be mentioned here. "Being a good pupil" and "responsibility" as opposed to "success" have been among the most popular parental aims.[15]

I would not like to discuss to what extent the approval of common values can be treated as an indicator of the actual identity of female and male life-worlds. Instead, I would rather stress the fact that in both explanations proposed by Tatur the process of social comparison is influenced by dimensions other than gender which are perceived as more important. Both in the case of the authorities-society division as well as the

[12] She points to the fact that the "new" women's movement is no longer based on the assumption of equal rights for equal individuals, but it demands the right and the "social space" to articulate and realize the female identity and life-world.

[13] Elżbieta Nasalska and Zbigniew Sawińska, Przemiany celów i dążeń życiowych społeczeństwa polskiego w latach 1977-1986 (The Change of Life Aims and Goals of Polish Society, 1977-1986)," *Kultura i Społeczeństwo* 1 (1989): 169-183.

[14] Irena Reszke, "Prestiż społeczny a płeć. Kryteria prestiżu zawodów i osób (Social Prestige and Gender: Criteria of the Occupational and Personal Prestige)," *Wrocław* (1984).

[15] Jadwiga Koralewicz-Zębik, "Wartości rodzicielskie a stratyfikacja społeczna (Parental Values and Social Stratification)," *Studia Socjologiczne* 3-4 (1982): 237-262.

public-private one, men and women are perceived as belonging to the same *social category*. In the first case, they are elements of society, fighting against the communist state for the recognition of their civil rights. In the second case, the orientation of both genders toward the private sphere of social life makes them partners rather than competitors. In both cases, the interests of men and women are perceived as common by virtue of the fact that they are completely different from the interests of the other side of the social division or the interests related to the other sphere of social life.[16]

If the perception of deprivation depends on social context, does that not mean that with the fall of the communist state the logic of social comparison should return to its "normal" shape, and women should discover their social discrimination? Yes and no. Yes, if the perception of gender discrimination depends only on the relative importance of various dimensions of social differentiation. It seems, however, that it also depends on the existence of a very special image of society. Essential for the feminist movements in the West is the notion of society as composed of autonomous individuals whose rights are defined in terms of *achieved* social roles. In Poland, due to a long-lasting "private" opposition to the state,[17] a different notion has evolved. The society is perceived here as composed of families and family-like informal groups whose rights were illegitimately restricted by the state.[18] In this context, individual interests become subordinate to group goals, among which the well-being of one's family or in-group is of primary importance.

[16] For a more detailed discussion of the differences between "private" and "public" behavioral attitudes, see Mira Marody, "Antinomies of Collective Subconsciousness," *Social Research* 55:1-2 (Spring/Summer 1988): 97-110.

[17] It was not only opposition to the communist state. During the Second World War, Polish society had to fight for its survival against the Nazi state and earlier on, during the partition period (nineteenth-century), against the states which had taken away its national independence.

[18] Mira Marody, "State and Society in Poland Today," in J. Coenen-Huther and B. Synak, eds., *Postcommunist Poland: From Totalitarianism to Democracy?* (Commack, NY: Nova Science Publishers, Inc., 1993).

Such a notion promotes the formation of a social identity in collectivist rather than individualistic terms. Indeed, data collected in Polish sociological surveys supports this hypothesis. In the '80s, the hierarchy of concepts with which respondents defined themselves looked as follows: a man, a Pole, a parent, occupation, and gender.[19] A "man" can be interpreted as a singular form of collectivistic "people" since it was usually accompanied by an additional description such as "ordinary" or "average." A "Pole" and a "parent" are also singular forms of collectivist identities shaped on the basis of nation and family which for a long time were the main reference groups for Poles. Nowak wrote about the "social vacuum" meaning the lack of identification of a middle level in Polish society.[20] Many authors have also pointed to the "familialization" of occupational relationships in Poland.[21] A very telling anecdote is told by the author of a study on sexual harassment in the workplace.[22] He was employed in a plant as an ordinary worker (participant observation method), and one day he asked one of his male colleagues, "Look, why do men here grasp women's buttocks so often?" His colleague answered, "Because here we are like one big family." This story points clearly to the absence of other than "family" concepts which could be used as cognitive tools for describing various forms of gender relationships. A gender identity, as I mentioned earlier, is perceived mostly through its associations with family life.

The formation of identity in collectivistic rather than individualistic terms goes hand in hand with a specific type of moral orientation which has evolved in Polish society. The

[19] Krzysztof Koseła, "Deficyt społecznej tożsamości (Deficit of Social Identities)," manuscript, 1989.

[20] Stefan Nowak, "System wartohasci społeczeństwa polskiego (Value System of Polish Society)," *Studia Socjologiczne* 4 (1979): 155-173.

[21] Marody, "Antinomies."

[22] Krzysztof Konecki, "Flirtowanie pracownicze (Joking Relationships in the Workplace)," *Studia Socjologiczne* 1 (1989): 338-358.

results of research made by Jasińska-Kania,[23] in which she used so called "moral dilemmas" developed by Kohlberg,[24] show a striking difference with the comparable American data. According to Kohlberg's studies, a "law and order" orientation dominates the American adult population, especially people with higher education. In Polish society, the dominant type of moral reasoning is the orientation toward "consensus and interpersonal harmony" in an in-group, while the "law and order" orientation has been chosen by a surprisingly low percentage of respondents.[25] One can expect, therefore, that even legally guaranteed individuals' rights will be perceived as less important and unworthy of struggle when in conflict with in-group goals.

Both the formation of identity in collectivistic terms, in which the notion of family plays the most important role, as well as the significance ascribed to consensus and interpersonal harmony in interactions among the members of an in-group do not enhance the chances for developing a "feminist consciousness" in Poland. The former prevents women from looking at themselves as autonomous individuals endowed with specific needs and goals. The latter means that the struggle for women's rights, which by definition has to threaten interpersonal harmony, would be perceived as morally unjustified.

Conclusion

I did not become a feminist as a result of my American experiences, though I cannot say that they did not influence me at all. Those experiences made me aware of some forms of

---

[23] Aleksandra Jasińska-Kania, *Osobowość, orientacje moralne i postawy polityczne (Personality, Moral Orientations, and Political Attitudes)* (Warsaw: IS UW, 1988).

[24] Lawrence Kohlberg, *Essays in Moral Development, Volume 1* (San Francisco: Harper & Row, 1984).

[25] From zero to 16 percent and most often by women with only primary education.

gender discrimination present in my own society which I did not notice before. They have also forced me to reconsider my own attitude towards the "feminist issue" which I had regarded as well-grounded and beyond any discussion.

When speaking about feminism, I had in mind that popular version which one can see at American colleges and universities or among middle-class women. It is a form of social consciousness rather than a scientific theory. It influences the formation of female identity and other spheres of individuals' life to the degree which can only be compared with the role played by the family concept in my own society.

For American feminists, the most important goal in life seems to be a defense of their right to socially supported individual development. On the contrary, Polish women have a tendency to subordinate their own individual development to family goals, which they try to achieve by using private methods and tricks. Both attitudes contain in themselves their own negation. In Poland, we observe a growing disorganization of family life which accumulates socially neglected problems of individuals, whereas many American feminists seem to pay for the equality of their social rights with increasing private problems, a great many of which have their source in the disintegration of their families. Whatever may be said about the future of women in both societies, I cannot agree that a solution to their problems lies in the forced choice between individual's rights and happy family life.

A "Progressive" Movement Holding Sexuality Hostage

Marty Klein, Private Practice, Palo Alto

Correspondence should be addressed to Marty Klein, Ph.D., 881 Thornwood Drive, Palo Alto, CA 94303, (415) 856-6533.

In 1986, Katie Roiphe entered Harvard as an undergraduate, the feminist daughter of a well-known feminist. To her shock, the feminist culture she found on campus (and found again as a graduate student at Princeton) was rigidly dogmatic and preoccupied with sexual violence, rage at and fear of men, and the image of woman as victim. Her response was to write this revealing, insightful book.

The Morning After is nothing less than an ethnography of the way young women (and men) are socialized into today's sex-negative, victim-oriented campus feminist culture. With a compelling narrative style and engaging eye for detail, Roiphe describes the institutions of this socialization at colleges across America—date rape seminars, Take Back The Night marches, rape whistles, women's bathroom walls, and ideologically constructed statistics.

This social force—which Roiphe calls "Rape-crisis Feminism" (p. 62)—is ostensibly aimed at legitimizing women's pain. But it has resulted in women being encouraged to identify themselves primarily as the *victims* of this pain—not as powerful beings acting effectively in the world. This is "not the feminism I grew up with," writes Roiphe (p. 4). "This is not me," she recalls thinking at a date rape workshop during her first year in college. "This has nothing to do with me" (p. 5). Instead of advancing women's liberation, she maintains these "feminists are on the front lines of sexual regulation" (p. 171).

This social movement is mapping sexuality as an overwhelmingly negative force and instructing women in it at a particularly vulnerable age. Although this group says it is talking about violence, Roiphe notes that they're really talking about sex—which they seem unable to discuss without the context of violence. They're really addressing a new (and rather non-human) model of sex altogether: sex without persuasion or pursuit, sex without miscommunication or discomfort, sex that is completely rational, sex that lacks true female desire—or erotic surrender.

Roiphe details the movement's effort to present heterosexuality as dangerous, and to persuade women that they therefore need to be protected. In addition to needing protection from *physical* danger, however, women are seen as needing protection from *emotional* danger—from the range of disturbing and exhilarating feelings that all young men and women inevitably experience in the marketplace of dating, sex, and learning to relate.

One way that sexuality is being constructed as dangerous is through the increasingly broad definition of sexual trauma. Quoting student-orientation materials as well as academic literature, Roiphe shows how this philosophy asserts that if a woman feels exploited or harassed, she is; if she feels sexually uncomfortable, she has been assaulted; and if she feels any ambivalence or dismay after a sexual experience, her (male) partner should have taken responsibility sooner and interrupted it.

To have this danger taken seriously, Rape Crisis Feminism equates emotional bruises with physical ones, using expressions like "emotional rape" and "emotional incest." Catharine MacKinnon (1987, p. 82), for example, says, "I call it rape whenever a woman has sex and feels violated." A current pamphlet of the American College Health Association (1992) asserts that "unwanted sexual comments...are a form of sexual assault." Campus feminists then demand that colleges take appropriate steps to protect women from these allegedly damaging experiences.

The result, however, is to portray women as terribly sensitive and vulnerable to the commerce of everyday college life, as people who are so unable to take care of themselves that they need institutional protection. As Joan Didion (1979, p. 116) wrote, certain segments of feminism can breed "women too sensitive for the difficulties of adult life." Those of us who went to college in the '70s, '60s, or earlier can appreciate the irony of this sentiment, recalling how intent we were on having *less* institutional regulation and protection in our lives, particularly our sex lives.

One foundation of Rape Crisis Feminism is frequently-quoted statistics about sexual mayhem in America. The most widely mentioned is a *Ms.* magazine (1985, as cited in Roiphe, 1993) survey reporting that one in four college women is the victim of a rape or attempted rape. Roiphe challenges this figure by citing the critique of Neil Gilbert (1992), Professor of Social Welfare at the University of California, Berkeley.

In examining the *Ms.* study, Gilbert pointed out that 73% of the women categorized as rape victims did not define their *own experience* as "rape"—they were victims according to the interviewer. Gilbert also noted that 42% of the women identified in the study as rape victims had sex with the supposed "assailant" some time *after* the supposed rape. Thus, the so-called "rape epidemic" on campuses is more an interpretive phenomenon than a physical one. It is more about sexual politics than sexual behavior.

Examining the allegedly high frequency of date rape, Roiphe notes that "According to common definitions, even verbal coercion or manipulation constitutes rape" (p. 67). Although it may create a convenient statistical epidemic of sexual violence, defining behaviors like verbal pressure as date rape trivializes the suffering of those violently coerced. "By protecting women against verbal coercion," Roiphe writes, "these feminists are promoting the view of women as weak-willed, alabaster bodies, whose virtue must be protected. The idea that women can't withstand verbal or emotional pressure infantilizes them" (p. 67). It suggests, she concludes, that "men are not just physically but intellectually and emotionally more powerful than women" (p. 68).

Furthermore, this model implies that, under ideal conditions, all emotional risk can be removed from sexual interactions. Not only is this untrue, it limits the range of sexual experiences people can create—involving, for example, self-exploration, self-expression, spirituality, and consensual power play. Integrating the reality of sex—with its true risks and rewards—is an adult developmental task requiring years of psychological work. The fantasy of risk-free sex is attractive, but it eliminates this possibility.

The Morning After has only a few small weaknesses. The short book calls for a bit of fleshing out: interviews with a wider range of female students, interviews with male students about their response to the anti-date-rape machinery, and references to literature on socialization processes and identity formation.

These additions would have helped Roiphe analyze why young women respond so deeply to Rape Crisis Feminism. Is it, for example, because it helps them articulate amorphous anxieties about their burgeoning sexuality? Is it because it speaks of boundaries at a time in life when they are losing the comfort of parental limits? This brand of feminism, after all, is not simply about male-female relations; it is about how young women define and feel about themselves. If men and their disrespectful passions represent dangerous sexuality, Rape Crisis Feminism represents control and safety.

Roiphe also missed the chance to connect campus education on sexual violence with other ostensibly progressive social institutions that really teach that sex is dangerous, such as fear-based school sex education, TV talk shows, library censorship, and media bans on contraceptive advertising. Similarly, Roiphe does not discuss the campus fashion of glamorizing victimhood in the context of a similar trend in the larger society. This trend can be seen in movements involving recovery from dysfunctional families, codependence, recovered memory, sex addiction, and battered woman's syndrome defense (now extended to the parenticidal Menendez brothers). This kind of socio-cultural context would have added meaning to the phenomenon she describes.

But these weaknesses do not take away from the book's exquisite accomplishment: a clear, straightforward description of how one kind of campus feminism betrays women's personal and sexual power. The writing is clear, the anecdotes and descriptions of campus life are colorful and revealing, and the book moves relentlessly forward without getting bogged down in ideological mud.

It is important to note that Roiphe does *not* claim there is no rape, date rape, sexual harassment, or predatory men. Those who charge this have either not read the book or they refuse to believe that anyone who takes these problems seriously could critique the rape crisis movement.

Thus, Roiphe has been virulently attacked as part of the anti-feminist backlash. She has been accused of denying the existence and seriousness of sexual violence when she clearly expresses her concern for and loathing of it. The argument should ring familiar to sexologists,

who are often attacked by society as not caring about certain problematic behaviors because we see fit to study them rather than simply condemn them.

Just as importantly, however, this phenomenon goes on *within* the profession of sexology. Those of us who criticize the model of sex addiction are attacked as "in denial"; those who reject the concept of repressed/recovered memory are attacked as "in collusion" or "sexist." And those of us who urge our colleagues to use more scientific language on surveys or in therapy—terms like *adult-child sexual contact* instead of *molest,* or *unwanted sexual attention* instead of *harassment*—are often accused of nasty motives.

These attacks eerily echo Roiphe's experience: just as some feminists imply that critiquing the movement intrinsically dishonors the pain of victims, some sexologists say we inevitably deny the damage of pornography, prostitution, and rape if we critique conservative, sex-negative censorship, laws, and clinical models. This is what the mainstream press refers to as "political correctness."

The Morning After is a thought-provoking, valuable book. Reminding us that not all feminists are "Rape Crisis Feminists," it adds an important, urgent viewpoint to today's dialogue about gender relations and sexuality. Those who claim to speak on behalf of "women" have an intellectual obligation to listen to *this* woman's voice: that sexual violence exists and is abhorrent, but that women should not adopt an identity of feminine weakness as the price of being protected from it.

References

American College Health Association. (1992). *Acquaintance rape.* Rockville, MD: ACHA.

Didion, J. (1979). *The white album.* New York: Farrar, Straus and Giroux.

Gilbert, N. (1992). Realities and mythologies of rape. *Society,* 29.

MacKinnon, C. (1987). *Feminism unmodified.* Cambridge, MA: Harvard University Press.

Muehlenhard, C., & Schrag, J. (1991). Nonviolent sexual coercion. In A. Parrot & L. Bechhofer (Eds.), *Acquaintance rape: The hidden crime* (pp. 115-128). New York: John Wiley.

Roiphe, K. (1993). *The morning after: Sex, fear, and feminism on campus.* Boston: Little, Brown.

Acknowledgments

Jeger, Lena. "Has It Made Any Difference?" *New Statesman* (Feb. 16, 1968): 198–99. Reprinted with the permission of Statesman and National Publishing Company Ltd.

Weller, Robert H. "The Employment of Wives, Dominance, and Fertility." *Journal of Marriage and the Family* 30 (1968): 437–42. Copyright 1968 by the National Council of Family Relations, 3989 Central Avenue, NE, Suite 550, Minneapolis, MN 55421. Reprinted by permission.

"Sex Unwanted." *Economist* (Dec. 7, 1968): 47. Reprinted with the permission of Economist Newspaper Ltd.

Potter, Ralph B., Jr. "The Abortion Debate." In *Updating Life and Death: Essays in Ethics and Medicine*, edited by Donald R. Cutler (Boston: Beacon Press, 1969): 95–105, 109–11. Reprinted with the permission of Beacon Press.

Gilder, George F. "Introduction" and "Chapter 18: The Woman's Role." In *Sexual Suicide* (New York: Quadrangle, 1973): 1–8, 239–50, 263–64, 285–86.

Morgan, Marabel. Excerpts from *The Total Woman* (Old Tappan, N.J.: Fleming H. Revell, 1973): 53–73. Reprinted with the permission of Fleming H. Revell Company.

Bryant, Anita. "Lord, Teach Me to Submit." In *Bless This House* (New York: Bantam Books, 1976): 43–50.

Cummings, Scott. "Class and Racial Divisions in the Female Population: Some Practical and Political Dilemmas for the Women's Movement." *Sociological Symposium* 15 (1976): 99–117. Reprinted with the permission of *Sociological Symposium*.

Schlafly, Phyllis. Excerpts from *The Power of the Positive Woman* (New Rochelle, N.Y.: Arlington House, 1977): 9–21. Copyright © 1977 by Phyllis Schlafly. Reprinted by permission of Crown Publishers, Inc..

Bolin, Winifred D. Wandersee. "The Economics of Middle-Income Family Life: Working Women During the Great Depression." *Journal of American History* 65 (1978): 60–74. Reprinted with the permission of the *Journal of American History*.

Elshtain, Jean Bethke. "Hobbesian Choice: Feminists Against the Family." *Nation* 229 (1979): 481, 497–500. Reprinted from "The Nation" magazine. Copyright the Nation Company, L.P.

Falwell, Jerry. "The Feminist Movement." In *Listen, America!* (Garden City, N.Y.: Doubleday and Company, Inc., 1980): 150–64. Copyright © 1980 by Jerry Falwell. Used by permission of Doubleday, a division of Bantam Doubleday Dell Publishing Group, Inc.

Decter, Midge. "The Intelligent Woman's Guide to Feminism." *Policy Review* 16 (1981): 45–54. Reprinted with the permission of the Heritage Foundation.

Connaught, Marshner. "Who Is the New Traditional Woman?" In *The New Traditional Woman* (Washington, D.C.: Free Congress Research and Education Foundation, 1982): 1–4, 12. Reprinted with the permission of the Free Congress Research and Education Foundation.

Yarbrough, Jean. "The Feminist Mistake: Sexual Equality and the Decline of the American Military." *Policy Review* 33 (1985): 48–52. Reprinted with the permission of the Heritage Foundation.

Wilkins, Shirley and Thomas A.W. Miller. "Working Women: How It's Working Out." *Public Opinion* 8, no.5 (1985): 44–48. Reprinted with the permission of the American Enterprise Institute for Public Policy Research.

Saknussemm, Arne. *The International Patriarchy* (San Francisco: The Almasi Scholars, 1986): 1–31.

"Why Can't a Woman Be More Like a Woman?" *Economist* (May 17, 1986): 43–44. Reprinted with the permission of Economist Newspaper Ltd.

Nicholas, Patricia. "Women Working and Divorce: Cause or Effect?" *Psychology Today* (Oct. 1986): 12–13. Reprinted with the permission of Sussex Publishers Inc.

Palisi, Bartolomeo J. and Claire Canning. "The Perceived Control of Well-Educated Women: 1972–1984." *Social Science Journal* 25 (1988): 337–51. Reprinted with the permission of JAI Press, Inc.

Heilbrun, Alfred B., Jr. and David M. Gottfried. "Antisociality and Dangerousness in Women Before and After the Women's Movement." *Psychological Reports* (Feb. 1988): 37–38. © *Psychological Reports* 1988.

Friedman, Marilyn. "Feminism and Modern Friendship: Dislocating the Community." *Ethics* 99 (1989): 275–90. Reprinted with the permission of the University of Chicago Press.

Snitow, Ann. "Pages from a Gender Diary: Basic Divisions in Feminism." *Dissent* 36 (1989): 205–24. Reprinted with the permission of the Foundation for the Study of Independent Social Ideas, Inc.

Wilson, Elizabeth. "Against Feminist Fundamentalism." *New Statesman and Society* (June 23, 1989): 30–33. Reprinted with the permission of Statesman and National Publishing Company Ltd.

Ebling, Kay. "The Failure of Feminism." *Newsweek* (Nov. 19, 1990): 9. Reprinted with the permission of Newsweek, Inc.

"Wrong on Rape: Neither Naming Rape Victims Against Their Will, Nor Broadening the Definition of Rape to Include Seduction, Helps the Cause of Feminism." *Economist* (May 18, 1991): 14–15. Reprinted with the permission of Economist Newspaper Ltd.

Bowman, James. "Perplexed by Sex?" *American Enterprise* 2, no.6 (1991): 46–51. Reprinted with the permission of the American Enterprise Institute for

Public Policy Research.

Bailey, William T. and Tracy L. Hamilton. "Feminism and Anorectic Tendencies in College Women." *Psychological Reports* (Dec. 1992): 957–58. © *Psychological Reports* 1992.

Taylor, Barbara. "Love and Trouble." *New Statesman and Society* (Feb. 12, 1993): 35–36. Reprinted with the permission of Statesman and National Publishing Company Ltd.

Fox-Genovese, Elizabeth. "From Separate Spheres to Dangerous Streets: Postmodernist Feminism and the Problem of Order." *Social Research* 60 (1993): 235–54. Reprinted with the permission of *Social Research*.

Bonilla, Margaret D. "Cultural Assault: What Feminists Are Doing to Rape Ought to Be A Crime." *Policy Review* 66 (1993): 22–29. Reprinted with the permission of the Heritage Foundation.

Marody, Mira. "Why I Am Not a Feminist: Some Remarks on the Problem of Gender Identity in the United States and Poland." *Social Research* 60 (1993): 853–64. Reprinted with the permission of *Social Research*.

Klein, Marty. "A 'Progressive' Movement Holding Sexuality Hostage." *Journal of Sex Research* 31, no.2 (1994): 146–48. Published by permission of the *Journal of Sex Research*, a publication of The Society for the Scientific Study of Sex, Inc.